THE MIRROR OF JUSTICE

THEODORE ZIOLKOWSKI

The Mirror of Justice

LITERARY REFLECTIONS OF LEGAL CRISES

PRINCETON UNIVERSITY PRESS, PRINCETON, N.J.

Published by Princeton University Press, 41 William Street,
Princeton, New Jersey 08540
In the United Kingdom: Princeton University Press, Chichester, West Sussex

Library of Congress Cataloging-in-Publication Data

Ziolkowski, Theodore.
The mirror of justice : literary reflections of legal crises / Theodore Ziolkowski.
p. cm.
Includes bibliographical references and index.
ISBN 0-691-02683-1 (CL : alk. paper)
1. Law in literature. 2. Law and literature. 3. Literature—
History and criticism. I. Title.
PN56.L33Z56 1997
809′.93355—dc20 96-28326

This book has been composed in Berkeley Book

Princeton University Press books are printed on
acid-free paper and meet the guidelines for permanence
and durability of the Committee on
Production Guidelines for Book Longevity of the
Council on Library Resources

Printed in the United States of America
by Princeton Academic Press

10 9 8 7 6 5 4 3 2 1

FOR

Elizabeth Ziolkowski

Robert Thurston

Lee Upton

CONTENTS

PREFACE

WE LIVE in an age permeated not just by a suspicion of lawyers as a profession but by a skepticism regarding the law as an institution. As lawyer jokes proliferate, applications to law schools decline. The legal fictions of William J. Coughlin, John Grisham, George Higgins, Steve Martini, Richard North Patterson, Barry Reed, Nancy Taylor Rosenberg, Robert K. Tanenbaum, Scott Turow, and many others enjoy their popularity not because they glorify the law but because they expose its moral ambiguities as well as abuses inherent in the legal system. The spectacle of televised celebrity trials has done little to enhance public respect for the institution or its practitioners. Many citizens, and not just those on the radical left or the extreme right, regard every new law as yet another infringement of their personal liberties. The ancient adage *summum ius, summa iniuria*, widely voiced during the turbulent era when medieval customary law was being displaced by a modernized Roman law (see chaps. 5–7 below), might well be the watchword for those members of our own society who believe that the highest law of the land is truly tantamount to the greatest injustice.

In no small measure this situation has arisen because the processes of law and legislation, in the course of time, have become increasingly professionalized and hence more remote from normal daily experience, even as our lives are increasingly subject to regulation. Ours has become a society of externally imposed statutes rather than a community of internalized law known as a *Rechtskultur*. It is no doubt true that the complexities of corporate law, like the intricacies of medical science, require specialization. But the broader issues of human social behavior, as well as human health, should be a matter of vital public concern. The Romans, who laid the foundation for law as we know it in the Western world, regarded an active engagement with the law as the obligation and privilege of every thinking citizen. Jurisprudence is defined in the opening paragraph of Justinian's *Institutes* not in the specialized terms of a first-year law-school curriculum—contracts, torts, felonies, procedures—but as "the acquaintance with matters divine and human, the knowledge of what is just and unjust" (*Iuris prudentia est divinarum atque humanarum rerum notitia, iusti atque iniusti scientia*).

We have relinquished too readily the notion of the jurisprudent—that is to say, the individual who, while not a professional lawyer, is seriously interested in the nature and history of law. Law amounts to more than statutes and procedures: it constitutes the basis and expression of all social order. Many societies, from the Babylonians to the present, have left us the records of their laws—records that enable us to form an image of their aspirations as well as their organization. But laws, and systems of law, have also changed profoundly over time. The record of that change, of the forces that have produced that evolution, can often best be observed not in the law books but in literature.

What many masterpieces of world literature mirror are not simply the workings of the law but, more compellingly, the moments of crisis when society discovers that its laws have become problematic. This book addresses a group of widely read and influential literary works that reflect momentous crises in the evolution of Western law: the transition from prelegal to legal society, the Christianization of Germanic customary law, the conflict between customary and Roman law, the debate in antiquity and the Renaissance over law and equity, the Romantic disputes regarding codification, and the modern skepticism concerning the nature of law altogether. Thoughtful citizens concerned with the law today can look to the literature of the past to see how men and women of other ages came to grips with similar problems and questions. *Antigone* and *Reynard the Fox*, *The Merchant of Venice* and *Michael Kohlhaas* confront issues that are just as insistent at the end of our millennium as they were in fifth-century Athens, in twelfth-century France, in Elizabethan England, or in Prussia during the Napoleonic Wars, even though those eras observed wholly different legal systems. In this sense, literature provides a faithful mirror of justice that shows, moreover, that the finest literary works (the "canon") more often challenge than support the prevailing ideology.

Since antiquity, great writers have been drawn to questions of law and justice, but their works do not necessarily involve lawyers. There are no lawyers in *Antigone*; the only lawyer in *Reynard the Fox* is a minor figure of ridicule; the "lawyer" in *The Merchant of Venice* is an impostor. The message that cries out to us from the centuries that produced Aeschylus's *Eumenides* and *Njal's Saga* is that the law in its most generous sense—as "the knowledge of what is just and unjust"—is the urgent responsibility of all citizens and not the prerogative of specialists. Indeed, the interests of professionals are sometimes so narrowly focused that they lose sight of the broader issues. Most, though not all, of the legal thrillers that have enjoyed a notable success in the United States during the past decade do not deal at all with issues of justice: instead, they are concerned with courtroom tactics, with the lives and careers of lawyers, and with crimes that do not challenge the law but can be accommodated easily within its existing framework.

Daniel J. Kornstein, the lawyer-author of one of the liveliest and most original books on Shakespeare, wrote recently that "culture has been delegated too much to the experts" (*Kill All the Lawyers? Shakespeare's Legal Appeal* [Princeton, NJ: Princeton University Press, 1994], xiv). That is certainly true. Literary studies have benefited from the "Law and Literature" movement, which has arisen during the past two decades in analogy to such interdisciplinary areas as Religion and Literature or Medicine (including Psychoanalysis) and Literature. As practiced today in the United States, the field is represented largely, though by no means exclusively, by lawyers. These critics, approaching literature from the standpoint of law, are concerned primarily with law *in* literature (that is, depictions of law, lawyers, and legal procedures in literary works) and law *as* literature (that is, the rhetorical strategies of legal texts and the hermeneutics of their interpretation). Many law schools, as well as a few humanities departments, offer courses on Law and Literature. The energy of the field has generated such journals as the *Cardozo Studies in Law and Literature* and the *Yale Journal of Law and the Humanities*. Its adherents have developed a variety of methodologies, as exemplified by the anthology *Interpreting Law and Literature: A Hermeneutic Reader*, ed. Sanford Levinson and Steven Mailloux (Evanston, IL: Northwestern University Press, 1988). It has aroused its controversies, as attested by Richard A. Posner's *Law and Literature: A Misunderstood Relation* (Cambridge: Harvard University Press, 1988)—even its own "poetic ethics," as evidenced by Richard Weisberg's *Poethics and Other Strategies of Law and Literature* (New York: Columbia University Press, 1992). So flourishing is the enterprise that it has recently prompted a critical survey: Ian Ward's *Law and Literature: Possibilities and Perspectives* (Cambridge: Cambridge University Press, 1995).

This interdisciplinary activity (like Religion and Literature or Medicine and Literature) is too fascinating and important to be conceded to the lawyers. Issues of law are so central to human society that they dominate many of the landmark works of Western literature and thereby have a claim on the attention of all educated people. The approach that I employ is best characterized, in contradistinction to Law and Literature, as Literature and Law and differs from it not in subject matter but in emphasis. The approach is historical rather than theoretical: I am interested in locating each literary work within its own legal context rather than in challenging or revising our understanding of the work in the light of modern legal practices and controversies. It is based on the assumption that the issues in those works, being historically determined, cannot be addressed simply with the principles and methods of modern legal theory or practice. To approach them we need, beyond our passionate concern as social beings with values of justice, enough understanding of legal history to provide in each case an adequate and appropriate context for the literary work.

Second, my interest is substantive rather than rhetorical: although language—in particular the legal terminology of various cultures—is essential for my purposes, I focus primarily on the tensions between law and morality that arise at certain crucial junctures of history. Further, my texts and sources are comparative rather than (as in the case of most, though not all, Law-and-Literature studies) Anglo-American: all but one of the literary works I treat emerge from cultures outside the common-law system. Finally, my interest is concentrated on the literary work and on historical evolution, not on the theories and arguments of others. I have no desire to engage in the polemics that enliven many of the contributions to Law and Literature (such as the cited works by Posner and Weisberg) because they are largely tangential to the issues central to this book. I do not adduce the literary work in order to enhance a debate about modern law; I consult legal history in order to heighten my understanding of the literary work.

I do not regard my undertaking as a substitute for the project of Law and Literature but as complementary to it. It is, in sum, the mode in which a literary scholar with his particular qualifications and questions approaches the same conjunction of fields that has attracted so many lawyers with *their* qualifications and questions.

THIS BOOK revolves around seven major works (chaps. 2, 3, 5, 8–11) that reflect epoch-making upheavals in the history of law. In each case the literary work is related to its contemporary legal crisis in a conjunction justified whenever possible by biographical evidence concerning its author. (In several cases I have included plot summaries emphasizing the legal aspects of the works under discussion, on the assumption that not every reader will recall the details of the lengthy *Njal's Saga* or, say, the various versions of the legend of Reynard the Fox.) The introduction sets forth the principles according to which I selected those works and organized the sequence of presentation. Chapter 4 reviews the legal history indispensable for an understanding of the works taken up in the following chapters. Since the response to the reception of Roman law was so varied, it seemed useful to include a variety of authors and works in chapters 6 and 7 rather than to focus on a single central one. (Because many of the Latin texts have never been translated into English, I have paraphrased rather generously and cited key phrases in the original. All translations of texts treated, unless otherwise indicated, are my own.) The last chapter, finally, is intended as a representative sample rather than as a definitive survey: I hope that it will open possibilities of further exploration to readers curious about the field of Literature and Law.

MY INTEREST in this topic was first aroused by my studies in German Romanticism. I became aware, some years ago, that a surprising number of German writers in the Romantic era, including such major figures as Goethe, Kleist, and E.T.A. Hoffmann, were legally trained and had often practiced law. I first addressed this curious phenomenon in a talk entitled "Kleists Werk im Lichte der zeitgenössischen Rechtskontroverse" at the 1986 meeting of the Kleist-Gesellschaft in Berlin (*Kleist-Jahrbuch 1987*, ed. Hans Joachim Kreutzer [Berlin: Erich Schmidt, 1987]). The following year I delivered the more general "The Lure of the Law in German Romanticism" at the Seventeenth Triennial Congress of the Fédération Internationale des Langues et Littératures Modernes

(*Proceedings*, ed. G. D. Killam [Guelph, Ontario: University of Guelph, 1989]). That work eventually resulted in a chapter, "The Law: Text of Society," in my *German Romanticism and Its Institutions* (Princeton, NJ: Princeton University Press, 1990). These studies soon persuaded me that the subject deserved a much more extensive treatment, a treatment that needed to be both historical and comparative in scope if I was to succeed in demonstrating the two principles that I gradually came to see as constitutive in the development of literary works concerned with problems of justice: the evolution of law, and the dissociation of law and morality. My readings initially produced a review article, "Literature and Law" (*Sewanee Review* 99 [1991]: 122–32). I also benefited from discussions with various audiences, including many lawyers and judges, to whom I presented a slide-lecture, "The Figure of Justitia in Art and Literature"—a fascinating topic that I decided not to include here as a separate chapter lest it shatter the framework and continuity of this book. As the book assumed tangible shape, I had the opportunity of working through the material with the students in an undergraduate seminar, "Literature and Law," that I taught at Princeton University in the spring terms of 1994, 1995, and 1996. In 1995 I presented "Kafkas *Der Prozeß* und die Krise des modernen Rechts" at a Colloquium on Literature and Law sponsored by the Akademie der Wissenschaften in Göttingen (*Literatur und Recht. Literarische Rechtsfälle von der Antike bis in die Gegenwart* [Göttingen: Wallstein, 1996]). I am grateful to those audiences and to my students for helping me to sharpen my thoughts on literature and law in general as well as my understanding of specific texts. The Kleist-Gesellschaft and the Göttingen Akademie der Wissenschaften and their respective publishers have kindly given me permission to adapt in substantially revised and expanded form material first published in their volumes. I gratefully acknowledge permission to quote two passages, translated by my friend and colleague Robert Fagles, from *The Iliad* by Homer, translated by Robert Fagles. Translation copyright © 1990 by Robert Fagles. Introduction and notes copyright © 1990 by Bernard Knox. Used by permission of Viking Penguin, a division of Penguin Books USA Inc.

IT IS A PLEASURE to express my appreciation to the Rockefeller Foundation for a five-week residency in 1993 in that earthly paradise of the Bellagio Study and Conference Center. It was there, not far from the Lombard cities where around A.D. 1000 the modern study of law began, and a millennium later, that I outlined this book and wrote the introduction. Mary Murrell handled my manuscript from submission to publication with the gracious professionalism to which I have become accustomed through thirty years of association with Princeton University Press. Thanks to her initiative, I benefited from the enthusiasm and insight of two eminently knowledgeable readers coming from their respective fields of law and literature, Daniel Kornstein and Virgil Nemoianu. Authors at Princeton University Press, finally, have every reason to be grateful to its superb editors and designers. Lauren Lepow sharpened this manuscript through her discernment, punctiliousness, and subtle sense of style; Jan Lilly brought her award-winning talent to its design.

As usual, I am indebted to my family for encouragement and stimulation over the years. My daughter, Margaret C. Ziolkowski, brought to my attention several of the Russian works discussed in the last chapter. My son Jan M. Ziolkowski provided me with valuable bibliographical assistance concerning literature and law in the Middle Ages. My son Eric J. Ziolkowski in numerous conversations catalyzed my thinking on issues concerning law, morality, and religion. My wife, Yetta, whose judiciousness has enhanced my thinking and writing for many years, accompanied me from the Areopagus in Athens to Thingvellir in Iceland, from the former seat of the *Reichskammergericht* in Wetzlar to the isolated castle of Falkenstein in Saxony-Anhalt, where Hoyer II commissioned the German version of the *Sachsenspiegel*. It is a pleasure, finally, to acknowledge through the dedication to a book *on* law three special people who have come into our family *in* law.

Theodore Ziolkowski

Princeton, New Jersey
February 22, 1996

THE MIRROR OF JUSTICE

CHAPTER ONE

Introduction

The Origins of Law

Looming on the threshold of many civilizations, where myth gives way to history, stand the figures of the great lawgivers. In the mythology of India, Manu (whose name is cognate with the Indo-European word for "man") was the first human being, the first Hindu king, and the legendary author of the Sanskrit code of law. Menes, who flourished around 3100 B.C., founded Memphis and became the first ruler of a unified Egypt, which he conquered through military victories and then consolidated through wise administrative measures. Minos, the legendary sovereign of Crete, enjoyed a reputation for harshness among the Athenians because he exacted from their city an annual tribute of youths and maidens with which to appease the Minotaur; yet so just was his reign that, following his death, he was rewarded by appointment to the office of judge in the underworld. Moses—to complete the roster of fabled law-bringers with remarkably similar names—returned from his forty-day seclusion with the Lord on Mount Sinai bearing the two stone Tables of Law that have governed the people of Israel for over three thousand years.

While legendary lawgivers tower at the misty beginnings of civilization, great legal codes often mark the earliest stages of recorded history. We are acquainted with late archaic Sumeria and Akkadia largely through the code that Hammurabi (1792–1750 B.C.) caused to be inscribed upon an eight-foot pillar of black stone in the temple of Marduk in Babylon. The Covenant Code (Exod. 21.2—22.17), generally regarded as the oldest part of the Pentateuch or Torah (meaning "law"), constitutes a catalog of the earliest civil ordinances of the largely agricultural Hebrews following their arrival in Canaan. The Code of Gortyn, chiseled into the circular walls of a court in Crete, has preserved in its more archaic passages our earliest records of pre-Hellenic Greek society. The remnants of the Code of Draco (621–620 B.C.; reinscribed on stone in 409 B.C.) provide one of the primal documents in the history of Athens. The Twelve Tables, on which the early Romans recorded (451–450 B.C.) the customary law of their day, embody the foundations of Roman history.

For these reasons law has been regarded by many thoughtful observers as the most reliable index of any civilization. On the first page of his masterpiece

The Common Law (1881) Oliver Wendell Holmes wrote, "The law embodies the story of a nation's development through many centuries, and it cannot be dealt with as if it contained only the axioms and corollaries of a book of mathematics."[1] In the second volume of *The Decline of the West* (*Der Untergang des Abendlandes*, 1922) Oswald Spengler stated that "every legal system contains in concentrated form the worldview of its creators."[2] And A. S. Diamond concluded his comparative study, *The Evolution of Law and Order* (1951), with the conviction that "the law remains the distilled essence of the civilization of a people."[3]

Small wonder that many late-medieval collections of laws were known as "mirrors" because they were believed to provide the truest reflection of their respective societies and of societal values. In one of the earliest of these "mirrors," Eike von Repgow's *Sachsenspiegel* (written ca. 1220–35), the author reminds the reader in his preface that his book is called "Mirror of the Saxons" because Saxon law can be recognized in it just as women regard their countenances in a mirror:

> "Spegel der Sassen"
> Scal dit buk sin genant,
> went Sassen recht is hir an bekant,
> Alse an eneme spegele de vrowen
> er antlite scowen.[4]

In imitation of this widely circulated work, of which over 200 manuscript copies are known, Germany brought forth various other legal "mirrors": the South German "Mirror of the Germans" (*Deutschenspiegel*) of 1260; the "Mirror of Swabians" (*Schwabenspiegel*) of 1270–80, which was circulated in some 350 manuscripts and gradually became the generic term for written laws of any sort; Ulrich Tenngler's "Layman's Mirror" (*Layenspiegel*) of 1510; and Justin Gobler's "Mirror of Laws" (*Der Rechten Spiegel*) of 1550.

That an institution so fundamental to human society also found its reflection in works of literature is not surprising. The Greek preoccupation with law, and notably with legal principles, which is evident in Plato's *Laws* and Aristotle's *Politics*, informs Greek tragedy from Aeschylus's *Oresteia* to Sophocles' *Antigone*. The ancient Germanic obsession with law that impressed Tacitus around A.D. 100 remains broodingly omnipresent in the Old Norse sagas a thousand years later. The satirization of law by the various late-medieval adapters of the legend of Reynard the Fox, by Sebastian Brant in *The Ship of Fools* (*Das Narrenschiff*, 1494), and by Rabelais in his *Gargantua and Pantagruel* (1532–52), mirrors the disenchantment with customary law as well as the ambivalence that characterized the "reception" of Roman law in Renaissance and Reformation Europe. This literary fascination with the law has extended itself by way of Goethe, Kleist, Dickens, Trollope, Dostoevsky, Tolstoy, Kafka,

Camus, and Faulkner unabated into the present, when writers regularly reach the best-seller lists with novels about lawyers, and when television lures viewers to follow, day after day, the continued coverage of courtroom trials and, each evening, the adventures of policemen and lawyers in their quest for justice.

The venerable association of literature and law has hardly gone unremarked. Hegel famously oriented the discussion of divine and human law in his *Phenomenology of Spirit* (*Phänomenologie des Geistes*, 1807) around Sophocles' drama *Antigone*. In an early essay on poetry in the law ("Von der Poesie im Recht," 1815) Jacob Grimm observed that "law and poetry arose together from the same bed," the foundations of which were "wonder" and "faith."[5] Grimm went on to demonstrate, with copious examples from Roman as well as ancient Germanic law, that many of the technical terms in law and poetics are etymologically related and that much ancient law is characterized by such striking poetic devices as alliteration: *quod felix faustumque sit* and *aqua et igni interdicere*; or *eigen und erbe* and *gut oder gelt*. Henry Sumner Maine began his classic study, *Ancient Law* (1861), with the observation that "our best sources of knowledge [for ancient jural phenomena] are undoubtedly the Greek Homeric poems."[6] Rudolf von Jhering, in his influential tract *The Struggle for Law* (*Der Kampf um's Recht*, 1872), a widely translated argument for legal activism, illustrated his notion of justified legal claims with reference to Shylock in *The Merchant of Venice* and found his understanding of the instinctive sense of right (*Rechtsgefühl*) exemplified by the hero of Kleist's story *Michael Kohlhaas*.[7]

Law as the foundation of civil society and as the embodiment of a people's ethical values resides explicitly or implicitly at the core of many of the world's greatest literary works, either as their theme or as their condition of being. That being the case, how is a study of literature and law, or more specifically the reflection of law in literature, to make any selection without appearing arbitrary? How is it possible, to cite specific examples, to embark upon this topic without coming to grips, say, with that governing classic of German literature, Goethe's *Faust*, to whose jurisprudential issues one legal scholar has devoted an entire book?[8] Or with the "forensic fictions" of William Faulkner, in which lawyers play such a conspicuous role?[9] How can we avoid the appearance of the unselective catalog, which characterizes earlier works on this topic?[10] Or the random assortment of examples, which determines many recent works on the subject, both German and English?[11]

I believe it possible to establish rational criteria of organization that enable us to make a plausible selection of examples from the wealth of Western literature and to undertake comparisons that amount to more than the casual associations sometimes justified as "intertextuality." We can do so by drawing upon two basic principles of legal anthropology: the evolution of law, and the dissociation of law and morality.

The Evolution of Law

It has been understood since classical antiquity that systems of law can and do vary from society to society and at different stages in their development. Friedrich Schiller, in his lectures on the legislation of Lycurgus and Solon, regarded it as Solon's greatest insight "that laws are only the servants of culture [*Bildung*], that nations in their adulthood require a different guidance from that of their childhood."[12] Aristotle based his *Politics* on an analysis of the constitutions of 158 different city-states, which he classified according to several types (the positive forms of kingship, aristocracy, and polity in contrast to the negative forms of tyranny, oligarchy, and democracy). In these types and their various subtypes, in turn, he saw reflected the history and development of the individual city-states. The Romans restricted their law, which according to at least one widely accepted understanding of that ambiguous term was known as *ius civile*, exclusively to Roman citizens.[13] To regulate their extensive commercial relations with non-Romans, the jurists developed what became known as the *ius gentium*, an international law synthesized from practices and procedures common to the various systems of the foreign peoples with whom they dealt.[14] During the late years of their empire, moreover, the Romans were exposed directly to the laws of foreign peoples because the Germanic tribes that invaded and conquered the Italian peninsula brought their own laws with them but, in accordance with their policy of legal autonomy, allowed the Romans to continue to be governed by Roman law. In the Middle Ages it was proverbial that travelers moving across Europe were compelled to change laws more frequently even than they changed coins, and the late-medieval reception of Roman law was motivated in no small measure by the desire of rulers to establish a legal system common to all inhabitants of the emerging modern states.

However, interest in the history and evolution of law, as opposed to recognition of the differences among existing legal systems, did not begin in any meaningful way until the Age of Reason and the gradual emergence of what we now know as the modern historical consciousness.[15] Locke and Hobbes developed radically different theories on the origins of government, yet both presupposed an evolutionary process underlying those origins. In *Leviathan* (1651) Hobbes viewed men and women as essentially selfish beings who adopted certain covenants and established an external power to enforce them, not from any social impulse, but simply to protect themselves against one another in a life that is "nasty, brutish and short" (chaps. 13–14). Locke, in contrast, argued in the second of his "Treatises of Government" (1690) that government is only a "fiduciary power" established through a voluntary social contract by a free people living in happiness. In both cases, primitive man was seen as evolving from a prelegal condition into a state of contractual government.

It was Montesquieu who first came to grips with the circumstances controlling the evolutionary processes of law. In *De l'esprit des lois* (1748) Montesquieu dealt mainly, as his subtitle suggests, with the "rapport que les loix doivent avoir avec la constitution de chaque gouvernement, les moeurs, le climat, la religion, le commerce, etc. . . ." The book is remembered today principally for its rather Aristotelian distinction among republic, monarchy, and despotism; for its defense of the separation of powers, which exerted a powerful influence on the framers of the American Constitution; and for its theory of the political influence of climate. In the last five of the massive work's thirty-one books, however, Montesquieu turned his attention to the history of law and traced its development under differing circumstances in different countries.

In Germany of the Romantic era the scholarly historiography of law was firmly established and even appropriated for political purposes.[16] Gustav Hugo, inspired by Gibbon's *The Decline and Fall of the Roman Empire* (1776–88), turned away from the purely systematic treatment of Roman law that had prevailed for centuries and sought (in his *Lehrbuch der Geschichte des römischen Rechts*, 1790) to understand the "inner" development of that law, from the Twelve Tables to Justinian's great *Corpus Iuris Civilis*, as a reflection of the mentality of the Roman people.[17] Friedrich Karl von Savigny, the great historian of Roman law in the Middle Ages and the founder of what we now know as legal historiography, used his vast knowledge of medieval jurisprudence to oppose the codification of German civil law during the Napoleonic era. In his compelling polemic *Of the Vocation of Our Age for Legislation and Jurisprudence* (*Vom Beruf unserer Zeit für Gesetzgebung und Rechtswissenschaft*, 1814), he argued that law is an organic institution that cannot be modified or systematized by legislation. Holding that the talent for legislation emerges in different peoples at different times, he maintained that the Germans of his day were not yet mature enough to undertake anything as sophisticated as a codification. Rudolf von Jhering, while appropriating the evolutionary ideas of Hugo and Savigny, rejected their vague notions regarding a "spirit of the people" informing Roman law. Instead, he concluded in his own study of "the spirit of Roman law" (*Geist des römischen Rechts auf den verschiedenen Stufen seiner Entwicklung*, 1852–65) that it was essentially a product of the constant struggle of practical jurists seeking to mediate among competing interests.[18]

The Romantic sense of history also characterized the study of Germanic law. Jacob Grimm, a legal historian by training, was inspired by his teacher Savigny to collect the legal antiquities of the Germanic past—not the laws themselves, but legal practices and beliefs—in his still indispensable *Deutsche Rechtsalterthümer* (1828). His contemporary, the distinguished reformer, patriot, and statesman Karl Freiherr vom Stein, initiated the still standard collection of *Monumenta Germaniae Historica* (1828–), the second part of which comprises the primitive legal codes of the early Germanic peoples.

Building on this base of legal historiography and specifically on the works of Savigny, whom he cites respectfully, the British jurist and scholar Henry Sumner Maine created the field of comparative law with his magisterial study *Ancient Law: Its Connection with the Early History of Society and Its Relation to Modern Ideas* (1861). Maine, working on the premise that social development generates the evolution of legal concepts, interpreted ancient Roman law in the context of the existing Hindu law with which he had become acquainted as a colonial administrator in India. Through his comparison of those two great systems as well as more primitive ones, he reached his famous conclusion that "the movement of the progressive societies has hitherto been a movement *from Status to Contract*."[19] Maine's theory appealed to the Victorian era because it was consistent with many of the prevailing ideas of the day, especially in its emphasis on patriarchy and family in the development of legal institutions. But his ideas were also compatible with the theories of evolution that were transforming geology and biology, and they seemed to confirm Hegelian idealizations of a humanity moving ever forward toward freedom.[20]

A profound sense of historical evolution also informs Oliver Wendell Holmes's *The Common Law* (1881), whose principles as set forth in its opening lines are fully consistent with those proclaimed by Savigny (whom Holmes cites):

> The life of the law has not been logic: it has been experience. The felt necessities of the time, the prevalent moral and political theories, intuitions of public policy, avowed or unconscious, even the prejudices which judges share with their fellow-men, have had a good deal more to do than the syllogism in determining the rules by which men should be governed. The law embodies the story of a nation's development through many centuries, and it cannot be dealt with as if it contained only the axioms and corollaries of a book of mathematics.[21]

Similar thoughts are evident in the works of several prominent legal scholars of the next few decades, notably the three-volume set of readings, *Evolution of Law* (1915–18), by Albert Kocourek and John Henry Wigmore; Wigmore's own two-volume illustrated *Panorama of the World's Legal Systems* (1928); and Arthur Linton Corbin's *The Law and the Judges* (1914), which emphasizes the role of community in lawmaking. As Dennis Lloyd has observed, "Each society will inevitably see its law, just as it will see its God, in its own image, and even within the same society there will be a constant process of flux and development."[22]

In recent decades evolutionary models and metaphors have again held a special appeal for some of the most creative American and Continental legal scholars, in whose work various approaches can be differentiated: social, doctrinal, economic, and sociobiological theories.[23] A similar evolutionary process has been noted by many recent students of justice. David Miller argues in his influential study that conceptions of social justice differ radically among three basic types of human society: primitive, hierarchical, and market.[24]

The evolutionary theory of law and justice yielded a particular usefulness as a tool for scholars in other social sciences, notably sociology and anthropology.[25] In his classic work *Gemeinschaft und Gesellschaft* (1887) Ferdinand Tönnies assumed that a process of legal evolution accompanied the shift from community to society that characterized the history of modern Europe. Emile Durkheim and Max Weber were not interested primarily in the evolution of law; but both took for granted an evolutionary theory of law as the foundation of their sociological thought. Durkheim's *De la division du travail social* (1893) begins with the premise that social solidarity is a moral phenomenon inaccessible to precise observation. Durkheim argues that it is necessary to substitute for the inaccessible inner circumstances an exterior fact that symbolizes the former. "Ce symbole visible, c'est le droit."[26] Since law reproduces the principal forms of social solidarity, he continues, it is simply necessary to classify the different species of law in order to determine the different species of social solidarity that correspond to them. In the course of his book he has recourse to such classic systems of law as those embodied in the Old Testament, the Twelve Tables, and the accounts in Tacitus's *Germania* in order to make his sociological discriminations. Finally, in the seventh part of his posthumously published *Wirtschaft und Gesellschaft* (1922), Weber cites Maine as well as Savigny while establishing a comparative typology deriving legal organization from legal thought. In the chapter on "legal honoratiores," for instance, he characterizes the thinking of such different types of "law-speakers" as judges, priests, and professors, and analyzes the effects upon legal thought exercised by such different systems as the guildlike method of training English lawyers, the rationalization of law in countries based upon Roman jurisprudence, and the limitations imposed by sacred law in Hindu and Mosaic countries.[27]

While the absolute types and patterns proposed by earlier evolutionists are no longer accepted by legal anthropologists in view of the diversity of social patterns in human history, the basic evolutionary principle assuming a correlation between the legal and social order of given societies has become a commonplace in social thought. In *Primitive Law* (1935) and several subsequent works, Arthur S. Diamond combined the history of ancient law with modern sociological typologies and recent anthropological data to generate a theoretically innovative paradigm of comparative law. Using reports on the legal practices of often illiterate peoples of Africa, Australia, and South America, Roman accounts of the early law of Germanic tribes as well as explorers' reports on the practices of North American native tribes, and the recorded history of the great legal codes of antiquity, Diamond proposes a model that enables us not only to understand the evolution of legal systems historically within specific groups but also to make appropriate comparisons among different peoples who, at radically different points in chronological time, have attained the same relative level of legal sophistication.

Diamond's evolutionary history of law is based on several assumptions.[28] Logic as well as anthropological observation suggest that legal development is related to the growth of social organization. A society that has not advanced beyond the household or the hamlet requires laws of a different order of complexity from one based on such larger units as clans, tribes, or nations—not to mention those that have evolved into states and empires. Nomadic tribes, whether pre-Canaanite Hebrew or early Germanic or nineteenth-century African, need regulations of a different sort than do settled societies with towns, real property, and markets. In general, the sophistication of the legal system corresponds to the size and density of the population, whether in ancient Babylon, classical Rome, or modern states. (Homogeneity of the population also plays a role: the essentially homogeneous peoples of the Greek city-states or the people of tenth-century Iceland shared the moral assumptions upon which their laws were based to a degree unknown among the diversified populations of the later Roman empire or the United States today.)

The evidence is overwhelmingly persuasive that societies at the same level in their evolution, regardless of their chronological position in history, develop laws that display remarkable similarities. Among the most primitive food-gatherers and hunters, wherever we encounter them, the offenses regarded as *crimes* meriting the attention of the community are those that potentially affect the welfare of the group: notably incest, witchcraft, and sacral offenses. At this level one can hardly speak of "law"; we are dealing with customs enforced by community sanctions, usually death. Homicide, bodily assault, adultery, and theft, in contrast, are regarded as offenses with no *public* consequences: affecting only the injured party, they are left to be settled by the individual and his family. Theft is still a relatively inconsequential matter because individuals own hardly anything worth stealing. Homicide is normally dealt with by retribution against the murderer or his family. Adultery in flagrante delicto is avenged on the spot by the offended husband.

As societies evolve—say, to the level of the first-century Germanic tribes described by Tacitus or the equivalent level among certain African tribes of the nineteenth century—the "legal" practices change. Homosexuality and sodomy are universally added to the list of public crimes, as witness the abominations that bring down the wrath of the pre-Mosaic God upon Sodom and Gomorrah in Genesis 19. As for civil wrongs, with the acquisition of property among these cattle-keepers, theft has become a more common offense and is normally punished by manifold restitution of the amount stolen, or its equivalent. ("Do not men despise a thief if he steals to satisfy his appetite when he is hungry? And if he is caught, he will pay sevenfold; he will give all the goods of his house" [Prov. 6.30–31].) Families begin to prefer compensation in return for the death or injury of a group member rather than simple retaliation, which all too easily devolves into a cycle of violence. The Early Codes at this level, as evidenced by the Icelandic sagas or as recorded by anthropologists from the still unwritten laws of certain early-twentieth-century African tribes, display a high degree of sophistication in the compensation for various delicts, ranging from the intentional homicide of a man (fourteen cows and one bull) or a woman (seven cows and one bull) by way of unintentional homicide (half of the above) to injuries causing the loss of a finger or an eye (one cow and one bull), loss of a tooth (one goat), or loss of both testicles or the penis (fourteen cows and one bull).[29]

As a sense of national solidarity transcending family, clan, and tribe begins to appear—for example, among the Merovingian Franks of the sixth and seventh centuries or the Zulus of the nineteenth—the situation changes appreciably. Among these migrant peoples the "king" or chieftain is head of the people and *not* ruler of a particular geographical space, but their codes of law show that certain hitherto private injuries are increasingly coming to be regarded as criminal or public offenses. Accordingly the king or tribal leader begins to take an active interest in the judgment and punishment of homicide and similar crimes that affect the group's welfare.

During the next stage—which can essentially be identified with feudalism in western Europe, but also with Hittite society of the mid–fourteenth century B.C. as well as various African peoples of the recent past—pronounced changes take place. In these Central Codes more and more offenses become criminal: breach of the peace on the king's highway or in his palace, treason, murder, robbery, attack on private dwellings, and neglect of military service. Even though some of the sanctions are mild (fines), the fact that they are exacted by the central authority and not by an individual or the family indicates a significant evolution in the notion of law and order.

We reach, finally, the great written codes that stand at the beginning of many civilizations: Hammurabi's Code (ca. 1792–1750 B.C.), the Covenant Code of Exodus (ca. 900 B.C.), the Code of Draco in Athens (621–620 B.C.), the Twelve Tables of Roman law (451–450 B.C.), but also the great codifications of law in thirteenth-century Europe as well as Abyssinian law of 1935. The social and legal similarities among these Late Codes, all of which are essentially collections of case law ("dooms," *themistes*, *mishpatim*), is astonishing. In almost every case we are dealing with late feudal societies divided into three classes—aristocracy, commoners, and slaves—and the laws distinguish precisely among the privileges, responsibilities, and punishments appropriate to each. In these increasingly wealthy families the laws of marriage, inheritance, and property play a proportionately major role; and in the new market society accompanying the emergence of towns the law of contracts assumes a sudden prominence. Because these societies for the first time have a clerical class of priests and scribes, legal transactions begin to be written, and not merely witnessed with an elaborate ritual. As the feeling emerges that financial payment is no longer an honorable compensation for a death, the normal sanction for intentional homicide is death: "Moreover, you shall accept no ransom for the life of a murderer, who is guilty of death; but he shall be put to death" (Num. 35.31).

It is at this stage that the notorious principle of talion (*lex talionis*) makes its first appearance in most of the codes and enjoys its brief legal life. Thus we read in Hammurabi's Code: "If a seignior has destroyed the eye of a member of the aristocracy, they shall destroy his eye" (§196).[30] "If he has broken a[nother] seignior's bone, they shall break his bone" (§197). "If he has destroyed the eye of a commoner or broken the bone of a commoner, he shall pay one mina of silver" (§ 198). According to the Old Testament: "When a man causes a disfigurement in his neighbor, as he has done it shall be done to him, fracture for fracture, eye for eye, tooth for tooth; as he has disfigured a man, he shall be disfigured" (Lev. 24.20). (The appearance of the principle in the much earlier code of Exodus at 21.23–24 is widely regarded to be an interpolation from later times.)[31] Similarly the Twelve Tables provide that "If [a man] has broken a member, unless he makes his peace with him [i.e., through compensation] there shall be like for like." (SI MEMBRUM RUP(S)IT, NI CUM EO PACIT, TALIO ESTO.)[32]

The *lex talionis* has often been misunderstood: these dreadful mutilations are not so much an expression of bloodthirsty vengeance as, rather, society's attempt to legislate and restrict the degree of vengeance for specific crimes.[33] The legal prescriptions are generally meant to state a principle of limited reparation in kind in place of specific or ceaseless vengeance. Thomas Jefferson understood this principle well when he wrote, in his "Bill for Proportioning Crimes and Punishments in Cases Heretofore Capital" (1779), that a criminal "after suffering a punishment in proportion to his offence is entitled to [society's] protection from all greater pain, so that it becomes a duty in the legislature to arrange in a proper scale the crimes which it may be necessary for them to repress, and to adjust thereto a corresponding gradation of punishments."[34] Solon presumably had something similar in mind when, according to legend, he discarded the harsh measures of his predecessor Draco, who reputedly imposed the death penalty for almost every crime, and replaced them with milder penalties. (It is now widely assumed that Draco was not so bloodthirsty as legend would have it; it is simply the case that he concerned himself exclusively with homicide laws, which were in fact retained by Solon.) Since these societies knew as yet no such institution as the prison, the punitive options were few: essentially death, fines, or exile. From the Early to the Central Codes, as we have seen, the number of crimes meriting death had increased dramatically. But the death penalty now came into conflict with the new religious or ethical view among Babylonians, Hebrews, Romans, and Christians alike that human life is sacred. Mutilations scaled according to the principle of analogy were devised to provide a state-sanctioned punishment other than death, but one that was still proportionate to the seriousness of the offense.

Our concern is of course with societies that have developed a literature as well as law: those that Diamond calls the Early, the Central, and above all the Late Codes. It is not necessary to accept the economic criteria underlying Diamond's pathbreaking work in order to make use of his evolutionary typology of law.[35] Similar analogies have become a commonplace in the history of jurisprudence. One recent textbook of Roman law notes that the relation between the Roman law of the classical period and English law constitutes "a natural relationship stemming from similarity of national characteristics; the national attributes which enabled the English and the Romans to govern the world are the same as those which formed their law."[36] Another scholar finds a common denominator among the communitarian aspirations for social justice of the German Anabaptists, the American Amana societies, and the Zionist kibbutzim.[37] Similar analogical thinking is common in other fields as well, as when a distinguished French scholar in his *Histoire de l'education dans l'antiquité* (1948) compares society in Homer's time to that of Carolingian, prefeudal Europe and emphasizes the parallels between the development of Athens and that of modern western Europe[38]—comparisons that are precisely analogous to those in Diamond's model. Such temporal relativism, it goes without saying, is implicit both in Spengler's notion of cultural "synchronicity" (*Gleichzeitigkeit*) and in Toynbee's "contemporaneity" of societies.

Along with recent legal theorists, literary scholars can make fruitful use of Diamond's historical typology for their own purposes. Taken not as an absolute rule but as a tendency, it enables us to organize our material in a rational rather than a merely impressionistic or "intertextual" manner. As we shall see, both *The Eumenides* and *Njal's Saga*, though separated by seventeen centuries, are in Spengler's phrase "relatively simultaneous"—that is to say, written by authors looking back from the vantage point of their own Late Code societies at legal institutions just emerging from the stage of Early Codes. We therefore follow a natural evolutionary progression if we move directly from Aeschylus to the author of the Old Norse saga because both share the same assumptions about their legal institutions, which in turn are remarkably similar in their procedures. Sophocles and Shakespeare, in contrast, are both writing at a point in the evolution of their national legal systems when circumstances have caused them to question central provisions of the existing Late Codes. Accordingly it makes sense to consider *Antigone* and *The Merchant of Venice* as relatively simultaneous and, in both cases, as representing a significantly later stage of evolution than either *The Eumenides* or *Njal's Saga*.

This book will take up its texts, in other words, in a sequence that reflects the evolution of the legal institutions upon which the individual works are based. The feudal customary law satirized in the various legends of Reynard the Fox represents a stage (Central Code) in the evolution of law that is more advanced than the Early Codes of *The Eumenides* and *Njal's Saga* but still not at the level of the Late Codes attacked by the writers of the Renaissance and Reformation. *Michael Kohlhaas*, though set in the sixteenth century, was written by an author whose legal thinking was determined by the modern codification process of the late eighteenth century, while Kafka's works display all the ambivalence of the heated legal controversies of the fin de siècle.

To establish the principle that law evolves and to take that principle as the organizing criterion of this book is simply the first step. Given the centrality of law in human affairs, legal issues play a very large role in literature. Which works do we single out from the great evolutionary chain for special consideration? Here we need a second principle in order to determine our criterion of selection.

The Dissociation of Law and Morality

It is a commonplace of legal anthropology that, at the beginning of their evolution, law and morality are not yet separated and that the development of law amounts to a process of continual dissociation of those two social forces.[39] In archaic cultures law was essentially an item of faith, and "morality" meant basically "religion."[40] Henry Sumner Maine, in his lecture "The Sacred Laws of the Hindus," recognized that the code of Manu, "though it contains a good deal of law, is essentially a book of ritual, of priestly duty and religious observance," and that this combination is by no means peculiar to the Hindus.[41] "There is no system of recorded law, literally from China to Peru, which, when it first emerges into notice, is not seen to be entangled with religious ritual and observance." Maine adduces the Twelve Tables of Rome to show that several of its rules are religious or ritual in nature; and he might equally well have cited the Ten Commandments, which conflate religious laws governing man's obligations vis-à-vis the deity with secular laws specifying various civil obligations and criminal prohibitions. His lecture "Religion and Law" begins with the claim that the professions of lawyer and priest were essentially identical in the earliest recorded usages of the Celts, Romans, and Greeks.[42] Indeed, the authority and truth of law, its claim to the obligation to be obeyed, derives originally from the belief that all law is God-given.[43] This is made explicit in the Ten Commandments, but the same primitive assumption is attributed to the Cretan at the beginning of Plato's *Laws*. Asked by the Athenian whether the laws of Crete were instituted by god or man, he responds, "Indubitably a god." A similar belief in the identity of law and religion underlies Calvin's sixteenth-century Geneva as well as late-twentieth-century Iran. But the *auctoritas* and *veritas* informing the law are not necessarily religious: they can derive from any moral conviction that is shared by a unified social order of the type that Tönnies called *Gemeinschaft*. To take an example from recent history, the *Reichsstrafgesetzbuch* of Nazi Germany based its law, in cases not covered by existing statutes, on the "sound sense of the people" (*nach gesundem Volksempfinden*). According to §2 of that code, "Anyone who commits an act that the law declares punishable or that merits punishment according to the basic conception of a penal code or the sound sense of the people, will be punished."

At the other end of the scale, and of the process of legal evolution, many thinkers have sought vigorously to separate law and morality, precisely because of the dangers inherent in the "sound sense of the people," whether in the courts of Nazi Germany or in a lynch mob in the United States. This move toward disjunction had its beginnings in antiquity when community solidarity first began to be shattered by individuals thinking for themselves. It took a major step forward during the High Middle Ages as the new concept of "justice" began to take shape and as professional lawyers began to differentiate themselves from local law-speakers who represented the voice of their communities.[44] But it gained real momentum during the Enlightenment. Thus Kant made a distinction between the juridical and the ethical or between legality and morality (in his *Metaphysics of Morals*).[45] By the end of the nineteenth century Kant's view had been radicalized into an absolute dissociation of law and morality advocated by leading thinkers both in Europe and in the United States. In a talk entitled "The Path of the Law" and delivered in 1897 at the dedication of the Boston University School of Law, Oliver Wendell Holmes confided, "For my own part, I often doubt whether it would not be a gain if every word of moral significance could be banished from the law altogether, and other words adopted which should convey legal ideas uncolored by anything outside the law."[46] In Austria, as we shall see, similar views culminating in the so-called Pure Law movement were popularized by the satirist Karl Kraus, who in 1908 published a collection of polemical articles entitled simply *Morality and Criminal Justice* (*Sittlichkeit und Kriminalität*), in which he lampooned any intrusion of law into the domain of private morality.

In practice, of course, the separation is never so absolute as theory proposes: the relation of law to morality is more accurately described as two intersecting circles whose area of overlap varies from society to society.[47] Yet it is precisely the tension between law and morality that produces the evolution of law. As long as the two are in total harmony, there is no need for the law to modify itself in its fundamentals. But when law and morality fall out of phase, especially as the law in modern welfare states has invaded every corner of public and private affairs, then the law begins to be challenged by individuals or by minority groups within the society.[48] The law is an institution whose essential conservatism is symbolized by the wooden tablets or bronze columns or stone pillars upon which it is engraved or the codes and constitutions within which it is embedded. The law is modified only when the sense of the community evolves to a point at which an unbearable tension develops between the law and the ethos it is supposed to reflect. As James Gould Cozzens has a wise judge put it in his novel *The Just and the Unjust* (1942), the jury protects the court in the ancient conflict between liberty and authority. "It doesn't matter how wise and experienced the judges may be. Resentment would build up every time the findings didn't go with current notions or prejudices."[49] Thus when social and religious morality began to put a higher value on human life, as we saw, the *lex talionis* was introduced as a deterrent to blood vengeance. Our own time has seen similar tensions between the existing law and personal or group morality produce profound legal crises: for example, the debates over civil rights, abortion, affirmative action, euthanasia, gay rights, and the death penalty.

It is at those moments when the tension between law and morality is increased to the breaking point that the law is changed and its evolution lurches forward again. And it is precisely those epoch-making moments that great literature reflects. There are hundreds of works in the history of literature that deal with law: from Cicero's orations and Apuleius's *Apologia* down to the late-twentieth-century novels featuring the figure of the lawyer. But the existing law suffices for the needs of most of those works; they express no sense of dissatisfaction with the system; the pleasure of these forensic fictions arises from their skillful use or abuse of the existing system. In such works, characteristically, it is not the law as such that is at issue but the determination of facts within its framework (for instance, in the traditional courtroom drama).

But there is a much smaller group of legal works in which it is not the facts that are in question but the values by which the facts are to be judged. Orestes and Antigone and Shylock do not for an instant deny or contest the facts of their deeds; they take exception to the values and laws by which those deeds are being condemned. It is works like these that reflect those moments of crisis in the evolution of law when the entire system is being challenged—the moments of tension when a society moves, as in *The Eumenides*, from a prelegal community of blood vengeance to a society of legal institutions; or, as in *Njal's Saga*, from pagan Germanic law to its humanization through Christianity. Similarly in the legends of Reynard the Fox we witness the late-medieval challenge to Central Code customary law.

Law rarely operates in a vacuum: despite the hopes and theories of the Pure Law movement, as the influence of religion and morality declines, its authority is replaced by politics and government. Indeed, the relative influence of morality and politics can be charted over time as falling and rising lines on a graph representing the evolution of law on a historical scale.[50] In *Antigone* we sense the stresses of a society in which law and religion have moved apart, creating a space where politics seizes the upper hand. Similarly, *The Merchant of Venice* exposes the anomy of a society in a state of social and legal disarray because, in the absence of religious authority, the competing claims of religious and political criteria come into conflict. In *Michael Kohlhaas* the crisis stems not from any deficiency in the law, which has been fully secularized, but from the fact that the law is not respected by the very agents charged with its enforcement: the hero's morality requires him, paradoxically, to break the law in order to force its restitution. By the time we reach Kafka's *The Trial* the bureaucratization of the law has become so complete that it represents pure form without content: Josef K. is never informed of the crime that he is alleged to have committed. It is works such as these, works reflecting not the unproblematic functioning of the existing law but the crises that precipitate its evolution, that constitute the focus of the present work.

In one sense—and hence the title of this work—the process reflected in these works is the reestablishment of justice at a new stage following its temporary dislocation. But that claim raises a question concerning the understanding of justice itself. In his *Critique of Pure Judgment* (*Kritik der reinen Vernunft*, 1781) Kant observed that "jurists are still seeking a definition for their concept of right."[51] And the definition of justice is equally perplexing, having been formulated so often in so many different ways.[52] Aristotle recognized in the *Nicomachean Ethics* (5.7.5) that the rules of human justice, in contrast to natural law, are not the same everywhere since the forms of government vary from place to place. No one has discussed the dilemma that "there are justices rather than justice" more insightfully than Alasdair MacIntyre, who has written of "a set of conflicting conceptions of justice, conceptions which are strikingly at odds with one another in a number of ways."[53]

In this wilderness of definitions I propose to understand justice—structurally, of course, and not substantively—as the perfect equilibrium of law and morality, an equilibrium suggested by the balances that Justitia has held in her hand since antiquity. In this understanding I take law to signify the existing legal code in any society and morality to designate the individual's or the community's sense of right and wrong, whether informed by religion or any other value and whether understood as retributive or distributive. I believe myself to be in agreement with Dennis Lloyd, who points out in his discussion of "legal injustice" that "injustice will arise when the law . . . is itself unjust if judged by whatever value system may be applied to test the substantial justice of the legal rule."[54] Similarly, Ronald L. Cohen notes, "Different interpretations of justice and disagreement over the existence of injustice and what it demands have transformed individual lives, relationships, policies, and entire societies, and there is every reason to expect this to continue."[55] If a court's decision is consistent with our sense of right and wrong, we call that decision just; if it is at odds with our sense of right and wrong, we feel that an injustice has been done.

Law and justice are bound in a tension that is almost sexual in its force. This was well understood by the ancients, who envisioned the mythic lawgivers and the great lawmakers and codifiers as male: Manu, Menes, Minos, Moses, but also Draco, Solon, Justinian, and so on down through history. Justice, in contrast, is invariably female: the Egyptian Maat, Greek Themis or Dike, Roman Justitia. (A close analogy is evident in the parallel between the fathers of the State—Washington, DeGaulle, Bismarck—and the female embodiments of the Nation: Liberty, Marianne, Germania.)

Justice in the modern sense is a relatively recent concept, one that emerges only when the dissociation of law and morality makes urgent the need for another authority in which we can lodge our appeal for right. To put it another way, justice is a *moral* concept, not a legal one: it can be applied to law and to legal decisions but it is not inherent in them. The earliest deities characterized as goddesses of justice, Maat and Themis, are actually representatives of order in heaven and on earth and only by extension the keepers of justice or right. (Appropriately the very term "right"—which is cognate with the words for "law" in the Romance languages, French *droit* or Italian *diretto*—stems from the Latin words *rectum* and *directum*, which define a spatial order of things.) Similarly Dike, whose name is often translated as "Justice," is in Homeric Greek the spirit of vengeance who avenges crimes against the community and its values. The Romans were not very much interested in justice as a concept: the word occurs in the first sentence of Justinian's *Institutiones*—the famous words *Iustitia est constans et perpetua voluntas ius suum cuique tribuens*—and rarely thereafter.[56] There was no cult of Justitia nor were there temples dedicated to her. Justice in her recognizably modern hypostasis, with the attributes of sword and scales, first came into existence around 1250, just at the point in history when the state was beginning definitively to replace religion as the authority of law.[57] Yet the figure representing that coincidence of law and morality is always represented as a young woman—usually, like Maat, Themis, Dike, and the Roman Justitia, clear-eyed in her vision. (Justice acquired her blindfold for the first time in the woodcuts for Sebastian Brant's *The Ship of Fools* [*Das Narrenschiff*] in 1494.)

Hence it is no surprise that the literary representation of legal crises, the dislocations of law and morality, often take the form of a struggle between men and women—a struggle that usually displays pronounced sexual or gender overtones, as in the battle between matriarchy and patriarchy in the *Oresteia*. In pagan societies, where "justice" still amounts to little more than the thirst for the sanctioned blood vengeance that will set aright the social order dislocated by a murder, it is often the case that the female representatives of justice—the Erinyes in *The Eumenides* or Hallgerd and Bergthora in *Njal's Saga*—must be restrained in their blood lust by the representatives of law (Apollo, Athena, the citizens of Athens, Gunnar and Njal). When law has become institutionalized, in contrast, it is the figure of justice who strains against the law, as in the case of Creon and Antigone. Shakespeare, as we shall see, achieves paradoxical effects in *The Merchant of Venice* by inverting the normal expectations associated with male and female, law and justice (chap. 9). Kafka finds the appropriate image for what he sees as the legal anarchy of his society in a figure of Justice who has reverted to type and become a vengeful huntress (chap. 11). Finally, the anarchism reflected in Heinrich Böll's novel *End of a Mission* (*Ende einer Dienstfahrt*, 1966) is symbolized by a Justitia who is described as being part whore and part goddess (chap. 12).

IN SUM, the following chapters deal in their historical context with literary works reflecting major crises that punctuate the evolution of law in Western civilization. The crises are precipitated in each case by dislocations in the relationship between law and morality as the truth of religion gradually gives way to the authority of the state, as community is increasingly fragmented into a society with different ideologies competing within the bland structures of bureaucracy. This is the trajectory that we see reflected in the Mirror of Justice: a tragic trajectory extending from the trial of Orestes, which constitutes the cornerstone of Western civilization, to the trial of Josef K., which undermines the foundations of that entire noble edifice—from that moment in classical antiquity when blood vengeance is replaced by trial by law to the moment in the twentieth century when law reverts once more to blood vengeance. The evolution of law has come full circle, from a primitive community so totally integrated that law and morality are one to a society so totally bureaucratized that "everything," as Kafka wrote in *The Trial*, "belongs to the Court."

CHAPTER TWO

The Birth of Justice from the Spirit of Tragedy

AESCHYLUS'S *Oresteia* marks the cornerstone of Western civilization. The students of myth and primitive religion who see in it a movement from matriarchy to patriarchy,[1] the Jungians who sense there an evolution from the unconscious to consciousness,[2] the Nietzscheans who detect a tilt from the Dionysian toward the Apollonian[3] or from chaos to cosmos,[4] the social anthropologists who register a shift from shame-culture to guilt-culture,[5] the legal historians who trace a progress from irrational to rational law,[6] from retaliation to retribution, or from strict liability to liability based on fault[7]—all attribute to this powerful dramatic trilogy what Freud called "the decisive step in human culture: the replacement of the might of the individual by the might of the community."[8]

IT IS of course not the case that society in archaic Greece was lawless: even the most primitive society has its laws. But it was a prelegal society in which homicide, along with most major delicts of a nonreligious nature, was still a civil offense of small concern to the community. Accordingly any sanctions, even though supported by custom, had to be executed by the individual and his family. In his "world poem"[9] Aeschylus celebrates, and provides the ritual occasion for the entire Athenian community to celebrate, the moment in their collective history when their archaic prelegal tribal society became a civilized society of laws and completed the "rite of passage from savagery to civilization"[10]—what has been called the journey from the Lion's Gate of Mycenae to the Erechtheum of the Acropolis.[11] One prominent scholar has sought to shock the bourgeoisie, or at least the classicists among them, by stating that "The cliché we have heard repeated all our lives, that the *Eumenides* depicts the transition from the vendetta to the rule of law, is utterly misleading."[12] This statement, while literally correct, is also very much beside the point, attacking as it does a cliché accepted by few thoughtful readers of the *Oresteia*. The trilogy marks a transition not from lawlessness to law but, rather, from a tribal culture ruled by customary law enforced by individual might to a civilized society governed by constitutional law enforced by state institutions. To that extent the trilogy mirrors a critical moment in the history of Western civilization.

The Law of Blood

Blood vengeance, as a form of retribution sanctioned by customary law, is common worldwide in primitive communities with no fixed authority, from archaic Greece and Germania to pre-Islamic Arabia down to modern Polynesia and Africa.[13] A practice that can be eliminated only by strong political authority, it has notoriously managed to maintain itself down to the very recent past in such Western societies as Corsica and the Balkans. Anthropologists have ascertained that blood vengeance occurs less frequently among hunting and fishing peoples, who have few possessions, than among shepherds and husbandmen with their flocks and property. Along with property comes the related custom of *composition*—that is, financial or real compensation for the committed offense, including murder. (Paradoxically, although composition or wergild was originally introduced in order to avoid the escalating spiral of blood vengeance feuds, it was subsequently rejected by more advanced peoples, such as the ancient Hebrews and modern Corsicans, who felt that money was an inappropriate compensation for human life.)

Blood vengeance as well as composition was evidently known to the earliest Hebrews, for reminiscences of the practice show up in their oldest stories and laws.[14] When Cain was expelled from the Lord's presence to wander as a fugitive on earth, he realized immediately that he would be exposed to blood vengeance for slaying his brother: "whoever finds me will slay me" (Gen. 4.14). Accordingly the Lord put a protective mark on him as a sign of divine mercy. (The author of Genesis does not make it clear precisely who is potentially threatening Cain with blood vengeance since he has just killed his only brother.) Similarly, the cities of refuge established in Numbers are intended to restrain the execution of blood vengeance until and unless it has been sanctioned by the courts, a provision that implies the general practice of blood vengeance.

> And the Lord said to Moses, "Say to the people of Israel, When you cross the Jordan into the land of Canaan, then you shall select cities to be cities of refuge for you, that the manslayer who kills any person without intent may flee there. The cities shall be for you a refuge from the avenger, that the manslayer may not die until he stands before the congregation for judgment." (Num. 35.9–12)

The law distinguishes carefully between murder and manslaughter. If the congregation finds evidence of premeditated murder, then the vengeance-seeker is himself permitted to inflict the death penalty.

> But if he stabbed him suddenly without enmity, or hurled anything on him without lying in wait, or used a stone, by which a man may die, and without seeing him cast it upon him, so that he died, though he was not his

> enemy, and did not seek his harm; then the congregation shall judge between the manslayer and the avenger of blood, in accordance with these ordinances; and the congregation shall rescue the manslayer from the hand of the avenger of blood. (Num. 35.22–25)

Already here we note the unwillingness to accept a composition for murder: "You shall accept no ransom for the life of a murderer, who is guilty of death; but he shall be put to death" (Num. 35.31). But essentially murder is still a private matter, which is merely regulated by the congregation; it is up to the avenger to exact the penalty. The evolution of murder from a family affair to a community concern occurs only when people begin to believe that unavenged blood pollutes the land: "and no expiation can be made for the land, for the blood that is shed in it, except by the blood of him who shed it" (Num. 35.33). Even the man guilty of manslaughter must remain in the city of refuge for a specified period (normally until the death of the high priest) to allow the land to be purified—a development that takes place also in archaic Greece[15] and that we shall encounter in Aeschylus's *Oresteia*.

It is within this context that we must understand the principle of retaliation as it occurs in the Covenant Code of Exodus, notably the provision governing conflicts: "If any harm follows, then you shall give life for life, eye for eye, tooth for tooth, hand for hand, foot for foot, burn for burn, wound for wound, stripe for stripe" (Exod. 21.23–25). It is now commonly understood that the *lex talionis*, wherever and whenever it came into existence, was meant not as a vehicle of vengeance but, rather, as a means to limit vengeance. A man or woman who is merely wounded should not seek a life in return. Indeed, it is precisely in such cases that some sort of compensation may be appropriate.

Homeric Greeks occupy a slightly more primitive level on the anthropological scale than the Hebrews whose history is recounted in the Pentateuch. Although they are acquainted with both blood vengeance and composition, vengeance is still strictly a private matter. They have not yet advanced to the cultural level at which murderers may seek refuge in special havens or at which killing has religious implications of pollution.[16] When Ajax and Odysseus are sent by the Achaeans to persuade the sulking Achilles to join the battle against the Trojans, Ajax finally gives up in frustration.

> Why, any man will accept the blood-price paid
> for a brother murdered, a child done to death.
> And the murderer lives on in his own country—
> the man has paid enough, and the injured kinsman
> curbs his pride, his smoldering, vengeful spirit,
> once he takes the price.
>
> (*Iliad* 9.772–77)[17]

But Achilles remains stone-hearted against his fellow warriors' entreaties on the grounds that Agamemnon has stolen a girl from him. Ajax's astonishment at this behavior suggests his expectation that most Greeks of the time would accept composition for a slain relative. And the composition satisfies not only the injured kinsman but also the entire community, since no pollution has taken place.

A second example is found in the famous description of the shield created for Achilles by Hephaestus at the request of his mother Thetis in *Iliad* 18.[18] Among the various scenes depicted on its vast surface we find the representation of what must have been a typical court situation.

> And the people massed, streaming into the marketplace
> where a quarrel had broken out and two men struggled
> over the blood-price for a kinsman just murdered.
> One declaimed in public, vowing payment in full—
> the other spurned him, he would not take a thing—
> so both men pressed for a judge to cut the knot.
> The crowd cheered on both, they took both sides,
> but heralds held them back as the city elders sat
> on polished stone benches, forming the sacred circle,
> grasping in hand the staffs of clear-voiced heralds,
> and each leapt to his feet to plead the case in turn.
> Two bars of solid gold shone on the ground before them,
> a prize for the judge who'd speak the straightest verdict.
>
> (18.580–92)

The main uncertainty in this passage concerns the precise issue in the dispute. The language permits two readings: the murderer claims that he has already paid the blood money while the kinsman claims that he has not received it; or the murderer offers to pay a certain amount which the kinsman refuses to accept—either because it is too small or because it is unworthy. But the general situation is quite clear. A man has been murdered; blood money, or wergild (*poinê*), is supposed to be paid; the contenders take their dispute to court, where it is to be arbitrated under the guidance of a jurisprudent (*histôr*) who supervises the judges seated on stone benches in the sacred circle (*hierô eni kyklô*). The judges, having heard the two disputants, rise in turn to offer their opinions. The one whose decision (*dikê*) is accepted as the most satisfactory receives the specified payment. The scene, in sum, portrays a society that has reached the stage in blood vengeance at which a murder may be satisfied by composition but at which there is not yet any question of pollution. In the words of Wilamowitz, "the lustre of Homeric poetry should not deceive us as to the fact that it transfigures a cruel world."[19] This is not inconsistent with

Werner Jaeger when he states, with reference to this passage as well as the *Odyssey*, that "in Homeric thought *dikê* was the line between savagery and civilization."[20]

Blood Vengeance in the *Oresteia*

The same attitude toward murder and blood vengeance is evident in the story of the Atridae as it was known in eighth-century Ionia, the traditional home of "Homer." (Homer is not familiar with the earlier family horrors of cannibalism and incest going back from Atreus and Thyestes by way of Pelops to Tantalus.) In the *Odyssey* the story of Agamemnon, murdered at the instigation of his faithless wife, is almost routinely adduced in drastic counterpoint to the tale of Odysseus, who is able to return after twenty years to his faithful wife Penelope. In the opening lines of the epic (1.29–43) Zeus, addressing the other gods, makes an instructive example of Aegisthus, who has just been slain by Orestes. Mortals, he points out, constantly accuse the gods for their misfortunes; yet Aegisthus brought his death upon himself because he had been explicitly warned by Hermes not to kill Agamemnon or to woo Clytemnestra. In the last book, when the slain suitors join the other spirits in the land of the dead, the ghost of Agamemnon utters a paean to Odysseus (24.191–202), who is fortunate to have such a virtuous wife as Penelope, in contrast to Clytemnestra, who has brought ill repute upon all women as a result of her evil deeds. At several points in between, the story is repeated in whole or in part. We learn (3.253–75) that Clytemnestra initially resisted Aegisthus's seductions, especially since Agamemnon had left behind a bard as guardian of her morals. But eventually Aegisthus removed the bard, the queen succumbed to his importuning, and they began to plot against Agamemnon. Aegisthus posted a guard to watch for Agamemnon's return from Troy (4.524–37). Alerted by the guard to Agamemnon's landing, he hides men in ambush in the palace while he prepares a feast of welcome. Having greeted the returning hero at the shore, he accompanies him back to the palace, where he feasts his guest and then kills him, "as one slaughters an ox," along with all his companions. Afterwards he rules in Mycenae for seven years (3.305). We hear of Clytemnestra only indirectly—as the coconspirator, the treacherous woman, and the murderer of Cassandra (11.409–34). Accordingly, Orestes takes his just revenge upon Aegisthus; there is nothing to suggest that he personally kills his mother, although we do hear of the funeral banquet with which Orestes honored the men of Argos following the burial of "loathed Clytemnestra and feeble Aegisthus" (3.309–10).

Orestes' blood vengeance not only involves no pollution; it brings him great honor. At the outset (1.298–300) Athena consoles Telemachus with the example of Orestes and the fame (*kleos*) he received for slaying his father's murderer. Later Nestor, using virtually the same formulaic words (3.196–98), points out to Telemachus that it is a fine thing for a son to survive when a man dies, as when Orestes slew "crafty Aegisthus, the murderer of his father."

The allusions to the Oresteia in the *Odyssey* constitute a story that differs appreciably from the version made famous by Aeschylus. Clytemnestra does not slay her husband; Orestes does not murder his mother; there is no sister Electra and no friend Pylades; there is no sense of guilt and no pursuing Erinyes. We have instead a straightforward case of retaliatory killing wholly consistent with the customary law of blood vengeance.

Whether or not we accept Wilamowitz's controversial conjecture of a seventh-century Delphic epic dealing with the Oresteia,[21] we have persuasive evidence from such independent sources as the post-Homeric epic cycle, the poetry of Stesichorus and Pindar, pre-Aeschylean Attic vases, and sarcophagus reliefs that a major change took place in the material in the course of the seventh century. We know the five books of *Nostoi* (Homecomings), traditionally attributed to Agias of Troezen, only in an abstract by the fifth-century (A.D.) Neoplatonist philosopher Proclus. But the original seventh-century Ionic work, which recounted the stories of the Homeric heroes in the years before and after the *Iliad* and the *Odyssey*, evidently contained an account of the Oresteian matter, which Proclus recapitulates in one sentence: "Then comes the murder of Agamemnon by Aegisthus and Clytaemnestra, followed by the vengeance of Orestes and Pylades."[22] Already here the plot has been enhanced: Clytemnestra shares at least equal guilt for the murder of Agamemnon, and Orestes is assisted by his friend Pylades in the blood vengeance. But there is still no hint, at least not in Proclus's retelling, of guilt or Erinyes.

The earliest textual evidence stems from the extant fragments of the heroic hymn in two books entitled *Oresteia* and written early in the sixth century by Stesichorus.[23] The Sicilian poet has shifted the action from Mycenae to Lacedaemonia, where Agamemnon is slain with an ax by Clytemnestra, who is driven to the horrendous deed not by the purely political motives of Homer's Aegisthus but by her brooding anger over Agamemnon's sacrifice, ten years earlier, of their daughter Iphigeneia. Here, too, we find the sister Electra, who remains behind in the palace when the nursemaid Laodamia, perhaps with the assistance of Talthybios, rescues Orestes, who later returns and murders Clytemnestra in an act that she foresees in a dream. The fact that Orestes is given a golden bow by Apollo to ward off the Erinyes suggests that the authority of the god and his Delphic oracle have here been introduced to justify the terrible act of matricide and that the Erinyes have appeared as avengers of the murdered Clytemnestra.

A century later in his eleventh Pythian ode (474 B.C.) Pindar followed Stesichorus in locating the action in Laconian Amyklai near Sparta. Again it is a nurse, here named Arsinoë, who rescues Orestes and carries him off to safety at the home of his friend Strophios near Parnassos when Agamemnon along with the prophetess Cassandra is cut down by the merciless Clytemnestra. The poet is uncertain whether she was motivated by anger at the slaughter of Iphigeneia or simply by the moral corruption of her licentious behavior with her lover. Some time later Orestes returns and, in vengeance, slays both his mother and Aegisthus.

By the time Aeschylus wrote his *Oresteia* the legend had grown well beyond the form we first encounter in the *Odyssey*. There, traditional heroic practices prevail: Agamemnon is murdered, for political and personal reasons, by Aegisthus, who in turn is slain in the appropriate response of blood vengeance by Agamemnon's son Orestes; matricide, guilt, the gods, and the Erinyes play no role whatsoever. We are dealing with a straightforward blood feud as known from the heroic age in every culture. In the course of the seventh and sixth centuries the plot is modified and expanded: it is Clytemnestra who now slays her own husband for reasons of matriarchal revenge; the cast of characters is enlarged to include a sister, a nurse, and a supporting friend; Orestes' act of vengeance, which now involves not merely murder but matricide as well, is justified by the exhortation of the god Apollo; and vengeance for Clytemnestra's murder is now sought by the Erinyes.

This is the point at which in 458 B.C. Aeschylus took up the legend as the basis for his *Oresteia*, the only intact trilogy from the entire corpus of Greek literature. In a grand simplification it can be said that the first two dramas—*Agamemnon* and *The Choephoroi* (*The Libation Bearers*)—do not carry the plot beyond the point it had already reached. This statement does not refer, of course, to the sheer poetic excellence of the work: the subtle characterization that in Clytemnestra has created one of the most memorable figures of all drama; the sophisticated structure (with its varied patterns of threes); the powerful language of the dialogues and the exuberant choral odes; the vivid imagery (notably of animals and hunting); and all the other elements that distinguish one of the greatest works of world literature. But from the standpoint of plot alone nothing has been added. To be sure, the motivation is made more explicit and plausible: Clytemnestra, brooding over the sacrificial slaughter of Iphigeneia, and Aegisthus, seeking vengeance for the ancient family crime that Agamemnon's father, Atreus, inflicted on his own father Thyestes, have compelling reasons to seek Agamemnon's death. When he returns, triumphant, from Troy, she lures him into the bath where she stabs him as he lies entangled in his robes, and then, with the same sword, murders the captive Trojan princess Cassandra, who has become innocently involved in the tragic fate of the Atridae. In the second drama Orestes, who has been raised at Phokis near Delphi, returns to Argos with Pylades to seek blood vengeance for his father's murder, as ordered by Apollo. Encountering Electra at their father's tomb, he is strengthened in his resolve by his sister and his friend. Tricking Aegisthus into returning to the palace without his bodyguard, Orestes first kills him and then, over his body, stabs his mother to death. The mirror-image choreography is magnificent: in the *Agamemnon* the mother kills first her husband and then his concubine; in *The Choephoroi* the son kills first the paramour and then his mother. In both plays, however, we remain essentially in a moral realm that is as Homeric as the setting in Argos to which Aeschylus, in contrast to Stesichorus and Pindar, has returned the action. The ruling principle is *lex talionis*. The vocable *dikê*—which in older Greek designates customary right or the proper order of things and only later takes on the specific meaning of "justice" as well as more technical legal meanings[24]—is equivalent to "vengeance" whenever it occurs in the first two plays, as the context makes amply clear.[25]

Both works begin, characteristically, with talk of revenge. In the *Agamemnon* the chorus of elders reminds us of the quest for vengeance that initially sent Agamemnon and Menelaus to Troy. The messenger announces Agamemnon's return as the tool of avenging Zeus (lines 525–26: *dikêphorou Dios*).[26] As Clytemnestra's women spread the royal carpet on which Agamemnon is persuaded to enter the palace, she says with a fierce irony that justice/vengeance (911: *dikê*) shall show him the way. While Clytemnestra and Agamemnon are inside the palace, Cassandra understands that blood money (1223: *poinê*) is being demanded for all the crimes committed earlier in this family and foretells that an avenger (1281: *poinatôr*) will come to avenge his father on the mother. When the palace doors open to reveal Clytemnestra standing over the bodies of Agamemnon and Cassandra with sword in hand, the image must have reminded the Greek audience of Dike in her Orphic aspect of Vengeance, as we know her from ancient vase-paintings.[27] A few moments later she tells the chorus that her terrible deed was prompted by the "fierce ancient spirit of vengeance" (1501: *palaios drimus alastôr*) reaching back to the terrible feast of Atreus. Similarly, when Aegisthus emerges from the palace, he gloats at the gladsome light of the "day of vengeance" (1577: *hêmeras dikêphorou*). Aegisthus calls himself "the righteous plotter of this murder" (1604: *dikaios toude tou phonou rhapheus*) and says that it was justice/vengeance (1607: *dikê*) that brought him out of exile to avenge his family on the house of Atreus. The chorus spells out this *lex talionis* most explicitly when it predicts to Clytemnestra the future vengeance for her own act of murder, saying that "it is law that the [evil]-doer must suffer the consequences" (1564: *pathein ton erxanta: thesmion gar*).

The Choephoroi, which amounts to a veritable hymn to vengeance, continues this theme of unremitting revenge, which has taken on an association with pollution: "What atonement is there for blood that has fallen on the earth?" (line 48: *ti gar lutron pesontos haimatos pedoi*). In Orestes' first speech he appeals to Zeus to aid him in his quest for revenge. The chorus of women encourages Electra to summon some god (119: *daimôn*) or mortal down upon the offending Clytemnestra and Aegisthus. When the still innocent maiden asks whether it should be a judge or an avenger (120: *dikastên ê dikêphoron*), the women define him simply as "one who kills in return" (121: *hostis antapoktenei*). The identification of justice (*dikê*) with vengeance is, if anything, even more powerful in this second drama. Apollo has commanded Orestes to kill (274: *antapokteinai*) his father's murderers "in like manner," warning him that avenging Erinyes have arisen from the paternal blood. Electra appeals to Zeus to extract justice from the existing wrongs (398: *dikan ex adikôn*), and she is reinforced by the chorus, who recall the "law" (400: *nomos*) that any killing that spills blood on the ground demands more blood in return. Orestes, Electra, and the chorus whip themselves up into a frenzy of vengeance that they routinely label "justice" (*dikê*). When Clytemnestra finally appears at the palace gate to welcome the strangers, she offers them the warm baths with which she had years earlier welcomed Agamemnon, soothing beds, and—with sublime irony—the presence of Justice's eyes (671: *dikaiôn t'ommatôn parousia*). After Orestes has killed Aegisthus, he hesitates for an awful moment before striking down his mother, appealing to Pylades for advice. His friend, in the only words that he utters in the entire drama, exhorts him to keep in mind the prophecies of Apollo and the oaths he swore and to risk alienating all men by his actions rather than to incur the wrath of the gods by failing to keep his word. As Orestes drags Clytemnestra into the palace, the chorus stands outside and observes that "justice" (935: *dika*), identical with "harsh revenge" (936: *barudikos poina*), which finally came to the house of Priam, has at last returned to Agamemnon's house at the command of the Pythian god. "Wily blood vengeance" (947: *doliophrôn poina*) was assisted in its struggle by the "true daughter of Zeus" (948–49: *etêtymos Dios kora*) whom men call Justice (*Dika*). With similar words Orestes justifies his own deeds. He carried out the act of matricide "justly" (988: *endikôs*) and "not without justice" (1027: *ouk aneu dikês*), and Aegisthus received his "justice" (990: *dikê*) "as the law required" (*hôs nomos*). It is therefore a surprise to him when the Erinyes suddenly appear in the last moments of the drama, their eyes dripping with hateful gore. The chorus, to whom the Erinyes are invisible, is equally puzzled because Orestes has after all fulfilled the letter of the law, appeasing his father's spirit by his acts and vanquishing his enemies. Assuming that it is simply the wet blood on his hands that has disquieted him, they advise him that there is one cure for his pollution: Apollo's touch. As the raving Orestes rushes off to Delphi, the chorus wonders yet again where this misery of the Atridae will end.

THUS FAR the essentially heroic legend of blood vengeance that we know from Homer, the Homeric *Nostoi*, Stesichorus, Pindar, contemporary visual arts, and the first two works of Aeschylus's trilogy. But with the introduction of the notion of a blood guilt pursuing Orestes in the form of the Erinyes, a new element enters the plot. And there was no obvious traditional solution to this problem. Sophocles and Euripides, both writing an *Electra* some forty years after Aeschylus (in the penultimate decade of the fifth century), offered radically different responses to the dilemma posed in the last lines of *The Choephoroi*.[28]

Sophocles' *Electra* (written between 418 and 410 B.C.) is almost Homeric in its consciously archaic motivation. Orestes, acting here out of purely personal motives and without any divine behest (albeit with the acquiescence of the gods), celebrates a political triumph and suffers no guilt or pursuit by the Erinyes. In his drama Sophocles shifts the focus of interest from Orestes to Electra, so terrible in her furious lust for revenge; he thus creates a new tradition that extends down to Hugo von Hofmannsthal's *Elektra* (1904), which provided the libretto for Richard Strauss's opera, and to Eugene O'Neill's *Mourning Becomes Electra* (1931).[29]

Euripides, who wrote three plays relevant to our theme, remains closer to the religious motivations that concerned Aeschylus. (*Iphigeneia in Aulis*, which was produced posthumously in 405 B.C., is not germane, dealing as it does with events prior to the Trojan War.) In his *Electra* (417, or possibly 413) it is again the hate-filled sister who provides the center of action. At the end she is married off to Pylades, and almost as an afterthought we learn that Orestes is being pursued by the Erinyes. But in the final scene the Dioscuri appear as *dei ex machina* and send Orestes to Athens, with the promise that Athena will protect him from the onslaughts of the Erinyes and that the Areopagus will clear him of the crime of matricide. In *Iphigeneia in Tauris* (ca. 412) he chose a variant of the traditional legend, according to which Iphigeneia was rescued from death at Aulis when Artemis substituted a hind for the sacrificial victim and transported Iphigeneia to Taurus to serve as her priestess. Orestes, crazed by the Erinyes, has been commanded by Apollo to rescue the sacred image of his sister and take it back to Athens. Following the recognition of brother and sister and their perilous escape, Athena appears to restrain the angry Thoas, king of the Taurians, from his pursuit; she foretells that Orestes will be freed from the Erinyes and that Iphigeneia will remain the priestess of Artemis in her new shrine at Brauron. In 408 B.C., almost as though he wished to compensate for his earlier neglect of Orestes for the sake of the two sisters, Euripides wrote an *Orestes*, which otherwise has no counterpart in the tradition. The action takes place on the sixth day following the murder of Clytemnestra and Aegisthus. Orestes has gone mad, and Euripides gives a detailed and convincing portrayal of his condition. Orestes, Electra, and Pylades have been sentenced to death by the citizens of Argos for their deeds. In their continuing lust for revenge they try to kill Helen, the ultimate source of all the evils; but since Helen has disappeared, they set the palace on fire and turn their fury upon her daughter, Hermione. At this point Apollo appears and sets matters aright: Electra marries Pylades; Orestes must spend a year in exile, but then, cleared of all guilt by the court on the Areopagus, he will return to marry Hermione. Apollo takes it upon himself to reconcile the citizens of Argos with these resolutions.

In sum, the events at Argos—the matricide and the murder of Aegisthus—produce in Sophocles' eyes no problem at all, while they represent for Euripides an essentially religious issue that is resolved by theological means (notably the restoration of the statue of Artemis). (In several other primitive traditions, which did not receive literary shaping, Orestes cures his madness by various other religious means: by sitting on a stone fetish, by gnawing off one of his fingers, or by seeking the counsel of nine men of Troezen at a holy stone of Artemis.)[30] The legal implications do not exist for Sophocles, and for Euripides they are of minor interest: in both *Electra* and *Orestes* the *dei ex machina* who appear at the conclusion speak of a trial on the Areopagus; but it is purely routine and Orestes' acquittal is taken for granted. A similar indifference to, or denial of, a legal dimension prevails in all subsequent treatments of the theme.[31] In Robinson Jeffers's "New Oresteia," *The Tower beyond Tragedy* (1925), Orestes exemplifies the hero who transcends all feelings of guilt and enters the state of philosophical detachment that Jeffers subsequently labeled Inhumanism. Jean Giraudoux's *Électre* (1937) constitutes virtually an attack on the notion of justice. In his amoral version of the legend the past killings and notions of revenge have lost their relevance: everyone, including Orestes and the representative of law, is at peace with the situation—everyone except Electra, whose lust for vengeance and "justice" disrupts the harmonious society and ultimately causes Orestes, after she has goaded him into matricide, to curse her and commit a suicide of despair. In Sartre's *Les Mouches* (1942) his Oreste carries out the murders as an act of defiant freedom against a hostile state and its protecting deities. Oreste regards remorse as cowardly: "Le plus lâche des assassins, c'est celui qui a des remords" (act 3, scene 2). In the closing scene he freely assumes the burden of the Erinyes (the flies of the title) in order, like the Pied Piper, to liberate Argos from their plague. And in the *Elektra* that constitutes the third part of Gerhart Hauptmann's *Atriden-Tetralogie* (1944) Orestes, having been driven to kill his mother by his sister's lust for revenge and by Clytemnestra's own frenzied attack, strides out into the dawn and freedom, leaving Electra behind with the murderous ax in her hand.[32] The major twentieth-century adaptations of the Oresteia are as conspicuously unconcerned with its legal implications as were most classical versions.

Aeschylus and the Areopagus

Alone among dramatists ancient or modern, Aeschylus wrote a *Eumenides*—that is, a work that gives the Oresteia an explicitly legal dimension in addition to its theological or philosophical resolutions and that thereby displays the shift from a prelegal society of blood vengeance to a society of laws as the basis of civilization. Aeschylus's preoccupation with law is evident even in the language and imagery of the trilogy. We have already noted that the word *dikê* and its derivatives occur with notable frequency in the *Agamemnon* and *The Choephoroi*. But it shows up almost twice as often in *The Eumenides*, with eighty occurrences as contrasted to forty-nine and forty, respectively, in the first two plays.[33] Particularly conspicuous are the genitive metaphors involving *dikê* in the magnificent choral odes: examples include *domos dikas* (line 516: "the House of Justice"), *bômon dikas* (539: "the altar of Justice"), and *hermati dikas* (564: "the reef of Justice"). Why should this have been the case?

Aeschylus (525–456 B.C.), born at Eleusis to a noble family of Eupatridae, experienced personally the extremes of Athenian political forms, witnessing during his boyhood the tyranny of Hippias and coming to manhood during the democratic reforms of Cleisthenes. Familiar from childhood with the Eleusinian Mysteries, he was to make dramatic use of mystical ideas especially in the *Oresteia*.[34] Aristotle tells us (*Nicomachean Ethics* 3.2) that he was even tried and acquitted by the Council of the Areopagus for revealing secrets of the cult of Demeter.

The Areopagus, the "Hill of Ares" situated to the northwest of the Acropolis, got its name, according to one legend, from the tradition that Ares was tried there for the murder of Poseidon's son Halirrhothios, who had seduced Ares' daughter. (Another version has it that the hill was named for the *arai* ["curses"] who inhabited its caves and who were worshiped under the benign names of *semnai* ["venerable ones"] or *eumenides* ["gracious ones"].) Its name apart, the Areopagus from the earliest days of Athens was the site of the *boulê* or council of elders that ruled the city.[35] Originally no doubt equivalent to the council of nobles who advise the leaders in the Homeric poems, the *boulê* was at first chosen exclusively from the Eupatridae and represented the aristocratic-conservative pole in the movement toward democracy that Aristotle traces in the early chapters of his *Constitution of Athens* (*Athênaiôn Politeia*).[36] During the eighth and seventh centuries, under the monarchs and oligarchy, this council of nobles had the responsibility of supervising the laws, of administering important municipal affairs, and of punishing by penalty or fine all infringements of public order and morality. It was also traditionally responsible for trying cases of homicide. Even though a new system of recruitment in the seventh century caused the council gradually to become less exclusively aristocratic, tensions inevitably arose between its members and other classes, who were often reduced virtually to serfdom by its taxes and laws. When Draco undertook in 621 B.C. the first systematic codification of Athenian law, he shifted the responsibility for lesser crimes to other popular tribunals but, in an effort to replace private vengeance by public justice, left the authority for cases of murder with the venerably ancient Areopagus. In the movement toward democratization, other institutions were gradually established that competed with the political authority of the council: notably the *Ekklêsia* or citizens' Assembly that met in the Agora. Under Solon's constitution (594) a new democratic *boulê* of four hundred was established as a check on the original council, which henceforth became known as "the Council of the Areopagus" (*hê ex Areiou pagou boulê*). Toward the end of the century, in the course of his extensive democratic reforms, Cleisthenes enlarged the popular council to five hundred, further eroding the authority of the aristocratic Areopagus. The city had reached this point in the development toward democracy, Aristotle tells us (chap. 23), when the Council of the Areopagus once again came to power as a result of the Persian Wars. When Xerxes, ten years after Marathon, mounted a second huge attack on land and sea, the military strategists were at a loss and urged the Athenians to look out for their own safety. The Areopagus raised the necessary funds to man the fleet that destroyed the Persian ships at Salamis in 480 B.C. and established command of the seas. Regaining public confidence and authority as a result of this success, the Areopagus remained in control of the government for some seventeen years following the Persian Wars.

The year 462 B.C. witnessed one of the most critical events in the history of Athenian democracy, although almost every word of Aristotle's account (chap. 25) is regarded by historians as controversial. Ephialtes, the leading spokesman of the people and a man with a reputation for incorruptibility and loyalty to the state (*dikaios pros tên politeian*), attacked the Council of the Areopagus, bringing suit against some of its members for alleged misconduct in office. He succeeded in stripping the Areopagus of most of its powers—notably its supervision of the magistrates, its guardianship of the laws, its control of education and censorship of morals—which were transferred to more democratic entities: the Council of Five Hundred, the popular Assembly, and the various tribunals of law. The Areopagus retained little more than its ancient charge of trying cases of homicide and the supervision of various cultic affairs, under which Aeschylus had presumably been tried. Ephialtes himself was assassinated within a year by his aristocratic opponents. We can hardly appreciate today the civic trauma that these events represented: the social and political balance between classes achieved by the previous isonomy was upset as the nobility lost power in the new democracy. For the first time in history, the *polis* was ruled by the people, and not by tyrants or the nobility.[37]

It is generally agreed that Aeschylus, the scion of a noble family as well as an intensely patriotic and politically engaged citizen, must have had strong feelings about the reforms of 462 B.C. and that he chose to express those feelings in *The Eumenides*. But opinion is sharply divided about the nature of that response. Is he defending the changes[38] or opposing them?[39] Or is his position intentionally ambiguous and his sole goal to reconcile democrats and conservatives to the newly reduced authority of the Areopagus as a return to its original function as the judge of homicide?[40] One of the most sensible views proposes that Aeschylus was less concerned about any specific political effect of Ephialtes' action and more about its general implications for the traditional order of the *polis*.[41]

However we choose to interpret the work, it is clear that this major crisis of Athenian legal history prompted Aeschylus in *The Eumenides* to rethink the history of the institution under challenge—to review the development that led from the essentially prelegal society of Homeric Greece to the new society of democratic Athens, that is, a civilization governed by law. Indeed, the whole movement of his trilogy and the thrust of its great concluding piece makes it clear that Aeschylus regarded the establishment of legal institutions as the very foundation of civilized society. In his effort to accomplish this he rewrote the history of the Areopagus, making its establishment as the first court of law the high point and culmination of the ancient legend of the Atridae.

From Tribe to Tribunal: *The Eumenides*

The Eumenides is in many senses a troublesome work. Notwithstanding its mystery and power, it is (even allowing for several missing lines) not just the shortest of Aeschylus's plays; at 1,047 lines it is the shortest in the entire extant corpus of thirty-one Greek tragedies.[42] (The *Agamemnon*, by way of comparison, one of the longest plays, weighs in at 1,673 lines.) Yet moving as it does from Delphi to Athens and from the Acropolis to the Areopagus, it fails to adhere to the basic unities of time and place that Aristotle demanded of the ideal tragedy. As a result of the shift of scene, moreover, the chorus is required to enter not just once, as in most other Greek tragedies, but twice: first at Delphi and then again in Athens. It was not only such ancient theoreticians as Aristotle who were compelled to ignore *The Eumenides* because it did not fit their expectations. Contemporary students of tragedy, noting its exceptional nature, have also omitted it from their consideration: George Steiner is unable to accommodate its compromising conclusion to his understanding of tragic catastrophe.[43]

The action of the play is easily recapitulated. The "hypothesis" or plot outline (by Aristophanes of Byzantium) preceding the play is conspicuously brief: "Orestes, surrounded in Delphi by the Erinyes, goes on the advice of Apollo to Athens to the temple of Athena. Having won his case with her counsel [or even perhaps: with thanks to her newly established Council (*hês boulêi*)?], he returns (from exile) to Argos. Having soothed the Erinyes, Athena addresses them as Eumenides."[44] (The hypothesis notes in conclusion that this particular plot occurs in neither Sophocles nor Euripides.) We can expand this recapitulation. As *The Choephoroi* ends, we recall, Orestes, crazed at the sight of the Erinyes who have been attracted by the blood on his hands, rushes off to seek purification through Apollo's healing touch. The action of *The Eumenides* begins accordingly at Delphi, where the temple of Apollo was the acknowledged authority on sacral law, religious rituals, and specifically on rites of purification. As the drama begins, the priestess of Apollo, following her daily prayer, enters the temple and almost immediately rushes back out in horror to report that she has seen a suppliant sitting on the omphalos, his hands and his sword dripping with blood, and surrounded by a sleeping horde of hideous women, part Gorgon and part Harpy. When the doors open to reveal the inner shrine, we recognize Orestes and the Erinyes, whom Apollo has charmed to sleep while he performs the ritual of purification, pouring pig's blood over Orestes.[45] Although Orestes has been purged of his pollution by this sacred ritual and can once again approach men and gods without contaminating them, Apollo warns that the primal Erinyes will not be satisfied by this Olympian religious ritual, and advises him to travel to Athens to be judged and freed of their pursuit. (It is important to understand that the act of purification does not clear Orestes of the crime: it simply entitles him to appear unsullied before a court of fellow men; he still stands accused of murder.) He goes, guided by Hermes and guarded legally by the safe-conduct—that is, the "right of outlaws" (line 92: *eknomôn sebas*)—that protects those seeking sanctuary.

Following his departure the ghost of Clytemnestra appears and with bitter reproaches rouses the Erinyes from their sleep. They quarrel furiously with Apollo, who again promises protection to the matricide whom they swear to hound with their vengeance. Already at this early point we realize that the ancient blood feud of the Atridae, which hitherto despite the support of various deities has taken place wholly at the level of human conflict, has been transformed into a transcendental struggle between divine forces—the deities of the underworld and of the heavens, of the past and the future, of the "Olympian and Chthonic Rituals" that Jane Harrison has brilliantly explored.[46] We prepare ourselves, therefore, to read the coming drama on two levels: human and theological.

The scene changes to the temple of Athena on the Acropolis at Athens where, after long and wearying journeys, Orestes has just arrived. (It is worth noting that this is presumably the only play whose action Aeschylus located in Athens.) He reminds us that he is in no need of religious purification (237: *ou prostropaion*) and has come at Apollo's bidding in order to clear himself legally. Almost immediately the Erinyes enter in hot pursuit of their victim, whom they espy clinging to Athena's wooden image. The relentless Furies, insisting that neither Apollo nor Athena can save him from their grasp, chant a binding spell (first stasimon) to paralyze their prey.[47] When Athena enters, the Erinyes state their case—which is based on Orestes' matricide—and make what they regard as a legitimate and absolute claim upon their victim. When Athena points out that only half of the case has been presented, they tell her indignantly that Orestes refuses to take an oath, the ancient legal procedure (also common in ancient Germanic law) by which an accused man could swear his innocence. Orestes, quite reasonably, sees no need to swear an oath since he is not contesting the actual deed. He maintains, however, that it was an act of justifiable homicide: a murder, in short, whose motivation needs to be judged. In words that he subsequently repeats for emphasis he asks Athena to decide whether or not he acted justly (468: *ei dikaiôs eite mê*; 612: *ei dikaion eite mê*)—a usage that clearly indicates that we are now in a different world from that in which *dikê* meant simple vengeance. Following this discussion (which is analogous to the preliminary hearing before the magistrate that the Athenians called *anakrisis*) the goddess, overwhelmed by the awesome responsibility of deciding between two equally persuasive arguments, decides to establish an altogether new institution to try the case: she will choose "the best among my citizens" (487: *astôn tôn emôn ta beltata*) to hear the witnesses and to assess the evidence. When Athena has left to make her arrangements, the Erinyes denounce the new system of justice in their second stasimon. But they have little choice other than to participate in the trial that begins directly thereafter with Athena as presiding magistrate, Orestes as defendant, Apollo as a witness for the defense (576: *marturêsôn*), and the Erinyes as prosecutors (583: *diôkôn*). (Some scholars believe that the jury of Athenians must have been represented by an additional chorus or by a number of mute actors;[48] but it seems more appropriate to the ceremonial nature of the performance to assume that the actual audience of Athenians understood itself in the role of the jury on the momentous occasion when that institution was created by their forefathers.[49] It has been persuasively suggested that the most conspicuous feature of the *Oresteia* is "this organic union between the drama and the community out of which it had emerged and for which it was performed.")[50]

The prosecution begins by interrogating the defendant about the circumstances of the crime: Orestes concedes (what?) that he killed his mother, (how?) that he struck her in the throat with a sword, and (why?) that he did so at the behest of Apollo. When challenged that they did not hound Clytemnestra during her lifetime, the Erinyes explain that they pursue only those who are guilty of killing blood relatives and that Clytemnestra was not related by blood to her husband, Agamemnon. (They do not point out the paradox made clear in *The Choephoroi*: that they would have harried Orestes had he failed to avenge the death of his father.) Confused in the face of these plausible arguments, Orestes calls upon Apollo for support, whereupon the god acknowledges that he did indeed order Orestes to carry out the murder (which, in turn, was ordained by Zeus). But he makes the point that the killing of a great man under such humiliating circumstances—by a woman in the bath—is a particularly heinous crime, one that overrides the normal considerations of filial respect for the mother. Then he presents his main argument: that Orestes is not actually related by blood to Clytemnestra since according to Pythagorean genetic theory only the male is the begetter and the female nothing but the vessel in which the newly begotten child is nurtured. (This argument, which long struck modern ears as absurd and logically embarrassing, was an essential principle of patrilineal inheritance law in Athens and hence quite plausible to Aeschylus's audience;[51] indeed, it became a favorite topic for rhetorical debates. It sounds less far-fetched to today's readers accustomed to court hearings involving the rights of surrogate mothers and in vitro fertilization.) Both parties sum up their arguments with only slightly veiled threats of vengeance against the citizens of Athens if the verdict turns out badly for them.

With a certain trepidation Athena hands the case over to the jury, urging them to find a middle ground between anarchy and despotism while not rejecting altogether the healthy notion of fear espoused by the Erinyes. In support of this idea she cites a proverb to the effect that men who fear nothing cannot be just (699: *tis gar dedoikôs mêden endikos brotôn*). As the jurors deliberate the case and prepare to cast their pebbles, Apollo and the Erinyes mutter further threats while Athena states the important principle that, in the case of a tie, her own vote will go to the defendant. (A considerable bibliography has arisen surrounding the grounds for Athena's vote;[52] but for our purposes it suffices to note that Aeschylus was concerned mainly with the etiological justification of the existing practice in Athenian law, according to which the *archôn* cast his vote, in cases of a tie, for the defendant—the ancient Roman principle *in dubio pro reo*.)

Since it turns out that the votes are equally distributed,[53] Athena rules in favor of the defendant, and Orestes is acquitted on the charge of homicide. (Again Athena uses a legal *terminus technicus*: 752: *anêr hod' ekpepheugen haimatos dikên*.) Orestes, pledging an oath of peace between Argos and Athens—a topical allusion to the recently (461 B.C.) formed alliance between the two cities against Sparta—departs for home and disappears from the play. Orestes' acquittal represents formally the end of the tragedy of the Atridae: and we are never allowed to forget, in the course of the trilogy, that the sequence of crime and guilt and vengeance embraces at least three generations, extending back from Orestes and Electra by way of Agamemnon, Clytemnestra, and Aegisthus to Atreus and Thyestes. But even if the human action has ended in a legal resolution, there still remains the possibility of tragedy on the higher level of deities. It is to the resolution of this theological tragedy that Aeschylus turns in the concluding two hundred lines of his drama.

The Erinyes, furious at what they regard as an insult to justice, threaten a terrible vengeance upon the land that has mocked them so grievously. But after a lengthy exchange with the courteous and respectful Athena, whose lips are guided by the goddess Persuasion (*Peithô*), the goddesses finally agree to accept a position of honor and sanctuary in Athens.[54] Following the third stasimon, which embraces several hymns in which they bless the city, the Erinyes are conducted in solemn procession to their new abode at the base of the Areopagus, where they will henceforth be known under the more propitious name of "The Venerable Goddesses" (1041: *Semnai Theai*). (It has often been remarked that the name *Eumenides* ["gracious ones"] does not occur in the text of the play—only in its title and in the "hypothesis.")[55] It is important to note that they have not been wholly disenfranchised: they will continue to exercise their pursuit of murderers, not on their own initiative, however, but only as agents of the court, as police of the new civilized society of laws[56]—in the word of Heraclitus, *Dikês epikouroi* ("hirelings" or "auxiliaries" of Justice).[57]

In the barely one thousand verses of his play Aeschylus accomplished two astonishing etiological feats. He established for the first time a link between the dreaded Erinyes and the venerable *Semnai* or *Eumenides* who traditionally inhabited caverns at the base respectively of the Areopagus and the Acropolis, thereby transforming the fearsome bounty hunters into peaceful bailiffs.[58] And he accounted in a new manner for the origins of the judicial function of the Areopagus (which had previously been explained mythologically by reference to the trial of Ares) by representing the trial of Orestes as the first trial for bloodshed in human history. We have already noted the pronounced emphasis on law and justice in *The Eumenides*, such as the frequent references to *dikê*. But there are more specific indications. The speakers employ, as we have seen, a good number of legal technical terms. And the procedures outlined by Athena and followed in Orestes' trial are consistent (albeit not fully identical) with contemporary legal practice in Aeschylus's times.[59] Indeed, one critic has suggested that Greek tragedy in general "seems to suggest as its informing image a theatre shaped more by the law-court than by the altar."[60] Some scholars, to be sure, have argued that *The Eumenides* is "but a dubious authority" on the details of Athenian law.[61] But it does not follow that Aeschylus was not passionately interested in the history of law and the grand civilizing shift from a culture of primitive blood vengeance to a society of laws. In any case, our concern is not with the niceties of fifth-century legal procedure as evident in *The Eumenides* nor with allusions to such contemporary events as the treaty with Argos or Ephialtes' reform of the Areopagus; it is, rather, with the reflection in Aeschylus's "world poem" of his sense of origin and crisis in Athenian legal history.

The play betrays a powerful historical consciousness and opens with a prayer that amounts to a genealogy of prophetesses from Gaia and Themis by way of Phoebe down to the present priestess of Apollo. When Athena concludes that the trial for murder is too weighty a matter for her alone to judge, she decides to establish an institution that will endure "for all time" (484: *thesmon, ton eis hapant' egô thêsô chronon*). Later she admonishes the citizens of Athens that they are hearing "the first trial" (682: *prôtas dikas*) for bloodshed and thereby founding an institution—"this Council of Judges (684: *dikastôn touto bouleutêrion*)—that will remain forever (*aiei*) for the people of Athens. But this institution, the fountainhead of Athenian justice, does not come into existence without controversy: indeed, the argument over its justification constitutes on the transcendental level the true dramatic conflict of the play.

The argument against the "new" institution proposed by Athena is enunciated by the Erinyes, who represent the most powerful personage of the play and the vehicle of Aeschylus's most profound thoughts on history and tradition. (The Erinyes and Clytemnestra are the only figures who have a role in all three parts of the trilogy, which might more appropriately be known as the *Clytemnestreia*.) We have already seen that the trilogy's first two plays are dominated by the principle of blood vengeance. It seems as though that principle is so self-evident that it does not need to be embodied by the Erinyes: invisible in the first two plays, they are seen only by Cassandra on the roof of the palace at the end of the *Agamemnon* and by Orestes in the closing moments of *The Choephoroi*. But in the third play, where the principle of absolute blood vengeance that they represent is called into question, they assume the loathsome form that up to this point has only been described but not presented and—like the unicorn in Rilke's poem—come into being because the people's belief in them is so fervent.[62] In fact, that belief was so ardent and their representation so powerful that, according to the ancient Life of Aeschylus, members of the terrified audience witnessing the first performance fainted and women miscarried.[63] (Aeschylus was apparently the first artist who actually described and portrayed these beings who had long been known by name and reputation.)[64] Accordingly Aeschylus must disarm their fearsomeness by transmuting them at the end into "venerable goddesses" (*Semnai Theai*), by characterizing them with a series of adjectives involving the prefix *eu-* (implying graciousness), and by co-opting them into the new system of justice.

The Erinyes embody unadulterated primal vengeance, which rises from any blood spilled on the ground—Agamemnon's as well as Clytemnestra's. They are monstrous women who kill their victims by sucking the blood from their bodies. When we first glimpse them, in their long black garments, their eyes dripping with gore, and awakening from the drugged sleep into which they have been charmed by Apollo, they are dreaming uneasily that they are hounds pursuing their quarry; appropriately their first words are the terrible cries of the hunt: "Seize him, seize him, seize him, seize him, watch him!" (130: *labe labe labe labe, phrazou*). (Consistent with this pervasive image of the hunt, the words characterizing Orestes often invoke the pursued fawn or hare.)[65] As they make clear in the great binding song, they understand themselves as the strict guardians of righteousness (312: *euthudikaioi*). They know absolutely no doubt in their mission of strictly constructed law, to which they were appointed at birth; the "eternal children of Night" (416: *Nuktos aianê tekna*), they repeatedly stress their ancient authority (394: *geras palaion*)—in particular to watch over acts of domestic violence and to pursue "the killers of their kin" (421: *brotoktonountas ek domôn*).[66] (Even though their anthropological origin can be traced back to a primitive Aegean matriarchal society, they never restrict their vengeance to matricide or to matrilineal murder.) Since Clytemnestra has no surviving kin to avenge her, that role has fallen to their lot. When they first arrive at Athens, they make an absolute claim upon the life of Orestes because he murdered his mother. In their eyes the law of strict retaliation still obtains: blood demands blood. The ancient law that they represent recognizes only guilt or innocence and makes no such distinction as that to which Orestes appeals between wanton murder and justifiable homicide. (For that reason Athena accuses them of preferring the appearance of legality to true justice.)

When Athena, by establishing the new court, acknowledges the possibility that some acts of homicide may be justifiable, they see it as the end of human society. The second stasimon begins with their lament over the ruin and catastrophe that will result from these new laws (490–91: *nun katastrophai neôn /thesmiôn*). If Orestes wins his case and is acquitted of the crime of matricide, then all parents in the future must quake in terror before their children. The very House of Justice will be undermined by these concessions. Reverence and respect for law and order result only from the sure knowledge that terror and dread await all violators.[67] In a series of proverbs they remind their listeners that one should praise neither anarchy nor despotism but the middle way of moderation, and that wanton violence (534: *hubris*) is the child of impiety. The altar of Justice must be maintained along with constraints upon transgressions. It is this conservative belief in absolute summary justice (= vengeance) that they carry into the succeeding interrogation of Orestes, in which Apollo, as we have seen, proposes justifications for the act of matricide. It is not a question of absolute guilt versus innocence but of justifiable homicide.

It is important to remember that Athena, as the tutelary deity of Athens and the presiding magistrate in the proceedings, does not unthinkingly take sides. On the contrary, she embodies the very moderation and the middle way upon which the Athenians prided themselves. Accordingly she sees merit in both arguments: indeed, it is precisely this ambiguity that characterizes all tragic dilemmas and all true tragedy. Her charge to the jury virtually recapitulates the Erinyes' words to the effect that justice requires a certain degree of fear. At the same time, her decision to institute a deliberating body of jurors rather than simply to hand Orestes over to the Erinyes indicates that she appreciates the other side of the case—the possibility that Orestes' deed, and hence in principle any act of homicide, can be justified.

Athena's own ambivalence is reflected in the fact that the vote is split: at least half the jury is persuaded by the Erinyes' appeal to the old law of absolute vengeance. Even Orestes wants the assurance of the court that his act was justified. His repeated question as to the righteousness of his deed reminds us of his hesitation in *The Choephoroi* to strike his mother down, a hesitation that must be dispelled by Pylades' reminder of his duty and his oath to Apollo. For that reason one critic has seen the central moment of the trilogy in *The Choephoroi*: "the whole world and the fate of mankind hang in that act of hesitation."[68] It may well be true that the development of individual moral consciousness is evident in Orestes' hesitation, which is so unlike the unwavering and almost gleeful sense of vengeance that motivates Clytemnestra in the *Agamemnon*. But the essential step out of primitive tribalism toward a society of laws takes place only when morality moves from the private to the social realm—when the personal excellence that Homeric Greeks prized under the name of *aretê* develops into the commitment to social justice that the Athenians knew as *dikaiosynê*.[69] At that point, for the first time, a tribunal of peers can be assembled to acknowledge that homicide is no longer an act merely of concern to the individual and his immediate family but a threat to the society as a whole, and that crimes must be judged in their social and psychological context and not simply and unthinkingly handed over to the absolute vengeance-claims of the past.

This debate between primitive blood vengeance as embodied by the Erinyes and civilized trial by jury as proposed by Athena is regarded in the play as being clearly a struggle between the old order and the new. (We may accept without difficulty the qualification that Apollo's act of purification at Delphi represents a transitional aristocratic stage between the blood feud of tribal society and the trial by jury of democratic Athens.)[70] Apollo as well as Athena, both of whom claim their authority from Zeus, represent the newer Hellenic hierarchy of Olympian deities, in contrast to the ancient Mediterranean divinities evident in the Erinyes. In his first speech Apollo identifies the Erinyes as "ancient, antiquated maidens" (69: *graiai palaiai paides*) despised by men and gods alike. Later the Erinyes, furious that Apollo has helped Orestes to escape, call him a "young" god, who has trampled upon aged deities (150: *neos de graias daimonas kathippasô*), whereupon he orders them out of his temple and accuses them of barbaric practices of torture unacceptable to civilized Greeks. Apollo tells them contemptuously that he shall be victorious since they are without honor (722: *atimos*) among the new and old gods. This motif—the conflict between young and old, between the new justice and ancient vengeance—persists to become the principal theme of the great stanzas in which the Erinyes accuse Athena and the younger gods of trampling the ancient laws and snatching them away (778–79 and repeated 808–9: *iô theoi neôteroi, palaious vomous / kathippasasthe kak cherôn heilesth e mou*). They rage, in two identical strophes, at the land that has so dishonored their ancient wisdom (838: *eme palaiophrona*) and complain to Mother Night that the new Uranian gods have deprived them of their honor. Athena, shrewd in her assessment of their feelings, reassures them (848–49) that she understands their anger and concedes that they are more ancient (*geraitera*) and wiser (*sophôtera*) than she. But she goes on to make them an offer they can't refuse so that they will not be able to say that any ancient deity (883: *theos palaia*) such as they was driven away in dishonor by younger gods and the citizens of Athens. At length the Erinyes are persuaded by her arguments and agree to accept an abode in the city, where they shall continue to watch over all human affairs (930: *panta gar hautai ta kat' anthrôpous*)—in particular, crimes of blood vengeance and homicide.

Thus the ancient spirit of vengeance is co-opted into the new civil society, and the fury of the Erinyes—under their new title of Venerable Ones—is channeled into the service of the institution of law, thereby completing an astonishing and epoch-making process of social development. "Regarded originally as a tort to be redressed by the kinsmen of the victim, and subsequently as a pollution to be expiated by the prescriptions of the aristocratic priesthood, the offence of homicide is now a crime to be submitted to the judgment of a legally appointed committee of the people."[71] What began as a family tragedy and then became a struggle between the old and the new gods emerges ultimately as a drama of mankind. The juridical defeat of the old gods by the new ones does not result in the chaos that they feared but produces rather a typically Athenian compromise of the sort that Aeschylus witnessed in the course of his own lifetime: a democracy mediating between anarchy and the despotism of terror.

It is this transition, marking the shift from tribal culture to civic society, from individual blood vengeance to the controlled legality of the city-state, from private morality to social justice, that Aeschylus celebrates in his great trilogy. Other works (including Aeschylus's own *Suppliants*)[72] may tell us as much or even more about actual fifth-century legal practice or contemporary political events. Ephialtes' reform of the Areopagus was the occasion but not the reason for the *Oresteia*. Whether or not Aeschylus agreed with the reforms becomes immaterial in the face of his majestic paean to a society based upon justice. Aeschylus's trilogy is not a political commentary; it is a profound meditation on the philosophy of history, the history of law, and the theory of politics, which offered Athenians an opportunity to reflect on the political choices they had made and not made in recent decades.[73] "Later generations listened with awe to the austere warnings of Aeschylus in *The Eumenides* to keep the fear of the law and its majesty always alive in the hearts of the citizens, for that alone would enable them to steer the middle course between the extremes of tyranny and anarchy which threatened to destroy the liberty of both the community and the individual."[74]

Albert Camus once remarked that "tragedy is born in the West each time that the pendulum of civilization is halfway between a sacred society and a society built around man."[75] In the crucible of Aeschylus's genius the dialectical interplay between freedom and community, between individual and institution, which in the first two plays of the trilogy remains implacably tragic, succeeds in transcending tragedy, whose otherwise irreconcilable forces are here reconciled for the first time in human history in the Court of Justice.[76]

CHAPTER THREE

The Ambivalence toward Pagan Law

The Saga Age in Iceland

The Icelandic "family sagas" (*Íslendinga sögur*) constitute perhaps the most remarkable literary corpus of the Middle Ages and, as such, Scandinavia's greatest gift to world literature. These forty-odd prose narratives, written mostly in the thirteenth century, relate the often interconnected stories of the great families that settled Iceland during the so-called Saga Age from 930 to 1030. The histories of these houses represent, as W. P. Ker put it a century ago, "the last and also the finest expression and record of the spirit and the ideals belonging properly to the Germanic race in its own right, and not derived from Rome or Christendom."[1] Most other Germanic tribes, passing through Roman territories in the course of their migrations or living close to the Roman *limes*, were affected early by their contacts with the great empire to their south: the Goths had a translation of the Bible in the fourth century; the Burgundians, Lombards, and other tribes began to accommodate their laws and political organization to Roman practice and the Latin language from the fifth century onward; the Saxons produced a religious epic, the *Heliand*, based on the life of Jesus as early as the ninth century. The Scandinavian tribes were least directly exposed to Roman influences—and the Icelanders last of all. As a result, at a time when the Goths and Vandals were already extinct or totally absorbed by Mediterranean peoples and when the Franks and Saxons had long since adopted the imperial ways of Rome, the farmers of Iceland were living in a stateless and pre-Christian society that had more in common with the Germania described by Tacitus around A.D. 100 than with the Continental kingdoms.[2] The analogy of heroic society in tenth-century Iceland to the society of Homeric Greece has been noted by more than one observer.[3]

Although the island had occasionally been visited in earlier decades by pagan Norsemen and Irish Christian hermits, the first permanent settlement was established around present-day Reykjavik in A.D. 874 by a Norwegian named Ingolf.[4] Many of the settlers who colonized Iceland over the next two or three decades, as we know from such early sources as the *Landnámabók* (Book of settlements) and the *Íslendingabók* (Book of Icelanders), were local warlords resisting the efforts of King Harald Fairhair to impose his rule on the traditionally independent landholders as well as farmers from southwestern Norway fleeing the incursions of marauding vikings. By 930 the habitable coastal areas ringing the island were fully settled by colonists from Norway as well as other descendants of Norsemen who had been living for a generation or two in Ireland and the Hebrides.

Initially the settlers were content to live autonomously on their farmsteads—there were no towns or villages in medieval Iceland—in loose liege arrangements with chieftains who were known as *goðar* (singular *goði*, "priest") and maintained the pagan temples for their areas. Neighboring householders attended sacrifices in the temples, participated in public meetings called by their chieftains, and enjoyed a relationship of reciprocal support and protection. However, as the population increased—in the course of the tenth century, it has been estimated, the number of inhabitants reached some 50,000—the disputes inevitably extended beyond the authority of the local chieftains. While settlers who had emigrated to avoid a tyrannical king had no desire for a centralized government, they soon felt the need for a coordinated legal system that would be valid for the entire country. Sometime around 927 they sent a representative named Ulfljot abroad to compile a code based on the law of western Norway (from the law province known as Gulathing) with which most of them were already familiar.

Ulfljot's code, formally adopted in 930, provided for a General Assembly, or *Althing* (*alþingi*), that was held annually for two weeks in midsummer at Thingvellir ("Assembly Plains") in southwestern Iceland. Here the thirty-six "ancient" chieftains (later increased to thirty-nine), each accompanied by two advisers, constituted a legislative council (*lögrétta*) that enacted new laws and made any necessary changes in older laws. The chieftains also elected a lawspeaker (*lögsögumaðr*—a uniquely Icelandic institution) who served for renewable periods of three years and whose principal responsibility it was to recite the (still unwritten) laws to the people from the Law Rock (*lögberg*)—one third of the code each year—and to serve as arbiter in matters of legal interpretation: what Max Weber called "Law Prophet" or charismatic "declarer" of the law.[5] The Icelandic code of law rapidly developed into the most elaborate and systematic code used by any Germanic people. In fact, their cultural predisposition for law and lawmaking turned Iceland into what has been termed "a distinctly oversanctioned society."[6] Like the Romans, the Icelandic people evidently enjoyed the process of legislation as well as the rhetoric and rituals of judicial procedure, which played a major role in their lives and literature. These farmers were shrewd businessmen who were constantly involved in lending money, collecting debts, managing inheritances, planning marriages and divorces with complicated dowries, handling property disputes, arranging settlements and compensations for killings, bearing witness and taking oaths, and engaging generally in practices that almost daily involved the law. However, in the absence of any central executive authority—there was no army or police force—it was left up to the individual to enforce any judgments or sanctions (usually fines, banishment, or outlawry) imposed by the sophisticated legal procedures. Since enforcement could normally be achieved only by violent means, the legal system in Iceland has been called "stylized feud,"[7] "at best an uneasy substitute for revenge,"[8] and "aggression projected outward and codified."[9]

In 965 the country was divided for administrative convenience into four geographical districts or "quarters," each of which convened its own local Thing twice a year. Three quarters (East, South, and West) convened three district Things every spring and fall, while the North Quarter had four, each presided over by three chieftains. Although courts for local disputes were convened at all the district Things, a court representing each quarter also met at the Althing—outdoors, with the judges seated on rocks arranged in a circle—where cases were heard in which the litigants belonged to different districts or in which no decisions had been reached at the district level.

Because cases at the Quarter Courts sometimes ended in divided judgments, in 1005 a so-called Fifth Court (*fimmtardómr*) of forty-eight judges (thirty-six acting plus twelve alternates) was instituted by the powerful lawspeaker Skapti Thóroddsson to meet at the Althing as a Superior Court of Appeal. Around the same time the number of chieftains was increased to forty-eight. This constitutional system, perfected in all essentials in 1005, prevailed during the entire commonwealth period of Icelandic history—that is, from 930 until the Norwegian kings took over the island in 1262 and introduced new codes. Although for the first two centuries the law was purely oral, it was codified in writing in the early twelfth century (1117–1118) and was preserved in two expanded revisions around 1250 in a work that came to be known, in analogy to an older Norwegian code, as *Grágás* ("gray goose," presumably either from the color of its binding or from the quills used to inscribe it). (These manuscripts of *Grágás* had no status as formal legal codes; they were simply transcriptions, commissioned by private individuals, of the oral tradition.)

It was this "semianarchy,"[10] then, that characterized the Saga Age of Iceland, a republic of free farmers, taking pleasure in their elaborate system of laws but frequently, even routinely, resorting to the violence of blood feud to enforce the judgments of the district assemblies or the Althing. Even the official conversion to Christianity, formally accepted in the year 1000 at the Althing, had little immediate impact on everyday political and social life.[11] (The Church began to play a larger role only after the election of the first native Icelandic bishop in 1056 and after the law of tithes, passed in 1096, provided a sound financial basis for the Church.)

NJAL'S SAGA

Of the three dozen or more accounts of the great families written down in the thirteenth century, the most popular, the longest, and the most famous is the late *Njal's Saga*, known also as "The Saga of Burnt Njal" (*Brennu-Njáls saga*, literally "The Saga of Njal of the Burning") or, familiarly in Icelandic, simply as *Njála*. Superlatives hardly suffice to express the enthusiasm of its admirers, who at an early date caused it to be copied in many manuscripts and, later, to remain steadily in print. It has been called "the most profound and the most powerful"[12] as well as "the mightiest of all the classical Icelandic sagas."[13] Others have termed it "the culmination of Icelandic literature"[14] and "one of the great prose works of the world,"[15] written by "the Shakespeare of saga literature."[16] It has been said to enjoy "almost the character of a sacred book, and is read with reverence."[17] The title scarce does justice to the subject matter. Although the work culminates with the powerful scene in which Njal and his family are burnt alive in their farmhouse, the narrative contains much more: the preceding heroic adventures of Njal's friend Gunnar, the subsequent fanatical quest for vengeance undertaken by his son-in-law Kari, an account of the conversion of Iceland and the establishment of the Fifth Court, a depiction of the famous Battle of Clontarf near Dublin in 1014, as well as accounts of numerous viking expeditions. Covering over half a century (from ca. 960 to ca. 1016) and including some two dozen vividly memorable characters, the saga truly embraces the Saga Age of Iceland. (In fact, over six hundred characters, most of whom are related by extensive genealogies and complicated kinships, are mentioned in the course of the saga.) The work is so long and so exhaustive in its portrayal both of Gunnar's life and of Njal's family tragedy that older commentators believed that it resulted from the conflation of two separate epics. Today, however, it is generally accepted that it was "conceived and written as one saga."[18] Yet although the saga constitutes a powerful unity, its 159 chapters can usefully be seen as a trilogy preceded by a preface or a double prelude.[19]

Njal himself is introduced surprisingly late, uniquely so in saga literature, for a title figure: he first appears in chapter 20[20]—"a wise and prescient man" and "a gentle man of great integrity" whose advice "always turned out well for those who followed it"—as the good friend of Gunnar Hamundarson, who himself had entered the saga only one chapter earlier: a man so heroic and skillful that "it has been said that there has never been his equal." The preceding chapters tell the stories—interesting in themselves but only loosely linked to the following action—of the marriage of Gunnar's kinswoman Unn and of the first two marriages of his future wife Hallgerd. When Unn divorces her first husband Hrut, who as the result of a curse is unable to consummate their marriage, he refuses to return her dowry. Her father takes the matter to court at the Althing, but Hrut challenges the older man to an unequal single combat and intimidates him into forsaking his claim. At roughly the same time (around 960) the beautiful but haughty Hallgerd successively marries two men, both of whom are murdered by her foster father when she goads them through her behavior into slapping her. Gunnar enters the saga when, advised on legal procedures by Njal, he wins back from Hrut the dowry of his kinswoman Unn. (Unn later marries again, and her son, Mord Valgardsson, turns out to be the villain of both sections.)

Following his viking adventures, Gunnar returns to Iceland as a wealthy man and, despite Njal's warnings, marries Hallgerd, who is by now rid of her first two husbands. Soon thereafter the evil-tempered Hallgerd quarrels with Njal's wife Bergthora over the seating arrangements at a feast. In revenge for the perceived insult Hallgerd sends a slave to kill one of Bergthora's slaves, and this incident initiates an escalating series of killings commissioned by the two women over the next few years: following each incident Gunnar and Njal make amends by paying generous compensations for the slain men, but each time their wives—usually while their husbands are away at the annual Althing meetings—commission an even more grievous murder. The compensations increase, in accordance with the standing of the victims, from 12 ounces of silver for a slave to 100 ounces for a freeman to 200 ounces for a member of the family. Finally Njal's three sons, goaded by their mother, kill two of Gunnar's kinsmen, who had composed taunting poems about them. Despite all this hostility between members of their families, Gunnar and Njal continue to arrange appropriate settlements and refuse to let their friendship be destroyed.

When Iceland is beset by a famine, Gunnar in his generosity gives away most of his family's provisions. While he is away at the Althing, Hallgerd sends a slave to steal two horseloads of food from a neighboring farmer named Otkel—a deed that precipitates the events leading to Gunnar's death (and incidentally fulfills her uncle's first-chapter prophecy about her *þjófsaugu* ["thief's eyes"]). When he finds out about her theft, Gunnar slaps Hallgerd and, as in the cases of her two previous husbands, earns her deadly wrath. Immediately he rides to his neighbor's farm and offers to make amends for the stolen goods, but Otkel, advised by friends envious of Gunnar, refuses to accept any compensation. Instead, he summons Gunnar to the next Althing to answer to the shameful legal charge of receiving stolen goods. On that occasion Gunnar challenges his opponents and forces them to accept his compensation. The following spring, while Gunnar is sowing grain in his fields, Otkel and a group of friends pass Gunnar's farm. Otkel's horse gallops out of control, causing Otkel to wound Gunnar with his spur. At first Gunnar is inclined to keep his peace, but Otkel's companions circulate the rumor that Gunnar had wept in an unmanly fashion. (Taunts about sexuality were regarded as especially demeaning.) On their return past his farm Gunnar and his brother Kolskegg kill Otkel and his seven companions. At the Althing the matter is resolved equitably: the compensations for Otkel's killing and Gunnar's wound cancel each other out, and the other killings are assessed on the basis of each individual's worth. Gunnar gains much credit from the outcome, but Njal warns him that it will be the start of an escalating spiral of killing unless Gunnar makes sure never to kill more than once in the same family and to honor every settlement made between himself and other men.

During a horsefight Gunnar's horse is blinded by one of the contestants, and the resulting dispute arouses deep enmity between Gunnar and the men of Thrihyrning. They ambush Gunnar and his brothers, who kill fourteen of their attackers and wound many others. While Gunnar consults Njal about his defense at the Althing, his old enemy Mord urges Thorgeir Starkadarson and the other men of Thrihyrning to initiate legal proceedings against Gunnar. At the assembly, where both groups appear in great strength, settlements are arranged for the wounds and killings. But Thorgeir, unhappy with the settlement, approaches Mord, as Gunnar's bitterest enemy, to seek support and advice. For months Thorgeir Starkadarson, along with Thorgeir Otkelsson (son of Otkel, whom Gunnar had earlier killed), plot and scheme against their common enemy. Finally the two Thorgeirs and their followers ambush Gunnar and his brother Kolskegg. Gunnar and Kolskegg drive off their attackers, but when Gunnar kills Thorgeir Otkelsson in the process, he violates Njal's warning about killing twice in the same family. At the Althing a settlement is arbitrated for the killings, and Gunnar and Kolskegg are sentenced, on pain of outlawry, to banishment for three years. Njal urges his friend to heed the settlement: if so, he will return as a man of great renown. But Gunnar, as he sets out for the ship that is to take him abroad, pauses to admire the landscape around his farm at Hildarend and, overcome by a sudden sentiment in a famous (and uncharacteristically lyrical) passage, decides that he cannot tear himself away from the lovely slopes and golden cornfields of home. At the next Althing, accordingly, he is declared a full outlaw, who may be killed with impunity. His enemies meet and decide to get rid of Gunnar once and for all. That fall, when all his men have gone off for haymaking and Gunnar is at home alone, his enemies attack him in his house. The mighty Gunnar would still have been able to withstand them all, but his bowstring breaks. When he requests from Hallgerd a strand of her long hair with which to replace it, she refuses, reminding him maliciously of the blow he had given her months earlier. As a result, he is finally overwhelmed and killed.

Following Gunnar's death, Njal and his family are unable to undertake legal proceedings against the killers because Gunnar died as an outlaw. Njal's son Skarp-Hedin and Gunnar's son Hogni therefore attack the killers and avenge Gunnar's death through blood feud. At the next district assembly, settlements are negotiated for the killings; Gunnar's son Hogni gets married and, according to the customary formula, "is now out of this saga" (*ok er hann ór þessi sögu* [196]); his brother Kolskegg goes to Denmark, where he becomes a Christian and also leaves the saga, which now turns to the tragedy of Njal's family.

THE SECOND part of the saga begins, as did the first, with a number of chapters only loosely related to what follows. The deep-rooted enmity between the Njalssons and the Sigfusson family is explained as the result of an incident abroad involving Earl Hakon of Norway, Thrain Sigfusson, and Njal's sons, Grim and Helgi. When the Njalssons return to Iceland, their friend Kari, who had assisted them in their Norwegian troubles, marries their sister Helga and becomes linked to the family. Kari joins them when they plot against and eventually kill Thrain Sigfusson. Njal consults with Thrain's brother Ketil to arrange full compensation for the killing and, in his effort to preserve the peace, adopts Thrain's son Hoskuld, whose behavior even as a boy exemplifies his almost saintly goodness.

The narrative is briefly interrupted by the introduction of the powerful chieftain Flosi and his family. When Njal looks around for a suitable marriage match for his foster son Hoskuld, he asks for the hand of Flosi's niece, Hildigunn. Hildigunn—like Hallgerd, a beautiful but arrogant woman—reminds Flosi that he had promised never to marry her to a man without the rank of chieftain. Njal asks for three years to find a solution, but he is unable to persuade anyone to sell a hereditary chieftainship for Hoskuld. At the next meeting of the Althing, therefore, he undertakes a legal stratagem highly uncharacteristic for a man famed for his good counsel (chap. 97). Instead of helping to resolve the unusually large number of litigations, he gives advice that leads to deadlocks and quarrels, causing many plaintiffs to leave the assembly dissatisfied. The following year at the Althing, people are reluctant to undertake lawsuits because progress in the courts is so unsatisfactory. Using the ancient common Germanic alliterative phrase *með oddi ok eggju* (242; "with spearpoint and sword-blade"), they threaten to settle their claims with weapons. Arguing that Iceland must not become lawless, Njal says that the lawmakers of the land have an obligation to resolve the difficulties. At the meeting of the *lögrétta* Njal points out to the chieftains that the Quarter Courts are so overworked that few decisions are possible. He therefore proposes the establishment of a Fifth Court as a Court of Appeals to which cases from the Quarter Courts may be referred, and he explains that appointments to the new court could be made from new chieftainships to be established in each quarter—chieftainships to which thingmen would have the right to transfer their allegiance from old liege-chieftains. When the Fifth Court is approved and incorporated into the Constitution, Njal obtains permission to institute one of the new chieftainships at Hvitaness for his foster son Hoskuld, who is henceforth known as Hoskuld Hvitaness-Priest. This action clears the way for Hoskuld's marriage to Hildigunn.

Thrain Sigfusson's brother-in-law, Lyting, is unhappy because he received no compensation for Thrain's death. To avenge it, therefore, he kills a member of Njal's family, a bastard son also called Hoskuld. Goaded by their mother, Njal's sons pursue Lyting and his brothers and manage to kill one of them. Lyting goes in fear to Hoskuld Hvitaness-Priest and asks him to intercede for a settlement, to which Njal agrees. The narrative is now interrupted by six chapters relating the conversion of Iceland and the formal adoption of Christianity at the Althing to assure that all men in the land may be governed by one law. Paradoxically, the first reported act of Christian miracle supports the pagan law of vengeance. At a district assembly Amundi, the blind son of

Hoskuld Njalsson, encounters his father's killer, Lyting, and swears that, if his eyes were blessed with sight, he would demand compensation for his father or take blood revenge. As he leaves the booth, his sight is suddenly restored by the will of God; he rushes back up to Lyting and kills him with an ax-blow to the head and then immediately becomes blind again as he walks away. Following the usual compensations (of which half is remitted because of the justness of Amundi's claim) peace prevails for a long time.

The cycle of violence is set spinning again when Valgard the Grey—Unn's second husband and Mord's father—returns to Iceland, which he had left some years earlier in opposition to the Christian conversion. When he expresses to his son his consternation at the decrepit state of their district and their booths at Thingvellir,[21] Mord explains that, as a result of the Fifth Court and the creation of new chieftainships, many former liegemen have withdrawn their allegiance from him and transferred it to the new chieftain, Njal's foster son Hoskuld Hvitaness-Priest. The crafty Valgard carefully instructs his son how to go about seeking revenge and then, going on a rampage against Mord's crosses and other Christian images, dies. Mord begins to carry out the plot, which involves winning the friendship of the Njalssons with false words and gifts. Despite their father's warnings, the Njalssons are turned against their foster brother by Mord's slander. While Hoskuld Hvitaness-Priest is sowing grain one morning, Skarp-Hedin and his brothers attack and kill him. The gentle Hoskuld, making no effort to defend himself, sinks to his knees in a most unpagan manner, saying, "May God help me and forgive you all" (chap. 111). Njal, grieving at the death of his beloved foster son, predicts that this murder will lead not only to his death, but to the death of his wife and all his sons.

Mord, lying about his complicity in the killing, initiates the proceedings for a hearing at the Althing. Meanwhile Flosi, angered by Hoskuld's killing and incited by his niece Hildigunn, who taunts him with Hoskuld's bloodied cloak, agrees to press her claims at the Althing—even though she makes it clear that, like Bergthora and Hallgerd before her, she really wants blood, not compensation. Foreseeing that her demands will lead to much death, he reluctantly agrees. Both Flosi and Njal ride to the Althing with strong support, and for several days a great deal of politicking goes on as both sides try to win further allies. After much negotiation and complicated legal maneuvers and seeming deadlocks, a full settlement for Hoskuld's death is announced at the Law Rock. It involves, at the suggestion of wise men, an unusually large compensation (six hundred ounces of silver) so that men will begin to appreciate the cost of wanton killing. But when Njal and his sons arrive at the law council (*lögrétta*) to deliver their payment, Flosi cracks a joke at Njal's expense, to which the grim and ironic Skarp-Hedin responds with a nasty riposte implying a sexual perversion on Flosi's part. Flosi angrily rejects the settlement, whereupon Njal predicts disaster for everyone—correctly, as it turns out.

Flosi demands from his followers an oath to support the Sigfussons against Njal. Abandoning all subtlety, he proposes to ride straight to Bergthorsknoll the following fall and attack the Njalssons "with fire and sword" (*með eldi ok járni* [318]). At the appointed time Flosi and his men ride to Bergthorsknoll, where Njal and his family, alerted by portents of disaster, are making their preparations. Even though the Njalssons are so strong that Flosi knows his forces cannot defeat them in open battle, Njal orders everyone to go into the house, assuming that honorable men would never resort to the illegal and contemptible device of arson.[22] After heavy fighting, however, Flosi decides to set fire to the house—a drastic action by which Njal along with six members of his family perishes and from which only his son-in-law Kari manages to escape.

While Flosi foresees dire consequences from the Burning for himself and all his followers, Kari sets out to recruit allies for his retaliation. It is decided that Mord, involved through his own initial schemes against Hoskuld, will take over the legal proceedings against Flosi, advised by Thorhall Asgrimsson, one of the three greatest lawyers in Iceland. Flosi, meanwhile, rides ahead to the Althing and wins the services of Eyjolf Bolverksson, reputedly another of the three greatest lawyers in Iceland. Following many pages of legal maneuvering, in which Kari's side repeatedly seizes the advantage, Eyjolf succeeds in getting Flosi off on a technicality that Thorhall had not anticipated. (Eyjolf had earlier advised Flosi, as a last resort, to change his legal residence secretly to a different quarter, with the result that the charges are invalidated by being brought and heard in the wrong court.) At this point Thorhall, incapacitated in his booth with an injured leg, advises his side to bring charges in the Fifth Court of bribery against Flosi, who had presented Eyjolf with an expensive bracelet in return for his services. Once again, however, Eyjolf succeeds in having the charge dismissed through a legal technicality. (In a trial at the Althing each side was supposed to exclude six of the judges from the full court of forty-eight; otherwise the proceedings were invalid. Mord dismisses six, but when Eyjolf fails to dismiss his six, Mord neglects to exercise his right and duty to exclude another six, and the verdict against Flosi is therefore invalidated because it is rendered by forty-two rather than the proper thirty-six judges.) Thorhall is so infuriated at this abuse of the law that he springs from his sickbed and rushes to the Fifth Court, where he kills the first of Flosi's kinsmen that he meets. At this point a great battle takes place between the two sides—a battle so extensive that the narrator, as he laconically notes, is unable to relate all that happened. Following much killing, peace is negotiated when a respected chieftain, Hall of Sida, sets a splendid example by foregoing compensation for his own son and offering pledges of peace to his adversaries. The settlement is referred for arbitration to a panel of twelve wise men, who propose a judiciously balanced payment:

> Njal was to be paid for with treble compensation, and Bergthora with double compensation. The killing of Skarp-Hedin was equated with the killing of Hoskuld Hvitaness-Priest. Grim and Helgi were each to be paid for with double compensation, and there was to be single compensation for every other person killed. No settlement was made concerning the death of Kari's son, Thord. (322)

In addition, Flosi and the Burners are ordered, on pain of outlawry, to leave the country—Flosi for three years and the others for life.

The agreement is confirmed by everyone except Kari, who refuses to equate the shameful deed of arson with normal killings. Along with Njal's nephew Thorgeir, Kari rides in pursuit of the Sigfussons, kills five, and puts the rest to flight. Through the mediation of Hall of Sida, Flosi's father-in-law and an early convert to Christianity, a binding truce is arranged between Flosi and Thorgeir, but Kari continues his relentless pursuit of the Burners. With the assistance of a clownlike farmer named Bjorn, he kills those of the fugitives remaining in Iceland and then sails south in search of the others. At Orkney, in the residence of Earl Sigurd, Kari catches up with one of the Burners, Gunnar Lambason, and decapitates him. Fifteen more arsonists die in the Battle of Clontarf outside Dublin. When Kari hears this good news, he sets sail for Wales, where he finds and kills Kol Thorsteinsson, the last of the Burners except Flosi. Flosi makes a pilgrimage to Rome, where he is absolved by the pope, and then returns to Iceland, having fulfilled all the terms of the settlement, including his three years of exile and compensation. Kari, having also been granted absolution in Rome, makes his own way back to Iceland. Shipwrecked on the shore close to Flosi's farmstead at Svinafell, he walks directly to Flosi's house to put his nobility to the test. The two Christianized vikings, both now absolved by the pope, celebrate a full reconciliation, which is cemented by Kari's marriage to Flosi's niece Hildigunn, the widow of Hoskuld Hvitaness-Priest (whose killing initiated the entire tragic sequence of events). The narrator reports briefly that Flosi lived to be an old man and then died at sea. Kari, who had lost his son Thord in the Burning, had three more sons and established an outstanding family line. And there, the narrator tells us, I end the saga of the Burning of Njal (*Ok lýk ek þar Brennu-Njáls sögu*).

Legal Reality and the Aesthetics of Law

Even a brief recapitulation of the lengthy saga reveals that it is thoroughly saturated with law and legal procedures. It becomes rapidly apparent that a reputation as a learned lawyer entitles a man to great respect in tenth-century Iceland. In the second sentence of the saga we are told, for instance, that Unn's father Mord was a powerful chieftain and "so skilled a lawyer (*svá mikill lögmaðr*) that no judgment was held to be valid unless he had taken part in it."

In chapter 20 Njal himself is introduced as "so skilled a lawyer that no one was considered his equal" (*Hann var lögmaðr svá mikill, at engi fannsk hans jafningi*). And in chapters 135 and 138, to underscore the importance of the trial of the Burners, the opposing counsels, Thorhall Asgrimsson and Eyjolf Bolverksson, are each said to be "one of the three greatest lawyers in Iceland" (*Hann var inn þriði maðr mestr lögmaðr á Íslandi* [359]). (Earlier, to be sure, Thorhall is reported to have been taught law so well by none other than Njal that he became unqualifiedly "the greatest lawyer" [*mestr lögmaðr*] in Iceland [chap. 27].)

The presence of these legal giants is more than simply honorific. Their expertise is needed to supervise the great lawsuits that constitute much of the action, from the controversy regarding Unn's dowry (chaps. 8, 22–23) and the succession of trials in which Gunnar is involved—Otkel's summons to Gunnar for receiving stolen goods (chaps. 50–51), Gunnar's trial for killing Otkel and his followers (chap. 56), the lawsuit between Gunnar and the Sigfussons (chap. 66), and Gunnar's settlement for killing the Thorgeirs (chap. 74)—to the celebrated trials of the second half: between Njal and Flosi (chaps. 119–23) and against the Burners (chaps. 141–45). Many lesser accommodations are arranged privately without formal procedures at a district assembly or the Althing, such as the series of compensations agreed upon by Gunnar and Njal in response to the killings commissioned by their wives. An entire lengthy chapter (chap. 97) is devoted to one of the most significant episodes in the history of Icelandic law: the establishment of the Fifth Court along with the consequent constitutional changes. In addition to the direct and indirect characterization of saga figures through their legal dealings, the plot itself is often moved along by such legal affairs as the inheritance claims that take Hrut to Norway or the marriage settlements that bring Gunnar into the plot and that link Flosi to Hoskuld Hvitaness-Priest.[23]

The saga also contains several statements about the importance and centrality of law that have attained proverbial status in Icelandic thought. In defending Gunnar against the Thorgeirs (chap. 70), Njal remarks that it is no breach of settlement for a man to have lawful dealings with another. "With laws shall our land be built up but with lawlessness laid waste" (*með lögum skal land várt byggja, en með ólögum eyða* [172]). Later (chap. 97), when he is urging the establishment of a Fifth Court, he responds to the threat that disgruntled people will settle their claims with weapons by saying that it would be intolerable to have no law in the land (*ok hlýðir þat hvergi at hafa eigi lög í landi* [242]). Njal is not the only figure in the saga who speaks for the nobility of the law. When the Icelanders, divided by the process of conversion, threaten to renounce their community of laws, the Christian law-speaker, Hall of Sida, asks the heathen priest Thorgeir to give his opinion on what the law should be (chap. 105). Following a day of deliberation Thorgeir utters his solemn opinion at the Law Rock, saying that it would be unacceptable should all Icelanders not have one and the same law. "If the laws are divided, the peace will be divided" (*ef sundr skipt er lögunum, þá mun ok sundr skipt friðinum* [271]). As a result, it becomes the first precept of the new laws (as iterated in the first article of *Grágás*) "that all people in this country must be Christian and put their trust in one God, Father, Son, and Holy Ghost."[24]

This centrality of law in *Njal's Saga* has not gone unnoticed.[25] Over a century ago a leading Icelandic scholar called it "The Saga of Law *par excellence*."[26] Heusler, in his epoch-making study of law in the Icelandic family sagas, acknowledged the idiosyncratic position of *Njal's Saga* and called it "the veritable lawyer's saga" ("die wahre Juristensaga").[27] More recently Lars Lönnroth summarized the scholarly opinion of the past hundred years by stating, "It is generally recognized that the judicial sections of *Njála* are unlike those of any other saga."[28]

The basic question underlying most studies of law and legal procedures in the saga concerns the degree to which they may be regarded as historical evidences of legal practices of the tenth and eleventh centuries, rather than projections back onto that early period of thirteenth-century legal attitudes. (The question regarding oral tradition versus written law is simply an aspect of the larger issue.) Older scholars of the so-called Icelandic School were passionately committed to the historical validity of the sagas, arguing that the trials of *Njal's Saga* amounted to contemporary reports that had been preserved more or less intact for almost three centuries. But one of the earliest scholarly monographs devoted to *Njála* demonstrated over a century ago that many of the legal formulas and procedures used in the saga are based upon thirteenth-century written sources and projected back into the Saga Age.[29] This "German" view, accepted with certain modifications by most subsequent scholars, was summed up by Heusler, who regards *Njála* as the richest and, at the same time, the most clouded source of ancient Germanic legal materials.

> This lawyerly saga is no naive extension of the law of the Saga Age. It projected a great deal more Late Icelandic law—that is, *Grágás* law—into older times than all the other narratives taken together. The *Njála* and it alone sought on a large scale to shape sections of ancient law, namely, court procedures, according to the official law of the thirteenth century.[30]

As a result, as Einar Ól. Sveinsson has more recently observed, "many a lawyer from the time of the Commonwealth (930–1262) would not always have been impressed with some of his legal machinations, and the author of *Njála* would have devised them quite differently if he himself had been better versed in the law of Njál's day."[31]

The findings of Lehmann and Schnorr, Heusler, and Einar Ól. Sveinsson have been repeatedly verified. It has been demonstrated, for instance, that the entire debate concerning the establishment of the Fifth Court (chap. 97) amounts to a "collage of quotations from the *Grágás*."[32] The legal trick used by Eyjolf to win Flosi's acquittal on technical grounds (chap. 144) depends on a paraphrase in chapter 97, which is taken directly from the *Grágás*, where the law is clearly and explicitly stated:

> The man who has a case to prosecute before the Fifth Court is to dismiss six men from the court and name witnesses to it and name them all and say, "I dismiss you from the court and I am not content that you should have a seat in the court for this case"—and state what case it is. And they are to withdraw from the court, and if they will not withdraw from the court they are fined and what they say is invalid. The man who has a case to defend before the Fifth Court is also to dismiss six men from the court and name them all by name. "I am not content that you should have a seat in the court for this case which he has brought against me," and name the other man who brings the case against him by name and state what case it is. And they have to withdraw from the court and sit within the circle of judges while the case is judged. They are not to go away unless it is on a necessary errand. But if they will not withdraw from the court, the penalty is a fine and what they say is invalid. If he will not dismiss them from the court, the prosecutor is then to dismiss both groups, and if the prosecutor will not dismiss them from the court, his case is void.[33]

It is also conceivable that the author knew perfectly well that legal advisers in Iceland were permitted to be paid but that he introduced a provision against bribes (*ef menn bjóða fé eða taka* [244]) into his depiction of the establishment of the Fifth Court simply in order to anticipate the lawsuit between Kari and the Burners and Kari's accusation of bribery against Eyjolf.

However, it is not our task to determine the sources of Icelandic law and legal procedures as they occur in *Njal's Saga* or to assess the correctness of their use: that task has been carried out by generations of literary, legal, and social historians of the past century. We can assume as a given that the author not only had an enormous respect for law but was also well enough versed in the law—both the *Grágás* and the more recent Norwegian codes—that he was easily capable of adducing the appropriate material that applied to the legal situations as they arose in the stories of Gunnar and Njal.[34] At the same time, we should keep in mind Einar Ól. Sveinsson's caution that the author's fascination with and enthusiasm for the law often exceed his knowledge of it.[35] But criticism of the author's legal expertise, while important to historians, is not relevant in the present context. We are concerned, rather, with the author's use of law *within* his work and with the implications of that use for his view of law and Icelandic history. We can take as a governing principle the statement of Magnús Magnússon and Hermann Pálsson that "the only valid 'historicity' in the sagas is not so much what it tells us about the history of Iceland as what it tells us about thirteenth-century attitudes to the history of Iceland. The saga-writers were not trying to write history in our sense of the term; they were trying to create an acceptable image of the past."[36] The appropriate question in our context is this: Why was the late-thirteenth-century author of our saga so profoundly interested in the law, and what is his attitude toward the law, the lawmen, and the legal procedures that he portrays so extensively?

Several recent critics of the saga have suggested that the author's attitude toward law displays not the confusion and ignorance attributed to him by older scholars but a knowledgeable ambivalence that perceived in the law "in theory a force for order but in practice often a force working towards disorder."[37] It is worth our while to take this insight a step further.

Early Icelandic society exhibited a predisposition toward lawmaking that was unusual even among other Germanic peoples. One scholar has observed with reference to *Grágás* that "Some of the rules themselves display a rococo complexity that suggests sheer pleasure in the formulation of law almost as if it were for law's sake alone."[38] Now, it is generally acknowledged that the author of *Njála*, like most young men of good family, was so thoroughly steeped in the law of the land that, in the tradition of the law-speakers, he had learned great chunks of *Grágás* by heart—passages that later came easily to his mind as he needed them in his composition. The likelihood that he often quoted from memory rather than copying from a written source suffices to explain the occasional inaccuracies and inconsistencies in the text.[39] But some readers have sensed in the saga an obsession with law that goes beyond the needs of the plot: Heusler, for instance, believed that the forms of legal process often become absolute, "an end in themselves" ("Selbstzweck").[40] Certainly, to the extent that Njal reflects his author's predilections, we sometimes note in his dealings a pleasure in law for its own sake. His advice to Gunnar on the means to retrieve Unn's marriage settlement (chap. 22) goes well beyond any reasonable procedure and betrays a joy in pettifoggery and manipulation per se, as does his scheming to produce the need for a Fifth Court (chap. 97).[41] Moreover, since injuries were normally "published" by both the offender and the injured party, the trials rarely needed to establish "guilt" and "innocence"; and since the penalties were prescribed by law, the juries had little latitude. It was their function, rather, to consider justification and, above all, procedural precision according to the formula: *qui cadit a syllaba, cadit a tota causa*.[42] Hence the author's meticulousness in recounting the procedural details: that is where the skill of his lawyers is evident and where the interest of this audience lies.

On the one hand, then, we have an author whose national predisposition toward the law is enhanced by personal predilection—an author for whom the law has literally become an autonomous value whose history and compilation is sufficient unto itself. He is a citizen, after all, of the same century that produced Henry de Bracton, Eike von Repgow, Philippe de Beaumanoir, and other authors of the thirteenth-century legal renaissance of which he, as an educated man, may well have been aware and certainly constituted a part. This attitude could easily account for the sheer *joie de livre*, unique among saga writers, with which he narrates the history of Icelandic law, rehearses the laws themselves when they are relevant to his story, praises famous lawmen, recapitulates famous trials, and frames his entire action within a generally legal context.

However, the author's juridical joy, which derives an aesthetic pleasure from the work of pure law, is matched by a sense of realism, an awareness that, in early Icelandic society, sometimes nothing worked but violence. His ambivalence is therefore directed not so much against the law—which, almost like a poem, is regarded as beautiful but often useless—as against the society in which it is meant to function. It is not the law that is defective, but the men who are supposed to live by it. According to an often-cited calculation by Heusler, the sagas display a marked preference for processing disputes by blood rather than by law or arbitration. Out of some 520 cases in the family sagas enumerated by Heusler, 297 led to blood vengeance, 104 to arbitration without prior recourse to law, and 119 to lawsuits. Of these 119 legal actions, only 50 led to a judicial decision; 60 ended up being arbitrated out of court and 9 others reached no conclusion, usually because the court was scattered by violent disruption.[43]

These proportions are borne out a fortiori by *Njal's Saga*, where no dispute is ultimately resolved by court action. The saga begins with an episode in which a perfectly legal claim to Unn's marriage settlement brought in the divorce action by her father Mord, who is introduced as a highly experienced lawyer (*mikill lögmaðr*), is lost by the threat of violence: the challenge to a duel that the older man, despite derision and ignominy, does not feel qualified to take up. The lawsuit is subsequently won by Unn's kinsman Gunnar—not by a peaceful settlement but by another challenge to single combat, which was not abolished as a means of legal decision making until the time of the Fifth Court.[44] This opening episode sets the tone for all that follows, down to the moment when another great lawyer, Thorhall, is so enraged by the legal maneuvers of Flosi's defenders that, although ill, he takes spear in hand and charges to the Fifth Court where he slays Flosi's kinsman.

The law is known to everyone, and the cases are meticulously presented in the courts; but if matters do not turn out satisfactorily, even the greatest lawyers resort to violence. Njal and his friend Gunnar try to resist the general tendency to vengeance and violence, but all their compensations cannot stop the killings commissioned by their ruthless wives. A perfectly satisfactory settlement is reached, following complicated negotiations, for Gunnar's deadly assault against Thorgeir, but it falls through when Gunnar is unable to abide by its terms and thus becomes an outlaw, subject to being killed without penalty. Because Gunnar cannot be avenged legally, Skarp-Hedin and Hogni take unlawful revenge by killing his murderers. In the second part, following complicated legal maneuvers, a hefty compensation is finally arranged for Hoskuld's killing, but the settlement fails because of the taunts of Skarp-Hedin and Flosi. Following the Burning another elaborate settlement is worked out, but it is rejected by Kari, who is not satisfied until he has exacted blood vengeance from all the Burners but Flosi, with whom he is finally reconciled. With the exception of various private reconciliations the action of the saga leaves us with the distinct impression that violence is the most effective way to settle a dispute. In other words, there is still no real identity of law and community values (or sense of justice).

The violent conclusion results even in those cases in which the law is apparently manipulated successfully by clever lawyers. In a complete rewriting of Icelandic legal history the author attributes to Njal the conception of a Fifth Court and reduces Skapti Thoroddsson, the historical creator of that institution, to the mere executor of Njal's proposals. Njal undertakes this major constitutional change, we are given to understand, mainly in order to obtain a chieftaincy for his foster son Hoskuld (a political ploy that would not have appeared so unscrupulous to Njal's realistic contemporaries as it has done to many modern readers). But even though Njal succeeds for the moment and Hoskuld gets his chieftaincy and his wife, in the long run violence prevails. Only a few years later the killing of Hoskuld Hvitaness-Priest is plotted by Mord Valgardsson out of spite for Hoskuld's new position. Similarly the elegant legal maneuvers that culminate in the Burners' acquittal at the Althing are in vain. Every one of them but Flosi is hunted down and killed by Kari. The final impression left by the work is that the law is as lovely and as central to Icelandic life as a perfect skaldic poem—and just as irrelevant to the realities of its violence. Or, as Heusler put it, "the law of the sagas represents the reality and the law of *Grágás* the theory."[45] In this sense the saga can be read, if not as "an indictment of the legal system of medieval Iceland," then at least as "a condemnation of the ruthless men who subverted it for selfish reasons."[46]

Pagan Ethos and Christian Ethics

Heusler has spoken of the fundamentally non-Christian nature ("das innerlichst Unchristliche") of ancient Germanic attitudes as manifest in Icelandic society, which was characterized by an overwhelming sense of personal pride and honor coupled with an incessant striving for power.[47] This attitude, which dominates most of the older sagas, undergoes a change in *Njal's Saga*. Although the pagan attitude governs most of the figures and drives much of the action, an end to the *circulus vitiosus* of vengeance and killing occurs in those cases when the law is undergirt by a social attitude that renounces pagan honor in favor of Christian ethics. It is no accident that the enduring settlements that occur at the end of the three main parts of the saga are tied conspicuously to Christianity. The first part ends with a report about Gunnar's brother Kolskegg, who was condemned along with Gunnar to banishment as punishment for the killing of Thorgeir Otkelsson. While Gunnar remained in Iceland to be outlawed and killed, Kolskegg went first to Norway and then to Denmark, where he was baptized. (Iceland had not yet been converted at that time.) Afterwards, we are told, he traveled to Constantinople, where he ended his life in the service of the emperor as a leader in the Varangian Guard. The second part concludes with a settlement that brings peace to all the participants in the great battle at the Althing (except for the Burners hounded by Kari). Appropriately, this settlement is initiated by Hall of Sida when he renounces compensation for his own slain son: Hall and his household were the first to embrace Christianity (chap. 100); Hall accompanies the evangelists on their tour of Iceland and lends his influence to their conversion efforts (chap. 101); and he is chosen by the Christians as their law-speaker at the Althing at which the conversion of Iceland is debated and approved. The third part ends after Flosi and Kari have both made pilgrimages to Rome, where they are absolved by the pope. In all three cases it appears to be Christian ethics, not pagan law, that accounts for the final settlement. Kolskegg renounces the career of vengeance that he might have undertaken in response to Gunnar's killing because he has become a Christian knight. Hall of Sida accomplishes the peace through the model of his own Christian renunciation. Flosi and Kari are able to overcome the terrible burden of death in their own past—the Burning and the blood killing of the arsonists—only because their Christian faith has been confirmed in Rome.

In addition to these cases of explicit conversion two other figures are portrayed virtually as proto-Christians in their behavior even before the conversion. Exceptionally in the saga, neither Njal nor his foster son Hoskuld ever commits an act of violence or pagan heroism. Hoskuld's death at the hands of the Njalssons is described as a Christian martyrdom.[48] Similarly, Njal's death by burning is a martyrdom that he voluntarily takes upon himself: Flosi seeks revenge only from his sons and offers Njal his escape, which Njal declines on the grounds that he is too old (roughly eighty) to seek vengeance for the death of his sons. The death of an innocent man, who chooses that end over violence and revenge, can also be seen as a Christian act, if not as a Christ analogy.

Such a reading enables us to understand the interpolation of the otherwise seemingly incongruous six chapters on the conversion of Iceland. These chapters, appropriated almost wholly from the *Íslendingabók* of Ari the Learned, were regarded by Heusler as a "disturbing alien element" ("störender Fremdkörper").[49] Yet if this late saga does in fact seek to portray a shift in Icelandic history, from pagan ethos to Christian ethics, then these chapters can be regarded as the central turning point of the entire saga.[50] It is true enough that the Christianization itself is portrayed with a certain ambivalence. The evangelists enforce conversion aggressively with the sword, killing those who oppose them—notably sorcerers, poets, and berserks (chaps. 102–3). We also misunderstand medieval Christianity if we believe that it condemned vengeance killings. As we have already seen, the first miracle of newly Christianized Iceland was the temporary healing of Amundi's sight so that he could slay his father's murderer (chap. 106). In general, blood feud and private vengeance were regarded as perfectly legitimate in Christian Europe from the sixth century to the fifteenth.[51] It may be perfectly true that *Njal's Saga* is never tendentious in a political or religious sense.[52] Yet the author seems to suggest that the law became a force, and not merely an entrancing game, only when it began to be animated by the power of Christian ethics. Only at this point, in other words, did law and justice become identical in the Icelandic consciousness.

NJAL'S SAGA portrays a series of events that took place in the heart of the Saga Age, from about 960 to 1016. But it was not written down until almost three hundred years later (around the year 1280) by a writer conflating oral tradition, written documents, the impact of contemporary events, and personal experience.[53] To put matters in perspective, it is as though an American writer of the 1990s set out to explain, say, the Salem witch trials based on legendary accounts and seventeenth-century tax documents; nineteenth-century legal practices; modern views of religion, psychology, and society; and his own acquaintance with the town and its landscape. In a provocative comparative analysis Denton Fox has pointed out that the three-hundred-year time lag between the events depicted and the actual composition of *Njal's Saga* is roughly analogous to that in the cases of several other great Western epics: notably *Beowulf*, the *Chanson de Roland*, and presumably also the *Iliad*. "At the time the saga was composed Iceland, like the societies which produced the epic poems, was moving away from a heroic age."[54] Heusler was making much the same point when he described the author of the saga as "a Romantic who wanted to paint a vanished earlier age . . . as a venerable slice of antiquity."[55] Lönnroth has remarked that Icelanders of the thirteenth century, although they were Christians, "revered the pagan era as a kind of Golden Age" and treasured their laws and political institutions as "a legacy from these pagan ancestors."[56] However, the author was not simply attempting to depict a vanished Golden Age of Icelandic history. His account reflects at many points, including his view of law, his reaction to his own society.

The Age of the Sturlungs rivaled in its complexity other periods of history, like the Renaissance or Romanticism, in which great creative energy was coupled with political, social, and military turmoil.[57] Around the year 1200, radical changes were taking place in the economic, political, and social life of Iceland. A series of ecological disasters undermined the economy: climatic change, volcanic eruptions, epidemics, deforestation, and a decline in sheep farming owing to overgrazing. As the balance of trade shifted in favor of Norwegian merchants, many families were compelled to sell off their farmsteads and chieftainships. As a result, economic and political power became concentrated in the hands of a few mighty families, including notably the ambitious and rapacious young family of Sturlungs from which the entire age was to take its name. The commonwealth, in which for over three hundred years the power had been distributed among forty-eight chieftains and several thousand prosperous families and in which affairs had been conducted with at least the semblance of democracy at the district and annual Things, came increasingly to resemble the fiefdoms of medieval Continental Europe. The Althing itself was reduced to a rubber stamp for the desires of the ruling families, whose arrogance and ambition could no longer be restrained by law. Social life was characterized by treachery, by moral depravity, by sexual license, and by atrocities and maimings of a sort portrayed fully in the stories of the *Sturlunga Saga*.

For decades the Norwegian kings had been eyeing the remote island republic to which many of their most capable subjects had fled in the tenth century and which had in the meantime attained a level of literacy and intellectual culture unmatched on the mainland. By the mid–thirteenth century the situation in Iceland, exacerbated by struggles between the Church and the wealthy landowners as well as recurrent wars between private armies of powerful chieftains, had become so intolerable that the people readily agreed in 1262 to a treaty uniting Iceland with Norway, which under the rule of King Haakon IV had become a model state without feuds, with a flourishing trade, and with a rational administration. After Haakon's death in 1263 he was succeeded by his son, Magnus VI, who as a result of his new law codes became renowned as "the Law-Mender." The first of his codes, *Járnsíða* (Ironside—probably because the volume was encased in iron), was imposed on Iceland in 1271, only to be replaced ten years later by the *Jónsbók* (1281), named for the *lögmaðr* who brought the code from Norway. The new laws did not wholly invalidate the traditional Icelandic laws as formulated in *Grágás*, but they made important constitutional changes: the chieftains, replaced by royal administrators, became obsolete; and the decline of the Althing was initiated when the country was divided into twelve judicial districts and the lay judges replaced by trained legal experts.

These were the circumstances under which the author of *Njála* composed his saga, which reflects his ambivalence toward the Age of the Sturlungs as well as Saga Iceland. As a learned man with a taste for history and law, he was unhappy with the loss of traditional values—the decline of the Althing and the diminution of the old laws of *Grágás*, which he had studied and memorized as a young man. In order to preserve that vanished culture he depicts in his saga the Iceland of the early commonwealth years and the founding of the institutions upon which it was based. In order to portray the legal culture of that age, which by now had receded into history for a generation familiar only with *Járnsíða* and *Jónsbók*, he relied by analogy on *Grágás* whenever the oral sources of the story failed him or were inadequate or no longer comprehensible. In any case, *Grágás* itself extended back to the beginning of the twelfth century, if not to the founding era. At the same time, his aversion as a Christian to the unbridled violence and vengeance, including the unlawful and maligned burnings, that had marked the recent Icelandic past is evident in his depiction of the overturning of lawful order by men and women motivated by irrational passions and hatreds and jealousies. The modern reader does not need much imagination to understand that Njal's proverbial words apply to the Age of the Sturlungs at least as aptly as to the Saga Age: "With laws shall our land be built up but with lawlessness laid waste" (chap. 70).

In *Njal's Saga* the author's ambivalence toward his material is a double one. His saga depicts the inadequacies of a law and legal system not yet informed and motivated by a strong sense of Christian ethics. The Golden Age is tarnished by its own pagan ethos. At the same time, the fulfillment of the union of pagan law and Christian ethics as promised by the reconciliation of Kari and Flosi is suppressed. The author relies on his audience's knowledge of Icelandic history to supply the fact that a long period of peace began in Iceland shortly after the events portrayed in the saga.[58] Yet the author's ambivalence toward his own age suggests that the fulfillment was only short-lived and disappeared again in the stormy turbulence of the Sturlungs and their counterparts. To the extent that the stories of Gunnar and Njal can be read as analogies to the author's own present, he seems to hope that the pagan excesses of the early thirteenth century will give way, under law, to a new Christian community of the sort implicit in the life of Njal and the reconciliation of Kari and Flosi.[59] Yet the healthy realism of Icelandic culture and the author's pervasive irony must have qualified even that hope with ambivalence.

Njála and *Oresteia*

It is evident from the discussions of the preceding two chapters that the *Oresteia* and *Njal's Saga* share a number of conspicuous similarities—similarities that can be attributed in no small measure to the relative simultaneity of the societies being portrayed as well as the societies from whose perspectives the writers view their material. What leaps immediately to mind are the many parallels of character and plot. Few women in world literature can match Clytemnestra and Hallgerd in their fierce haughtiness and lust for vengeance, which in both cases leads directly to the slaughter of their husbands, Agamemnon and Gunnar. Orestes and Kari dominate the last third of these works as the ruthless avengers who are ultimately healed and redeemed by the religious authority of, respectively, Apollo and the pope. In both works two figures related by their innocence and powers of prophecy—Cassandra and Njal—are caught up and destroyed by tragic forces that they foresee but cannot forestall. And in both works supernatural figures of ancient tribal belief embody the imminent tragedy: in the *Oresteia* the Furies and in *Njála* the various visions witnessed before the Burning (chaps. 124–26); a striking example is the ring of fire with a man on a gray horse inside the circle riding furiously, who rushes past Hildigunn with a blazing firebrand (chap. 125).

We have also noted obvious similarities in the legal practices of societies at the same stage of development: the *boulê* constituted at the end of *The Eumenides* corresponds closely to the *lögrétta* of *Njal's Saga*, and both bodies meet on a prominence: the Areopagus and the Law Rock. Similarly, the procedures of the Homeric Greeks (as described on the shield of Achilles in *Iliad* 18) are virtually identical with those followed at the Althing.

In both works we are dealing with authors looking back at a heroic past from the social and political turmoil of their own present—the controversy surrounding Ephialtes' democratic reforms in Aeschylus's Athens and the tumult of the Sturlungs, settled finally by the Norwegian kings, in thirteenth-century Iceland. Onto that past both authors projected contemporary legal procedures in an effort to explain etiologically the origins of their law and its civilizing force. To that extent, the trials in both works can be called "a constructive parody, a re-creation of court procedure which reminds us of its flaws and flexibility."[60]

Above all, in both works we have seen portrayed the evolution from a prelegal tribal community to a society governed by laws and a sense of civic justice. To represent that movement both authors favored a tripartite structure: the trilogy of Aeschylus's plays, in which the first two present the past while the third depicts the redeeming shift; and the saga portraying in its first two parts the death through blood vengeance of the pagan hero Gunnar and the innocent Njal, and representing in the concluding third the reconciliation in Christianity of Flosi and Kari. It is the double perspective of the authors that creates in the *Oresteia* and *Njála* the characteristic ambivalence: toward a past venerated for its simple heroic virtues but condemned for its blood vengeance (it is no accident that the first trial on the Areopagus ends with a split verdict and that Iceland is torn between paganism and Christianity) and toward a present at once informed by the civilizing power of Athena's justice and Christian forbearance yet disrupted by modern ambition and political turmoil (in the persons of Ephialtes and the Sturlungs). This tension between the writer's present and a distanced subject establishes a pattern that we will have occasion to observe repeatedly in the legal literature of the following chapters. The distance can be temporal, as in Kleist's *Michael Kohlhaas*; it can be spatial, as in *The Merchant of Venice*; or it can be parodic, as in *Reynard the Fox* and Kafka's *The Trial*. But that distance offers writers a perspective through which to view with critical detachment the legal crises that they witness in their own societies.

CHAPTER FOUR

The Role of Rome

JUSTICE GAZES most often into her literary mirror at times when she has been disheveled by the winds of social and political upheaval. Accordingly our examples tend to concentrate themselves in periods when the existing law has just undergone, or is threatened by, a major transformation: when, for one reason or another, the law finds itself out of phase with the prevailing community passions, and justice is wracked. This was the case in fifth-century Athens and in thirteenth-century Iceland. It will also be the case in northern Europe of the late Middle Ages, in Napoleonic Germany, and in fin-de-siècle Austria.

This thesis is paradoxically confirmed by the fact that from a civilization with such an extraordinary talent for law as ancient Rome we have inherited no major literary works that revolve in any important sense around legal crises. Certainly Seneca offers no tragedy of law to compare to the *Oresteia*, nor does Virgil in his national epic betray any jurisprudential obsession of the sort that motivates the author of *Njal's Saga*. It is almost as though the jural passion of the Romans had spent itself in the generally juristic atmosphere of Roman society and in the legal education from which most prominent Romans, including the major literary figures, benefited. Greece bequeathed to posterity the profound and often troubled ruminations of Plato's *Republic* and Aristotle's *Nicomachean Ethics*, which still today absorb all serious thinkers of jurisprudence; the Romans shaped the history and politics of Western civilization through the substantiality of their *Corpus Iuris Civilis*.

In Rome, essentially the same legal system enjoyed a thousand-year period of uninterrupted and steady development from the Twelve Tables (451–450 B.C.) down to Justinian's codifications (A.D. 529–34). The Twelve Tables, albeit partly obsolete, remained formally in force down to the *Corpus Iuris Civilis*. To be sure, the law produced many of the most distinguished examples of Latin prose: for instance, Cicero's juridical orations or Apuleius's *Apologia*, in which the urbane young intellectual, educated at Athens and Rome, successfully defended himself against the charge of magic and in the process ridiculed the legal ineptitude of North African country bumpkins. But Cicero, Apuleius, and the other great Roman jurists were making brilliant use of the existing law, not commenting on its deficiencies or inequities. Mere mortals may be deficient in their morality or in their observance of the law, and the Roman moralists and satirists found frequent occasion to lampoon the moral degeneration of the people. But the law itself is not challenged. On the contrary, several of the most celebrated purple passages of Latin literature are dedicated to the sanctity of the law.

In the vision of horror that presents itself to Virgil, writing his *Georgics* during the tumultuous decade that ended with the Battle of Actium (31 B.C.), the cities take up arms against one another in violation of the legal agreements that bind them (*vicinae ruptis inter se legibus urbes / arma ferunt* [1.510–11]). The same work ends (4.560–62) with a paean to Octavian, who has stormed victoriously across the East and brought Roman law to peoples eager to receive it (*Caesar dum magnus ad altum / fulminat Euphraten bello victorque volentis / per populos dat iura*). For Virgil and his contemporaries the law is the unquestioned possession of the Romans, the basis of their civilization, their principal bequest to mankind. When, early in the *Aeneid*, Jupiter assures Venus that her ward, Aeneas, will survive his present tribulations to found a new kingdom, he foretells a time when wars shall cease, harsh ages will be gentled, faith and integrity will prevail, and Romulus and Remus, as the founding fathers of the city, will lay down laws: *aspera tum positis mitescent saecula bellis: / cana Fides et Vesta, Remo cum fratre Quirinus / iura dabunt* (1.291–93). Horace knew that law unsupported by morality is useless: *quid leges sine moribus / vanae proficiunt?* (*Odes* 3.24.35–36). In his Roman Odes he bemoans the licentiousness that has corrupted the nation. But, like his friend Virgil, he felt confident that under Augustus custom and law had eradicated the stain of sin: *mos et lex maculosum edomuit nefas* (*Odes* 4.5.22). His *Carmen Saeculare* (17 B.C.), the great national hymn of Rome, celebrates the emperor's new decrees sanctifying marriage: *patrumque / . . . decreta super iugandis* (17–18). Ovid, finally, broods from his exile on the Black Sea over the offense that has cost him his former happiness in Rome; but he never questions the legality or justice that the emperor exercised in sending him away. Thus in the apostrophe that opens his *Tristia* (1.1.25–26) the poet warns his little book of laments not to take his part even though it is attacked in biting words, for his case is not a strong one and cannot be saved by any legal defense (*tu cave defendas, quamvis mordebere dictis; / causa patrocinio non bona maior erit*).

In Roman literature, in sum, we see no reflection of legal crises but rather an affirmation of the great system of law that incorporated the national sense of morality and that constituted the firm basis of Roman civilization. Unlike Athens and Iceland, what Rome bequeathed to posterity was not a great literary work mirroring a crisis or even a simple change in the history of its law but that law itself. The *Corpus Iuris Civilis* furnished the language and form for the customary law that governed Europe in the Middle Ages and was adopted a thousand years after the decline and fall of Rome as the model for the law shaping the emerging modern states of Europe.

From Codification to Customary Law

It is one of the melancholy facts of history that the great codification of law, which represents perhaps Rome's most enduring bequest to Europe, took place at a moment when the empire was already in precipitous decline. When Justinian set his commissions to work shortly following his accession to the throne in Constantinople (A.D. 527), the western half of the empire was already under the control of barbarian tribes—the Ostrogoths in Italy, the Franks in Gaul, the Visigoths in Spain, the Vandals in Africa, and the Anglo-Saxons in England—and plunging rapidly into the Middle Ages. In an important sense the great Byzantine compilation that came to be known as the *Corpus Iuris Civilis* marked the end of the empire.

The paradox is perhaps insufficiently appreciated that Justinian's monumental work, which provided the model for all subsequent codifications, was itself based on a system of case law as inductively and experientially practiced, and dependent upon precedent as greatly as Anglo-American common law. When the codifying commissions approached their monumental task, they had to come to grips with a legal tradition extending back more than a thousand years to the Twelve Tables (451–450 B.C.) and beyond. This tradition consisted of several huge masses of material: the statutes or *leges* promulgated over centuries by the Roman assemblies, along with the later *consulta* of the Senate; the annual edicts of the magistrates, in which they announced their procedures and policies for the year of praetorial activity; and the mandates, decrees, and rescripts (known collectively as *constitutiones*) through which the emperors communicated their legal intentions and opinions. Added to these were hundreds of volumes of commentary in which learned jurisconsults expounded their interpretations of the often terse and conflicting formulations of the various laws, edicts, and constitutions. (The most important of these were written in the late second and early third centuries by such frequently cited jurists as Gaius, Papinian, Paulus, Ulpian, and Julian.)

As practiced in daily life, Roman law was case law that depended not on legal theory but on the magistrates'—and the jurists'—knowledge and understanding of specific laws and past rulings. It was not until the fourth century that the first attempts were made to collate the vast masses of imperial enactments in *codices*, most of which have been lost. The first task undertaken by Justinian's commission, under the direction of Tribonian, the chief of the imperial chancery, was the revision of the ninety-year-old code of Theodosius, which had to be updated, consolidated with other codes, and edited for clarity. This *Codex* and its revision, both of which appeared in 529, consisted of twelve books subdivided into titles under which, for the first time, an attempt was made to systematize the material of the imperial enactments. Justinian then appointed a sixteen-member commission to consolidate into one *Digest* the mass of juristic interpretations that had arisen in the course of the past six centuries: the experts read some two thousand writings by thirty-nine jurists in order to compile their fifty books, subdivided into titles containing excerpts from various authorities on specific points of law. The *Digest*, published in 533, was meant to supersede all earlier commentary, from which it was henceforth prohibited to make citations (and which, accordingly, tended to be lost to history). That same year also saw the publication of the four volumes of *Institutes*, a textbook for beginning law students based on the famous *Institutes* of Gaius and beginning with the famous definition: *Iustitia est constans et perpetua voluntas ius suum cuique tribuens.*[1] The fourth and final part of the great compilation consists of the *Novellae Constitutiones* that Justinian continued to issue until his death.

In what is still perhaps the best introduction to the subject, Paul Vinogradoff has written, "Within the whole range of history there is no more momentous and puzzling problem than that connected with the fate of Roman Law after the downfall of the Roman State."[2] Even before the *Corpus Iuris Civilis*—the Codex, Digest, Institutes, and Novels—was completed, Roman law had lost its influence in most of western Europe. Not wholly, of course. Roman law remained in effect in certain Italian cities still under Byzantine control, notably in the south around Naples and in Romagna around Ravenna. In 506 King Alaric II ordered a compilation of barbarized Roman law for the use of populations under Visigothic domination in southern France and Spain. Unlike northern Europe, where feudal circumstances prevailed, the Lombard cities maintained a kind of municipal life and a sense of historical continuity with the Roman past throughout the waves of Germanic invasion that swept across the plains of northern Italy for centuries. The Lombard law that evolved from the seventh to the eleventh century amounted to an amalgam of traditional Langobardic laws, vulgar Roman law, and later Frankish additions ("capitularies").[3] Even before the year 1000, centers of Lombard law had formed at Pavia and of Roman law at Ravenna, where law was not so much taught formally as studied and discussed by the learned nobility. (It was only after the rediscovery of the *Digest* in the eleventh century that legal study could be pursued on any sort of systematic basis.)[4]

The methodical study of Roman law began in the eleventh century as European society evolved, economically and socially, to a postfeudal stage at which it again required the sophistication of an advanced legal learning. Hastings Rashdall's assertion that "the work of the School of Bologna represents the most brilliant achievement of the intellect of medieval Europe"[5] has been often repeated. By the middle of the twelfth century the city had become famous all over Europe for its law faculty, exemplified by Irnerius, who perfected the techniques of commentary or "glosses" that determined the study of law for centuries to come, and by Gratian, whose *Decretum* provided the basis for the canon law that was studied with the same glossatorial methods—that is, using the tools of language and history to elucidate texts that were by now some six hundred years old and that contained excerpts dating back more than a millennium. As a result of these developments the cultivation of law achieved enormously great prestige, and students flocked to Bologna from all over Europe in order to accredit themselves in this exciting, and profitable, new profession. By 1158 the number of foreign students at Bologna was so great that Emperor Frederick Barbarossa had to issue a special charter or privilege of protection. A century later, in 1265, the guild of foreign students, the so-called *universitas ultramontanorum*, comprised scholars from fourteen different nations, mostly Germans. (The original three Italian guilds of Lombards, Tuscans, and Romans were gradually collapsed into a single *universitas citramontanorum*.) Originally the "university" was identified only by its student guilds, but by 1215 we have evidence of a joint faculty of the professors of civil and canon law, and by 1219 there was a recognized system of degrees. In 1253, finally, the existence of the "university" at Bologna was confirmed by a papal bull. Although the documentary evidence is patchy, the position of Bologna was so dominant that it fostered daughter institutions at Vicenza (1204) and Padua (1222), and in the course of the thirteenth century law faculties were established elsewhere in Italy as well as in France and Spain.[6]

As the systematic study of Roman law spread to other universities and countries, the scholarly work of the glossators gave way in the fourteenth and fifteenth centuries to the initiatives of such scholars as Bartolus de Sassoferrato and Baldus de Ubaldus. In a barbarous Latin style that lent itself easily to parody and with copious citation of often contradictory sources, these *commentatores* sought to reshape ancient law, with the tools of scholastic didactics, into a body of legal doctrine suitable for the late-medieval world. As the French satirist Bonaventure Des Periers remarked, the Italian scholars were *non commentatores, sed tormentatores juris*.[7]

It was this so-called *mos italicus* that attracted foreign students by the thousands, including many Germans, to the Italian universities in the thirteenth and fourteenth centuries, and that prepared the way for the "theoretical" reception of Roman law that preceded its subsequent reception in practice. Accordingly, the "Roman Law" that began to be received in northern Europe was not Justinian's *Corpus Iuris Civilis* per se but certain parts of it surrounded by a mass of commentary. The commentary often obscured the material's classical sources and took over a law in total ignorance of the social needs in antiquity that had initially brought it forth and that sometimes were no longer relevant.

In southern France and Provence, which had been subject to Roman rule since classical antiquity, written Roman law, in the form of the *Breviarium Alaricianum*, had acquired the force of customary law. In contrast to this *pays de droit écrit* south of the Garonne, the north was still governed by customary law similar to medieval German law and based on Frankish law going back at least to Charlemagne. In the mid–fifteenth century the *pays de droit coutumier* was ruled by about sixty general customals—including notably Philippe de Beaumanoir's thirteenth-century *Coutumes de Beauvaisis*—not to mention some three hundred more local customals.[8] Yet this customary law was subtly infiltrated by Roman principles, in what Vinogradoff has called "an intelligent reception" whereby "Roman views were modified, combined with native ideas, or entirely rejected."[9] This "prophylactic innoculation"[10] of French customary law by Roman law meant that any revolutionary reception was resisted as unnecessary by northern French jurists well into the seventeenth century. At the same time, at French universities a new way of studying the *Corpus Iuris Civilis* had emerged—the *mos gallicus*, personified by such distinguished humanists as Cujacius (Jacques Cujas), Budaeus (Guillaume Budé), and the Italian Alciatus, who moved to France because his approach was uncongenial to colleagues in Italy. These scholars, who approached Justinian's compilation not as a guide to modern law but as an invaluable source for insights into the moral and social thought of ancient Rome, established at Bourges the most distinguished center for the study of Roman law in the modern manner known as "elegant jurisprudence."[11]

In England the situation was different.[12] In the second quarter of the twelfth century the Lombard scholar Vacarius (1120–1200) arrived from Bologna as the first known professor of Roman law in England.[13] By 1149 he was lecturing (presumably at Oxford) to students for whom he prepared a compendium of Justinian's *Codex* and *Digest*—a textbook that became known, thanks to the indigence of the students, as *liber pauperum*. The coherence of the *Tractatus de legibus et consuetudinibus Angliae* (ca. 1188) traditionally ascribed to Ranulf de Glanvil, chief justiciar of England, can be explained only by its author's familiarity with the rationality of Roman law, so different from the chaotic medieval law books that preceded it.[14] Thomas à Becket's struggle with Henry II stemmed from his insistence, as archbishop of Canterbury, on the priority of Roman canon law over the temporal English law. And Henry de Bracton took as the model for his epoch-making treatise *De legibus et consuetudinibus Angliae* the expositions of the distinguished Bolognese glossator Azo, from which he was able to adduce general principles underlying the English case law that he described. As Holdsworth summarizes, "Roman doctrine is used to illustrate and explain the principles of law, or is worked, in a modified form, into its substance."[15] The fact that English law experienced an "intelligent reception" during the legal renaissance of the twelfth and thirteenth centuries obviated, as in France, a more revolutionary reception according to the Continental model in the sixteenth century. When England perceived the need to modernize its legal system, it turned back to its own law books—notably Glanvil and Bracton—rather than to the Continental commentators. And the new administrative bodies that were needed were developed from existing institutions.[16] In addition, the strong centralized authority precluded the territorial disarray of law that characterized northern France and Germany. And the gradual growth of the Inns of Court with the concentration of legal power in London strengthened the position of common lawyers to such an extent that they were easily able to resist the incursion of jurists trained in Roman law.

The Situation in Germany

Of the Three R's that characterized northern European history in the late fifteenth and early sixteenth centuries, the Reception of Roman Law is perhaps less familiar than the Renaissance and Reformation. Yet even in countries that ultimately rejected it, as we shall see in England, the debate produced significant political realignments as well as a strengthening of the indigenous common law. In Germany, where a form of Roman law wholly displaced the existing patterns of Germanic law, the effect on legal, social, and political life was immeasurable.

The Three R's were of course interrelated to no small degree. The Reception depended extensively on the humanist revival of learning, through which the Latin texts of Roman law were rediscovered, edited, and glossed. In addition, the Reception constituted part of the general reform movement that permeated the age in its social, religious, and political life. Indeed, long before Luther the term *reformatio* was used widely as a label for the renewals of legal codes—urban, territorial, and imperial—that took place in the course of the fifteenth century all over Germany.[17] As a result, the Reception cannot be viewed in isolation from the other movements that characterized the transition from medieval to modern in northern Europe. And to the extent that the Reception was a phenomenon that touched all citizens in their daily lives, it was reflected in the literature of the age—most conspicuously in Germany, but also in England and northern France.

During the nineteenth century the German scholars who created and nurtured the historical study of German and Germanic law (and hence became known as *Germanisten*, in contrast to the *Romanisten*, who dealt with Roman law) concluded that the Reception was a phenomenon largely restricted to Germany—one that came swiftly and with disastrous consequences for a society that thereby lost an indigenous law written in the vernacular, administered by respected laymen, and centered on the concept of the freedom of the individual.[18] The notion that the Reception was "a national misfortune, a violation of innocent Germania by the brutal Roman," persisted into the twentieth century down to the Nazis, who found Roman law alien to the German conception of law and right.[19]

We understand today that the Reception affected many countries, albeit to differing degrees. We also know, thanks to many specialized studies of specific towns and regions, that even in Germany it proceeded at a different pace and with a differing reaction in the towns and in the territories, in south and north, among the princes and among the peasants. And we appreciate that, across the social and political spectrum, the response varied from eager acceptance to indignant rejection.[20] Many questions remain, and opinion varies widely on the relative weight attributable to various factors to be discussed below: Roman law versus customary law, written law versus oral law, *mos italicus* versus *mos gallicus*, *Professorenrecht* versus *Juristenrecht*. Above all, it is still a matter of dispute whether the Reception amounts in the last analysis to a system imposed from above by authority (like the Prussian reforms of the late eighteenth century) or demanded in a revolutionary swell from below by the peasants and the bourgeoisie. However, for all the variety that colored this complex phenomenon that took place throughout much of Europe over a period of several centuries, the basic outline is nonetheless generally clear.[21]

It was only in Germany that the indigenous law was displaced by a Roman law that had undergone extensive revisions in medieval Italy, a phenomenon that amounted to a large-scale transformation of German cultural life. It was not so much the changes in actual content of the law that mattered as, rather, the scientific rationalization of law—that is, a general "transformation in the categories of legal thought, involving the sudden appearance within the medieval legal world of a 'scientific', rational or academic view of law."[22]

In the fifteenth century the vast lands of the Holy Roman Empire were still governed by a highly fragmented system of overlapping and often conflicting sets of laws. On one level citizens were subject to the laws of their own towns (*Stadtrecht*), to territorial rule (*Landrecht*) as represented, for instance, by Eike von Repgow's compilation of Saxon law (*Sachsenspiegel*), and by a rather weak imperial law (*Kaiserrecht*). In addition—and this marks one of the most important differences between Roman and Germanic law—each estate or social group was bound by its own set of laws: the *Lehnrecht* of the knights, *Zunftrecht* of the guilds, *Bauernrecht* of the peasants, or the *Hofrecht* of the manors. The whole complex system, based essentially on ancient Germanic principles and procedures, was regulated by often minimally trained judges presiding over tribunals of elected lay judges (*Schöffen*), who were frequently stymied at the start by issues of competence. The system was most highly fragmented in the southwest; in the north, the *Sachsenspiegel* played the unifying role that was fulfilled in northern France by Beaumanoir's *Coutumes de Beauvaisis* and in England by Bracton's *De legibus et consuetudinibus Angliae*.

By the end of the fifteenth century many Germans were deeply convinced of the need for change. In many rapidly modernizing towns and cities the *Stadtrecht*, in a series of "reformations," had already been adapted to the demands of commerce and business. The princes were dismayed at the medieval practice of feud, which still constituted the normal—and fully legal—means of resolving territorial or even personal disputes, especially for the free knights, who clung to their treasured *Lehnrecht*. And the merchants were distressed by the legal uncertainties that made business between cities and countries unnecessarily complicated and dangerous. Accordingly, toward the end of the century, and notably following the Diet of Frankfurt in the spring of 1486, the princes, under the leadership of Berthold von Henneberg, archbishop of Mainz, began demanding certain reforms in return for their support of the emperor in his war against the Hungarians.[23] Specifically, the estates demanded a Perpetual Public Peace (*Ewiger Landfriede*) forbidding feud justice, and a reorganization of the Imperial Chamber Court (*Reichskammergericht*), making it a permanently established court with judges not subject to the whim of the emperor. These goals, which were consistent with imperial desires to impose a unified code of written law on the patchwork of largely unwritten "customary" law, were finally achieved with the agreement of the new emperor, Maximilian, at the Diet of Worms in 1495. Maximilian's initiative was reinforced successively by two comprehensive criminal codes, the *Constitutio Criminalis Bambergensis* of 1507, written for the prince-bishop of Bamberg, and the *Constitutio Criminalis Carolina*, published in 1532 over the seal of Emperor Charles V, both of which strengthened central government by introducing the methods of Roman law.

The *Reichskammergericht*, in contrast to the earlier royal conventions or *placita generalia*, had a regular seat: first at Frankfurt, from 1495 to 1527; then at Speyer; and from 1693 until its abolishment in 1806 at Wetzlar. This court, originally instituted to hear cases involving parties directly responsible to the emperor, applied Roman common law to all cases not covered by the traditional local statutes.[24] Initially only half of the assessors had to be *doctores* while half were still chosen from the knights' estate; but very soon it was expected that even the knights should have had some legal training. This produced far-reaching social effects.[25] The trend appealed greatly to the army of lawyers newly trained in the *mos italicus*, either in the Italian universities or in the recently established German institutions. It also gratified the humanist scholars who were working toward the revival of classical antiquity in all its aspects, including the law. The written common law was further justified by the appeal to its rationality, which provided a constant standard in contrast to the fluctuations of instinct or inclination under the old system of customary law.

Because the affairs of the empire were increasingly dominated by trained jurists, the princes also felt the need of knowledgeable advice. As a result, the princes began to include jurists as advisers in their trains; during the reign of Frederick III (1439–1493) complaints were increasingly heard about the predominance of jurists at the imperial court. Meanwhile, in the territorial courts the learned *doctores* gradually displaced the lay justices (*Schöffen*), who had hitherto managed legal affairs according to their understanding of the old Germanic customary law. (Because the jurists held themselves to be above the trivia of local law, the smaller courts continued to be ruled by traditional customary law—with the result that the frequency of appeals to the higher courts increased dramatically.) Also displaced were the lower ranks of the nobility, the knights, who had previously depended for much of their support on positions as princely councillors. As a result of these changing circumstances around 1500 Roman law was prominently replacing the older system of customary law; but this displacement brought with it many complaints about the old law and the new law alike,[26] and these complaints are reflected in the popular literature of the time, as we shall have occasion to observe in the following chapters.

Various factors have been cited to account for the different nature of the Reception in Germany: the desire of the emperors to establish their central authority by an appeal to the legal system representing the *imperium*; the establishment of the Imperial Chamber Court (*Reichskammergericht*); the codifications or "reformations" of existing legal codes in order to bring them into conformity with modern circumstances; the influence of the trained jurists; and inherent weaknesses in the existing German legal system(s).[27]

In addition, certainly, there were powerful negative factors. Unlike England, Germany had no centralized political or legal authority that could resist the imposition of an alien law. The absence of a trained legal cadre meant that, unlike France, Germany had no legal intelligentsia to direct the course of affairs—no scholars, with the notable exception of Ulrich Zasius (1461–1535) in Freiburg, to compare with Alciatus, Budaeus, or Cujacius. To be sure, hordes of German students had migrated to Italy in the thirteenth and fourteenth centuries to study law, and their numbers were so great that special provisions had to be made at Bologna and Padua for the *natio Germanica*. But by far the majority of these students were members of the clergy, who returned to practice canon law in ecclesiastical courts and exerted little influence on courts of secular law.[28] Only canon law was taught at the earliest German universities (Prague, Vienna, Heidelberg, Cologne, Erfurt), and it was displaced by Roman law only toward the end of the fifteenth century with the establishment of such universities as Basel (1460) and Tübingen (1477). But during the fifteenth century the teaching of law at most German universities was notoriously bad, making it the subject of ridicule by the humanists and the object of frustrated contempt by citizens who suffered at the hands of poorly trained lawyers. Indeed, the inadequate training of lawyers and judges in Germany during the fifteenth and sixteenth centuries produced a flood of handbooks and summaries dedicated specifically to remedying their deficiencies in substance as well as procedure.[29]

A combination of these various factors, plus the desire to join the growing European community of lawyers linked by their common commitment to Roman law,[30] produced in Germany by the middle of the sixteenth century the so-called *usus modernus pandectarum*. This system, combining Roman law, canon law, and elements of the indigenous customary law, represented a total break with the medieval past. It was not the case that specific points of the old German law did not continue to be observed. Rather, the new academic jurisprudence characteristic of the Roman legal system introduced into German legal thinking a disciplined rational approach that was utterly distinct from the older Germanic conceptions based on personal freedom and a great range of circumstances varying according to social status.[31] During the Middle Ages, canon law with its universalizing tendencies had provided the legislation needed for the still limited international agreements that transcended local and territorial law. But when, as a result of the Reformation, the influence of canon law declined in Germany, the Roman civil law tended to expand in order to assume those functions.[32]

That this profound social and intellectual turmoil left its mark on the society is evident from the conspicuous role that law and lawyers play in the literature of the age. Indeed, one could argue that the Reception and Reformation absorbed so much of the creative energy of the early sixteenth century in Germany that the finest literary documents of the period amount to satires of existing circumstances, orations on the present, and utopian visions of a better future.

As a result of the confusions and controversies produced by this encounter between two legal systems, and exacerbated by the incompetent lawyers and judges who exploited the situation, ordinary citizens in German-speaking countries toward the end of the fifteenth century had no reason to believe that their interests were being served by Roman law or by the indigenous customary law. *Summum ius, summum iniuria*—this saying, which already enjoyed proverbial status by the time Cicero cited it in his *De officiis* (1.10.13), was frequently quoted by Erasmus, Luther, and other theologians of the age.[33] The sentiment precisely exemplified both the disenchantment with customary law and the simultaneous Reception of Roman law.

CHAPTER FIVE

The Disenchantment with Customary Law

The Ironization of Ordeal

Trial by ordeal, whether in the form of judicial duel or some other variant, is characteristic of the most ancient legal practices and is known over much of the world.[1] But it is especially prominent in the earliest recorded laws of the barbarian Germanic tribes.[2] In the *Lex Burgundionum*, a compilation undertaken by Gundobad, king of the Burgundians from 474 to 516, trial by combat is decreed in cases when perjury is suspected. "For it is just that if anyone shall say without delay that he knows the truth of the matter and shall offer to take oath, he should not hesitate to fight" (Title 45).[3] Faith in the *judicium dei* is implicit in the justification that, regardless of the outcome, "one may delight in truth rather than falsehood." A certain influence of Roman law is evident even in this code of the Burgundians, who had crossed the Rhine less than a century earlier, in 413, and established a kingdom in the Rhone valley in Roman territory. We note already, for instance, a tendency to use financial compensation, or composition, in place of the blood feud so beloved by the barbarian tribes.[4] But in this early fusion of Germanic and Roman law the influence does not yet extend to such sacred customs as oath taking and ordeal.

The situation looks entirely different when we turn to the Lombard laws of the seventh and eighth centuries. The Langobardi did not enter northern Italy until A.D. 568, where they were slow to assimilate to the Roman Catholic culture. Nevertheless, many of the Germanic customs—notably *faida* or blood feud—were not suitable for the more sophisticated Mediterranean town life that they encountered in their new home. By the time their laws were codified in 643 by King Rothair (*Rothair's Edict*) and supplemented from 713 to 735 by King Liutprand, the influence of Roman law in curtailing the practice of judicial ordeal was much more extensive. Rothair still accepts *camfio*, or judicial duel, in accusations of capital crime (Title 9). But in many lesser cases, such as accusations of illegitimacy, pleas for guardianship, and even uxoricide (Titles 164–66), the edict accepts the testimony of oath-helpers. "For it seems to be unjust that such an important case should be settled by a duel between two men."[5] King Liutprand still acknowledges trial by combat, but he also knows that the practice is subject to abuse. Accordingly (Title 71.II), "If anyone with evil intent challenges another man to combat—a thing often done by evil persons," the challenger must take an oath that his action is based on a positive suspicion of some appropriate crime.[6] Five years later the doubts emerge more strongly (Title 118.II). According to Lombard law, a man who kills a fellow freeman loses all his property. "As a result, there have been some men who sought to prove by combat—as provided by the earlier law—that one of their relatives who had suffered some illness and died in his bed was actually deliberately killed" (by poisoning).[7] Liutprand and his judges therefore decree that henceforth in such cases, if the accused man or his champion should be defeated, rather than losing all his property he shall pay suitable composition to the accuser. "For we are uncertain concerning the judgment of God [in this matter] and we have heard that many men have unjustly lost their cause through combat; however, on account of the customs of the Lombard people we are unable to abolish this law."

It is difficult ever to know precisely to what extent ancient law reflects contemporary reality—whether, that is, it amounts to an accurate description of present practice, the definition of an ideal, or a sentimental recollection of the past. In fact, despite its gradual suppression in written law the practice of the judicial duel continued for centuries before finally giving way to the illegal duel. Huizinga recounts in all its comic-pathetic detail a celebrated combat between two burghers of Valenciennes as late as 1455 under the formal auspices of the Burgundian court.[8] Even when the legal documents fail, moreover, we know the precise detail of the judicial ordeal in the Middle Ages from literary monuments. As one scholar has observed in connection with medieval France, "There are few sustained narrative works belonging to the twelfth and thirteenth centuries that do not contain a trial"; and most of those trials depend upon ordeal of one sort or another.[9]

In the memory of many readers the *Chanson de Roland* (written around 1100) ends with the tragic tableau eternalizing the death of Roland and the twelve paladins, along with 20,000 French soldiers, in the pass at Roncevaux. But in fact almost half of the poem's four thousand verses still remain, of which the concluding three hundred are devoted to the trial of Ganelon, who betrayed Roland and the French rear guard to the Saracens. The conduct of the trial follows in precise detail the procedures used in early-twelfth-century France and England, and not necessarily the Frankish practices that may have been used in 778, when the incidents upon which the poem is based actually occurred.[10] Because the charge is treason—that is, a crime against the empire—Charlemagne summons vassals from every part of the empire to constitute a proper court, a so-called *placitum generale*, which opens at Aix (Aachen) on Saint Silvester's Day. Ganelon does not deny the charge of seeking Roland's death: it is his defense that he betrayed Roland not as an act of treason against the emperor but, rather, out of justified vengeance for earlier deeds ("Venget m'en sui, mais n'i ad traïsun," 3778).[11] As the Frankish lords withdraw to confer, Ganelon asks his kinsman Pinabel to serve as his advocate. Seeing this, and out of fear of Pinabel, the jurors seek a compromise: Roland is dead, and no compensation will bring him back. No sensible man would seek a duel at this point. They beseech the emperor to forgive Ganelon and to take him back into his services. Charlemagne is dismayed and angered by their recommendation for clemency. Thierry, the duke of Anjou, takes the emperor's side and rejects the argument that a private quarrel may be settled against a knight involved in the emperor's service. Accusing Ganelon of perjury and treason and of deserving a felon's death by hanging, he declares himself ready to defend his accusation by the sword. The two contestants give Charlemagne their right-hand gloves as a pledge, and thirty kinsmen stand bond for Ganelon. After a long battle, in which Thierry appears to be the underdog, Pinabel is slain, and the Franks cry out that God has worked a miracle ("Deus i ad fait vertut!" line 3931). Now that the trial by combat has revealed the divine judgment, the Franks eagerly condemn Ganelon's thirty kinsmen to death by hanging. Ganelon himself is drawn and quartered. The entire procedure appears to have followed in good order. But three circumstances alert us to a certain sense of disquiet regarding the justice of the proceedings. First, the jury is swayed to its initial recommendation of leniency by fear of the defendant and his kinsmen. Second, Charlemagne does not accept the judgment of his jury; the trial by combat results from the failure of a negotiated compromise. Finally, the poem ends by stating not that *justice* was accomplished but that "the emperor has done *his* justice" ("l'emperere ad faite sa justise," 3988). In the words of one critic, the poem seems to acknowledge "the political ability with which lords were able to manage courts in their own interest quite as much as in that of some abstract justice."[12]

In sum, the *Chanson de Roland* contains not only a precise record of judicial proceedings of customary Anglo-Norman law but also the seeds of discontent with that law. This discontent may reflect the tension produced in European society in the twelfth century as a new process of rationalization—exemplified by Glanvil in England and the glossators in Italy—began to systematize or otherwise to contend with traditional oral law. It is worth noting that the Middle High German adaptation of the material, the *Rolandslied* by the so-called Priest or Pfaffe Konrad (ca. 1170), adds a few details that are characteristic of Germanic legal procedure and, in particular, calls attention to Charlemagne's role as the creator of German law.[13] But the major change is evident in the shift in motivation: in the heated atmosphere of the early Crusades Genelun is found guilty principally because he betrayed Christian knights to Saracen heathens.

The questioning of customary trial by ordeal, tentative in the *Chanson de Roland*, becomes explicit and even satirical in works of the thirteenth century, as is evident in one of the most memorable scenes in Gottfried von Strassburg's courtly epic *Tristan* (written between 1200 and 1210)—a scene not familiar to those who know the story only from Richard Wagner's treatment.[14] Three-quarters of the way into the 20,000-line extant fragment of the work, King Marke of Cornwall, having yet again become (justly!) suspicious that his wife Isolde has been committing adultery with his nephew Tristan, summons an ecclesiastical court (*concîlje*, rather than a *placitum generale*) to London to advise him. (This is normal procedure: as in the *Chanson de Roland*, the council is summoned not to adjudicate a case, but to hear the accusation and to recommend an appropriate trial—normally by oath or ordeal.) Since the accusation, inasmuch as it involves an offense against the king, also raises the possibility of treason, as in Ganelon's case, the court also includes secular representatives with royal authority. One of the wisest of the princes skilled in Church law, the bishop of Thames, offers his advice (lines 15,350 ff.). Although Tristan and Isolde have been accused of a serious offense, no proof has been offered. (Medieval law had severe penalties, usually death, for adulterous couples caught in flagrante delicto; but mere suspicions or accusations could often be rebutted by oath-takers.)[15] In effect, however, he continues with a shrewd realism, people are just as eager to listen to lies as to truth. The present uncertainty is intolerable, especially in light of the political implications. He proposes that the queen be summoned to the palace to answer to the charges, which he repeats in her presence.

Isolde, responding that she is far from her home in Ireland (an allusion to her legal nonstatus in Cornwall and the absence of supporting witnesses) and among strangers who are prepared to believe the worst of her, declares herself willing to submit to any legal process that might clear her name: "swaz gerihtes man mir ûf geleit" (15,511).[16] King Marke immediately states that he will be satisfied if she will undergo the ordeal of the hot iron ("daz gerihte / zem glüejenden îsen," 15,524–25), known technically as *judicium ferri candentis*.[17] Isolde accepts the decision, and the trial is set to take place six weeks later in the town of Caerleon. Isolde, under no illusions about her guilt, is desperate. Entrusting her plight to the merciful Christ, she conceives a deceitful plan that depends upon God's courtly nature:

> in disen dingen haete Isôt
> einen list ir herzen vür geleit
> vil verre ûf gotes höfscheit.
>
> (15,550–52)

She writes to Tristan and instructs him to come in disguise to the place in Caerleon where her ship is to land.

On the appointed day Tristan appears in pilgrim's garb. When Isolde spots him, she asks him to carry her from ship to shore, telling her entourage that under the circumstances she did not want to be borne by a knight. As he does so, she whispers that, when they reach the shore, he should fall down with her, and he does so in such a manner that he comes to rest in her arms beside her on the ground. When her followers rush to punish the pilgrim for his clumsiness, she defends him and points out that he fell out of weakness and illness. Making a joke of the matter, she says she can no longer prove that no man besides Marke ever lay in her arms. Meanwhile, at Caerleon the iron has been placed in the fire. Isolde, putting aside all her jewelry and fine garments, clothes herself in a hair shirt and woolen cloak in order to win God's favor so that he will overlook her true guilt and restore her honor:

> daz got ir wâren schulde
> an ir niht gedaehte
> und sî z'ir êren braehte.
>
> (15,648–50)

With her sleeves rolled up above her elbows and with bare arms and feet—the prescribed deshabille to prevent any concealed devices—she arrives at the cathedral, where, laying her hand on the sacred relic, she swears an oath that she has carefully formulated: that never a man has known her body and that never a living man besides the king has lain in her arms or at her side—apart from the one that she cannot deny, the poor pilgrim that he saw with his own eyes. King Marke, satisfied with the oath (although it is unusual for the accused to formulate the oath), orders her to take the iron in her hand. Seizing it in God's name, she carries it without being burned ("und truog ez, daz si niht verbran," 15,732). Gottfried plays down in one quick verse the act itself; so we know neither the weight of the iron nor the number of steps taken—details normally spelled out by customary law. Indeed, Isolde is immediately exonerated although normally the court waited for three days to determine whether the wound was healing (innocent) or festering (guilty). Instead he goes on to add an almost blasphemously ironic moralizing conclusion to the effect that almighty Christ is as tractable as a cloak in the wind, adapting himself pliantly whenever he is nicely asked.[18] Whether in earnest or in play, he always obliges just as one wishes, as is evident in Isolde's case. "She was saved by her deception and her perjured [literally: "poisoned"] oath" ("ir trügeheit / und ir gelüppeter eit," 15,747–48).

For the time being, at least, she is restored fully to trust and honor. Whether or not we question the outcome of the trial from a modern ethical standpoint, the essential matter from the medieval point of view is that the trial was legally impeccable. To be sure, not every detail is depicted; we do not see, for example, the actions preliminary to the oath and ordeal, which do not involve Isolde, the *benedictio ignis* and the *benedictio ferri in igne*. In general, however, the legal proceedings—from the summoning of an advisory council and the recommendation of the proper test to the trial by ordeal itself—are carried out and portrayed with precise and accurate attention to judicial procedures in early-thirteenth-century Germany.[19]

The ordeal of carrying a glowing-hot iron a certain number of steps without being burned, widespread in world cultures, is known to us from Hindu ordeal books as well as Germanic customary law, from which it was adopted into Christian legal practice. However, just at the time when Gottfried was writing, Christian opinion was sharply divided on the legitimacy of *judicium ferri candentis*. In 1211, over eighty Catharist heretics were tried by this ordeal in Strassburg, and most were found guilty. This notorious case prompted Pope Innocent III, in January 1212, to forbid the practice pending its formal rejection at the Fourth Lateran Council of 1215.[20] But what was initially accepted and then subsequently rejected by Church doctrine continued to thrive in the popular imagination as a telling example of the manipulability of certain practices of traditional law.[21] The administrators of ordeals in all societies have long been aware of various means of calibrating the pain of ordeal by fire and thus insuring the guilt or innocence of the accused.[22] And these ancient legal practices, notoriously subject to abuse, were regarded with particular skepticism as customary law came into contact with increasingly sophisticated societies.

Not long after Gottfried von Strassburg, the early-thirteenth-century Middle High German minstrel known as "Der Stricker" wrote a short verse anecdote (*maere*) in which he secularized the ordeal by fire, shifted it into a noncourtly private realm, and inverted the circumstances.[23] In this short narrative, which consists almost wholly of dialogue, a wife tells her husband that she fears he will leave her for another woman. If she could only be certain that he has never possessed another lover, she would be reassured and would make him happier than any other woman could. Despite her husband's consoling words, she begs him to demonstrate his love by undergoing the test of the hot iron. The husband complies good-naturedly, and the iron is heated and laid on two stones, "as custom required" ("daz ez nâch sînem rehte lac," line 67). But the canny husband has earlier concealed a piece of wood in his sleeve, upon which he holds the iron and carries it "more than six steps." He shows his unwounded hand to his wife, who now concedes that he has proven his faithfulness. At this point, however, the husband demands that she demonstrate her own faithfulness in the same manner while the iron is still hot. The wife pleads that men have greater willpower than women and are able to resist temptations to which women succumb. Before she picks up the iron, she begs him to overlook one man, swearing that otherwise she has never slept with anyone but him. The husband readily agrees, but then his wife asks him to forgive her for two more lapses, as well as a sum of money that she has secretly put aside. Again he declares his willingness but insists that she pick up the hot iron. She finally does so and burns herself so severely that she screams with pain. When he tries to bandage her hand, she complains that it is so badly burned that she can no longer use it as before. (In other words, she concedes her guilt even before the usual three days have passed.) Her husband promises that in the future he will behave in such a manner as to fulfill all her worst fears. Again, then, the motif of ordeal by hot iron is used to show how this common practice of customary Germanic law can be abused—with the result that the law itself is brought into disrespect.

But the motif continued to exert its literary appeal. Some three hundred years later Hans Sachs updated the Stricker's comic narrative in a dramatic farce entitled *The Hot Iron* (*Das heiss Eisen*, 1551), which shifts the niveau to the peasantry. It is essentially the same plot, but here an older woman is introduced to whom the peasant wife confesses her anxieties and who recalls the ancient custom ("wie man vor Jahren Gwohnheit hätt").[24] Again the husband, who proclaims his innocence in a monologue, is compliant, being aware of his wife's caprices. Again, being realistic, he conceals in his sleeve a stick of wood on which he carries the glowing-hot piece of iron. The wife is fully satisfied until the husband turns the tables and demands that she undergo the same ordeal—and with precisely the same results, although Hans Sachs heightens the comedy by having the wife confess to affairs with seven men, not counting the bachelors(!). She burns her hand, of course, but Hans Sachs gives his playlet a comic twist. The husband tells the neighbor that he had known all along of his wife's infidelities, but he is now prepared to forgive her if the neighbor will help to keep his wife faithful for the rest of her life. The two conspirators go off to drink a conciliatory glass of wine together.

The example of trial by ordeal, as it makes its way from heroic *chanson* by way of courtly epic through medieval popular narrative to early-modern folk theater, not only reflects the reduction of an originally serious legal procedure to no more than a quaint old practice used to chasten a gullible woman. It also attests the public disenchantment with the uncertainties that characterized the rituals of traditional customary law and hence, to a certain extent, with customary law itself. We observe a similar skepticism made far more explicit when we turn to one of the most popular stories of the late-medieval world.

The Trial of the Fox

In 1796 Goethe jotted down a distich headed "Reineke Fuchs," in which he expressed his astonishment that a poet could have written this work centuries ago since the subject matter is so contemporary:

> Vor Jahrhunderten hätte ein Dichter dieses gesungen?
> Wie ist das möglich? Der Stoff ist ja von gestern und heut.[25]

Goethe had been familiar since youth with the medieval legends regarding the shrewd fox known variously as Renart, Reinhart, Reinaerde, or Reynke, and in 1782 he had read aloud to friends in Weimar J. C. Gottsched's modern prose translation of the late-fifteenth-century Low German version.[26] Only two years earlier he had published his own treatment of the material, a twelve-canto poem in heroic hexameters entitled simply *Reineke Fuchs* (1794). As he tells us in his account of the unsuccessful German military campaign against the French revolutionary troops (*Campagne in Frankreich 1792*, 1822), Goethe turned to the subject in January 1793 in an effort to save himself from the sorry circumstances of the world by gazing into this "Mirror of Courts and Sovereigns" ("Hof- und Regentenspiegel").[27] "For even if humanity exposes itself here in its undisguised animality, still everything happens in an exemplary and even serene manner, and one's good humor is nowhere disturbed." Thirty years later he recalled the consolation and joy that he drew from his work on "this unholy secular bible" ("dieser unheiligen Weltbibel").[28] In particular, he found the political realism and social cynicism of the medieval satire appropriate to the deplorable state of contemporary world history, and his close adaptation required only the most trivial modifications to make its relevance apparent to his enthusiastic readers.

Goethe was not alone in sensing the modern implications of this medieval matter. In the two hundred years since the publication of *Reineke Fuchs* many other writers have returned to the subject as a vehicle of social and political criticism. Thomas Carlyle was obviously under Goethe's influence when he focused on *Reynard the Fox* in the introduction as well as the conclusion of his *German Literature of the Fourteenth and Fifteenth Centuries* (1831), which opens with the claim that "the Apologue of *Reynard the Fox* ranks undoubtedly among the most remarkable Books, not only as a German, but, in all senses, as a European one."[29] His survey culminates in his discussion of the Low German *Reineke* as "a rude, wild Parody of Human Life, full of meaning and high moral purpose." Paradoxically, it was precisely the satirical aspect of the late Low German beast epic that dismayed Jacob Grimm, who in 1834 wrote the first (and still indispensable) scholarly study of the material, and led him to prefer the gentle irony of the earlier versions.[30] But his younger contemporary, the prolific Berlin satirist Adolf Glassbrenner (1810–76), published a *Neuer Reineke Fuchs* (1846) in forty-five cantos, adapting the old tale to contemporary events. For almost four hundred years, he begins (ignoring Goethe's treatment, which is not an updating), the world has heard nothing about the fox. So he proposes to report as well as possible how our hero has gotten along in the meantime and how he carried on in recent times:

> So will ich denn bestmöglichst melden,
> Wie es ergangen unserm Helden,
> Und wie er in der jüngsten Zeit
> Sich wieder machte groß und breit.[31]

It is no accident that scholars in the former German Democratic Republic were drawn to the theme in studies that, beginning with analyses by Marx and Engels of the early-sixteenth-century peasant rebellion, saw in the fox an oppositional hero and in the poem(s) an exposure of the corrupt feudal society.[32] The continuing appeal of the material is evident from the existence of the International Reynard Society, which since 1988 has been publishing its own *Reinardus Yearbook*.

If it has been mainly as a vehicle for general social satire that the material has attracted writers and critics since Goethe, medieval poets were fascinated in particular by the legal implications of the story. Goethe's adaptation was based on the most popular late-medieval treatment: the Low German *Reinke de Vos* published in Lübeck in 1498—a work he knew in Gottsched's prose translation with its reprint of the Low German text.[33] It was this work, and notably its 1519 and 1539 reprints in Rostock, that assured the enormous European success of the poem, which was straightway translated into High German, Danish, Latin, English, and other languages.[34] But this Low German version, itself an adaptation from an earlier Dutch version, merely marked the final stage of a development that had begun over three centuries earlier.

The medieval world knew various tales concerning the clever fox. In 1834, as the appendix to his study of the legend, Jacob Grimm reprinted a number of representative fables in Latin and German from the twelfth to the fourteenth century.[35] But the first sustained narratives were two anonymous Latin beast poems revolving around the wolf and involving only secondarily the fox. The mid-eleventh-century *Echasis captivi* (*The Captive's Escape*, probably composed around 1045 in the Moselle valley) tells the story in some 1,200 lines of a foolish calf who escapes from his stall, is captured by a wolf who threatens to eat him, and is then rescued by his herd assisted by the wily fox. Almost exactly a century later (1148–49), and somewhat to the north in the Low Countries, another poet composed a much longer Latin narrative (almost 6,600 lines) linking a dozen different tales about the wolf *Ysengrimus*, most (but not all) of which involve his battles with his crafty vulpine opponent, who is here first called Reinardus (a Germanic name going back to the forms *Reginhart* and *Raginohard*, meaning "counselor" or "adviser"). Apart from the fact that these two popular Latin poems revolve around the wolf and not the fox, it is their crucial characteristic that they are both fundamentally satires of the clergy.[36] The calf is the novice who seeks to throw off monastic restraints and lands in the clutches of the devil's wolfish henchman until he is rescued by his fellow monks. And *Ysengrimus*, according to the most recent scholarship, amounts to a satire on monasticism, monastic life, and specific monks, unified by the metaphor of the wolf-monk.[37] Even though the two works contain many specific references to monastic rules and occasional passing allusions to secular law, neither can be said to concern itself primarily or even significantly with legal issues.

The Old French Renart

The case changes dramatically when, a few decades later, we reach the *Roman de Renart* and the imitators it engendered. The relationship between the Old French work and the preceding Latin *Ysengrimus* has been subject to much debate.[38] It is still not known, for instance, whether the French work was directly influenced by the Latin poem or whether both were based on still older tales. In the present context the point is irrelevant because the legal satire, which had no importance in the monastic satire of the Latin works, suddenly becomes the central issue in virtually all treatments of the Renart theme. Indeed, as the epic develops, the basic Renart story, the framework embracing all the other episodes, is a courtroom drama.

The designation *Roman de Renart* is misleading because, unlike most Old French courtly romances, it is not a unified narrative by (usually) a single author but a cycle of some two dozen versified tales by various hands.[39] When Pierre de Saint-Cloud composed the first of these tales around 1176, he announced to his listeners that he was departing from the courtly tradition of romances about Troy or Tristan, with which they were familiar. Instead, he continued, he intended to tell them a story they had never heard about the long-lasting and inexorable feud between Renart and Ysengrin:

> Mais onques n'oïstes la guerre,
> Qui tant fu dure de grant fin,
> Entre Renart et Ysengrin,
> Qui moult dura et moult fu dure.
>
> (II.10–13)[40]

Pierre's story of some 2,500 lines was so popular that it virtually established a new narrative genre. By 1180 his imitators had already produced several more tales, or *branches*, about Renart. These were gathered into a collection that, though now lost, was known to the Alsatian poet Heinrich der Glichezaere, who used it as the basis for his Middle High German version of the legend.[41] By 1200 various authors had added many more *branches*, which in the course of the thirteenth century were gathered into three extant collections under the common title *Roman de Renart* although each used a different number and succession of episodes.[42] However, the earliest *branche* (combining the ones now numbered II and Va) by Pierre de Saint-Cloud, which initiated and provided the framework for all the others, is essentially a legal drama.

Much of the text (the 1,396 lines of *branche* II) relates various of Renart's adventures with Chantecler the rooster, an unnamed titmouse, Tiebert the wildcat, Tiecelin the raven, and Ysengrin the wolf. In the last of these episodes Renart invades the wolf's lair, where he makes sexual advances to Ysengrin's wife Hersent and then urinates on his children. The episode culminates with Renart's rape of Hersent, an act that he brazenly denies, and he offers to prove his innocence with an oath. These events lead (in *branche* Va) to their indictment of Renart at the court of King Noble the lion. Ysengrin is confident that he can win the case not only because he is wise and experienced ("Que molt ert voiziez et sages," Va.295) and skilled in several languages; he is also the king's chamberlain ("conestable"). At the *placitum generale*, at which the entire kingdom of animals is represented, Ysengrin begins his complaint with a general comment on the worsening state of law, on the mutability of truth, and on the unreliability of a word of honor:

> "Rois, justise va enpirant:
> Verites est tornee a fable,
> Nule parole n'est estable."
>
> (316–18)

He goes on to accuse Renart of breaking the royal ban against adultery, an accusation that Hersent supports, saying that Renart has pursued her since her girlhood. The king, hearing about the previous relations between Renart and Hersent, is inclined to a more cavalier interpretation of the circumstances but determines that Renart must be judged by the rules of the kingdom. He turns for advice to the camel Musart, a papal delegate from Lombardy and learned in jurisprudence ("Molt fu sages et bon legistres," 451).[43] In broken French mixed heavily with Latin legal terms, Musart sternly recommends the most severe penalties: if Renart will not make amends, he should be dispossessed of his property, stoned to death, and burned. If the king is unwilling to carry out right and justice ("reison ne droit," 481), he is not a proper monarch and should withdraw into a monastery.

The barons are divided in their response to these strong words, but the king tells them to deliberate the charges, which he rephrases in the manner most favorable to Renart: whether someone overwhelmed by love can be blamed for an act that is excused in his partner. After the barons withdraw, Brichemer the stag speaks first. Though sympathetic to Ysengrin, he reminds the barons that it is customary in such cases to hear a third witness lest someone make unfounded accusations. Since his wife will say whatever Ysengrin orders, he must produce another witness. But Brun the bear argues that Ysengrin is such a respected figure that he should be trusted on his own word alone. Baucent the boar supports Brichemer, but Plateax the buck points out that the case also involves the complaint that Renart abused Ysengrin's property and children and owes satisfaction to the wolf. Brun then interpolates a long story (of more than 150 lines) to demonstrate Renart's iniquity. The boar objects that the story is irrelevant to the case at issue: they must judge the facts before them. It would be sinful and wrong to mix up cases in court:

> "Que nos les melomes en cort:
> Que pechiez seroit et grant tort."
>
> (783–84)

This one cannot be decided until Renart has had an opportunity to defend himself. Cointereax the monkey supports this view, but the bear, convinced in advance of Renart's guilt, argues that Renart should be seized forthwith, bound hand and foot, and thrown into prison. The proper penalty would be whipping and castration so that he might never commit violence against another woman. But he fears that justice is dead ("Dont sai je bien, justice est morte," 842). The boar, sensing that many are speaking out of fear of the violent wolf, pleads for mercy and a reconciliation. Brichemer, seeking a consensus, proposes that they set a day for the reconciliation ("acordement") when Renart shall offer the promised oath and make amends. When a crime cannot be unequivocally proved, no trial should ensue—only a compromise. Since the king will be absent, Roonel the dog can act in his stead because he is an honorable man. All agree to this proposal, which Brichemer announces to the king, emphasizing that they have acted according to the customs of the land ("Selonc la guise de la terre," 894). He thereupon gives a concise and accurate summary of the deliberations. The king accepts the recommendation, happy to be relieved of the responsibility of judgment, and appoints Grinbert the badger to summon Renart for the following Sunday. Grinbert bears these tidings to Renart in his retreat at Malpertuis, and Renart agrees to all the terms.

Renart in his arrogance is utterly unconcerned about the outcome, but Ysengrin is not so casual in his confidence. Approaching Roonel in advance, he explains the arrangements and asks the dog, as his friend, to take his side until Renart has fulfilled all the terms of the agreement. Above all, he needs a sacred relic upon which Renart can swear his oath. Roonel proposes a solution: on the appointed day he will go out from the town and lie in a roadside ditch as though dead. Ysengrin will ask Renart to swear his oath on Roonel's tooth. Then Roonel will seize Renart by the wrist; and if Renart refuses, Roonel will have a bevy of dogs in hiding to capture him. Thereupon Ysengrin pays personal visits to all his friends—including the leopard, whom the king has designated as his personal representative—and asks them to swear to support him. On the appointed day Renart and Ysengrin appear with their supporters at the determined place near the ditch. Brichemer, as the leader of the baronial court, tells Renart that he must take an oath on the tooth of Saint Roonel, swearing that he neither deceived nor tricked Ysengrin in any way and that he has been unjustly accused. Renart rolls up his sleeve as though prepared to take the oath, but in fact he has perceived from the motion of the dog's flanks that Roonel is alive and well. When Renart hesitates, his ally the badger, who has also noticed the deception, asks the barons to make way so that Renart can approach the relic. But as soon as the others step back, Renart makes a tricky maneuver and flees, his enemies in hot pursuit. Although the dogs tear him bloody in thirteen places, he manages to make his escape and reach the security of his sanctuary at Malpertuis. Thus the story ends.

In the following years other writers added episodes: *branches* III (1178) and IV (1178). The anonymous author who in 1179 wrote what is now known as *branche* I begins by telling his audience that Pierre de Saint-Cloud, who devoted his imagination and art to the verses about Renart and his cousin Isengrin, left out the best part: the complaint and judgment rendered at King Noble's court regarding the sexual outrage that Renart inflicted on Hersent the she-wolf:

> Perrot, qui son engin et s'art
> Mist en vers fere de Renart
> Et d'Isengrin son cher conpere,
> Lessa le meus de sa matere:
> Car il entroblia le plet
> Et le jugement qui fu fet
> En la cort Noble le lion
> De la grant fornicacion
> Que Renart fist, qui toz maus cove,
> Envers dame Hersent la love.
>
> (1–10)

The entire lengthy *branche* (1,620 verses) is dedicated to that judicial proceeding. The following spring, when the king once again summons all his barons to his palace for a *placitum generale*, Ysengrin reminds him that he has still received no satisfaction for the injuries done him by Renart. The king, still not fully convinced of Hersent's innocence, is inclined to dismiss the matter, but Brun the bear, introducing a new aspect, reminds him that Renart's actions constitute a breach of the general peace, the *pax regis*, that has recently been declared. He challenges the king, as ruler of the land, to make peace in this feud and among his vassals.

> "Mes vos estes prince de terre:
> Si metes pes en ceste guerre!
> Metes pes entre vos barons."
>
> (65–67)

Requesting a judicial hearing on the matter, he proposes at least a financial settlement. At this Bruiant the bull becomes indignant, saying that a mere compensation in return for all the evil that Renart has done would be quite unsatisfactory: he should be castrated and tossed into a swamp. The badger argues that they are making a mountain out of a molehill, that the case has grown out of all proportion. He himself would be prepared to pay any fine if the case should be reopened, but that would serve only to bring further disgrace upon Hersent. Hersent, in what is surely a parody of the recently popularized story of Tristan and Isolde, offers to undergo an ordeal to demonstrate her innocence—an offer that the king urges Ysengrin to accept. But the wolf refuses, lest his wife be burned in the ordeal and her shame publicly attested (as in the Stricker's *maere*). He threatens to undertake a feud against his enemy before autumn, whereupon the king, angered, reminds him of the public peace that has been sworn ("la pes juree / Dont la terre est aseüree," 263–64).

Matters stand in Renart's favor when suddenly a procession of chickens led by Chantecler enters, bearing a litter with a dead hen who has just been killed by Renart. Following their account the king swears vengeance for the murder and the social disorder caused by the fox:

> "Quar j'en voil fere grant justise
> Del omecide et du desroi."
>
> (376–77)

When the corpse has been ceremonially buried, the king sends Brun the bear to summon Renart. Much of the following narrative is taken up with uproarious accounts of the tricks by which the clever and malicious Renart deceives first Brun (445–720) and then Tibert the wild cat (742–921), who is sent with the second summons. To deliver the third and final summons the king sends Renart's friend and relative, Grinbert the badger, who takes along a letter displaying the royal seal and containing a stern order. Renart, who has caused great distress and trouble ("grant ennui et grant contrere," 999), is summoned to appear on the following day to give satisfaction to the king. He is ordered to bring neither gold nor silver nor followers in his defense—nothing, in fact, but the rope with which he shall be hanged. Renart is terrified, and Grinbert offers to hear his confession, whereupon the fox launches into a lengthy catalog of his past iniquities (1029–96). Following his absolution, Renart bids farewell to his wife and children and, with abject prayers, sets out with Grinbert to the king's court. (Even in his terror, and to Grinbert's dismay, Renart longingly eyes a yard full of chickens that they pass.) So profound is Renart's fear of the king that his heart pounds and his horse stumbles in sympathy.

As soon as Renart arrives at court, many animals eagerly come forward with their complaints against him. Renart speaks in his own defense with a partly hypocritical and partly reasonable argument involving corruption among the nobles at court, the inherent weaknesses of his individual accusers, his personal loyalty to the king, and his advanced age. Unfair as the proceedings are, he has appeared out of respect for his sovereign and is prepared to accept his punishment, whether burning or hanging, even though any such judgment would be subject to much gossip. The king, having lost all patience, insists that this time Renart shall be judged without fail. The badger reminds him that Renart has appeared under safe-conduct ("par conduit," 1308) and must be tried fairly according to law and justice ("par loi et par jugement," 1306). He demands that Renart be given the opportunity to respond in a proper legal procedure ("A respondre par jugement / En vostre cort voiant la gent," 1311–12). All of Renart's enemies—Ysengrin, Tibert, Roonel, Tiecelin, Chantecler, and others—leap to their feet. When the king cries for silence and asks his barons what punishment Renart deserves, they unanimously demand death by hanging (the most common punishment of the day, even in the case of nobles, especially for treason, as we saw earlier in the case of Ganelon). The king agrees and orders them to proceed quickly, for if Renart should escape he would never come back.

While his enemies are erecting the gallows on a nearby hill, Renart turns to the king and declares that he is about to be hanged without having perpetrated a crime ("sanz forfet," 1384). At the same time (in a major distinction), he confesses to having committed many great sins ("molt grant pechez," 1385) for which he wishes to atone. He begs leave to take the cross and make a pilgrimage overseas in search of penance. If he should die under way, he would be redeemed; but to be hanged now would ensure damnation. He throws himself at the king's feet, and Grinbert joins his plea. The king relents and promises to release Renart if he will promise never to return. The other animals are chagrined at this turn of events, but the king forgives him his crimes. With all outward signs of repentance—the cross on his shoulder, a pilgrim's staff in hand, and the ritual scarf around his neck—but with contempt in his heart, Renart accepts a ring from the queen and sets out. When he reaches the top of a hill overlooking the valley, Renart halts his horse and wipes his bottom with the pilgrim's scarf, hurling insults down at the king and his court. Enraged, the king sends his barons after Renart, but the clever fox again manages to elude his pursuers and makes his way back to the safety of Malpertuis.

Over seventy years ago it was asserted by a French literary historian that "we perhaps know the true forms of feudal justice under the reign of Louis the Young better after having read the Trial of Renart than in attempting to reconcile what modern legists have sought to teach us about it."[44] More recently a distinguished Swiss jurist has demonstrated the extensive "agreement that claims our attention between the episodes concerning the accusation and trial of Renart and the system of criminal procedure that is evident in the juridical works and the customals of the twelfth and thirteenth centuries."[45] Other scholars have been more precise in their discriminations. We have learned that Pierre de Saint-Cloud takes considerable, and knowledgeable, pleasure in the details of legal debate and procedure whereas the anonymous trouvère of *branche* I is much less concerned with such niceties.[46] The earlier creator admired the legal institutions that he described while his successor regarded them with a more sharply satirical eye.[47]

However, in their eagerness to demonstrate agreement (a case that is convincingly made), these scholars downplay the clear signs of dissatisfaction with the legal system upon which both works are based. The symptoms are blatant. It is true that Pierre de Saint-Cloud pokes fun at the sole representative of Roman law who appears in his work, the learned camel Musart, who argues for the most severe penalties in his broken French interspersed with

Latin legal phrases. But most of the satire is reserved for the practices and procedures of the dominant customary law. At the first thought of a trial Ysengrin counts on political clout rather than on his legal skills to assure his victory over Renart. The initial grand jury deliberations are described with a shrewd psychological acuity that brings out not only the character of the individual barons but also the fears and cronyism that determine their decisions. After the first ruling—the decision to try Renart by oath—Ysengrin immediately pays a visit to the surrogate judge, Roonel, and succeeds in suborning him. The entire practice of oath taking is secularized, not to say trivialized, by the substitution of Roonel's tooth for a holy relic (a view consistent with the ironization of ordeal that we observed above). At the second hearing there is not even the pretense of neutral procedure: the barons cry for Renart's blood, and the enraged king readily accedes to their demands.

The development from the *Chanson de Roland* to the *Roman de Renart* exemplifies precisely the movement from the feudal belief in *judicium Dei* to the new secularized concept of the individual that began to emerge as an important aspect of the twelfth-century Renaissance.[48] Instead of the ordeal of combat, where both sides put their lives on the line, we have in Renart's trial an inquest pitting the individual against the state—an outsider against the ruling classes. Indeed, the very possibility of appeal emerged only when judicial administration moved from the divine ordeal (which of course admitted of no appeal) to the secular monarch.[49] To this extent the *Roman de Renart* is an exemplary work. But to the extent that it also embodies a critique of the state, of its customary legal system, and of the religious faith upon which it depended, *Renart* moves well beyond exemplarity and begins to undermine the very system that it portrays.[50]

The Middle High German Reinhart

Some twenty years after Pierre de Saint-Cloud's brilliant creation an Alsatian minstrel named Heinrich, who assumed the pseudonym "der Glichezaere" ("trickster" or "dissembler"), adapted the earliest Old French *branches* into a verse narrative of some 2,300 lines known as *Reinhart Fuchs* (written sometime between 1192 and 1200).[51] Although the work shares a few episodes with *Ysengrimus*, the principal source is the *Roman de Renart*.[52] But the author has made a number of changes in order to accommodate his narrative to the practices of German customary law, to the extent that they differ from the French.[53] Following a moralizing preface that stresses Reinhart's sly malice and the exemplary nature of the narrative ("do man bi mag bilde /Nemen vmbe manige dinc," lines 4–5), Heinrich begins, as does Pierre, with an account of the fox's adventures with the rooster, the titmouse, the raven, and the cat (11–384). The story then turns to Reinhart's attempt to seduce Ysengrin's spouse Hersant, who—conspicuously more virtuous than her French counterpart—indignantly rejects his advances, saying that she loves her handsome husband and pointing out that Reinhart is too weak for her in any case ("So werest dv mir doch ze swach," 433). This contemptuous rejection precipitates a series of misadventures involving Ysengrin and based on the early *branches*. When Reinhart causes the wolf to lose his tail, an event much bewailed by Hersant, it is the last straw: Ysengrin declares a feud (*vrlevge*, 1066) against his enemy.

At this point—and here we encounter the first major alteration—their common relative the lynx, saddened by their quarrel and the illegal threat to the secular peace, offers to act as an intermediary to bring about a reconciliation. Ysengrin says that he could forgive everything, even the loss of his tail, if Reinhart would swear an oath that he has not propositioned Hersant. (Slander is one of the most heinous offenses in Germanic law generally.) Hereupon follows the episode, familiar from Pierre de Saint-Cloud, of the dog's tooth. But in contrast to the French version, where the incident has formal legal status, sanctioned by the king and his court of barons, the German narrative employs a less formal, unofficial procedure involving friends and relatives (*mage*, 1100 and 1147) rather than judicial officers. The episode ends in the same manner, with Reinhart's escape; but the escape is more realistically motivated when Reinhart, having noticed the deception, interrupts the proceedings to request a private consultation with his advisers, a procedure perfectly acceptable in German law. It is only at this point, in the pursuit following Reinhart's escape, that he rapes Hersant and taunts Ysengrin with the fact. This leads to the formal indictment and trial, based on *branche* I, which takes up almost the entire second half of the poem (1239–2250). This sequence and balancing of events—the attempt at private mediation preceding the formal legal accusation—corresponds precisely to the practice known in medieval German (but not in French) law as "Minne und Recht" (in its Latin formulation *per amorem vel per justitiam*, or *per concordiam vel per judicium*).[54]

The preceding events, we learn, took place during a secular peace (*lantvride*, 1239, a term used here for the first time in German) declared by the lion, King Vrevel. (The king's name is a word that in Middle High German can mean either "courage" or "violence" and "arrogance." The predominance of the second meaning symptomizes the political feelings of the anti-Hohenstaufen author.) The king, we learn, had sought to appropriate an ant-castle imperialistically into his kingdom and, when the inhabitants refused, had destroyed it, killing a thousand citizens. When the ruling ant returns and learns what King Vrevel has done, contrary to all known law, he takes his revenge by crawling into the lion's ear, where he causes him great pain. The king realizes that he is being punished by God for his failure to act justly.

"Ich weiz wol, iz ist gotes slac,
wen ich gerichtes niht enpflac."

(1319–20)

(Otherwise only Reinhart, who has secretly witnessed the scene, understands the cause of the king's anguish and the roars that terrify the kingdom.) In an effort to set things right, he proclaims a royal court that is to take place six weeks hence (the normal period of time between proclamation and *placitum generale*). When the king is seated on the chair specially built for the occasion (*hochgestvle*, 1328) and all the animals (except Reinhart) have appeared, the king calls for silence in words close to the medieval legal formula:

> der kvnic selbe gebot,
> Daz sie ir brechten liezen sin.
>
> (1364–65)

Ysengrin is the first to claim his rights. In sharp contrast to the Old French version, in which the wolf is reputed to be a skilled orator and speaks for himself, the German narrator causes Ysengrin, in accordance with German legal practice, to request a spokesman or *prolocutor* (*vorspechen*, 1367) to represent him. (This practice was common generally in Germanic law, which depended heavily on formal precision in legal matters and where even a simple procedural violation, such as misspeaking, mispronouncing, clearing one's throat, stumbling, or making the incorrect gesture, could invalidate the entire proceeding and even carry severe consequences. As a result, it was customary for the parties to be represented by a friend or relative skilled in speaking and experienced in the ways of the law.)[55] Again, the words in which Brun agrees to serve as speaker "by law and favor" ("Dvrch recht vnd dvrch iwer gvte," 1371) have formulaic strength. Thereupon Brun brings forth Ysengrin's complaint against Reinhart, the loss of his tail and especially the fox's advances against Hersant during the declared period of *pax regis* ("in dem vride, / den ir gebvtet bi der wide," 1383–84), in an effort to transform the private offense into a public one and to justify the more severe penalty of death. (It is worth noting that even at this time, around 1200, the same complaint could be addressed either as criminal or civil.)[56] Krimel the badger then rebuts the accusations one by one. In particular he argues that, since Hersant is so much larger than Reinhart, he could not have violated her against her will—that the complaint therefore could not be punishable. The king then asks Randolt the stag "under oath" ("bi dem eide," 1413; another detail from German legal procedure) for his judgment, and the stag, as in the French original, demands death by hanging, a decision that is almost unanimously seconded by the other barons. The only opponent is the camel, who is pious, wise, and aged—and, in contrast to the French source, an expert in customary rather than Roman law. The camel reminds the king, again "under oath," that anyone who is accused at court during his absence must be summoned three times to appear. A majority of the other animals (another Germanic practice) are persuaded by this reminder when suddenly Schantecler and his kin appear with the corpse of their murdered daughter.

An interesting legal contretemps ensues. The king, enraged by this wanton act of violence and persuaded by the *physical* evidence of the corpse, forgets the earlier decision to summon Reinhart three times to answer for his other crimes; by German law he banishes Reinhart upon penalty of death. This satisfaction having been rendered, the relatives are now free to bury their murdered daughter. Afterwards, however, in apparent contradiction the king appoints Brun to deliver the first summons to Reinhart, with the familiar result. When Brun returns to tell his story, the king in his fury wants to condemn Reinhart to death and confiscate his property, a decision approved by many followers. This time it is the elephant who reminds him of the earlier decision, taken irrevocably under oath. The others agree "because it was legally right" ("wan iz was reht," 1645). The king sends Dieprecht the cat, who desperately tries to avoid the assignment by appealing to the local law. (It is not clear from the context whether Dieprecht seeks to refuse because Reinhart is his relative or because he is not legally qualified.)

> "daz lantrecht ist mir niht kvnt.
> Herre, er ist min kvllinc."
>
> (1650–51)

However, he is ordered to deliver the second summons, again with the familiar result. On Dieprecht's return the angry courtiers once more demand Reinhart's life, but the badger reminds the king of his earlier decision. This time the king dispatches the badger, who returns to court with Reinhart.

Heinrich's story now takes a wholly different twist. As the other animals scream for his execution, Reinhart calmly turns to the king and says that he has not responded to the summons before now because he has been abroad for the past seven weeks, in the renowned medical center of Salerno, seeking a remedy for the king's terrible headache. The king's wrath immediately dissipates, and he eagerly accepts Reinhart's prescriptions, which involve a terrible revenge upon his enemies. In order to cure the king he requires the hides of a wolf, a bear, and a wild cat as well as a cooked hen, a slice of boar, and a strip of venison—requisites taken from Ysengrin, Brun, Dieprecht, Schantecler's wife, Randolt, and an (unnamed) boar. The court disintegrates into total disarray as the other animals, fearful for their own lives, creep away stealthily. When the king is cured—the ant is driven out of his ear by the heat of a hot bath—the king promises rewards to Reinhart and his allies. The elephant receives a kingdom in Bohemia, but he is killed there by the inhabitants. The camel is appointed abbess of a cloister, but she is beaten by the nuns and chased into the Rhine, where she drowns. Finally, Reinhart prepares a poisoned drink for the king, who dies in agony realizing Reinhart's treachery. Heinrich concludes his poem with moralizing remarks to the effect that no one should have been surprised at Reinhart's behavior since, at court, many a scoundrel is held in higher regard than the man who has never done evil:

Daz sol nieman klagen harte,
waz want er han an Reinharte?
Iz ist noch schade, wizze krist,
daz manic loser werder ist
Ze hove, danne si ein man,
der nie valsches began.

(2175–80)

Heinrich der Glichezaere has given us the most profoundly serious, even tragic version of the legend, an account that exposes with utter moral conviction the power of evil in the world. The king betrays his supporters, who in the end are flayed and even eaten. Reinhart betrays his friends, who are sent away to imagined benefices, where they are immediately killed. The king himself is destroyed by the treacherous vassal to whom he unthinkingly, and with no concern for principle, turned in his distress. Reinhart himself is no longer the shrewd but lovable rogue: there is no ambivalence in his pursuit of Hersant and other innocents; he is evil personified.[57] The work constitutes a radical social satire written from an anti-Hohenstaufen standpoint. (The disparaging portrayal of King Vrevel was understood as a direct attack on Emperor Frederick Barbarossa.) At the same time, the author has such a detailed grasp of medieval German law that he must have participated actively in legal procedures, perhaps as an advocate.[58] But it is precisely the subversion of this law that enables Reinhart to outwit and ultimately destroy his enemies and victims—that enables evil, in sum, to subvert society. If *Reinhart Fuchs* is not a satire of law itself, it is a terrible commentary on the society that permits its laws to be abused in such an outrageous fashion. Perhaps because of this dark view *Reinhart Fuchs* had no successors or imitators. The version of the beast epic that was destined to survive gloriously returned, instead, to the brighter versions of the *Roman de Renart* where, for all their usually well-deserved suffering, the figures live on to another day.

The Flemish Reinaert

Sometime in the first half of the thirteenth century a Flemish poet calling himself Willem set out to translate *branche* I of the *Roman de Renart* into Flemish, making the adjustments necessary to accommodate the story to local circumstances. The identity of the author(s) as well as the time of composition continue to pose vexing and contested questions.[59] But the work that resulted, *Van den Vos Reinaerde* or more simply *Reinaert de Vos*, provided the basis for the beast epic as it subsequently became known, enframed by the legal drama. The first 2,000 of its almost 3,500 verses rehearse the story with which we have already become familiar. King Nobel has summoned his vassals to a *placitum generale* in order to hear their complaints and to pass judgment. Several animals—Isingrijn the wolf, Cortois the dog, and Pancer the beaver speaking for Cuwaert the hare—lodge complaints against the absent Reinaert. The charges are being successfully answered by the fox's relative, Grimbeert the badger, when Canticleer the rooster appears with his family bearing the corpse of his daughter. After her burial the scandalized vassals decide to summon Reinaert to court, and the three summonses are delivered, with the familiar results, by Bruun the bear, Tibeert the wild cat, and Grimbeert. When Reinaert finally appears in court, he begins by presenting a defense, but the vassals, persuaded by the accusations of the other animals, sentence Reinaert to death by hanging. Bruun, Isingrijn, and Tibeert go off to erect the gallows, while Reinaert's kinsmen, unwilling to see their relative hanged, leave the court.

At this point the story takes such an unexpected turn that some scholars have argued that a different narrator now takes up the account. While his worst enemies are away at the gallows, Reinaert begs leave of the king and queen to confess his sins, unfolding a tale that involves both a hidden treasure and a conspiracy against the king by Isingrijn, Bruun, Tibeert, and Grimbeert. The queen persuades Nobel to pardon Reinaert in return for the treasure, which is hidden in a remote part of Flanders. But Reinaert tells them that he will be unable to guide them there himself because he was excommunicated three years earlier for urging Isingrijn to leave his monastery. He is obligated to make a pilgrimage to Rome to seek absolution. The king has the wolf and the bear seized when they return from the gallows, and Reinaert takes his leave wearing boots made from the wolf's hide and carrying a purse of bearskin, accompanied by Cuwaert the hare and Belijn the ram. At home Reinaert and his wife kill and eat the hare and implicate Belijn in the murder by sending him back to court with the hare's head in his satchel. He then leads his family into the safety of exile while, back at court, the deceived king, finally comprehending the fox's treachery, exonerates Bruun and Isingrijn.

The legal sophistication of *Reinaert de Vos* has long been recognized. It has been presented, on the basis of detailed textual parallels with canonical and secular law, as a reliable introduction to medieval Germanic law.[60] It has been read, on the basis of the same data, as a poem exemplifying the abuse of law, especially by King Nobel.[61] Still another study has reconciled the two positions, demonstrating persuasively that the text displays an intimate familiarity with thirteenth-century Flemish law specifically and that the departures from normal legal procedures serve the satirical ends of the author.[62] The charges brought against Reinaert involve four of the six major felonies or *causae arduae* enumerated in the Flemish *Keures* or charters of customary law: murder, arson, theft, robbery, crimes against women, and breaking the peace. The procedures are consistent with those practiced at the *curia comitis* of the count of Flanders, and in particular all important legal matters in the epic—including charges, summonses, Reinaert's pardon, the transfer of the treasure to the king, and so forth—are "couched in the phraseology of strict legal formulation."[63] For instance, when Isingrijn brings his charges, he and his kin stand before the king, and the wolf appeals to the king in formulaic language stressing the king's nobility and honor as well as his sense of justice and mercy:

> "coninc here,
> dor u edelheit ende dor u ere
> ende dor recht ende dor ghenade
> ontfaerme u miere scade
> die mi Reinaert heeft ghedaen
> daer ic af dicke hebbe ontfaen
> groten lachter ende verlies."
>
> (65–71)[64]

(King, my Lord, by your glory and honor, in the name of justice and mercy, avenge the wrongs that Reinaert has done me, from which I have often suffered great injury and grief.)

Formal accommodations of this sort are not unlike those undertaken by Heinrich der Glichezaere to adapt his version to late-twelfth-century German law. Perhaps the most important and revealing of the legal manipulations is the author's use of the provision in a thirteenth-century Flemish legal charter to create a plausible connection between the first and the second parts of his narrative. According to the *Keure* of Poperinghen (1233) a twice-relapsed thief could escape the gallows only by proving that his accusation resulted from a conspiracy or plot against him (*quod contra eum esset conspiratum*).[65] Originally this provision was meant to bring notorious felons swiftly to justice by making any pardon contingent upon the remote possibility of a conspiracy. It is typical of the inversions and abuses of the law in this telling that Reinaert is able to exploit this remote possibility in order to save himself and to incriminate his enemies, and that the king is gullible (and corrupt) enough to believe him. It should be pointed out, by the way, that the substitution of a fine for capital punishment was legally permissible in Flanders at the discretion of the judge[66]—a loophole that Reinaert exploits when he invents a fictional treasure in whose existence the king and queen are avaricious enough to believe.

In sum, *Reinaert de Vos* makes knowledgeable use of thirteenth-century Flemish law, proceedings that are for the most part oral. At the same time, the text alludes in several places to written documents, as when Canticleer complains that Reinaert tricked him by means of a letter with the king's seal ("enen brief . . . daer u seghele ane hinc," 358–60). Such passages remind us that the work was composed during a period of transition in Flemish legal history—a period when codification and rationalization were introducing elements of Roman legal thought into the customary-law system, gradually reducing the importance of such traditional elements as oath taking, and increasing the authority of the written law in the form of the *Keures*.[67]

Over a century later, around 1380, an anonymous Dutch or Flemish writer updated and continued *Reinaert de Vos* in a version known from its penultimate line as *Reinaerts Historie*. This later version, making use of *branche* VI and more than twice as long as Willem's work, has generally been held to be vastly inferior in originality and quality. Since the continuation depends on Reinaert's presence at home, the unknown author has inserted a passage (3183–3203) in which Ermeline persuades her husband not to go into exile but to remain safe and cozy in their castle at Malpertuus. The continuation itself looks almost like a reprise of *Reinaert de Vos*. Again it begins with a *placitum generale* of Nobel's court at which a complaint is brought against Reinaert, this time by Lampreel the rabbit. The outraged monarch wants quick revenge, but his wife and advisers urge him to give the fox a hearing six days hence. Grimbaert goes to Malpertuus to warn his uncle, who again believes that he can lie his way out of trouble. On the way to court Reinaert tells his nephew several new stories about his exploits (based on other *branches*). When they arrive Reinaert first asks the king for an unbiased hearing, pointing out that he has enemies at court. He then makes up a total fiction about the withdrawal of his excommunication and concludes by declaring his readiness to prove his innocence through combat. When his accusers withdraw their charges, King Nobel himself accuses Reinaert of Cuwaert's death, whereupon the fox is expertly defended by his aunt, the she-ape Rukenau. This gives Reinaert the opportunity to fabricate another elaborate lie, involving several fables, in which he describes to the king various valuable gifts that he had allegedly sent back by way of Belijn. When the king appears to be prepared to forgive Reinaert, Isegrijn again accuses the fox of rape and demands satisfaction by duel. Following the ritual preliminaries, the battle is fought tooth and nail, and Reinaert—employing every dirty trick in the book—emerges victorious. Cleared by the judicial duel, Reinaert is appointed by the king to be his official adviser. Justice has been totally undermined in this work, which amounts to a satirical celebration of cunning and deceit abetted by shrewd abuse of the law. But here the king himself is not destroyed. The author leaves open the allegorical implication that Flanders continues to be ruled by a monarch advised by the most corrupt counselors.

We can end our story quickly, for *Reinaerts Historie* adds nothing essentially new to the legal implications of the beast epic. Indeed, the legal situation in all subsequent treatments of the tale is essentially the one established in the thirteenth century.[68] But it was this version that provided the foundation for the subsequent European success of this most popular of medieval tales. *Reinaerts Historie* was first published in a prose version, printed in 1479 at Gouda. (It was this prose version that William Caxton translated into English under the title *Reynart the Foxe* and published in 1481.) Around 1487 the original verse *Reinaerts Historie* was published in Antwerp in an adaptation by Hinrek van Alckmer, a pedagogue at the court of the duke of Lorraine. This adaptation did little but modernize the language and divide the poem into books and chapters with headings and didactic exegeses interpolated after every few chapters. All but some two hundred verses of this Flemish adaptation have been lost; but it provided the basis for the work that assured the worldwide popularity of the story, the Low German translation entitled *Reinke de Vos*, which appeared in Lübeck in 1498 and again in Rostock in 1519 and 1539. This version, translated into Latin by Hartmann Schopper under the title *Speculum vitae aulicae. De admirabili fallacia et astvtia vvlpecvlae Reinkes libri quattuor* (Frankfurt am Main, 1579), and into most other modern languages—including French, which appears to have forgotten its own original medieval versions until Méon's edition of 1826—was the version adapted by Goethe in 1794.

Shortly after its first appearance Martin Luther called *Reinke de Vos* "a vivid imitation of courtly life" ("lebendige contrafaktur des Hoflebens"),[69] a designation anticipating the title of the Latin translation as well as Goethe's characterization of it as a "Hof- und Regentenspiegel." But the work has also exposed itself as a mirror of the law—a mirror reflecting the uses as well as the abuses of the law of medieval France, Germany, and Flanders. During the centuries of uncertainty as the weaknesses of customary law and its procedures became evident to a Europe in which feudalism was being transformed by an emerging bourgeois society, in which medieval collectivism was giving way to a modern sense of individualism, no literary document exemplifies more vividly and with greater popular appeal than the adventures of Renart-Reinhart-Reinaert-Reinke in the reign of King Nobel-Vrevel the ambivalence made of nostalgia and contempt with which the old legal traditions were regarded. In the evolving society of the late Middle Ages the most reactionary force was the law—a law that despite local variants was basically uniform throughout Germany and the Lowlands.[70] In a very powerful sense, Renart's first appearance at court in 1176 marked the beginning of an evolution that ended with the displacement of customary law by Roman in Germany and Flanders soon after 1500.

CHAPTER SIX

The Reception of Roman Law in Germany

THE NEW Roman law was not welcomed as the legal panacea that would immediately heal all the problems identified in the traditional customary law. The view of Roman law and its lawyers in the 1490s is evident in influential works of two university friends and leaders in early German humanism, both of whom had become reluctant lawyers in order to support their humanist activities: Sebastian Brant and Johannes Reuchlin.

LAWYERLY SKEPTICISM: SEBASTIAN BRANT

Few readers today, looking for the first time at Brant's *The Ship of Fools* (*Das Narrenschiff*, 1494), a collection of 112 short chapters accompanied by woodcuts and loosely related by their focus on human folly, would suspect that the work was favorably compared by its contemporaries to Homer's *Odyssey*, to Dante's *Divine Comedy*, and to the satires of Horace, Persius, and Juvenal.[1] Nor was its appeal limited simply to classically educated humanists. The first German poetic work of truly European stature, it enjoyed huge international success unmatched for almost three hundred years until the publication of Goethe's *The Sorrows of Young Werther* (1774).[2] The book was an immediate triumph in Germany, where four pirated editions appeared in the first year alone.[3] A second edition was needed by 1495; six authorized editions appeared during Brant's lifetime; and the book has been steadily in print for the past four hundred years.

The influence of the work can be only partly measured by the German editions alone: its international success was due primarily to the Latin adaptation by Brant's student Jakob Locher, *Stultifera Navis* (1497), which was reprinted seventy times and served as the basis for several of the translations into other European languages: Low German (1497), French (1497), Dutch-Flemish (1500), and English (1509), all of which went through at least seventy editions. Indeed, the influence of Brant's work has extended into our own day. Although Michel Foucault, in his *Histoire de la Folie* (1961), concedes that the "ship of fools" was a literary image, he rather confusingly (and mistakenly) concludes that such vessels also had "a real existence" in the past and cites this "fact" to prove a point about the treatment of madmen in the late Middle

Ages.[4] Katherine Anne Porter's parable of good and evil in the twentieth century, *Ship of Fools* (1962), reprints on the title page a woodcut from Brant's work and states in a prefatory note that "The title of this book is a translation from the German of *Das Narrenschiff*, a moral allegory by Sebastian Brant (1458?–1521) first published in Latin as *Stultifera Navis* in 1494."[5] (Porter evidently did not realize that Brant's work was written and first published in German and that the Latin translation appeared three years later.)

The voluminous scholarship of the past century has been principally concerned with the apparent disparity between the enormous popular success of *Das Narrenschiff* and its less obvious literary merits, which have been flatly denied or historically relativized by many of its critics.[6] More recently, scholars have been fascinated by the relationship between the text and its woodcut images, most of which, it is now known, were created by Albrecht Dürer. Much less frequently remarked is the fact that the book was published by a man who proudly stresses both in his prefatory remarks and in his concluding words that he is a "doctor in both laws" ("in beyden rechten doctor")[7]—that is to say, that he holds the degree of *doctor utriusque iuris*, both in canon law and in civil law.[8]

An innkeeper's son, Brant was born in Strassburg in 1458 (or perhaps 1457). Though his father died when he was only ten, his mother saw to it that he received a good education and, in the excitement of early humanism, cultivated a strong taste for the classics. In 1475 he enrolled at the University of Basel, a new institution that, thanks to publicity generated by the recent Council of Basel (1431–49), was already competing with older German universities. During his first two years there Brant was a student in the so-called *Artistenfakultät*—the general humanities program based on the seven liberal arts that was the prerequisite for all further courses of study (theology, law, and medicine)—and supported himself by his duties as a *famulus* or assistant to Professor Jacob Hugonis. It was here that he formed his lifelong friendship with Johannes Reuchlin, his senior by two years, who tutored him in Latin and Greek. In 1477, when Brant received his baccalaureate, Reuchlin completed his own magister's degree and left Basel. Although Brant continued his humanistic activities—during the following years he wrote a number of occasional poems in Latin and also taught poetics in the *Artistenfakultät*—he was forced, in no small measure for economic reasons, to choose a profession in which he could support himself and his family: law. Early in 1484 he wrote ironically to Reuchlin that he was girding himself for his law exams and that he had fallen away from the Muses into the verbosity of law: *Ego a Musis in uerbosas leges incidi.*[9] In 1484 he received his licentiate's degree, which permitted him to practice and to teach law. For several years he supported himself by his law practice and by teaching humanities at the university. (In 1487 one of his Latin pupils was Jakob Locher, who was to translate *Das Narrenschiff* into Latin.)

In 1489 Brant was awarded his doctorate, a degree that in Basel automatically entitled him to become a member of the faculty of law. The university records indicate that Brant actually received the degree of *doctor iuris* and not *doctor utriusque iuris*.[10] This would strongly suggest that at Basel, which was noted for its emphasis on canon law, Brant's particular competence was in that field, and not in civil law. However, at the time when Brant received his degree, Roman law was still considered to be a unified whole, and students were trained in civil law along with canon law. Brant certainly believed in the importance of civil law. Almost immediately upon taking up his instructional responsibilities he published his *Expositiones siue declarationes omnium titulorum iuris tam Civilis quam Canonici* (1490; revised edition 1500), a textbook of Roman law—mainly civil but also canon—for beginning students and based on his own lectures at Basel. Not an original contribution to jurisprudence, Brant's presentation of the material was so skillful that it was reprinted frequently and continued to be used as a textbook well into the seventeenth century.[11] In 1492–93 Brant served for a year as dean of the faculty of law at Basel, commemorating the end of his term with a broadsheet ode to Saint Ivo (Saint Ives), the advocate of the poor and the patron saint of lawyers.[12] In sum, the author of *Das Narrenschiff*, who proudly designated himself as "doctor of both laws," was well entitled to that claim: a licentiate and doctor of the distinguished law faculty at Basel, he had earned a reputation as an excellent teacher, had published one of the leading textbooks of the age, and had served as the dean of his faculty.

During the decade of his tenure at Basel, Brant continued to turn out legal publications—notably a series of editions of canonical works, beginning in 1493 with an edition of Gratian's *Decretum*.[13] In 1501, following Basel's decision to leave the Holy Roman Empire and to join the Swiss Confederation, the imperial loyalist Brant left the university and returned to his hometown of Strassburg as city legal counsel and then, from 1503 until his death, as *Stadtschreiber*, a position combining the functions of municipal secretary with those of city chancellor. In this new position he continued his publicistic activities; but in view of the different emphasis of the practicing administrator (in contrast to the teaching scholar) he now concentrated on works written to help both court officials and ordinary citizens during the transitional period while Roman law was gradually displacing traditional customary law. In 1509 he composed an introductory poem to accompany the publication of *The Layman's Mirror* (*Layenspiegel*) by his friend Ulrich Tenngler, the provincial governor of Höchstadt.[14] It is worth noting that Brant expressly justifies writing his poem in German rather than Latin. Since he is a German layman (rather than a cleric) and works in a German chancellory—"so nu ain teütscher lay ich bin / Vnd in ainer teütschen Cantzley" (lines 52–53)—it does not seem appropriate to write on this occasion in the more scholarly tongue. Brant goes on accurately to describe the purpose of Tenngler's work. It is intended primarily as an aid for lay judges without formal legal training: to acquaint them, in written form, with the essentials of Roman as well as customary law and the appropriate procedures, so that the judges "will not vacillate in their opinions or believe that law grows on trees or dream that one does not need to heed what our parents thought":

> vnd nit in eüwern dunckenn schwencken
> Weenen ir das die recht auff baumen
> gewachsen sein, oder von traumen
> Dasz man nit auch muesz haben acht
> was vnser oeltern hond bedacht.
>
> (62–66)

In 1516 Brant reprinted Tenngler's *Layenspiegel* along with an older anonymous work, the so-called *Mirror of Complaints* (*Clagspiegel*, written a century earlier and first printed around 1460–70),[15] which was meant, in the words of Brant's versified introduction, to demonstrate "what is appropriate to court procedures and how every one may justify his suit":

> was zuom gerichtsgang dient vnd wie
> Ein yeder sein clag moeg begründen.
>
> (28–29)

It is unlikely that an author who spent his entire life as a legal scholar and practicing lawyer in both civil and canon affairs should not give evidence of this occupation in his literary works. If we peruse the poems that Brant wrote before or around the time of *Das Narrenschiff*, we find ample evidence. For example, the *Moretus*, a short didactic work meant for the moral instruction of the young (*Liber Moreti docens mores Iuuenum*) devotes sections to the various professions, including the law (*De iudice*).[16] The judge should, above all, remember that a higher power will pass judgment on him; he must take care lest his own unjust verdict condemn him. His verdicts should be strict and expeditious ("Er halt seyn vrteyl steyff vnd schnell," line 401) so that the wicked may be punished and so that his judgment may not be overturned upon appeal. By the same token, he should free the innocent, seek justice constantly, and reject any attempt at bribery. Finally, he should also see to it that the other officers of the court behave appropriately.

I have already mentioned Brant's broadsheet with the ode, elegy, and hymn to Saint Ivo, which portrays the righteous lawyer. In another Latin poem from the same period Brant addresses himself more satirically to the foibles of the lawyer (*de natura et moribus advocatorum*).[17] Addressed to his friend and colleague Hieronymus von Weiblingen, the canon of the church at Basel, the poem begins by stating that lawyers pursue cases and pointless lawsuits the way ravens flock around corpses strewn on the ground:

> Nempe solent lites perquirere, iurgia vana,
> Corvus ut assequitur sparsa cadavera humi.

But once they have the brief, they drag out the cases so as to increase their earnings. If anyone tries to circumvent them, they find ways to interfere, spewing out Lernaean venom, whipping up the furies, and assisting the adversary. They refuse to act without remuneration and spurn plaintiffs who come with empty hands. Whatever they do, they seize their booty with clawed fingers, like winged Harpies or Stygian hounds:

> Quicquid agunt, digitis praedam populantur aduncis,
> Harpyae volucres hi Stygis atque canes.

But if you bribe them to act on your behalf, they forget your case unless you constantly pay them. Should they finally take your case to court, they rant and rave in such a manner that you would think you were seeing the mouths of Anubis and hearing the waves crashing against the cliffs of Scylla:

> Si causas recitant, videas et Anubidis ora
> Et Scyllae scopulos vociferasse putes.

If you seek their advice, they change their waxen minds constantly, wiping out what they have already written. They rage like the truculent lioness or the bear with a new litter and easily explode in wrath. They know no mercy nor any work that would today be designated *pro bono* (*nec veniam novit nec pietatis opus*). Rather, they love luxury and leisure and consume the client's wealth like a savage bull, and if their nostrils catch the scent of gold, their vigilant eyes move like those of Argus. They will commit perjury for love of gold and carry out the most elaborate deceits:

> Laomedontea hinc periuria amore facescunt
> Auri, Naricii concipiuntque dolos.

The poem ends with an exhortation to lawyers and advocates to change their ways. For a long time Saint Ivo has stood at the portals of heaven awaiting colleagues of an uprightness like his own; but he will have to stand there for a long time before a just, pious, and faithful lawyer comes his way.

> Noster adhuc alios exspectans Ivo sodales
> Ante fores coeli tempora longa stetit,
> Stabit item, donec iustus, pius atque fidelis,
> Causidicus illi forsitan obveniat.

Not surprisingly, legal matters also play a conspicuous role in Brant's masterpiece, *Das Narrenschiff*. Not only does Brant devote several of the work's 112 chapters specifically to the law; beyond that, lawyers and the courts show up in so many various contexts that the reader has a sense of their total permeation of society. *Das Narrenschiff*—and hence its fame and lasting interest—amounts to a survey of European society and morals during the transition from late-medieval to early-modern times.[18] The framework fiction that accounts for its fame down to Michel Foucault and Katherine Anne Porter actually plays a minor role in the work: the motif of the ship is mentioned in the introduction, again near the middle (chap. 48), and finally close to the end (chap. 108). Otherwise the chapters have so little reference to the ship itself or its voyage to Fool's Land (*Narragonien*) that some critics have assumed that the device was added subsequently to unify a collection of fundamentally unrelated chapters. Indeed, Brant refers to various other possible organizing principles, calling his work a "Book of Fools" (*narrenbuoch*, chaps. 110 and 111) or referring to a "fools' order" (*narren orden*, chap. 111). Be that as it may, Brant's work portrays and satirizes pre-Reformation Germany in its breadth, from the point of view of an early humanist with a pronouncedly middle-class bias who still believes in the integrity of the Church and its dogma, who regards the Holy Roman Empire as the appropriate secular analogy to the Church, who has a strong nationalistic faith in Germany (and specifically Maximilian) as the logical standard-bearer for the empire, and who has little tolerance for a society in which morals and manners are declining at a dismaying rate. As we might expect from a Christian moralist, Brant deals conspicuously with the seven cardinal sins: the third chapter is devoted to *gytikeit*, or avarice, and others to lust (chap. 50) as well as hate and envy (chap. 53). On numerous occasions the scholar of canonical law cites Gratian's *Decretum*, which he had edited only a year earlier.[19] But side by side with arrogance vis-à-vis God (chap. 14), contempt of God (chap. 86), and blasphemy (chap. 87), he also deals with gambling (chap. 77), borrowing (chap. 25), and usury (chap. 93). A chapter on the sin of adultery (chap. 33) is matched by another on the misdemeanor of making noise in church (chap. 44), and bad manners (chap. 9) by bad table manners (chap. 110a.). The table of contents constitutes a veritable checklist of human sins and human folly. As one critic has aptly put it, the follies that Brant portrays are "nothing but the negative image of contemporary bourgeois ethics."[20]

In the course of his work Brant alludes to every form of law practiced in late-fifteenth-century Germany: customary German law, Roman law, canon law, and biblical law. But the common denominator in every case is a compelling sense of justice. Early in the book (chap. 2), as though to establish the thematic centrality of law, Brant discusses the theme "of good counselors" ("Von guten reten"). Many seek to become members of the council who understand nothing about law and grope about blindly. (Brant adduces Hushai and Ahithophel from 2 Sam. 16–17 as examples of the good and bad counselor.) But anyone who wishes to judge and counsel well must reflect and follow the law alone:

> Wer vrteln sol vnd raten schlecht
> Der dunck vnd folg alleyn zuo recht.
>
> (Lines 7–8)

It is not sufficient to advise how the law may be met minimally; the wise counselor will always consider the better alternative. If the law, and right, should be abridged, then there is no defense against God:

> Dann wirt das recht verkürtzet sust
> So hast kein woerwort gegen got.
>
> (16–17)

Each person is judged accordingly as he has judged. As you judge me and I you, so God will judge you and me.

> Wie du richtst mich, vnd ich richt dich
> Als wirt er richten dich vnd mich.
>
> (23–24)

Already, then, Brant ties secular law to divine judgment and the procedures of civil law to those of God. In another context (chap. 22) he paraphrases Proverbs 8 to make the point that divine wisdom is the creator of laws: "Durch mich, all gsatz mit reht vff ston" (14).

Brant cites legal examples to illustrate many of his chapters. The chapter on adultery (chap. 33) begins with the lament that this sin is nowadays taken very lightly: people have forgotten the commandment (the *Lex Iulia de adulterio*) that Emperor Augustus laid down for the Romans. The section on excessive loquaciousness (chap. 19) points out that the tongue is a powerful instrument in court: it can make crooked what seemed to be straight; and through it a fool can lose his possessions and be driven to the beggar's staff.

> Die zung die brucht man jn das recht
> Durch sie würt krum das vor was schlecht
> Durch sie, verlurt manch armer man
> Syn sach, das er muosz bettlen gan.
>
> (45–48)

True justice does not take friendship and social position into account (chap. 46: "On the Power of Fools") or discard truth and right for a scrap of bread. The wise man judges equitably: "Recht vrteyln, stat eym wisen wol" (41). The judge should recognize no one: justice should be blind to friendship. There are still too many judges of the sort that tried to undo Susanna (from the apocryphal story of Daniel).[21] True justice is cold: "Gerechtikeyt die ist vast kalt" (46). Brant is equally demanding of lawyers: the advocate who cannot advise us in our affairs is no better than the quack physician or the confessor who is unable to find the appropriate penance for each sin (chap. 55). In the section on haughtiness (chap. 92) he expresses his contempt for the fools who are inflamed with arrogance because they have studied abroad at Bologna, Pavia, Paris, Siena, Orleans, and elsewhere, as though it were not possible here in Germany to learn wisdom and art without attending foreign universities.

Als ob nit ouch jnn tütscher art
Noch wer vernunfft, synn, houbter zart
Do mit man wiszheyt kunst moecht leren
Nit not, so verr zuo schuolen keren.

(19–22)

The Romans once believed that teaching could be found only in Athens—until they discovered it at home in Italy. But now learning blossoms in Germany, and we would lack nothing as a nation were it not (and here Brant moves to another subject) for the national scourge of drunkenness that hinders us.

The author gives evidence of his knowledge of legal history. In the chapter on wicked women (chap. 64), to illustrate the dangers of too much talking, he cites the example of the notorious Calpurnia, who comported herself so boldly in court (by displaying her buttocks, according to one source), that Old German law henceforth prohibited women from appearing in court without an advocate (*Fürsprecher*).[22] Elsewhere (chap. 94) he alludes to the famous twelfth-century Italian legal scholar Bulgarus to illustrate the futility of hoping for one's inheritance: for Bulgarus was destined to be the heir of his own son. (Brant seems to be confusing this account with the circumstance that Bulgarus's wife predeceased her father and the scholar had to return her dowry to his father-in-law.)[23]

In the most extensive passage (chap. 71), finally, Brant lampoons those fools who always choose to go to court rather than to seek an equitable compromise and avoid the trial. This observation provides the author with the opportunity to satirize the entire legal system. In order to avoid justice men employ every device—here Brant uses a series of technical terms from civil and canon law ("bitten, triben, manen / Echten, verlüten, vnd verbannen," 7–8)—and try to bend the law to their purposes as though it were a waxen nose. But they fail to realize that they are the victims, the hare sauced for the court scribe; for all the officers of the court—the bailiffs, those having power of attorney, the procurators, and advocates—want to have a mess of fish for their table:

Nit denckend, das sy sint der has
Der jnn der schriber pfeffer kunt
Der vogt, gwalthaber, vndt fürmundt
Vnd aduocat, muosz zuo sym disch
Dar von ouch han eyn schlaegle visch.

(12–16)

These people know how to exploit every case, to make a full-blown suit out of the most trivial affair ("Das vsz eym saechle, wurt eyn sach," 19) and a river out of every brook. At this point—and here we sense Brant's national prejudice against pettifogging glossators from Italy—one must now hire expensive lawyers from abroad who complicate the issue and deceive the judges with their chatter:

Man muosz yetz koestlich redner dyngen
Vnd sie von verren landen bringen
Das sie die sachen wol verkluegen
Vnd mit geschwaetz, eyn richter btruegen.

(21–24)

They set many court dates so that their fees will be increased, and in traveling and eating they consume much more than the case is worth. In this manner the fool spends more than the settlement brings him and still believes that he is blinding the truth if he simply refuses to let the matter come to a quick conclusion. These are the contentious fools, Brant concludes, to whose bottoms he would like to see hackles attached:

Ich woltt wem wol mit zancken waer
Das er am ars hett haechlen schwaer.

(33–34)[24]

Throughout *Das Narrenschiff*, then, we hear the voice of the lawyer who is worried about the threats to justice in the German legal system: corrupt lay judges, incompetent advocates, exploitative foreign-trained lawyers, citizens who hope to abuse the system by clever legal maneuvers and by appeals from court to court, the ignorance of written law (German, Roman, canonic, and biblical), and most generally the decline in the sense of justice and ethics. We can only conclude, from the enormous success of Brant's work, that he was speaking the mind of many contemporaries during this critical period of transition from traditional customary law to the new Roman law.

Brant's work is epoch-making in another respect: in Dürer's accompanying woodcut, for the first time in literature or the visual arts, the figure of Justitia is depicted with a blindfold.[25] (In classical antiquity and in medieval art Justitia is inevitably portrayed as clear-eyed.) In the course of the sixteenth century the blindfold was rationalized into the now familiar image of judicial impartiality. But at this point the blindfold still has an emphatically negative association.

Professorial Disdain: Johannes Reuchlin

Johannes Reuchlin (1455–1522), the distinguished Hebraist among the early German humanists, is probably best remembered for his controversy with the anti-Semitic convert Johann Pfefferkorn and the Dominicans of Cologne concerning the study and teaching of the biblical language—a controversy that inspired his supporters to the *Epistolae obscurorum virorum* (1515–16). But Reuchlin, like his friend Brant, whom he had tutored at Basel, was also a trained and practicing lawyer by profession. Following his departure from Basel in 1477 he studied law at Orléans and then at Poitiers, where he received his licentiate's degree in 1481. Returning to Germany, he was engaged in 1482 as an interpreter by Duke Eberhard of Württemberg for a tour of Italy. He impressed the duke so favorably that, on their return, he was appointed as a lawyer to the court in Stuttgart, a position in which he fulfilled many important functions and missions. After the duke's death in 1496 Reuchlin, forced by court intrigues to leave Stuttgart, accepted the invitation of Johann von Dalberg, the bishop of Worms, to join the distinguished group of humanists who constituted the *Sodalitas litteraria Celtica* at Heidelberg. Reuchlin spent several happy and productive years teaching at Heidelberg, where he numbered Franz von Sickingen among his students. When political circumstances changed, he was recalled to Stuttgart, where from 1502 until 1512 he served as a judge in the high court of the Swabian League. Following the Pfefferkorn scandal Reuchlin taught Greek and Hebrew at Ingolstadt University and, in the year before his death, at Tübingen.

During his years at Heidelberg, Reuchlin occupied himself not only with teaching and with his translations from Homer, but also with original Latin verse compositions. He began in 1496 with a humorous diatribe against his friend Heinrich von Bünau, and its reception among his colleagues encouraged him to attempt a comedy entitled *Sergius vel Capitis caput*, ridiculing the Augustinian monk who had necessitated his departure from Stuttgart and, more generally, satirizing the monkish existence and the veneration of false relics. Reuchlin also intended his composition as a pedagogical vehicle for training his students in Latin elocution. Bishop Dalberg was amused by the play, but for diplomatic reasons prohibited its performance. Because the students were now eager to put on a theatrical performance, Reuchlin quickly wrote another comedy, which was acted on January 31, 1497.[26]

Reuchlin's "theatrical exercises" (*Scaenica progymnasmata*), known more commonly, from the name of the principal character, as *Henno*, do not constitute absolutely the first Latin school drama written in Germany. The work was preceded by Jakob Wimpheling's comic dialogue *Stylpho* (1480) and Johannes Kerckmeister's prose comedy *Codrus* (1485), as well as Reuchlin's own three-act *Sergius*. But Reuchlin is properly regarded, both by his contemporaries and by later scholars, as the founder of modern humanist comedy not only because *Henno* is the first work of dramatic liveliness but also because, with its fluid iambic trimeter and its choral odes separating the five acts, it is the first play in Germany to adapt the classic Terentian form of comedy.

While this early Latin comedy can hardly equal *Das Narrenschiff* in popular success, it had broad appeal and distribution.[27] Immediately circulated among humanists in manuscript copies, it was printed in 1498 with an accompanying poem by the author's former pupil Sebastian Brant. As the work became a mainstay of Latin instruction in schools all over Germany, it was repeatedly reprinted during the following decades. In 1512 Jakob Spiegel published an elaborate commentary, *Lucubratiunculae Progymnasmatum doctissimi Ioannis*

Reuchlin triumviri, intended for the use of students. Moreover, during the first half of the sixteenth century three separate German adaptations of the comedy appeared, beginning with the brilliant treatment by Hans Sachs (1531).[28] In sum, along with *Das Narrenschiff*, Reuchlin's *Henno* was one of the most popular works of the early sixteenth century and, moreover, represents the views of a typical humanist-turned-lawyer of early German humanism.

The plot of *Henno* was inspired by the most celebrated of ancient French farces, which Reuchlin probably saw during his years in France:[29] *La Farce de maistre Pierre Pathelin*, composed anonymously sometime in the two decades before 1470 and first published in 1486.[30] The enormously popular farce, which is still performed in France, concerns a wily lawyer, Pathelin, who dupes the draper Joceaume out of his payment for a piece of cloth, first by feigning illness and later by pretending delirium. When Joceaume gives up the attempt to collect his money, he discovers that his shepherd, Aignelet, has been swindling him by pretending that accidents have afflicted the flock. When he takes Aignelet to court, the shepherd hires Pathelin as his advocate. (Because Joceaume, confused by Pathelin's presence in court, mixes up the two cases, the judge calls his attention back to the case at hand with the words that have become proverbial: "Revenons à ces moutons.") The shepherd, following Pathelin's counsel and bleating ("Bee") in response to every question, is acquitted as mad. But when Pathelin tries to collect his fee, Aignelet outwits him by using the same tactic: he just bleats. While the farce ridicules the sleazy lawyer, it is important to note that it does not make fun of the law itself: the judge is competent, courteous, and incisive.

Though Reuchlin is clearly aware of the French farce, he has transformed the longer, looser play into a wholly new work in strict Terentian form. Following the author's prologue, act 1 introduces the peasant Henno, a drunkard who has stolen his wife's secret savings and given the money to his servant Dromo, who is commissioned to buy cloth for a new suit. Dromo agrees—but with the intention of keeping the money for himself, getting the cloth on credit from the draper, and selling it elsewhere for profit. When Elsa discovers the theft of her money, her neighbor Greta advises her to consult an astrologer. In act 2 the astrologer describes the thief so clearly that Elsa recognizes her husband. Meanwhile, Dromo has carried out his plan to cheat his master as well as the draper. He tells Henno that the draper has kept both the money and the cloth. When in act 3 the peasant and the draper meet, they realize that they have been duped by Dromo, who demands a decision in court. In act 4 the lawyer Petrucius advises Dromo simply to respond to the judge's questions with the syllable *Ble*. In the court scene that follows, the draper finally withdraws his claim because Dromo appears to be weak-minded and legally incompetent. In the last act, finally, Dromo uses the same tactic when Petrucius tries to collect his fee. And, to round off a subplot, Dromo confesses the truth to his employers: he deceived Henno because his master had stolen from his wife, he cheated the draper because he was known as a flagrant usurer, and he outwitted the lawyer because he was treacherous and a good-for-nothing (*perfidum et nequam*). Dromo marries Henno's daughter, keeping the money as a dowry, and everything is happily resolved.

The section of the play that is relevant for our purposes is act 4, in which Reuchlin satirizes lawyers as well as court procedures in language that makes use of contemporary technical terms.[31] As the scene begins (lines 296–322), Dromo appeals to the vanity of Petrucius, whom he calls skillful in the law, a protector of the poor, a public defender, counsel, orator, and jurisprudent:

> Salve perite iuris et miseris pater,
> Patrone, consul, rhetor et legum sciens.

Petrucius immediately corrects him, saying that he is a protector of the rich since his family requires a great deal of money. He tries to send Dromo away since a poor man cannot enrich him: *At vade pauper. Abi, miser me nil beat.* But when Dromo suggests that there might be some money in his case, he gets the lawyer's attention. Dromo explains that the draper Danista is taking him to court. The lawyer, his interests aroused, wants to know all the particulars (*Quare? nam oportet sciscitari singula*). Dromo recounts how he cheated his master and the draper. Now both are making accusations while he steadfastly denies everything (*Nunc postulant uterque, utrisque pernego*). But neither is able to prove his case (*Nequeunt probare uterque propositum suum*). Petrucius thinks that Dromo has a good case (*causam bonam foves*) and promises him a victory if he will pay him half of the eight gold pieces, but Dromo bargains him down to only two, begging pity for his poverty (*miserere paupertatulae*). Agreeing to the terms, Petrucius advises him to say nothing but *Ble*. "If I ask you anything, reply *Ble* and nothing else." (*Si quaero quae, tu redde Ble atque aliud nihil.*) Dromo agrees and promises to pay him the two gold pieces. Then they depart because the court is in session (*Iudex tribunal occupat*).

In the second scene (323–55) the judge, Minos, commands the court beadle to call for order and inquires about the litigants since his secretary is absent.[32]

> Praeco, iube silentium. Adversarii
> Vbi sunt? Abest nomencalator nominum.

Danista announces his presence and states that Dromo received fifteen ells of cloth from him without paying. He requests that Dromo therefore be required to pay eight gold pieces. When the judge asks Dromo why he says nothing, Dromo bleats and Petrucius points out that the poor man appears to be deaf.

> MI. Quid tu taces? DRO. Ble. PET. Apparet hic surdus miser.

The judge instructs Petrucius to advise (*patrocinare*) his client and warns the lawyers that they should be prepared with clear instructions for the litigation lest they get bogged down in procedures.

Curate vos causidici, ut unusquisque sit
Cum instructionibus paratus litium,
Ne ut antea turbemur in processibus.

Then he invites Petrucius, as the defending advocate, to begin. Petrucius points out that his client, being deaf and mute, is unable to confess or deny or even to speak. He insists that Danista must produce witnesses if he hopes to win his case.

Sed consulo, Danista causam testibus
(Si vincere optat et obtinere) iam probet.

Danista realizes that it does not matter whether Dromo speaks or is silent because no other witness was present. Since he is unable to prove his case, he requests that Dromo be required to swear an oath putting an end to the litigation by postponement or referral and affirming that the charge is untrue.

Igitur probare nil queo, sed hunc peto
Iurare decisorium et calumniam.

(In the commentary that Reuchlin appended to his teaching copy of the manuscript he explained any unusual technical terms. Here he defines *decisorium* as *iuramentum quod imponit finem liti et defertur sive refertur*.) But when the judge has Dromo brought forward for interrogation, the servant simply bleats in response to each question. Do you not wish to refute the charge? (*Non voles calumniam inferre improbe*.) Do you deny that it is true? (*Interrogatus vera ne negaveris*.) Have you made any use of a false proof? (*Sed probatione falsa ne utere*.) Have you bribed anyone with money? (*Neve quos pecunia corruperis*.) Does it seem to you that the case should be postponed? (*Differendam ne tibi litem pares*.) Dismayed by all the bleating, the judge advises Danista to drop his case against Dromo (*ut hunc missum sinas*). The draper complies and obeys, hoping that the thief will be damned[33] (*Ego obsecundor et obsequor, valeat latro*). Thereupon the judge informs the lawyer that his client is absolved (*Et ego, Petruci, absolvo sic clientulum*).

The act concludes with a choral ode (356–73) exhorting those who wish to have a tranquil existence to avoid the courts, pointing out that in the antechambers of Tartarus are Minos, Aeacus, and other noted counselors and advocates. Moreover, law is hostile to humanistic pursuits: the Muse forbids her followers to frequent the law courts, where cunning thrives, along with false accusations, lies, evil deceptions, and treacherous crimes.

Vetat Musa sequacibus industriis
Frequentare iuridici subsellia,
Vbi vigent versutia
Calumnia
Mendacia
Doli mali proditoriaeque fraudes.

Like his friend Brant, Reuchlin expresses the trained and practicing lawyer's doubts and concerns about his profession. He exposes the shyster who, for money, takes on the case of a man clearly guilty of fraud and helps him to win by tricks and cunning. Unlike the French source, he depicts a courtroom ineptly managed by a judge who knows enough legal terminology to get along but lacks the insight and wit to perceive and unmask sheer cunning. Finally, he concludes from all this, rather despondently, that decent men will simply avoid the courts altogether. Fortunately Reuchlin did not take his own advice. After the interlude at Heidelberg he returned to public service, where he functioned honorably as a judge for another decade while simultaneously pursuing his humanistic studies. But it would be unrealistic to discount the impact that his pedagogical play, with its satirization of lawyers and the law, must have had on the minds and opinions of many generations of impressionable students.

It is perhaps worth noting that Hans Sachs, who translated and adapted Reuchlin's comedy some thirty-five years later, intensified the satire against lawyers. Although Sachs does away with the choral odes, he introduces Petrucius loitering outside the courtroom and complaining in a brief monologue that, although court is now in session, no one has yet hired him as an advocate, and wondering if no one is going to grease his palm today:

> Man wird ietzt sitzen zu gericht.
> Bin doch von niemandt bstellet nicht,
> Dem ich daran sol procuriern!
> Wil niemant heut mein hendt mir schmiern?[34]

In general, the expansion of several passages indicating the corruptness of the lawyer and the incompetence of the judge suggests that the legal situation in Germany has not yet been resolved even by 1531.

Knightly Contempt: Ulrich von Hutten

How can we not respond to the exhuberance of the young man who exclaimed, in a famous letter to his friend, the Nürnberg humanist Willibald Pirckheimer: "O century, o learning! It's a joy to be alive, even if not yet to repose. Studies are thriving, minds are flowering. Accept your bonds, Barbarism, and get ready for exile." (*O seculum! o literae! Iuvat vivere, etsi quiescere nondum iuvat, Bilibalde. Vigent studia, florent ingenia. Heus tu, accipe laqueum, barbaries, exilium prospice.*)[35] There is no more attractive figure among the German Reformation humanists than Ulrich von Hutten (1488–1523), whose nobility of character was matched by his all-too-human contentiousness and obstinacy. An enemy of moral decay among the German nobility and of the corruption he witnessed at the court of Pope Julius II, he was capable of expressing his views in the best Latin written by any German of his age as well as a German matched in its vigor only by Martin Luther's prose. Respected for his writings by such humanists as Erasmus, More, and Budé, he engaged himself on the side of Reuchlin against the Dominicans with his *Epistolae obscurorum virorum* and was indicted with Luther in the papal bull of January 3, 1521. He dreamed of rehabilitating Germany according to the ideal image of ancient Germania as portrayed by Tacitus, but by the end of his short life the Fortuna that he often apostrophized in his letters and poems (such as *Fortuna* [1519]) had again turned against him: deserted by Erasmus, ignored by Luther, disappointed by Charles V, his knightly ally Franz von Sickingen dead, Hutten himself succumbed at age thirty-five to the syphilis with which he had been infected for many years.

Hutten was born in the duchy of Franconia into the estate of free knights whose principal raison d'être had been undermined by the growing use of mercenary troops in war and whose financial base from rents and revenues had been undercut by the growing class of urban merchants.[36] In addition, in their traditional feudal function as counselors to the princes they saw themselves displaced by the new class of jurists.[37] At age eleven Hutten—though the eldest son, he was of a sickly disposition—was sent for schooling to the monastery at Fulda, where he acquired the foundations of his excellent Latin but which he left in 1505 without having taken his vows. He thereupon embarked upon the goliardic life of an itinerant scholar, which led him to Cologne, Erfurt, Frankfurt an der Oder, Leipzig, Greifswald, Rostock, and Wittenberg in the course of an intellectual journey that began in medieval scholasticism and ended in Renaissance humanism. Acceding finally to the wishes of his father, who desired his son to prepare for a more reliable career, he left for Italy in 1511 to take up the study of law. But attracted by the humanists in Vienna, he spent a year there before proceeding to Pavia and Bologna, where war soon interrupted his studies. Back in Germany in 1513, he was promised a position by the archbishop of Mainz conditional upon his completing his legal studies. Returning to Italy two years later, he spent several months in Rome, where he witnessed the corruption at the papal court. Forced to flee following his murder of a French soldier in a tavern brawl, he returned to Bologna and continued his studies for a year; again, however, he had to leave the city, this time because of taunts that, as a student leader, he had directed against the city's governor. On his return to Germany in 1517, he stopped at Augsburg long enough to be named poet laureate by Emperor Maximilian, to whom he had earlier dedicated a volume of laudatory and patriotic epigrams. Without a law degree, but entitled by the imperial laurel to lecture on poetry and rhetoric at universities, he served for two years as counselor to Albert, the archbishop of Mainz, and observed the behavior of the courtiers at that court. By 1519, recognizing his unsuitability for a courtier's life, he obtained his release from the archbishop and spent the remainder of his short life involved in the conflicts generated by the Reformation. In 1522, finally, illness and political pressures forced him to flee to Switzerland, where he was given refuge by Zwingli and soon died on a small island in the lake near Zürich.

Hutten's combative and sometimes self-righteous temperament expressed itself in writings directed against many targets. Following the murder of his cousin by Duke Ulrich of Württemberg in 1515, he wrote a series of blistering attacks against tyrants in Germany, which led to the duke's ban and, eventually in 1519, his deposition by the Swabian League. His humanist convictions, combined with his contempt for scholastic narrow-mindedness, produced his memorable contributions to the second volume of *Epistolae obscurorum virorum* (1517). Following his experiences in Rome, he wrote a number of diatribes against corruption in the Church (for example, the "Roman Trinity" *Vadiscus* [1520]), which led to the inclusion of his name along with Martin Luther's in the papal bull. He railed against the Italians, whose influence threatened to undermine indigenous Germanic values as embodied in his beloved Arminius, to whom he devoted a poem. But no group evoked his wrath—and the venom of his pen—more furiously than the Roman jurists, whom he hated for a combination of reasons: they represented the abominated Italians and the Church; they sought to replace traditional Germanic values with foreign Roman codes; they were taking needed positions away from the free knights and elevating themselves socially to a position of equality with the lower nobility; they even sought to outlaw the precious right of feud, through which the knights had traditionally addressed their grievances. All these feelings against a group that he knew from his own years of study in Italy and from his years at the court in Mainz emerge vividly in Hutten's letters, poems, and dialogues.

Nemo is a sustained humanist joke in seventy-eight Latin distichs.[38] Drafted before 1510 and completed in 1515 after Hutten's first return from Italy,[39] the poem gets its title and its central conceit from the episode in the *Odyssey* (bk. 9) in which Odysseus blinds the Cyclops Polyphemus and then tells him that his name is *Outis*—that is, "no one," "nobody," "Noman," or *Nemo* in the Latin. The poet announces quite early that it is "nobody" who is speaking and saying nothing; and if the reader hears a sound, he should say that it is nobody's nothing.

> Qui loquitur, Nemo est; loquitur Nihil: at tibi siquid
> Insonuit, dicas Neminis esse Nihil.
>
> (Lines 13–14)

The poem consists of a series of statements on contemporary politics and morals, all of which are of course qualified and inverted by the fact that the speaker's name means "nobody." Thus at a time when the emperor was urgently seeking princely support for his war against the Turks—the principal topic at the Diet of Augsburg in 1518—"Nemo attacks the wild Turks in battle; and Nemo cares more for public welfare than for private gain":

> Nemo feros bello Turcas adit; et bona curat
>   Publica privato munere Nemo magis.
>
> (51–52)

The bitterness of the young humanist in an age concerned with other matters is evident is the statement that "Nemo does everything that pleases the stupid mob; Nemo receives rewards worthy of his excellent application to learning":

> Nemo quae placeant stupido facit omnia vulgo.
>   Nemo refert studiis praemia digna bonis.
>
> (57–58)

Or again on a personal level (from the young man already suffering from syphilis!): "In me trust is safe; he who desires his wife to be virtuous may dare to entrust her to Nemo's bed":

> In me tuta fides; audet committere lecto
>   Neminis uxorem qui cupit esse probam.
>
> (149–50)

The sequence of occasionally sophomoric jokes on political, moral, and social issues of the day constitutes a profoundly skeptical work that was more frequently reprinted than any of Hutten's poems, but it has nothing explicit to say about the law or lawyers—probably because it was initially conceived and drafted before Hutten went to Italy to take up his legal studies. The relevance for law and the Reception is made apparent, rather, in the letter to his friend and fellow author of the *Epistolae obscurorum virorum*, the humanist Crotus Rubeanus (= Johannes Jäger, 1480–1539), which was written around 1515 and included as a preface to the final edition of the work (1518).[40]

Referring to the line *Nemo refert studiis praemia digna bonis*, Hutten explains bitterly to his friend that when he arrived home from Italy, the rumor was already circulating that he had learned nothing and therefore amounted to nothing (*tuncque primum divagatus est rumor, nihil didicisse me ac esse nihil*, 176). Among the knights, "those erudite ignoramuses" (*ex istis vero indoctis doctis*, 177), his knowledge counted for nothing because he could not boast, like the trained lawyers and theologians, of "the Felini, the Baldi, the Bartoli, the Iasones, the Accursii, the Speculatores and that whole race of doctorlets," nor could he cite "the subtle Scotus, the seraphic Bonaventura, the twice sainted Thomas, the particularly magnus Albertus and the incontestable somebody, whose name escapes me through indifference" (177–78). Disgusted by those haughty dispensors of laws (*mihi stomachum moverunt isti olim superbi legum dispensatores*, 178), Hutten takes pride in his own humanistic learning and is contemptuous of the paltry knowledge and titles of which the Bartolists boast. But today what matters is to have a doctor's title, not to be learned (*Doctorem enim esse oportet nunc, doctum neque necesse est*, 178).

It is these vain and ignorant Bartolists, Hutten continues, who now attach themselves to the princes' ears like sponges (*quasi spongiae*, 179), by whose counsel states are governed, by whose precepts everything is done at home and abroad, who alone are considered *docti* and who alone reap the rewards of learning. How much better was Germany's condition before the lawyers, instructed by all their volumes, invaded the land; in the days when good Germanic customs counted for more than the written laws of the Romans (*tunc cum plus valerent hic boni mores, quam usquam scriptae leges*, 179). Indeed, he concludes, the state is best governed when these glossators are kept at a distance (*quanto ab ea longius absunt hi glossatores*, 179). Just consider the Saxons on the Baltic: how straightforwardly and justly they pronounce the law, without consulting the shysters, but according to ancient custom. (In fact, Hutten seems to have known very little about Saxon law despite the months he spent on the Baltic during his goliardic years.) Nowadays, in contrast, cases are dragged on for twenty years by thirty-six *doctores*. Of what use is legal learning if, after so many years and so many volumes perused, they are not able to find the law? Do we not begin vaguely to understand who it is that nourishes all these quarrels and discords in Germany, that links princes in domestic strife, that brings tumult into the republic, that fills everything with insurrections? Hutten goes on to ridicule the ignorance of jurisconsults, such as the "notable dolt" (*insignem asinum*, 179) he had known at Pavia: listening to a lecture in which many authorities were cited, including "Alexander de Imola and his followers [*ac sequaces*]," that particular fool assumed that Sequaces was the name of one of the glossators. Yet this same individual, recently returned from Italy and splendidly outfitted with books and vestments, is numbered among the *doctores* and turns his back on Hutten, although the latter understands much more about the law.

With a Ciceronian exclamation quite remote from the exuberance of his letter to Pirckheimer, Hutten laments the morals and the learning and appeals to the leaders of the times (*O mores, o studia, o temporis huius capita*, 180) to cast off the obfuscations and to see the truth. But the *doctores* take enormous pleasure in their commentaries, through which they involve the readily comprehensible field of law in a mist and render it more obscure with their Cimmerian shadows. They operate on the assumption that whoever clouds his books with a denser fog and darker night is regarded as a classic writer and held in admiration—not unlike Accursius himself, from whose gloomy mind a smoke has been poured over the body of civil law (*ex cuius tenebricoso ingenio hic offusus est iuri civili fumus*, 180). Any free-minded spirit would prefer anything rather than to plunge into such sordid affairs. Yet "we are nothing, Crotus, nor shall we cease to be nothing until we assume some role in this comedy" (*Sumus enim nihil, Crote, nec prius desinimus nihil esse, quam aliquam nobis in hac comoedia personam assumamus*, 180). If it were not for his desire for knowledge, Hutten might content himself with his position as a German knight (*Eques Germanus*, 180). In this age those who vaunt their learning know nothing. Those who are ignorant of humane letters presume to counsel us on what it is fitting to learn, and to act as advisers of our study. When such people inquire, "What is he?" the only suitable response is: *Doctor est, Magister est, Baculaureus est* (180). If none of the above applies, *Nihil est*. Nowadays people do not ask about one's qualities but about one's title (*Hodie enim non qualis quisque sit, sed quo vocetur nomine quaeritur*, 180). Circumstances and money count for everything, virtue for nothing. Why should anyone wish to be learned when in this day and age knowledge is regarded as the utmost insanity? (*cur igitur sapere quis velit, quando sapere extrema hoc tempore dementia est*? 180). This, Hutten concludes, is the source of that *Nemo* who dares with impunity to expose *Nihil*, since if someone is no one, what does it matter if he speaks his nothing? (*quia qui Nemo est quid obstat quo minus loquatur hoc suum Nihil?* 181).

Hutten goes on in the second part of his prefatory epistle to attack the theologians with equal energy. But by this point we can readily understand why, as he wrote later that year in his autobiographical letter to Pirckheimer, "certain people who regard themselves as jurisprudents, hotheaded and stupid men [*cerebrosi illi ac stolidi homines*], are defaming me because of my tale of Nihil and Nemo."[41] They tell stories and tales about Hutten (*qui de me sermones, quae fabulae sunt*, 211), while the unfortunate Nemo is the subject of mealtime conversations. People are so annoyed by his little fiction that they devote entire symposia to attacking him. But Hutten has nothing but an indecent gesture for those who are so dumb that they make a tragedy out of trivialities (*quibus ego medium digitum ostendo, sic insipientibus, ut in nugis tragoediam agant*, 211). Those who are truly learned have been amused by *Nemo* and understand that it is not a personal attack but a criticism of the age. Pirckheimer, if he hears criticisms, should defend his friend. Of what concern is it to Hutten if a certain Nemo resists the authority of Iason and attacks Accursius or if someone who is Nihil refuses to genuflect before the sepulchre of Bartolus? (*quid ad Huttenum, inquiens, Iasonis autoritati si quis Nemo refragatur, aut Accursium incessit, et ante Bartholi sepulchrum siquis Nihil qui est non congenudavit?*, 211). However, the situation is improving. Immediately before the exultant exclamation with which the letter ends (cited above) Hutten reminds Pirckheimer that Budé and Erasmus, those two Hercules of the day (*ecce tibi duos eadem tempestate Hercules*, 216), are simultaneously destroying the plagues of law and theology. Guilielmus Budaeus, the most scholarly nobleman and the most noble scholar in France (*nobilium in Gallia doctissimus, doctorum nobilissimus*, 216), is preparing his annotations to the Pandects. He has already declared war on the followers of Accursius in France and extirpated the whole breed of Bartolists (*debellavit ille Accursii in Gallia posteritatem et omne radicitus extirpavit Bartholistarum genus*, 216).

If the poem *Nemo*, and especially the accompanying letters to Crotus Rubeanus and Pirckheimer, display the humanist knight's contempt for the obfuscations of the Italian commentators and his rage at the ignorant *doctores* who currently wield such power in the princely courts, Hutten's dialogue *Praedones* (The brigands, 1521) exposes the class consciousness of the imperial knight who feels that the traditional rights and privileges of his estate are threatened by recent displacements of traditional law. Two years earlier, during the war of the Swabian League against his family's hated enemy, Duke Ulrich of Württemberg, Hutten had shared a tent with Franz von Sickingen (1481–1523), the imperial knight who for a decade had shrewdly utilized his powerful private army both to acquire a fortune in ransoms from besieged cities and to establish his political influence. In 1521, disenchanted with Maxilian's successor, Charles V, and named in the papal bull of 1521 to appear at the Diet of Worms to account for his anticlerical writings, Hutten was grateful to enjoy the protection of the powerful Sickingen. No doubt, Sickingen's example was already encouraging him to contemplate feud, outlawed by imperial decree since 1495, as a last resort for his own financial straits. In any case, his dialogue is firmly rooted in the circumstances of the moment.

The work, which has the lively language of a play, features three clearly characterized speakers: Hutten himself, Franciscus (= Sickingen), and Mercator, an unnamed merchant employed as an agent by the Fugger family.[42] As the dialogue begins, Hutten and the merchant are arguing about certain decrees and edicts issuing from the Diet at Worms. Though we do not yet understand the cause, Hutten is so enraged that the merchant has to remind him that they are in a free city, where violence is prohibited by law. It soon becomes evident that the merchant has indiscreetly accused the imperial knights, the traditional enemies of the towns and business, of brigandry. Franciscus arrives just in time to prevent the irascible Hutten from attacking the merchant, asserting that there are much worse brigands in other classes. He proposes to demonstrate that, in fact, four classes of brigand can be found in Germany (*Igitur quatuor sunt in Germania Praedonum genera*, 367). Hutten now jumps the gun and declares that the worst is the class of priests. But Sickingen suggests that they should start with the least objectionable and work their way up the scale to the worst: from common bandits by way of the merchants themselves and the lawyers to the priests.

Having dealt with bandits and settled the disagreements between merchant and knight—indeed, Sickingen hopes for his own political reasons to be the initiator of a pact of goodwill between the knights and the free cities (*author fiam ordini nostro perpetuae componendae cum liberis civitatibus gratiae*, 378)[43]—the dialogue goes on to the third category of brigands, the government officials and lawyers (*Scribae et Iureconsulti*, 378), who are more harmful than the merchants inasmuch as their range is broader. For no place is free of them, nor is there any place where they do not rob: in the courts of the princes, in the senates and bodies of the states, in public meetings and private consultations, in the military, at home, in war and in peace. Hutten impatiently interjects that such officials dominated Maximilian, abusing the prince's simple goodwill as they wished. Maximilian rewarded them royally, even giving them money that should have gone during wartime to the soldiers. He made them nobles and princes—even bishops, like the one whose father sold milk in Augsburg, but who is now so effete that he complains that the Fuggers have not imported enough exotic goods from abroad (379). And today similar sycophants are already clustering around Charles V and, corrupted by papal moneys, extorting from him edicts against Martin Luther. Sickingen and Hutten both express the hope that the young emperor's inherent character will assert itself and that, as other princes follow his example, the authority of the scribes and lawyers will gradually wither away. At present mean men are in power, who have no knowledge or skill in matters of state, no memory of the past, no experience of things, no industry of mind, and are endowed with no awareness of innocence, but who accede to the rule of public customs and laws by virtue of boldness and impudence and the worst devices (*qui nulla regendarum rerum aut ratione aut scientia, nulla antiquitatis memoria, rerum experientia, animi industria, denique haud ulla innocentiae conscientia praediti, verum sola temeritate et impudentia ac pessimis freti artibus ad publicum morum legumque regimen accedunt*, 380). These men control all access to the chancelleries, and their advice is sought as though from a divine oracle for all matters, public and private. They are, so to speak, the eyes of the kings, without which they see nothing and understand nothing (*qui sunt quasi quidam regum oculi, sine quibus nihil illi vident, nihil agnoscunt*, 380). And the worst things about these obfuscators (*fumivendis his*, 380), who cultivate their clothes more than their minds, is the fact that, out of self-defense, they hate no one more than truly educated and learned men. For they rightly suspect that these people recognize their ignorance and denseness and therefore keep them away from the princes.

But, Sickingen continues, the jurisconsults vex Germany even more slothfully than the palace officials. Ignorant though they are, they are popularly considered to be learned and vaunt their knowledge most odiously (*odiosissime superbiunt*, 381). Indeed, the immeasurable haughtiness of the lawyers (*fastus leguleiorum*, 381) surpasses that of any other group. If only the German princes would recognize how trivial their so-called learning is, there would be an end to the whole school of Bartolists (*actum de universa Bartholistarum schola fuerit*, 381). At present, however, their axioms are preferred to the opinions of honorable men. They are so stupid that their stupidity even corrupts the best minds when they have to deal with them. Those who are supposed to be prudent are devoid of all prudence, and all their discipline—if such it deserves to be called—consists in the most infantile loquacity. For what prudence is it if simple people are circumvented by deceit and if statutes are diverted by a clever interpretation of the law into a sense quite remote from the intent of the legislator, and equity is corrupted (*callida iuris interpretatione in diversissimam quamque sententiam a legislatoris mente derivantur leges, et aequitas corrumpitur*, 381–82).

Sickingen praises the Saxons, who despite their proclivity to drunkenness do not live without laws but rule without lawyers. The doctors today have no memory of the past; with their little red skullcaps (*cum rubris suis pileolis*, 382) they have invaded Germany like a tempest, and no one has yet appeared to oppose this pestilence. For a long time they have gotten away with all their projects, but this situation will not continue much longer. Sickingen believes that onlookers at the Diet of Worms have begun to comprehend the degree of injury perpetrated by the shysters who always ask, "What about the law?" (*quid iuris?* 382) but never find anything. Looking for the greatest difficulties in the simplest matters, they sweat away whole days and nights buried under mountains of books, whence they emerge, pale and exhausted with effort, and demonstrate with the testimony of texts what we were prepared to test with spoken words. Such a chore it is, Hutten recapitulates, to invert equity and injustice (*Tantus labor est aequum et iniquum pervertere*, 382), and what praise to defend a bad cause as though it were a just one! But for them no consciousness of right and wrong exists: whether someone is condemned or acquitted is only a question of words (*ita non est tuta per hos conscientia: in verbis situm est damnetur quis an absolvatur*, 382).

When Hutten asks about the usefulness of the vast heap of juridical books, Sickingen reminds him that the lawyers use them to fascinate and blind the judges. As wax is shaped by skillful hands, so they form the law and twist and retwist the statutes as they wish and to their own ends (*ut cera tractatus artificis manibus, ita formant ius hi ac leges torquent et retorquent quo volunt et quo ex re sua est*, 383). As a result, Germania is living more miserably under these dispensers of justice than if she had been defeated in war by tyrants. In other times, the knight continues, when men lived more simply and fraud had not yet come to be valued, the innocent were defended from violence and injury by the sword (and implicitly by the knights!). But now the violence with which justice is destroyed is sought in books. Therefore, it would be better if one day all the books should be burned up so that, with this instrument of crimes abolished, men might be less frequently distracted from equity. Hutten suggests that these learned ignoramuses might best be deported into Plato's Republic or into that Utopia recently described by Thomas More (*ipsi vero formularii et perverse prudentes isti atque indocti docti in Platonis civitatem aut illam nuper auditam Utopiam deportarentur*, 383) because they continue to repress truly learned scholars while empty titles enjoy honor. Nor do the princes realize that, through these good-for-nothings (*per nebulones hosce*, 383), they are being deprived of their own role: for if they were true princes, they would not derive their equity from written matter but from their inherent prudence, goodness, justice, and clemency. But at present whenever controversies arise, the princes send for the wise men (*Sapientes*, 383) who pass judgment and, nobility excluded, occupy the halls of the princes alone. Meanwhile the princes, so infatuated that they despair of ruling without these advisers, heap wealth upon them. Whatever they undertake, they are impelled by the lawyers' vapors and obsequiously obey their formulas and actions. This madness of the princes is inevitably followed by the oppression of the people. (*quam Principum dementiam vulgi oppressio sequitur necessario*, 384).

After Sickingen's disparaging remarks about the appearance and demeanor of the lawyers—they are no better than procurers (*meri lenones*, 384) with a truculent expression—Hutten suggests fatalistically that Germany must have been condemned by the gods to this destiny. He realizes that he is sometimes regarded as a nuisance by the knights for his continual warnings. But, he asserts, I shall never cease being the instigator for Germany to punish the wicked harshly (*neque unquam author esse desino Germaniae, ut male mulctet improbos*, 384). The lawyers have been a moral contagion, the supreme depravity of life, animating others by their advice to crime. They themselves persuade people to pursue litigation, and "never ceasing to prosecute calumny" is their term for pursuing the law (*ipsi lites sequi suadent et "non desistere a calumnia" ius persequi vocant*, 385). Hutten tells about a certain old shyster (*rabulam*, 385) he knew in Frankfurt who was conducting a case against Hutten's friend. "I won't promise, he said, what I can't accomplish: that is, to win. But I can promise to do what will shatter your adversary—to drag out the case for at least ten years." The merchant then cites approvingly the citizens of Nuremberg, who have closed their senate to the jurisprudents and keep them out of all public meetings since they cannot fail to be harmful (*tanquam innocentes esse qui nequeant*, 385). Hutten proposes making that action into a general principle: to exile lawyers throughout Germany and to exclude from governmental affairs all ignorant doctrine—to burn the works of Accursius along with those of his many followers. Surely then the homeland, now suffering a poor reputation because it has forsaken ancient customs and having lost the reputation of equity and justice among foreigners, might again return to its former honor and glory. The lawyers, then, are by far the worst brigands in Germany, the merchant agrees, because, while other merely carry off goods, they drive justice into the ground and destroy the laws and suck the blood from poor mankind, disturbing the tranquillity of all spirits. Hutten proposes that Germany should imitate its ancestors, those strong men who, having killed the Roman army and liberated the homeland, went on a fierce rampage against the lawyers (*in solos causidicos singulari quadam ferocitate saeviendum duxerunt*, 386). Perceiving that they had suffered the greatest injury and affliction from this breed, they cut out their tongues and stitched their lips together, saying, "Stop hissing, vipers!" (*sibilare, vipera, desine*, 386). The merchant hopes that the Germans will hear Hutten's admonitions to abolish and extirpate those whose supreme law (according to the Ciceronian tag) is the supreme injustice, and thereby liberate the country from their miserable oppression.

Sickingen now turns to the fourth category of brigands, the priests. But we have already heard by now the entire litany of often savage complaints against Roman law and its practitioners as viewed by the imperial knights, whose interests and influence were being threatened by the new breed. Hutten's appeal, of course, was romantically unrealistic; the day of the medieval knight was almost past, and the era of the lawyer and administrator working with the tools of the *usus modernus Pandectarum* had already begun. There remained nothing but a melancholy aftermath. Totally misunderstanding the historical moment, the new power of the cities and the social revolution of the peasantry, which was not sympathetic to the conservative views of the knights, Hutten undertook in the fall of 1521 a personal feud—strictly illegal according to the terms of the Perpetual Peace—against the Carthusians of Strassburg for their defamation of his character and actually received two thousand guilders in ransom. But subsequent attempts in the spring of 1522 to blackmail "the un-Christian, gold-greedy, thieving pack of courtesans" ("des vnchristlichen: goltgeyrigen Rauberischen Volcks der Curtisanen") failed,[44] and he joined Sickingen in the attempt to organize a league of Rhineland, Swabian, and Frankish nobility for the ostensible purpose of self-defense against the hostile forces emerging in the postmedieval world. Sickingen's last feud against the elector archbishop of Trier in September of that year ended in his defeat by the princes; outlawed for his offense against the Perpetual Peace, he retreated to his castle at Landstuhl where, mortally wounded during the ensuing siege, he died in 1523. Hutten died a few months later in Switzerland. The age of the knights had given way to the era of the *doctores*. Bound by his class prejudices against Roman law, Hutten never understood or appreciated the historical significance of the creation of the Imperial Chamber Court during the reign of his idolized knightly emperor, Maximilian.[45]

Humanist Ambivalence: Philipp Melanchthon

A different kind of ambivalence toward the Reception is manifest in the writings of Philipp Melanchthon (1497–1560), who more than any other major figure of the Reformation concerned himself with the law.[46] As the *Praeceptor Germaniae*, who became a professor of Greek at Wittenberg in 1518 at the age of twenty-one, Melanchthon was largely responsible for revising the German educational system in accordance with the convictions of the new revival of learning. And as Luther's friend and colleague, he became what amounted to the theological spokesman of the Reformation, producing in his *Loci communes rerum theologicarum* (from 1521) the first systematic codification of the new religious doctrine. The extraordinary breadth of Melanchthon's interests and erudition is perhaps most readily apparent in the famous orations (*declamationes*) that he wrote as models of humanist eloquence and that touched not only, as might be expected, on classical antiquity, rhetoric, and theology, but also on medicine, physics, mathematics, and current events (for instance, his funeral orations for Emperor Maximilian in 1519 and for Friedrich, the elector of Saxony, in 1525). Among these orations, which span a period of some forty years, no topic crops up more frequently than the law.[47]

Several factors help to account for Melanchthon's interest in legal theory and issues.[48] He was the nephew of Johannes Reuchlin and in 1508 (at age eleven!) staged a performance of the *scaenica progymnasmata* with his school friends at Pforzheim in honor of his uncle's visit.[49] As a student in Tübingen, Melanchthon had applied his encyclopedic mind to law, as well as philology, theology, and medicine. His mentor and colleague at Wittenberg was the distinguished jurist Hieronymus Schürpf, to whom Melanchthon devoted a moving memorial tribute (*Oratio de vita clarissimi viri Hieronymi Schurffi*, 1554). He maintained collegial relations with many of the prominent legal scholars of his day. His own philological scholarship—including his lectures on Cicero and his prolegomena to Cicero's *De officiis* (1530)—often involved him in the interpretation of legal texts. As a Reformation thinker he was compelled to take a position in the controversy concerning the compatibility of Roman law with Christian doctrine. Finally, the social turmoil of the age, exacerbated by religious fundamentalists eager to replace secular law with Mosaic law by violent means, made jurisprudence far more than a matter for abstract academic consideration. In sum, Melanchthon had strong reasons for taking up the burning issues of law in his popular orations addressed to the entire academic community of Wittenberg. And, as we know from the opening remarks prefixed to several of the orations, it was customary for speakers to use the occasion to speak of the dignity of law and to excite their listeners to a reverence for law: *Usitatum est hoc loco [et] in his spectaculis aliquid de legum dignitate dicere, ad quarum reverentiam certe excitari homines maxime prodest* (11:630; 234).

It should be kept in mind that the *declamationes* were written primarily as models of eloquence for Melanchthon's colleagues and students. Accordingly the emphasis rests on the formal treatment of the theme rather than on thematic originality; the thought is subordinated to the rhetoric.[50] Moreover, the orations were often written very quickly—sometimes to satisfy Melanchthon's own obligations to hold public lectures at Wittenberg, but often (as indicated in the titles) for other speakers on various occasions. As a result, we find in the orations less a development of Melanchthon's thoughts on law than a constant restatement of the same familiar themes. To the extent that Melanchthon is not so much a thinker or philosopher as a brilliant scholar and synthesizer, his orations reflect views on law widely held among the Protestant humanists.

The fundamental problem for many thinkers of the Reformation was the reconciliation of the divine law with *any* human law, whether Roman or customary. Because of the perceived disparity some evangelists even proposed that all human law should be discarded in a society governed again by Mosaic law. This problem does not exist in Melanchthon's Christian humanism, which sees God as the source of all law, whether divine, natural, or human. This distinction appears in the earliest of his *Loci communes* (1521), where he quotes Paul's epistle to the Romans to the effect that "there is no authority except from God, and those that exist have been instituted by God."[51] As he put it thirty years later in the oration *De legum fontibus et causis* (1550), using an image that recurs with leitmotivic frequency in other talks, "law is the ray of divine wisdom shining in this life" (*lux est radius sapientiae divinae fulgens in hac vita*, 11:917; 260). God has imprinted upon man certain, true, and immutable ideas drawn from his eternal mind, and since these are the sources of all law, it is certain that any laws congruent with these sources are divine (*Impressit igitur homini noticias certas, veras, immutabiles, sumptas ex sua mente aeterna. Hae cum sint legum fontes, certum est iura cum his fontibus congruentia divina esse*, 11:639). The evidences of this law, transmitted with the very light that is born with us and subsequently by the divine voice, are "the beginnings of law and of political order" (*initia legum et ordinis politici*, 11:919; 262). Indeed, all political order is the admirable work of the deity (*totus ordo politicus admirandum Dei opus [est]*, 11:914; 248).

Law is necessary because man in his depravity hates any restraint upon his natural desires (*Experimur in hac pravitate naturae humanae, odisse eam leges, tanquam carcerem, et malle concedi infinitam licentiam ludendi vanitate opinionum, et explendi vagas cupiditates*, 12:96; 283); this profound pessimism regarding human nature, stemming from a Christian awareness of original sin, grows stronger from the earliest to the latest orations. Just as the lovely order of nature suggests an underlying divine power, so too it is certain that human society and its restraints—governments, laws, the doctrine of virtue and justice, contracts, courts, and their administrators and interpreters—are established by God (*sic certum est a Deo societatem hominum et vincula societatis . . . poenas singulari opere ordinatas esse*, 11:919; 262). By the same token, God is displeased by societies without law and order, where blind passion rules: here the professor of Greek often adduces the Homeric example of the Cyclops (*manifestum est displicere ei cyclopicam vitam, quae sine ordine et sine legibus agitur, et quo caecae et dissimiles cupiditates impellunt, ruit*, 11:919; 263).

However, it is necessary to distinguish between biblical and political goverment (*Ingens discrimen est inter Evangelium et politicam gubernationem*, 11:921; 264). The Gospels constitute a divine voice revealing light and justice of the spirit to mortals wherever they may be. But since pious people live in different times and places, they also live in various empires and according to dissimilar laws (*Ut enim diversis dierum spaciis in diversis locis pii utuntur, ita in diversis imperiis ac dissimilibus legibus vivere possunt*, 11:921; 264–65). Accordingly, in civil life God permits mankind to make use of the laws of the governments in which they live (*in vita civili sinit nos [Deus] uti legibus imperiorum, in quibus vivimus*, 12:25; 257). Thus, as he adds in this oration, *De dignitate doctrinae legum et Iurisconsultorum* (1553), Joseph in Egypt passed judgment according to Egyptian laws, Daniel by Persian laws, Nebuchadnezzar by Babylonian laws, and Nahamam by Syrian laws (12:26; 258). It is not necessary for Christians to be ruled by Mosaic laws; they may use any laws that are consistent with natural law, even if they are founded by pagan jurists (*quod Christianis non sit necessarium uti legibus Mosaicis, sed quod liceat uti legibus quae iuri naturae consentaneae sunt, etiamsi ab Ethnicis Magistratibus conditae sunt*, 11:357; 221–22). Among the pagan legal systems, Roman law excels by far and constitutes a veritable philosophy (*Romanum ius antecellere legibus aliarum gentium, et vere quandam Philosophiam esse*, 11:358; 222). Indeed, Roman law is grounded upon the laws of nature just as clearly as is arithmetic upon the laws of proportion (12:22; 255).

Following the empire's fall, Roman law was lost in the West for five hundred years while the land was overrun by the Franks and Langobards. However, as Melanchthon relates in his great oration on the medieval jurisconsults Irnerius and Bartolus (1537), the law, which had been preserved and cultivated at Constantinople, has been restored to the courts as well as the academies, thanks to the efforts of scholars. And this restitution reformed the barbarian ways not only in legal affairs but generally in life (*revocatae sunt in forum et in scholas Romanae leges. Haec restitutio multos mores barbaricos correxit, non modo in iudiciis, sed etiam in reliqua vita*, 11:363; 227). Hence it is necessary for young men to study the law, for the written law is the most steadfast guard against tyranny (*Nam scriptum ius est firmum praesidium adversus tyrannidem*, 11:363; 227) and hedges off the liberty of the people against the avarice of the powerful (*Hoc muro septa est libertas populi adversus potentum cupiditates*, 11:363; 227). For these reasons, as Melanchthon argues in his impassioned exordium, this law, written by the wisest heads in the greatest republic and restored by the great counsel of the finest men, which is the most just and most consistent with reason, which arms us against tyranny, which is conducive to good morals, needs to be retained and defended with all vigilance (*Quare hoc ius, quod a sapientissimis viris in Repub[lica] praestantissima scriptum est, quod magno consilio summorum virorum restitutum est, quod est aequissimum et maxime consentaneum rationi, quod munit nos adversus tyrannidem, quod prodest ad bonos mores, retineamus, et omni studio propugnemus*, 11:363–64; 227).

Such a historical survey, repeated in several of the orations, traces the situation down to Melanchthon's early sixteenth century. Would that such counselors as Irnerius and Bartolus were living today! For since the prince is the custodian of laws and justice and the state needs written law, he is not able properly to understand his responsibility without the voice and advice of experienced legal minds (*Cum enim Princeps sit custos legum et iusticiae, et*

Resp[ublica] habeat opus scripto iure, non potest sine voce, sine consilio Iurisconsulti recte tueri suum munus, 11:356; 220). Today, however, the written law is being challenged on every side. In the confusion of the day there are "Cyclops and Centaurs [Hutten's term for the uneducated knights]" who call law vacuous and would prefer to see kingdoms seized by force and arms and ruled by the whim of the powerful: *in tanta confusione rerum humanarum, hoc totum quid vocamus legem, et politicam sapientiam, dicunt inane nomen esse, vi et armis rapi imperia, et regi arbitriis potentum* (11:630; 234). But history has shown how tyranny prevails when the rule of law gives way, as in the years following Solon and Augustus. In the oration *De stricto iure et aequitate* (1544) and elsewhere, Melanchthon defends the strict construction of the written law against those who would replace it by "equity" and the whim of the judges. Of what use is law, he asks in a vivid image, if judges are permitted to create equity from themselves just as spiders weave webs from their own excretions? (*si iudicibus tantum liceret ex sese fingere aequitates, ut araneae ex sese telas texunt*, 11:671; 276). Indeed, equity is acceptable only in those cases when the written law does not deal explicitly with the matter (*cum incidit casus, de quo lex non principaliter loquitur*, 11:222; 232). By the same token, he resists oversubtle interpretations, by which clever lawyers seek to deceive the voice of law, play tricks on the eyes and minds of men, and cover truth with shadows (*eludere legum vocem, offundere praestigias oculis ac mentibus hominum, veritatem tenebris involuere*, 11:674; 279).

Worst of all, he cries in his oration *De legibus* (1550), are those "new lawmakers" (*illi novi Nomothetae*, 11:915; 249) who seek to do away with the tried and tested Roman law and to replace it with new laws. In this context Melanchthon tells a story that he repeats on other occasions. An ape who has spent many years in captivity escapes and returns to his jungles, telling his fellows about the wonders of human civilization. The apes resolve to build houses to protect themselves against the elements and walls to guard against their enemies. They send out the young apes to begin the task, but they discover that they have no tools for cutting the wood or shaping the stones. Since they lack the arts of architectonics, circumstances force them to desist from the project that they foolishly undertook (*Denique ars tota architectonica deerat. Res igitur cogit eas id, quod stulte instituerant, omittere*, 11:915; 249). Those who dream that they can create laws better than those of the Romans, he concludes, are like the foolish apes. Indeed, the humanist has nothing but contempt, in his oration *De studio linguarum* (1533), for those would-be jurists who know nothing of classical antiquity: these "simple Solons without grammar, without dialectics, without a knowledge of religions, without eloquence, without philosophy—in short, without any humanity" (11:236–37).

It is an ancient dispute, Melanchthon concedes, as to whether it is better to be ruled by the arbitrary decisions of rulers or by a strict written law. But he argues strongly in every case for written law because, as he says in endless variations, men can be mistaken or corrupted, but law is equivalent to a mind without cupidity (*lex est mens sine cupiditate*, 11:220; 230).

In his appreciation of the great glossators and commentators, as well as such contemporary jurisconsults as Hieronymus Schürpf, Melanchthon values the editorial efforts needed to restore the written text to its original sense and the commentaries required to enable us to understand Roman law in its proper context. Accordingly he praises the scholars who, following the restoration of Roman law from the libraries and into the courts, have constantly provided them with commentary: *Laudanda est igitur prudentia summorum virorum, qui postquam Imperatoris Lotharii tempore rursus ex bibliothecis prolatae sunt humanae leges, et in forum, ac curiam revocatae, statim addere commentarios coeperunt* (11:220–21; 231).

But he reserves his most profound contempt for those who willfully distort the law in the service of their rulers—a contempt that emerges most strikingly in the early oration *De legibus* (1525). This youthful declamation, one of his longest, written under the impact of the nihilist and anarchist turmoil of the peasants' revolution, constitutes Melanchthon's most energetic, brilliant, and passionate statement on law and, at the same time, a résumé of his thought.

Melanchthon begins by defining his topic: he is going to talk about law, and specifically, about the law that presently prevails in the schools, and in the courts, of a good part of Europe. This law has already for some time been under attack by those who claim that the profession of profane laws is not appropriate for good Christians. But the situation is worsened at present by those little pedants (*Doctorculi*, 11:67; 190) who, albeit themselves virtually godless, nevertheless under the pretext of the Gospels make the case for tyranny and arbitrarily make and remake human as well as divine laws (*Evangelii praetextu tyrannidem gerunt, et pro libidine cum humanas, tum divinas leges figunt ac refigunt*, 11:67; 190). After a discussion of divine law Melanchthon reminds his listeners that there has long been a dispute in the academies regarding written law versus the decisions of magistrates. He points out that many ancient peoples—the Egyptians, Cretans, Athenians, Romans, as well as the Jews—had written laws (11:73; 196). But of what use is the law if it is not constant? No one would think of putting his life in the hands of a custodian not adequately known or trusted. When magistrates make decisions according to their own judgment without fixed laws, when the law is left to the power of rulers who are often dishonest, it can happen that through inexperience a magistrate will fail to perceive the difference between right and wrong. How often does not the appearance of right deceive? how often does not favor or ill will interfere with the judgment? (*Quoties recti species decipit? quoties iudicio gratia aut malevolentia officit?* 11:74; 197). Only fixed laws can restrain men and magistrates alike from violence. One might wish that society were ruled everywhere by wise Nestors, but in fact there is a paucity of the best princes. To make his point, Melanchthon quotes a saying that he cites elsewhere: you could engrave the images of all good rulers on a single ring (*Omnium bonorum Principum imagines in uno annulo sculpi posse*, 11:75; 198). And good laws not only protect the innocent; they also protect the magistrates against the importunities of the mob.

Laws also protect us against the worst plague on our states, civil discord (*Quae est autem pestis civitatibus perniciosior intestina discordia?* 11:76; 199). To make this point Melanchthon surveys the history of Athens and Rome. Because of the great power of habit it is not possible without considerable public turmoil to change laws to which we are accustomed (*Magna consuetudinis vis est, quae mores omnes, quibus assuefacti sumus, sine perturbatione publica mutari non sinit*, 11:77; 200). At the same time, law also has a positive momentum toward forming good morals (*Id adeo ad formandos mores, magnum habet momentum*, 11:77; 200). It is no shame to borrow from others: the Greeks took from the Egyptians just as the Romans took from the Greeks. We have already borrowed much from the Romans: our alphabet, the telling of time and the stars, music, architecture. Who would deny that our culture is now richer than it was during the barbarian age? If we have imitated the Romans in so many areas, why should we not appropriate their laws? Melanchthon points out that the Saxon written law has already emended much from Roman laws (11:79; 202).

What is more foolhardy, he continues, than for men to take part in government if they have no training in letters or law? After all, actors and musicians would never appear on the stage without proper preparation. And in these matters it is better to follow the jurisconsults than the philosophers because the latter are accustomed in the academies to permit themselves certain liberties that would not be feasible in public affairs. To be sure, there are in Europe some peoples (he has the English in mind) who make judgments according to not Roman law but vernacular laws. Yet even there, those who are going to take part in public affairs often study Roman law abroad, saying that they take on the spirit of the law, that is, the power of righteousness, so as to make better use of the native laws. Its opponents claim that Roman law is fragmentary and the text often corrupt. But fortunately we still have retained enough to understand the larger meaning of the law. And if the adversaries argue that Roman law has been defiled and distorted by the commentaries and emendations, Melanchthon replies that he heeds the laws, not the modern interpreters, who are sometimes as ill-suited to the refinements of legal language as an ass to the lyre (*quam ad lyram asinus*, 11:82; 205). After all, since the laws are written in Latin, how can anyone be skilled in them who does not command the language?

The humanist Melanchthon then states that a great power lies in the study of human letters (*Magna vis est in humaniorum literarum studio*, 11:83; 206), and he tells a story to illustrate the ineptness of those modern lawyers with no command of language or logic. A certain miller owned an ass, which emerged from the mill one day and descended to the river for a drink of water. Since the water at the edge was too muddy or too shallow for drinking, the ass stepped into a nearby boat to get closer to pure water. But the boat tore loose from its moorings, floated downstream, and shattered on a rock, whereupon the ass drowned. The miller sued the fisherman for the loss of his ass, but the fisherman claimed damages for the loss of his boat. The case was fiercely contested on both sides by hired advocates (Melanchthon uses the unflattering word *rabula*, 11:83; 206). The judge regarded the case as too complicated to decide and, rather than consulting the professors of law, turned it over to the lawyers (*leguleius*), who, according to Melanchthon, are probably still arguing it. I ask you, he concludes, are they not mad who plague themselves for so long with so ridiculous a case? The situation is due to the ignorance of the court, which is unable to discern law or right in many cases (*iudicii inopiam accuso, qua fit, ut nec ius nec fas in plerisque causis cernant*, 11:84; 206–7). The only solution, he exhorts his listeners, is to "explode" the unlearned commentaries and, cleansing the law of filth and squalor, to restore it to its pristine splendor. (At this point, in 1525, Melanchthon has not yet come to the appreciation of the glossators and commentators that is apparent in his later orations, such as the one on Irnerius and Bartolus.)

Melanchthon concedes that there are some men of questionable morals among the professors. But it is wrong to impute to the law itself the shortcomings of a few individuals. He hopes to hand over the task of teaching law to the most learned and finest professors in order to expel the sly and sycophantic practitioners (*extrusis veteratoribus et sycophantis illis*, 11:84; 207) and restore the courts to the power of good and learned men. At present, however, the subject is taught mainly by untutored vulgarians who know nothing, but whose words are accepted by students who are "heads without tongues, ignorant of the law and the power of equity" (*Capita sunt sine linguis, ius ipsi et vim aequitatis ignorant*, 11:84; 207). The clever lawyer leads them all around by the nose like cattle (*Leguleius illa naribus omnes tanquam bubulos trahit*, 11:84; 207). Given the sloth of the judges, they worm their way into the courts and take on the cases of the most fatuous advocates, extract cases from other cases, flay their clients, defraud the state, and deceive the unlearned judge repeatedly with new tricks. This deplorable situation will change only when educated and incorruptible judges are trained to enter our courts. The sanctity of the law is second only to that of the Church. To reinforce the point that laws should not be changed, Melanchthon tells the story from Demosthenes that in the well-ordered state anyone proposing a change in the laws had to do so with a noose around his neck: thus, if the citizens objected, he could be hanged straightway. In this connection he reminds us that Athens had its Nomophylakes, guardians of the law, whose responsibility it was to see that nothing was decided against the received laws. The oration concludes with an exhortation to study the laws bequeathed to us by the most prudent and learned men of the principal republic of the world.

In sum, as a humanist Melanchthon strongly affirms the value of Roman law, but he displays his contempt for the uneducated judges of his day as well as for the sly lawyers (*leguleius*) who deceive the courts by their tricky interpretations and procedures. As an educator, therefore, he repeatedly stresses the need for jurors who are trained in both the law and its language, Latin; and he recognizes the importance of the scholarly commentators who have helped to restore Roman law to its essential purity. Through his popular orations, in fact, Melanchthon probably contributed more than anyone to the principle of *Professorenrecht* over *Juristenrecht*, which prevailed for several centuries in German law.

BRANT'S enormously popular chapbook, Reuchlin's widely read school play, Hutten's slashing satire, and Melanchthon's influential orations mirror the wide range of opinion aroused by the Reception of Roman law in early-sixteenth-century Germany. At the one extreme stands the knight Hutten with his scorn of all things foreign, including the Italians and their law; at the other the scholar Melanchthon with his reverence for all things classical, including Roman law. Between them Brant and Reuchlin hold the more moderate position of practicing lawyers required to deal with both systems and seeking to ease the transition from one to the other. But all four share a contempt for greedy plaintiffs, unscrupulous attorneys, ignorant *glossatores*, and corruptible judges. Each in his own way exposes the prevailing tension between reality and the ideal, between law and social morality. Finally, the variety of literary forms employed by the four humanists suggests the diversity of the contemporary audiences for whom the struggle between traditional customary law and the new Roman law represented a lively issue.

CHAPTER SEVEN

European Variations

THE URGENCY and centrality of legal issues among humanists in early-sixteenth-century Germany becomes strikingly evident if we consider for comparison several works of a similarly satirical nature by three prominent non-German contemporary humanists.

DESIDERIUS ERASMUS

Erasmus (1466–1536) was already acquainted with *Das Narrenschiff* in its Latin translation when he was contemplating his composition of *The Praise of Folly* (1511).[1] In 1509, the year he wrote his great satire at the home of his friend Thomas More, two different translations of Brant's work appeared in England: Henry Watson's *The Shyppe of folles* and Alexander Barclay's widely acclaimed *The Shyp of Folys of the Worlde*. Certainly Erasmus's sustained narrative—spoken by Folly herself, written in an elegant Latin prose, and profoundly indebted to the satires of Lucian, some of which he and More had translated just four years earlier—displays conspicuous differences from the late-medieval broadsheet verse of Brant's work. His catalog of fools, which extends far beyond Brant's essentially middle-class German society, also includes lawyers. But they are cited almost in passing, for the sake of the categories under discussion, and not with the passion of direct experience. At one point Folly argues that the disciplines of learning are useless for mankind. After all, the simple people of the Golden Age, living by instinct alone, had no need for dialectics, rhetoric, or science. "To what end would jurisprudence be required since there were no evil habits, from which no doubt good laws are born?" (*Quorsum requireretur legum prudentia, cum abessent mali mores, ex quibus haud dubie bonae leges prognatae sunt?*)[2] In short, the good society needs no laws, for laws are produced as a response to human evil. As the innocence of the Golden Age passed away, however, the disciplines were invented, and among these the ones most highly esteemed are those that most nearly approximate common sense—that is to say, folly (*quae ad sensum communem, hoc est, ad stulticiam quam proxime accedunt*, 742–43). Accordingly such theoreticians as the theologians go hungry, the physical scientists freeze, the astrologers are ridiculed, and the dialecticians are ignored. But physicians are valued in an inverse proportion to their learning. "Following these the next place is given to the pettifogging lawyers [*leguleiis*, 749], and perhaps they should have first place because the philosophers are unanimously accustomed to ridicule their profession as being asinine [*asininam*, 750]." Yet big deals and small ones are settled by the decision of these asses, and their estates grow while the learned theologians starve.

Another passage occurs later when Folly is listing her followers among the learned, where again the lawyers have earned first place (*Inter eruditos iureconsulti sibi vel primum vindicant locum*, 142, lines 348–53). No one else is so smug and complacent (*neque quisquam alius aeque sibi placet*) as they assiduously roll along their stone of Sisyphus, weaving together in the same breath countless laws, whether relevant or not; heaping gloss on gloss and opinion on opinion (*glossematis glossemata, opiniones opinionibus cumulantes*), they act as though their profession were the most demanding of all. For whatever is toilsome they regard as admirable.

In these two passages we hear little more than the disdain of the humanist contemptuous of the mindless pedantry of the *mos italicus*. The same Renaissance impulse *ad fontes* that motivated Erasmus to edit the Greek text of the New Testament (1516) generated his contempt for moneygrubbing lawyers who know only the commentaries and not the true texts of Justinian's law. But the law is a purely secondary concern for this Christian humanist.[3] Indeed, Erasmus's view of law is neatly summed up by the saying *summum ius, summa iniuria*, which was frequently cited by the humanists, and on which he included a brief commentary in his lexicon of proverbs, *Adagia*.[4] His most sustained statement on law occurs in chapter 6 of his *Institutio Principis Christiani* (1516), which concerns lawmaking ("De legibus condendis aut emendandis").[5] But Erasmus is concerned there not with any system of existing positive law nor with the reception of Roman law but, more generally, with the philosophy of law. Basically he believes with Plato that the good society should have as few laws as possible; that those laws should be consistent with the law of nature (= the will of God); and that the laws should be so clearly written that there should be no need for lawyers. *Expedit igitur, vt leges sint quam paucissimae, deinde quam aequissimae et ad publicam vtilitatem conducibiles. . . . Postremo vt verbis apertis minimeque perplexis descriptae, vt ne magnopere sit opus questuosissimo isto hominum genere, qui se iureconsultos vocant et aduocatos*.[6] Erasmus provides a prime example for those historians who argue that humanism, through its indifference to the practice of law, actually hindered the Reception and contributed to the fateful separation of *Professorenrecht* and *Juristenrecht* that has characterized jurisprudence in Germany ever since.[7]

In any case, when Erasmus wrote his *Moriae Encomium*—a Greek title punning on the name of his friend, Thomas More—he was fresh from a three-year sojourn in Italy, where like Hutten he had been dismayed by the corruption at the court of the warrior pope Julius II. Accordingly, the monastery-trained humanist, who had absolutely no practical training in or experience of law, devotes by far the most space to his satire of the Church, its hierarchy and its theologians. In comparison with that rich subject, the lawyers offer poor material for Folly's ridicule.

Sir Thomas More

Unlike his friend Erasmus, Sir Thomas More (1478–1535), to whom *The Praise of Folly* was dedicated, was himself a lawyer and the son of a lawyer. Educated at Oxford and then trained at Lincoln's Inn, he had a brilliant career at the bar before entering Parliament in 1504 and then becoming successively privy councillor and lord chancellor to Henry VIII. His *Utopia* (1516) is as much an exercise in political philosophy as is *The Praise of Folly* a satire against the Church. Yet although More mentions the law and lawyers more frequently than does Erasmus, he remains basically as much a legal nihilist as his friend. The citizens of Utopia have very few laws because, given their education, few are needed (*Leges habent perquam paucas. sufficiunt enim sic institutis paucissimae*).[8] They see that other peoples are unfairly bound by laws too numerous to read through and too obscure to be understood. Accordingly—as did Plato from his Republic and Erasmus from his Christian community—they exclude from their communist paradise all lawyers, who cunningly manipulate cases and slyly dispute the laws (*porro causidicos: qui causas tractent callide: ac leges uafre disputent: prorsus omnes excludunt*). Instead, each man pleads his own case before a wise judge, who weighs the facts and assists simple people against the accusations (*calumnias*) of the crafty. Other peoples find it difficult to achieve this situation because they are burdened by a huge mass of the most complex laws (*tanto perplexissimarum aceruo legum*). But in Utopia each citizen is himself an expert in the law (*legis peritus*). Moreover, their laws are very few, and they regard as most equitable the interpretation that is most straightforward (*Nam & sunt (ut dixi) paucissimae: & interpretationum praeterea ut quaeque est maxime crassa: ita maxime aequam censent*).

If the citizens of Utopia make short shrift of law and lawyers (bk. 2), the book's narrator, Raphael Hythlodaeus, makes amply clear the deficiencies of legal systems in other nations. Following his eulogy to Utopia he contrasts the equity of that land with the "justice" of other peoples, among whom he can make out no trace of true justice or equity (*Hic aliquis uelim cum hac aequitate audeat aliarum iustitiam gentium comparare, apud quas dispeream, si ullum prorsus comperio, iustitiae, aequitatisque uestigium*, 238, lines 19–21). Indeed, as he looks around at the commonwealths flourishing in the world, he perceives everywhere nothing but a conspiracy of the rich (*conspiratio diuitum*, 240, line 20) to exploit the poor by means of laws (*publicis etiam legibus abradunt*), which they then call justice (*prouulgata lege iustitiam*).

It is hardly surprising, therefore, that Hythlodaeus's portrait of the English lawyer who staunchly defends his country's legal system turns into a parody. This lawyer—a layman, that is, a nonecclesiastical lawyer (*laicus quidam legum uestratium peritus*, 60, line 6)—praises the strict justice (*rigidam illam iustitiam*) according to which thieves are punished in England and approvingly cites cases when twenty at a time have been hanged from the same gallows. Hythlodaeus launches into a passionate disagreement, in which he points out that death is an inappropriate penalty for the crime of theft, and that the unusual number of thieves for which England is notorious has been produced in no small measure by the enclosure laws; these laws, benefiting sheep owners, have made the land unfit for agriculture and have thus impoverished many peasants while enriching the idle nobility. During this harangue the lawyer has been preparing his response and has decided to employ the method of disputants who simply repeat what they have heard rather than answering (*qui diligentius repetunt quam respondent*, 70, lines 14–15). The *iuris consultus* announces his intention, first, to repeat what Hythlodaeus has just said; then to demonstrate how he was misled by his ignorance of local conditions; and finally to dissect and destroy all his arguments (*rationes tuas omnes diluam atque dissoluam*, 70, lines 20–21). At this point their host intervenes and we are spared the lawyerly disquisition. More has succeeded in a few quick words in characterizing an advocate who repeats by rote rather than thinking and whose entire principle of justice is a defense of the status quo.[9] Yet his satire is much more restrained than the depictions we have seen by the German humanists. Certainly More's rejection of law and lawyers in his Christian communist utopia was not a response to the Reception of Roman law but, rather, a result of his exercise in pure political philosophy.

This difference was immediately noticed by the French humanist and legal scholar Guillaume Budé, who wrote a prefatory letter that was attached to the 1518 and succeeding editions of *Utopia*. Budé is so excited by More's observations that he is moved to say that the object of the legal and civil arts and sciences (*legitimarum . . . & ciuilium artium ac disciplinarum*, 5–6) is simply by all available means to deprive one's neighbor of his possessions. But he immediately goes on to point out that this tendency is even more pronounced in the courts of those countries ruled by Roman law (*Id adeo magis in ijs gentibus apud quas iura, quae ciuilia & pontifica uocantur, amplius in utroque foro ualent*, 6, lines 7–9). He continues in a passage worthy of Hutten (9–17) to depict the lawyers who deal with unwary citizens as the bird catcher does his prey (*inconsultorum ciuium aucupes*), who are artists in legal formulas, that is, tricky phrases (*formularum, id est excipularum opifices*), practiced in contract law, fixers of suits (*litium concinnatores*), and in sum the lawyers of a controverted, perverted, and inverted law (*iurisque contrauersi, peruersi, inuersi, consulti*). We need go no further to understand that the French observer regarded the barristers of English common law, as portrayed by More, as rather bland in comparison with the pettifogging, moneygrubbing advocates of Roman law.

François Rabelais

We sense the difference when we cross the Channel again to look, finally, at Budé's younger contemporary, François Rabelais (1494?–1553). By an odd yet symptomatic coincidence, it is a letter from Budé that contains the first datable information about Rabelais's life.[10] Writing in 1521 in response to a letter from the Franciscan monastery of Fontenay-le-Comte, where Rabelais had taken orders, Budé remarks that the humanistically educated young friar will understand a particular legal situation since he has himself studied law: *Ut nosti, qui juris studiosus fuisti.*[11] It is of course familiar handbook knowledge that Rabelais was a monk who subsequently gave up his calling in order to study medicine and to pursue an eminently successful career as a practicing physician. However, Rabelais's own works along with Budé's letter and other biographical evidence have led recent scholars to believe that "it was the law that seems to have had the more profound and lasting effect on his way of thinking and writing."[12]

Rabelais had an early acquaintance with legal terminology and procedures because his father, a licentiate of laws, was employed as an advocate at the court of Chinon. It seems likely, in view of Budé's letter, that Rabelais had studied law prior to his entry into the monastery in 1520, and certainly his works bear evidence of his familiarity with the law faculties at Bordeaux, Toulouse, Bourges, and Orléans. At the time of Rabelais's stay, Fontenay-le-Comte was a center of humanistic legal studies surrounding such advocates as Amaury Bouchard and especially André Tiraqueau, one of the most distinguished legal scholars of the day, at whose house local humanists regularly assembled to discuss law, ethics, philosophy, and literature.[13] At the time when Rabelais was a member of this cenacle, Tiraqueau and Bouchard were engaged in a lively controversy stemming from Tiraqueau's work *De legibus connubialibus* (1513)—a humorously pedantic dispute that subsequently provided material for the discussions of Panurge's wedding plans in the third book of *Pantagruel*.

In 1524 Rabelais took the unusual step of transferring from the Franciscan friars to the Benedictine Order—a decision presumably prompted by Franciscan hostility toward humanistic studies—and moved to the Benedictine house at Saint-Pierre-de-Maillezais near Poitiers. Here again the young monk with encyclopedic interests was in luck: his closest friend and sponsor at Poitiers was the humanist and poet Jean Bouchet, by profession a *procureur* or attorney at the courts of Poitiers.[14] Through Bouchet, Rabelais met the legal society of the Palais de Justice, the judges, advocates, counselors, clerks, bailiffs, and other figures who were to people his chronicles of Gargantua and Pantagruel. (Poitiers was proverbial for its lawsuits and litigious citizens.)[15] The university at Poitiers, where Reuchlin had received his licentiate's degree in 1481, was distinguished at the time for its law faculty, where both canon and civil law were strongly represented. Whether or not Rabelais was actually enrolled as a student (as was Judge Bridoye in the third book of *Pantagruel*!), many details in the works make it clear that Poitiers was the source of much legal lore as well as the locale for many of the juridical scenes in his works. By the time the first volume appeared in 1532, Rabelais—whether formally trained in law or not—had a firm grasp not only of legal procedures in France but also of the standard works of Roman jurisprudence. Indeed, it has been pointed out that, when the original *Pantagruel* was published in Lyons, it had the appearance of a law tome, bearing on its title page the classical framework familiar from law books long published by two Lyonese legal booksellers.[16]

Legal parody informs all five books of *Gargantua and Pantagruel*. The fun begins early in *Gargantua* (which, though the second volume to be published [1534], is the first in sequence as the reader of the complete work encounters them). In view of the unusual circumstance that his gigantic hero spent eleven months in his mother's womb, the author (chap. 3) cites a number of literary sources, from Hippocrates, Pliny, and Plautus, to Aulus Gellius and Virgil, to demonstrate precedents for this phenomenon. Then he goes on to cite various legal authorities to prove the legitimacy of a child born eleven months after the death of its father: "*ff. De suis et legit., l. Intestato §fi*, and *in Autent. De restitut. et ea que parit in xj mense*." He goes on to adduce "*Gallus, ff. De lib. et posthu., et l. septimo ff. De stat. homi* and several others that for the moment I dare not mention."[17] We should pause at this point to discuss the implications of Rabelais's method of citation.

Rabelais employs, here and throughout the five books of his work, the abbreviations that were customary in sixteenth-century law. The sign *ff*, probably an alteration of the Greek letter Pi, signifies the *Pandects* or *Digest* of Justinian's *Corpus Iuris Civilis*. The letter *l* means "law"; and § indicates the "paragraph." In its expanded form, then, the first reference would read: *Digest, De suis et legitimis heredibus, lex: Intestato*, in the paragraph concerning *filii* ("Concerning one's own and legitimate heirs" in the law on "intestate" and the paragraph on "sons"). (In fact, the full reference would be: *Digest*, book 38, title 16, law 3, paragraph 9.)[18] The second reference specifies the *Authenticae* or *Novellae*—in this case number 39: *De restitutionibus et ea quae parit in undecimo mense post mortem viri* ("Concerning legal restitution and the woman who gives birth in the eleventh month after the death of her husband"). The third refers to the so-called Gallus Law cited in the *Digest* (28.2.29) under the title *De liberis et postumis heredibus instituendis vel exheredandis* ("Concerning the legitimation and disinheriting of children and posthumous heirs"). The last one refers to the paragraph of the title *De statu hominum* ("On the human condition") in the *Digest* (1.5.12), which specifies that, according to the authority of Hippocrates, a birth occurring in the seventh month after conception is legal (*Septimo mense nasci perfectum partum iam receptum est propter auctoritatem doctissimi Hippocratis*).

Opinion among Rabelais scholars concerning these and many other similar passages varies sharply. While it is unquestionably clear that Rabelais was himself familiar enough with Roman law to identify passages that served his comic purposes, it is uncertain to what extent he expected his readers to understand the jokes. Some authorities maintain that the legal references are so highly technical that they would have been incomprehensible to any but legal experts.[19] Others believe that the references are sufficiently clear to have made their point for readers living in the legal culture of France in the early sixteenth century.[20] I am inclined to agree with the latter group. In the first place, it is evident that in some cases no specific meaning is intended: the point of the reference is nothing but the reference itself, as when Rabelais cites simply book and chapter for Pliny, Aristotle, and Aulus Gellius. He presumably does not expect his readers to look up the passages but merely to laugh at the pedantically excessive degree of documentation. In the second place, it is equally evident that Rabelais expected his humanistically educated readers to be able to complete many of the citations. For instance, the quotation from Virgil that immediately precedes the legal citations discussed above is a half-line specified only as *Egl.*: *Matri longa decem, etc.* Any sixteenth-century reader would have been able to supply the second half of the line from the fourth *Eclogue*, perhaps the most famous poem of the Middle Ages (*Matri longa decem tulerunt fastidia menses*), and to discuss the identity of the mysterious child whose birth, following ten laborious months of pregnancy, is there prophesied. Similarly, any reader with a knowledge of Latin and the general legal culture would have understood the citations that immediately follow to concern the legal status of children when the father dies intestate and women who give birth in the eleventh month—in both cases, then, more than enough information for the intended joke. (We shall return to this matter in another connection.)

Whereas the passage just discussed uses legal terminology for purposes of comedy, another passage close to the end of *Gargantua* (chap. 54) introduces the theme of judicial satire. Above the main gate of the abbey of Thélème, which Gargantua builds and endows, is engraved a lengthy inscription specifying those who may and may not enter the premises. Conspicuous among the latter (in second place after hypocrites and bigots) are dishonest shysters, clerks, members of La Basoche (the corporate body for clerks of the Palais de Justice), all of whom exploit the people; and ecclesiastical judges, scribes and Pharisees, as well as judges who condemn good people to the charnel house:

> Cy n'entrez pas, maschefains practiciens,
> Clers, basauchiens, mangeurs du populaire,
> Officiaulx, scribes et pharisiens,
> Juges anciens, qui les bons parroiciens
> Ainsi que chiens mettez au capulaire. . . .

We know from Gargantua's letter, in the second book, to Pantagruel (chap. 8) that he expected his son, as a well-educated Renaissance man, to study civil law, to learn the texts of Justinian's *Code* by heart, and to understand their philosophical basis. To this end Pantagruel visits various universities before arriving at Bourges, where he studies long and benefits from the faculty of laws. Adding another dimension to the critique of law, he observes (chap. 5) that the law books resemble a beautiful robe of gold, sumptuous and dazzling, but bordered with excrement ("brodée de merde"):

> "Car (disoit-il) au monde n'y a livres tant beaulx, tant aornés, tant élégans comme sont les textes des *Pandectes*: mais la brodure d'iceulx, c'est assavoir la *Glose de Accurse*, est tant salle, tant infâme et punaise, que ce n'est que ordure et villenie."
>
> ("For [he said] no books on earth are more beautiful, more ornate, more elegant than the texts of the *Pandects*: but the edgework—that is to say, the glosses of Accursius—is as filthy, as sordid, as noisome as ordure and dirt.")

Having become accomplished in the law, Pantagruel resolves (chaps. 10–13) the great legal dispute between Monsieur de Baysecul (Lord Kissass) and Monsieur Humevesne (Lord Whiffair)—a suit that for more than forty-six weeks had perplexed a special court consisting of the four greatest tribunals in France, the wisest university scholars of France, England, and Italy, as well as a host of other legal scholars ("Rabanistes"). Pantagruel agrees to adjudicate the case. But first he points out that they have obscured the case by applying the foolish reasons and inept opinions of the Italian commentators who never understood the least thing about the *Pandects*: "vous l'avez obscurcie par sottes et desraisonnables raisons et ineptes opinions de Accurse, Balde, Bartole, de Castro, de Imola, Hippolytus, Panorme, Bertachin, Alexandre, Curius et ces aultres vieulx mastins qui jamais n'entendirent la moindre loy des *Pandectes*." The entire heap of commentary, he adds, is nothing but chicanery, subversions of the law based on Cepola's textbook of diabolical legal ruses. Discarding the huge accumulation of documentation, Pantagruel permits the plaintiff and the defendant to address the court in their own words—words so utterly jumbled as to be an incomprehensible parody of legal language and procedure. Having heard them patiently and politely, Pantagruel then, using the most pedantic legal terminology, renders his judgment in language equally opaque, ending with the verdict that the two disputants should henceforth be friends, without costs and for cause. Both parties are satisfied with the judgment; the attending jurisconsults are ecstatic in their admiration of Pantagruel's wisdom, and the judgment is immediately printed, distributed to the world at large, and filed in the archives of the Palais de Justice. Rabelais makes clear through this comic lawsuit his opinion on pedantic legal terminology, on the ignorance of the glossators and commentators of *mos italicus*, and—in the opinion of one scholar—on the contemporary wrangling in the Paris Parlement on the limits of papal and royal authority.[21] It amounts to a comic variation of Melanchthon's critique.

The work contains many other examples of legal comedy. In book 4 Pantagruel journeys to the land of Procuration, where he encounters the "Procultous" (in Panurge's intentional deformation, which emphasizes the syllable "cul" [= "posterior"], a vulgar term for lawyers) and the "Chiquanous" (a pun on the root for "chicanery"). In these scenes (chaps. 12–16) Rabelais portrays a comic, and rather sadistic, inversion of the fact that, in France at the time, minor legal officials were often swollen with self-importance and were often assaulted for their insolence (as we observed earlier in the case of the first two messengers bearing summonses to Renart). The Chiquanous, Pantagruel learns, earn their living by hiring themselves out to be beaten. When a monk, priest, usurer, or advocate wishes harm to some gentleman, he sends a Chiquanou, who serves a summons upon him, insults him, and abuses him according to instructions. The gentleman, reacting normally, cudgels the rascal, whereupon the Chiquanou receives a reward sufficient to support him and his family for four months, while the gentleman must pay excessive damages so as not to end up in prison. In the fifth book (chaps. 11–15), finally, Pantagruel's travels bring him to the island named "Guichet" (= the wicket-gate of a prison), where his crew fall into the hands of the Chats-fourrez (the Furry Lawcats, named for the ermine gowns of court officials) and the sinister judge Grippe-minaud (a name that suggests a tomcat eager to seize prey in its claws). On this island, where corruption is the sole livelihood, the judge's every second word is "or ça!"—an expression that, taken in innocence, is a filler meaning no more than "eh! bien"; but which, in light of the judge's rapacious character, suggests "money here!"[22] (It is worth noting that this episode, first published posthumously in 1562, is the only legal satire in the whole work that displays genuine nastiness, in contrast to the manic gaiety of most earlier passages. This difference in tone, along with various other factors, has led many Rabelais scholars to question the authenticity of the entire fifth book.)

By far the most outrageously comic treatment of the law occurs in the famous episode in book 3 concerning Judge Bridoye (chaps. 39–44)—an episode that has been singled out as a striking example of Rabelais's style, which links reality to fantasy, coarse vulgarisms to erudition.[23] The judge's name, which is rendered as Bridlegoose in the English translations, literally designates a naive person capable of being led by the nose like a bridled horse (and thereby strikingly recalls Melanchthon's characterization of lawyers in *De legibus* [cited above]: *Leguleius illa naribus omnes tanquam bubulos trahit*). But Judge Bridoye's simplemindedness turns out to be not stupidity but something resembling *sancta simplicitas*.[24] Bridoye, we learn, has been sitting as judge for forty years and during that time has rendered over four thousand decisions, every one of which was appealed and then sustained by the high court. Now, for the first time, that same court has upheld the appeal against the decision that Bridoye rendered against a certain tax-assessor. Pantagruel, as an old friend of the judge, attends the trial at which Bridoye is asked by the Court of One Hundred Judges to explain and defend his decision.

The following chapters revolve entirely around procedure; we never learn the details of the case. The elderly Bridoye begins by conceding that his deteriorating vision was no doubt a factor in the case. When he sought to read the dice by which he meant to decide the case, he mistook a four for a five and ended up with the wrong decision. When the high president of the court asks in astonishment what dice he was talking about, it turns out that Bridoye had always been greatly impressed by the judicial saying concerning the hazards of justice (*alea judiciorum*). But taking the word *alea* literally rather than figuratively, he had invariably—for forty years and in over four thousand cases—decided his cases by a throw of the dice. When the high president inquires into his procedures, Bridoye explains at length, interjecting frequently that he proceeds "just as all of you do" ("comme vous aultres, messieurs"). The following paragraphs are filled with comic detail based on an intimate acquaintance with contemporary legal procedure:

> "First, I view and review, read and re-read, ponder, weigh, thumb and digest the bills of complaint, subpoenas, appearance by proxy, reports of hearings, investigations, instruments of deposition, petitions, articles of evidence, allegations, rejoinders, rebuttals, requests, inquests, surrejoinders, surrebuttals, confirmation of former testimony, acts, writs, bulls, exceptions taken, grievances, objections, counter-objections . . . confrontation of witnesses and accused; confrontation of the various co-accused . . . certificates, libels and apostoles requesting the judge to refer the case to another court . . . letters of attorney; royal letters; instruments of compulsion, forcing a clerk to produce a document . . . declinatories, questioning the court's competence . . . anticipatories, arguing the opponent's probable pleas . . . references to other jurisdictions . . . returns of cases to the judges that had referred them . . . conclusions, accessory contestations, appointments, appeals, confessions, notifications or executions of sentence . . . and all other such spiceries and sweetmeats."[25]

When the president asks why all these procedures and documents are necessary, since Bridoye ultimately bases his decision on a throw of the dice, Bridoye explains that, first, the proper forms must be observed; second, it involves a healthy amount of physical exercise; and, third, a certain expenditure of time is required to bring the case to maturity.

"Accordingly, like yourselves, gentlemen, I put off, delay and postpone my definitive sentence, so that the suit, having been thoroughly sifted, winnowed and thrashed out, may, in process of time, attain its full maturity. Thus, when the fatal throw of the dice takes place, the condemned party will bear its misfortune more cheerfully, according to *no. glo. ff. de excu. tut., l. Tria onera.*"[26]

Illustrating his argument with exemplary stories and proverbs, Bridoye explains that a lawsuit is at its inception "informe et imperfaict" (chap. 42), consisting of only one or two documents.[27] "But heap writ upon writ, pack and pile brief upon brief, and your lawsuit may be termed full-sinewed and well-boned."[28] He cites a current legal commonplace or brocard (the term *brocard* derived from "Burchard," the name of an eleventh-century bishop of Worms who made a compilation of canon law) to make his point:

Litigando jura crescunt;
Litigando jus acquiritur.

(Laws grow through litigation; the law accrues through litigation.)

When Bridoye has completed his defense, the court asks Pantagruel to pass judgment (chap. 43). Pantagruel points out that any proper decision must take into account not only Bridoye's advanced age and ingenuousness ("simplesse") but also his unblemished record of forty years. He therefore proposes that Bridoye give satisfaction to the injured party (a sum that he offers to pay himself) and that the court appoint a learned young lawyer to assist Bridoye in his office and to decide all future cases. If the court should decide to remove Bridoye altogether, then Pantagruel would be delighted to employ a man of his character in his own affairs.

In the final chapter of this episode (chap. 44) Pantagruel discusses the matter with his friend Epistemon. Conceding that in many cases the legal circumstances are so ambiguous that judgment by dice could not fail to be correct, he is nevertheless astonished that Bridoye was able to maintain his record for forty years. Epistemon—and here he defines the qualities of the good judge—suggests that Bridoye was so decent and sincere, so diffident about his own knowledge and capacities and so conscious of the antinomies and contradictions of the law, edicts, customs, and ordinances, that he appealed to God as the Just Judge, invoking his celestial grace and relying on the sacrosanct spirit with regard to the hazards and perplexity of definitive sentences. Accordingly, the Motivating Intelligences of the universe would cause the dice to fall to the advantage of the just party. In short, the divine will manifests itself through chance. Epistemon concludes that the iniquity and corruption of the judges in the *parlement* is so conspicuous that any decision by dice, no matter how it might fall out, would be as valid as a judgment passing through their bloody hands and perverse intentions. In a final slap at the glossators, Epistemon points out that the entire basis for their code was provided by Tribonian, a impious heathen, who was so pernicious, so perverse, so greedy, and so evil that he sold the law, pure and simple, to the highest bidder. In this manner he fashioned a legal fabric made up of scraps of laws while suppressing and abolishing the substance without which the law cannot form a whole—and he did this out of fear that, if the law remained whole and if people saw the books of the ancient jurisconsults on the explication of the Twelve Tables and the edicts of the Praetorians, his wickedness would be exposed to the public. The entire episode concludes with a passage startlingly reminiscent of Brant's image in his *Narrenschiff* of the fool with his hackles. It would be better, Epistemon states, for parties at law to walk upon caltrops ("chausses-trapes") than to submit their case to judges trained in this way. Epistemon cites Cato, who wished that the judicial courts of ancient Rome might be paved with caltrops.

The episode of Bridoye features, then, a fundamentally decent judge who arrives invariably at the correct decision explicitly by disregarding the cumbersome legal authorities that, out of respect for legal form, he lovingly and patiently assembles. Indeed, his use of dice to make his decisions excludes the very corruption that Rabelais otherwise indicts, and the failure in the case under discussion was not a failure of procedure but of eyesight. (It is important to note that decision by means of dice was at the time considered legally acceptable under certain conditions.)[29] Rabelais does not then simply savage the *mos italicus*; he portrays the ideal of the good judge who is in harmony both with the forces that determine the fall of the dice and, instinctively, with the principles of Roman law before they were contaminated by centuries of glosses, beginning with the very act of assembling the *Corpus Iuris Civilis*.[30]

The attack on the glossators is rendered comical, however, and not savage by its presentation: it is not shown being manipulated for sinister purposes by evil judges but being made irrelevant by good-hearted Judge Bridoye. It has been calculated that Bridoye's defense contains 121 legal references (including two repetitions) to Roman law, both civil and ecclesiastical; and one scholar, in an impressive display of learning, has identified the original sources in contemporary juridical literature for almost all (111) of them.[31] Now it is hardly surprising that Bridoye should be familiar with such references. After all, he obtained his legal schooling, as he tells us (chap. 41), at Poitiers, one of the most distinguished legal faculties in France. Accordingly the citations flow trippingly from his tongue (and without the explanatory expansions often included in modernizations and translations), as when he adduces (chap. 39) judicial support for his use of dice: *Doct. 26 q. ij. c. Sors; l. nec emptio. ff. de contrah. empt. l. quod debetur. ff. de pecul. et ibi Barthol.*—which conflates more or less relevant passages from Gratian's *Decretum*, the *Digesta*, and a gloss by Bartolus.

The question that has vexed the scholars is the extent to which Rabelais expected his readers to understand such references. Derrett concludes that the author "deliberately chose citations some of which many of his readers would know slightly or well, some of which a few of his readers would at once recognise, and some of which no reader would grasp unless he took down the book from the shelf."[32] However, Screech has made a convincing case for assuming that in fact the majority of Bridoye's references amount to legal maxims that would have been instantly familiar to most of the readers educated enough to appreciate his volumes—that, in fact, "the humour of the episode lies above all in Bridoye's abuse of commonplaces."[33] Screech points out that "legal knowledge was much more widely spread in the XVIth century than to-day." Most literate men had at least a minimal acquaintance with the law; humanists studied Roman law as an important aspect of classical civilization. The frequent citational abbreviations, which are confusing to modern eyes, would have presented no problem to Rabelais's readers.

But the main point of Screech's argument rests in his conviction that any educated man would have been familiar with most of the principal legal brocards. The fact that so many of his images and quotations appear in the works of such contemporaries as Brant and Melanchthon would seem to support this view.[34] No more than a basic knowledge of law of the sort available to any literate person of the age—if not Reuchlin's pupils, then certainly Melanchthon's students—was required for the appreciation of Rabelais's legal humor. The key, Screech suggests, lies in Bridoye's reference to his teacher at Poitiers, *Brocardium juris*, which is an allusion to a compilation of legal commonplaces entitled *Brocardia Juris* or *Brocardica Juris*.[35] This collection was often printed along with a similar compilation entitled *Flores Legum*, sometimes preceded by an introduction to the law and followed by a checklist of legal titles (*Tituli legales*) of the sort cited by Bridoye in his references. Screech has determined that "well over half the brocards actually quoted *verbatim* in Rabelais may be traced to these primers,"[36] which appeared in many editions between 1477 and 1536. Most of the others can be found in a few other well-known contemporary collections: notably Albericus de Rosate's *Lexicon utriusque Juris*, James Spiegel's *Lexicon Juris Civilis*, John Bellonus's *Communes Juris Sententiae*, and finally the *Commentarii de nobilitate et de jure primogeniorum* by Rabelais's friend Tiraqueau.

By 1546, when the third book was published, Rabelais was writing under circumstances utterly different from those that had motivated Sebastian Brant half a century earlier. Unlike Brant, who wrote for a public still largely ignorant of Roman law, Rabelais could count on an audience to whom the principles and procedures of that law were generally familiar. In contrast to the dark and vicious satire of the Germans, Rabelais remained (with the exception of the fifth book) on the lofty plane of high comedy. The distinction is important. Rabelais was familiar with most of the predecessors we have discussed. It is assumed by some scholars that Rabelais knew Brant's *Narrenschiff* at least in its French imitation by Robert de Balsac,[37] and that the more scurrilous tone of the fifth book is specifically due to the influence of the German work.[38] It has even been suggested that Bridoye's explanation of judicial hazard may be indebted to Brant's glosses in his edition of the *Decretum Gratiani*.[39] Rabelais refers frequently to the farce of *Pathelin*, which was Reuchlin's source; he alludes to More's *Utopia*, notably in *Pantagruel* (chap. 2), where it is recounted that Gargantua married the daughter of the king of the Amaurotes in Utopia. In 1532 Rabelais wrote an adulatory letter to Erasmus as the *pater amantissimme*[40] whose teachings have educated him; Erasmus's *Moriae Encomium* inspired many passages in the third book (Panurge's madness), and his *Adagia* constituted yet another important source for commonplaces quoted in the chronicles. Like many of his fellow humanists in other countries—Erasmus, More, Melanchthon—Rabelais admired and translated the satires of Lucian. And like other humanists he was appalled at the ignorance of the glossators, who defiled the *fontes* of classical antiquity with their irrelevant commentaries. But he never attacks Roman law per se, as did Hutten and other German nationalists. Rabelais would never have agreed that *summum ius, summa iniuria*. Instead, his criticism addresses itself to human weakness or malignity, which causes men to serve the law badly. Even in his most pointed attacks he manages to rise above the bitterness of satire to a sublime humor. In part this is due to the fact that the Reception in France took place, as we noted earlier, much less drastically than in Germany and yet more fully than in England.[41] The high comedy of the Tiers Livre represents the conclusion of a development that began half a century earlier with the rancor that greeted the initial incursions of Roman law into Germany. Rabelais was writing for a more highly educated audience than the masses who eagerly devoured Brant's chapbook verse. But he would have been unable to write about law and lawyers with equal ease and gaiety had he not been writing at the culmination of a European tradition that stretched back into the fifteenth century.

It is the ambivalent attitude toward customary law and Roman law alike that explains why, in the course of the sixteenth century, the image of Justitia began to show up, in paintings and sculptures on many public buildings, both with and without a blindfold—and in some cases as Janus-headed. Amid the clash of two great systems and in their distrust of both, the peoples of Europe were torn between two ancient attitudes: the noble Justinian belief that *Justitia est constans et perpetua voluntas ius suum cuique tribuens* and the cynical proverbial view that *summum ius, summa iniuria*. We shall have occasion to observe how Shakespeare exploited these two competing images to powerful dramatic effect.

CHAPTER EIGHT

Law and Equity I

PROBABLY no work in the history of world literature has been more assiduously debated by students of literature and law than that powerful fable of conflicting sexes, generations, laws, and religions in which a passionate and articulate young woman in the name of kinship and reverence advances the claims of equity and the mercy of unwritten tradition against the will of an older man who, in the name of civil order, demands the fulfillment of the law in all its rigor. I am speaking of course of *Antigone*—but also of *The Merchant of Venice*. We should not be misled by the reversal of roles—in one case the older man is the judge and in the other the younger woman—or by the fact that the heroine of Sophocles' tragedy dies and is followed into death by her fiancé Haemon while in Shakespeare's "comedy" Portia returns to Belmont and the embraces of her animated Bassanio. Both Shylock and Creon, widowed and rejected by their only offspring, are condemned to tragic survivals in which they must contemplate a costly wisdom purchased through suffering and a violation of their religious convictions. Portia, whose character is set in relief by her companion Nerissa, is no less relentless and self-righteous in her mission than Antigone in contrast to Ismene.

But the comparison is by no means merely "intertextual" in the loose sense in which the term is sometimes used. Both works appear at the same relative stage in the legal evolution of Athens and England. As a scholar of legal history has pointed out, "Western Europe was not ready to understand or absorb [the literature of classical Athens] till the fifteenth century."[1] If *Hamlet*, as a work portraying a stage in the progression from revenge to law,[2] might be fruitfully compared to *The Eumenides*, *The Merchant of Venice* enables us no less than *Antigone* to appreciate the conflict between law and equity in Athenian and Elizabethan society.[3] Moreover, we shall be able to make out a distinct chain of intellectual history linking *Antigone* to *The Merchant of Venice* and exposing Shakespeare's play virtually as a satirical inversion of Sophocles' tragedy.

ANTIGONE AS POLITICAL ICON

The figure of Antigone has fascinated readers and audiences for some twenty-five hundred years. The popularity of her story in classical antiquity is suggested by the many references in the course of seven centuries not just in

Greek and Roman drama but also in epic and lyric poetry, as well as scenes portrayed on vases, funeral urns, decorative reliefs, and sarcophagi.[4] As for the past two hundred years, George Steiner has observed that "It is not obvious that there is another work of literature which has elicited the strengths of philosophic and poetic interest focused on Sophocles' *Antigone* during the late eighteenth and the nineteenth centuries."[5] Sophocles' tragedy is the (largely unspecified) subtext in Hegel's *Phenomenology of Spirit* (*Phänomenologie des Geistes*, 1807). At the beginning of chapter 6, discussing the spirit that has not yet been alienated from itself by culture, Hegel argues that the ethical world ("die sittliche Welt") displays in its realization two aspects, human and divine law, which are exemplified by man and woman. It becomes evident from his quotation of a line from the play (*Antigone* 926) that Hegel identifies these aspects with Creon and Antigone and that he sees the outcome of Sophocles' tragedy as a synthesis reconciling the opposing thesis and antithesis. "Only in the mutual submission [*in der gleichen Unterwerfung*] of both aspects is absolute law/right [*Recht*] accomplished and the ethical substance emerges as the negative power that encompasses both aspects—or almighty and righteous destiny."[6]

The preoccupation with Sophocles' drama has continued unabated into the late twentieth century, wherein it has become par excellence exemplary for the resistance to tyranny.[7] It is remarkable, for instance, that *Antigone* was performed some 150 times in Nazi Germany in sixteen different productions between 1939 and 1944.[8] The performances were mounted as part of Germany's effort to preserve Western culture in the face of threatening barbarian hordes, and they were sufficiently archaized that any contemporary relevance was obscured for the general audience. Philosophically informed viewers saw in them a confirmation of the Hegelian idea that Creon represents the interests of state security against an unthinking Antigone who, caught up in her personal piety, makes no effort to understand the political realities that motivate the ruler. Still others, including the students of the "White Rose" group in Munich, savored the performances as a symbolic act of resistance against the oppressive dictatorship. The *Antigone* that Jean Anouilh produced in Paris in 1944 was tolerated by the Nazis, despite a heroine who clearly was meant to represent the French resistance, because the figure of Creon just as clearly exemplified the tragic dilemma of the German occupation authorities. For his postwar adaptation of *Antigone* (1948), Bertolt Brecht wrote a brief prelude highlighting the timeliness of the ancient drama: two sisters in Berlin in the closing hours of the war (April 1945) are apprehended by an SS officer in the act of cutting down their brother, who has been hanged on a meat hook for his activities in the resistance—a scene that prefigures Brecht's violent adaptation of Hölderlin's translation of Sophocles' original. Six years later an admirer of Brecht, the Swiss dramatist Friedrich Dürrenmatt, came to the even more depressing conclusion that in the totally bureaucratized states of postwar Europe "Creon's secretaries deal with the case of Antigone."[9]

Within the past two decades *Antigone* has been hailed by spokesmen from opposite political poles. In 1978 the left-liberal German writer Heinrich Böll wrote a brief satirical sketch entitled "The Postponed Antigone" in which a projected film of Sophocles' drama is rejected by a committee, comprising representatives from various political parties and church groups, on the grounds that Antigone and Ismene are "female terrorists" and that the play will be misunderstood by young people as "an exhortation to subversion."[10] Only a year later the French New Right philosopher Bernard-Henri Lévy, in *Le Testament de Dieu* (1979), presented Creon sympathetically—not as "the simple representative of a cold reason of state" but as a priest "occupying by himself the entire field of the sacred as it was conceivable in a city like Athens in the late fifth century B.C."[11] In performances of *Antigone* during the 1980s in such East Bloc countries as Poland and the German Democratic Republic, Creon was played as the embodiment of an old-style socialism blinded by its own dogma while Antigone exemplified the fresh breezes of Solidarity and Glasnost.[12] All in all, readers of the past two centuries have tended to regard Sophocles' tragedy as a mirror in which they see reflected their own concerns and ideologies. They have rarely troubled to locate the work within the context of contemporary Athenian law.

Antigone in Context

Few of the unwritten laws of Greek antiquity match in urgency the sacred commandment to bury the dead. The reason underlying this solemn duty is made clear in *Iliad* 23 when the ghost of Patroclus, slain earlier by Hector, appears in a dream to Achilles and appeals to him for a quick burial. Until he has been properly buried, the souls of the dead deny him entry into Hades and require him to wander alone before its gates. Even the rage of blood enemies cannot resist this powerful law: for which reason Achilles (in *Iliad* 24) restores to Priam the body of his hated antagonist Hector, whom he has recently slain and dragged around the walls of Troy. We know from Aeschines' oration *Against Timarchus* (ca. 345 B.C.) that Solon promulgated a law requiring a son to bury his father and perform the other customary funeral duties, even in cases when the father has abused his paternal responsibilities by hiring out the son for prostitution.[13] Executed criminals in Athens, though their bodies were tossed into a cleft beyond the Acropolis (the notorious *barathron*), could be recovered for burial by their relatives. The only two exceptions are consistent with the principle, known from legal anthropology, that the crimes which in any society first became of interest to the state involved incest, treason, and sacrilege: the bodies of traitors and of temple desecrators were exempt—though in practice they were simply tossed outside the city walls, where they could be taken by relatives for burial elsewhere.[14] In addition, as Thucydides informs us (4.97 and 5.11), during the general decline of morals resulting from the Peloponnesian Wars it was not uncommon for enemies to hold the bodies of the slain for many days, presumably to demoralize the enemy.

The conflict between this sacred commandment and the equally compelling law denying burial to offenders against the city sometimes produced a dilemma—and not only in Greece. In the apocryphal Book of Tobit the narrator tells us that, during his capitivity in Nineveh, he was forced to flee to escape the wrath of the king who discovered that Tobit was secretly burying the bodies of fugitives from Judea who had been killed and thrown outside the walls of the city. It is precisely this dilemma that provides the focal point for Sophocles' *Antigone*, a drama based on a local Theban myth still so undeveloped that Sophocles was free to use it as he chose in order to thematize an issue of great concern to him and his age.[15] Even if by Sophocles' time there had occurred a weakening of the strictly legal requirement concerning burial of the dead, it can be regarded as an even more powerful statement by Antigone (and Sophocles) in support of the ancient religious custom that she takes her obligation so seriously.[16] (Sophocles had already dealt with a similar issue concerning burial in his *Ajax*.) The fact that Antigone is able to satisfy her obligation by sprinkling a handful of dust on her brother's corpse underscores the symbolic importance of the act.

THE BACKGROUND to the action is familiar from other sources. Oedipus and Jocasta, following their fateful marriage, had four children: two sons, Eteocles and Polynices, and two daughters, Antigone and Ismene. Following the disclosure of Oedipus's crime and his ensuing deposition his sons agreed to share their royal inheritance by ruling over Thebes in alternate years. Having incurred their father's displeasure, however, they were cursed by him to die by each other's hand. When Eteocles completed his first year of kingship, he refused to make way for Polynices, who in the meantime had married the daughter of Adrastus, the king of Argos. Adrastus assembled an army headed by seven great warriors, the fabled Seven against Thebes, to pursue the rights of his son-in-law. Each of the seven champions led the attack against one of the seven gates of Thebes, which in turn were defended by Theban heroes. Eteocles himself took the gate attacked by Polynices. In the ensuing battle the Argive army was defeated, but the two brothers—in fulfillment of their father's curse—fell each at the other's hand, whereupon the rule of Thebes was assumed in normal succession by their maternal uncle, Creon.

This is the point at which the Sophoclean *Antigone* begins. (Euripides in his *Suppliants* and in the fragments of his own *Antigone* offers a radically different version of the events.) It is still night, and Antigone has summoned her sister Ismene outside the gates of the royal court to inform her of the proclamation just issued by Creon in his new office as commander or governor (*stratêgos*). Having ordered Eteocles to be buried "with righteous justice and according to law" (*syn dikêi . . . dikaiai kai nomôi*, lines 23–24), he has forbidden any Theban, under pain of death by public stoning, to bury the traitor Polynices. (Death by stoning was the customary punishment for harboring traitors.)[17] Despite this edict Antigone announces her intention to perform funeral rites for her brother and invites her sister to join her. Ismene, more timorous than Antigone, objects that she could not possibly carry out an act prohibited for the city (*aporrêton polei*, 44). She imagines the frightful death to which they would be condemned for acting in violation of the law (*nomou biai*, 59) and reminds her sister that they are mere women, too frail to oppose men. Introducing a motif that will occur frequently in the course of the drama, she uses the term "mindless" or "senseless" to designate Antigone's rash purpose (*ouk echei noûn oudena*, 68)—an accusation of madness that will subsequently be echoed both by Creon and by the chorus. Coldly rejecting her sister's timid evasions, Antigone states that she regards it as more important to please the dead than the living and that she has no intention of dishonoring the practices honored by the gods (*ta tôn theôn entim'*, 77). She rushes off to carry out the task that Ismene twice characterizes as "impossible" (*amêchana*, 90, 92).

Just as the sun rises, the chorus of Theban elders enters singing a hymn of thanks to Nike, who has brought victory to Thebes against the forces of Polynices that had hovered over the city like a bloodthirsty war eagle. At the approach of Creon, whom they, in contrast to Antigone, honor with the title of king (*basileus*, 155), they wonder why he has summoned this special assembly. Creon congratulates the elders for their unwavering loyalty to the royal family of Thebes: Laius, Oedipus, Eteocles, and (until his treason) Polynices. He now claims that same loyalty for himself even though he has not yet had the opportunity to prove himself—in character, in wisdom, in judgment—in the most appropriate way: by his skill in ruling and making laws (*archais te kai nomoisin*, 177). Explicating his own principles, Creon calls Zeus to witness that he could never befriend a man who threatens the city because the city-state is the greatest security (*hêd' estin hê sôzousa*, 189). Thus he justifies his first important proclamation: to bury with full honors Eteocles, who lost his life defending the city; and to leave unburied, as carrion for the birds and dogs, the body of the traitorous Polynices. The chorus concedes Creon's authority to make that ruling, and he in turn asks for their support against anyone who breaks the law.

At this point a rather clownish sentry rushes in to announce that Polynices' body has been given funeral rites—a sprinkling of dust—just before sunrise by persons unknown. The chorus suggests that the shocking deed might well be the work of the gods. But Creon angrily rejects any suggestion that the gods would wish to honor the man who attacked the city with the intention of burning their temples and abusing their laws. He claims, with the first hint of the paranoid suspiciousness that eventually consumes him, that it must have been a conspiracy of citizens, opposed to him and corrupted by money, who commissioned the deed. Threatening the sentry with torture and death, he sends him off to catch the culprit.

As Creon and the sentry leave the scene, the chorus sings its great Ode to Man, a recapitulation of human development from savagery to civilization that culminates in praise of those who succeed in interweaving secular laws with the oath-bound justice of the gods (*nomous perainôn chthonos theôn t'enorkon dikan*, 368–69). Such men rise to great glory in their cities (*hypsipolis*, 370). But the man who rashly practices evil will suffer the fate that in the eyes of the Greeks was the worst: he will be "uncitied" (*apolis*, 370).

As they end their magnificent ode, the sentry returns with Antigone, who has been caught in the act of consecrating her brother's corpse yet a second time with dust and libations. When Creon interrogates her, she defiantly confesses, acknowledging in particular that she was fully aware of the proclamation prohibiting such reverence, and goes on to justify her deed in a statement on "unwritten" and man-made law to which we shall return for closer analysis. Assuming that Antigone was assisted by her sister, Creon sends for Ismene, determined that they shall both suffer the specified punishment. Meanwhile Antigone cries out for death, saying that she has already earned glory by burying her brother and arguing that Hades demands the same rites for all the dead. When Creon objects that a distinction must be made between friends and enemies, Antigone utters the famous words: "Not to separate in hatred was I born, but to join in love" (*outoi synechthein, alla symphilein ephyn*, 523). When Ismene is brought in, she seeks to accept a share of the guilt, but Antigone harshly rejects her support, calling on Hades to testify to her sole accomplishment of the deed. Creon, still convinced that both sisters are guilty, dismisses with dark jokes Ismene's appeal to the fact that Antigone is betrothed to his son and sends them off to await their punishment.

Following the chorus's second ode (on the uncertainty of human destiny) Haemon enters and at first appears to accept his father's harsh judgment against the sisters. Pleased by his son's apparent filial submission, Creon delivers himself of a homily on the need for absolute civic obedience. Arguing that dread anarchy is the greatest of evils, he asserts that the ruler's commands must be obeyed unquestioningly, whether right or wrong. With great rhetorical skill Haemon praises his father's wisdom and at the same time suggests that human fallibility is possible. He reports that the citizens of Thebes, though afraid to say so publicly, secretly agree with Antigone. Urging Creon not to assume that the whole world is wrong and he alone in the right, Haemon tells his father that it is not shameful even for a wise man to learn new things. He implores his father to relent, and the chorus supports his gesture toward moderation. But Creon, angered at being lectured on politics by a callow youth and by untutored citizens, maintains that the city must be ruled by one man alone. When Haemon points out that his father, in his blind insistence on law, is riding roughshod over the honor of the gods, Creon is enraged and threatens to have Antigone executed immediately before Haemon's very eyes. Haemon rushes away while Creon prepares to carry out his sentence. The chorus prevails upon him to acquit Ismene, who is innocent of any crime. On his own, Creon transmutes Antigone's sentence from death by stoning (within the city walls) to burial alive in a vault outside the gates—to keep the city free of the pollution or defilement (*miasma*, 776) that would inevitably result from the spilling of blood.

After a brief ode to the power of love, the chorus engages in a lyric dialogue with Antigone, who reveals herself in a new light. No longer simply the single-minded rebel, she solicits the compassion of the elders for the young woman who, unmarried, is about to visit the banks of the Acheron. The chorus reminds her that she has brought her fate upon herself by her own insistence on being independent, a law unto herself (*autonomos*, 821), and shattering herself against the lofty pedestal of Justice (*hypsêlon es Dikas bathron*, 854). As the chorus continues relentlessly to point out that she has destroyed herself through her own self-willed passion (*autognôtos orga*, 875), Antigone succumbs momentarily to an existential anxiety about death that resembles nothing else in world drama so much as the prince's terror when he catches sight of his own grave in Kleist's *Prince Friedrich von Homburg*.

Creon, wearied by her laments, tells the guards to remove her quickly—but not before Antigone concludes with a bit of reasoning (904–20) so out of character that many scholars and readers including Goethe have questioned the authenticity of the lines.[18] Turning away from Creon, the chorus, and all living beings, Antigone addresses her remarks to the tomb that is soon to receive her and to her dead beloved: father, mother, Eteocles, and Polynices, on whose behalf she now is about to die. She observes that, had she been a wife or mother, she would never have defied the citizens' will (*biai politôn*, 907) in order to bury husband or children. She justifies this curious and seemingly self-contradictory assertion with a bit of sophistical reasoning based on an anecdote that Sophocles knew from his friend Herodotus.[19] If her husband had died, she might have taken another; similarly, she could have borne other children had the first died. But since her own parents are dead, she can never have another brother. For that reason Polynices deserved special honor. Unaware of any divine law that she has transgressed, she accepts her suffering, hoping only that those who punish her will suffer at least as greatly if in fact they are wrong. She leaves the stage for the last time saying that she is suffering her fate as a consequence of her reverence and piety (*tên eusebian sebisasa*, 943).

As the chorus sings an ode of condolence comparing Antigone to various mythological figures, the blind prophet Teiresias is led in pronouncing terrible omens. The birds he normally consults for his auguries have suddenly been overcome by a mad fury, the fires refuse to ignite for burnt offerings, and the altars themselves are fouled by carrion from the corpse of Polynices. He urges

Creon to relent, to pay homage to the dead, but Creon, attributing Teiresias's motives to a crass desire for money, still refuses even though the soothsayer had earlier given the correct advice for saving the city from the attack of Polynices' forces. Teiresias is compelled to reveal a dreadful prophecy—to foretell the death of Creon's own kin, "corpse for corpse" (*nekyn nekrôn amoibon*, 1067), in return for his own sacrilege, the inversion of proper natural relationships. For he has kept above ground the body of Polynices, which properly belongs to the dead below; and he has enclosed Antigone, who still belongs to the living, in a gravelike vault. With threats that the Erinyes are in pursuit of Creon while men and women hate him, Teiresias exits.

Creon, though reluctant to admit it, is profoundly shaken by the interview with the prophet. Urged by the chorus to free Antigone and to bury Polynices in order to redeem the city from the threatening disasters, Creon is finally forced to concede his fault and rushes off to honor the anciently established laws (*kathestôtas nomous*, 1113). The chorus, deluded into the hope that the final tragedy may yet be averted, sings an ode of joy to Dionysus. But a messenger appears and, after some introductory reflections on the vagaries of fortune, reports that Haemon has died by his own hand. Creon's wife Eurydice, having overheard the messenger's brief statement, comes out of the palace to ask for further details. As Creon's followers were washing and burying Polynices' corpse, he reports, they heard a keening voice in the distance and, on breaking into the burial vault to investigate, discovered Haemon clinging to the body of Antigone, who had hanged herself (in precise analogy to her mother Jocasta, as reported by Ismene at the beginning of the drama). Catching sight of Creon, Haemon sought to stab his hated father and, failing that, impaled himself on his sword in order to be united with his bride in the House of Hades.

Eurydice leaves the scene in silence, followed by the worried messenger, and shortly thereafter Creon appears with Haemon's body. Now, finally, he is prepared to recognize his own guilt (*emais dysbouliais*, 1269) and to confess that he has learned the meaning of justice (*dikê*, 1270) through his suffering and threefold rejection: by the representatives of clan (Antigone), city-state (Haemon), and religion (Teiresias). Just as he wonders what worse could happen, the messenger returns to announce the death of Eurydice, who fell on her sword and died with a curse on her lips for Creon, whom she blames for the death of Haemon as well as her other son, Megareus, who was killed in the fighting at the gates. Creon, shattered by these blows, accepts the full guilt for all that has happened. Reduced to a nothing (*ton ouk onta mallon ê mêdena*, 1325), he prays for death. But the chorus reminds him of the need to deal with present exigencies and points out that mortal men cannot escape their allotted destiny. As he departs, a broken man, the chorus reflects that the gods must be revered, that the mighty must pay for their arrogance, and—the Sophoclean message—that suffering teaches us wisdom.

Antigone and Creon

Despite the generations of readers since Hegel who have sought to reduce the work to the simplicities of allegory, *Antigone* as a drama depends upon enormously complex characterizations. Above all—and this is of central importance in connection with the legal implications—it is essential to understand that Creon must emerge as an appropriate counterweight to the obsessive energy of Antigone: that "Antigone's fate provides the foil for Creon and, in turn, Creon's fate becomes evident only against the background of Antigone's destiny."[20] Some readers have even felt that the balance of the work would be more accurately characterized by the title *Antigone and Creon*.[21] Indeed, in light of Creon's almost constant presence on the stage and the fact that he alone undergoes a decisive *peripeteia*, one could almost make a case for calling the work *Creon* rather than *Antigone*.[22] Be that as it may, Bernard Knox in his brilliant study has made a compelling case for Creon's adherence, until his unheroic collapse at the end, to the mold of the Sophoclean hero.[23] Both uncle and niece display the same unreasonable, stubborn resolve characteristic of Sophocles' heroes: *both* turn out to be "marvelous" and "terrible" (*deinos*) in the terms of the great choral Ode to Man. Her religious fanaticism is matched by his blind chauvinism. When their will is challenged, both are advised—Antigone by Ismene, Creon by the chorus—to seek a compromise that is in both cases angrily rejected. The second offer of compromise—to Antigone by Creon, to Creon by Haemon—simply hardens their resolve. Yet both ultimately question the principles upon which they based their earlier actions:[24] Antigone in her existential anxiety in the face of death, which prompts her reflections on the conditions governing her disobedience; and Creon, when he finally recognizes the tragedy brought about by his intransigence. Antigone clings to her relentless will while Creon succumbs to the pressure to relent. Yet both end in utter isolation: Antigone in the darkness of her burial chamber and Creon in the loneliness of the man who has lost his entire family and the respect of his community. For this reason it has been suggested that Creon fulfills the criteria of the Aeschylean hero, who is broken by destiny, while Antigone embodies the issue of Sophoclean tragedy: a stubborn hero unbent by fate.[25]

These powerful parallels, which Knox has exposed in elaborate detail, are essential to the structural beauty of the drama. Antigone and Creon undergo almost precisely the same process; she adheres doggedly to her will and he is shattered by it. Yet almost to the end he provides a worthy opponent to her will, the countervailing force that shapes her enterprise and, through its opposition, bestows dignity upon it. Without a powerful adversary her will could not emerge in its fullness.

At the same time, undeniable differences exacerbate the basic conflict—differences that far transcend such personality traits as Antigone's *philia* or "love"[26] (albeit more for the dead than for the living: she never mentions Haemon) and Creon's progressively crueler vindictiveness. Antigone does not dwell on the gender aspect to which Ismene points at the outset—the inherent weakness of women that precludes their effectiveness;[27] but Creon, with a misogyny so pronounced that modern analysts might suspect an underlying feeling of sexual inadequacy, returns obsessively to his unwillingness to be bested by a woman. He is equally angered, as an older man, at the prospect of being instructed by the young, whether Antigone or his own son Haemon. Indeed, his refusal to take counsel from others (*aboulos*, 1026; elsewhere [1050, 1098] it is his need of good counsel, *euboulia*, that is cited) is so extreme that it corresponds closely to Antigone's "madness." There is no doubt more than a hint of family tension in the relationship: Creon is not merely an older male authority figure; he is also Antigone's maternal uncle who has benefited dynastically from the death of her father and her two brothers. In Creon's eyes, in turn, Antigone embodies the hated family spirit of rebelliousness that caused Oedipus to slay his sister's first husband, that brought about the death of Jocasta, that generated the disagreement between Eteocles and Polynices, and that now threatens his authority in its first hours. Even the chorus agrees that she has inherited her wild spirit from an untamed father (*gennêm' ômon ex ômou patros*, 471). That Antigone opposes this intense family loyalty to Creon's powerful sense of patriotism and civic virtue amounts to a further calculated offense. It is no accident that Creon's language features so many images in which untrammeled nature (Antigone as a bird, for example, or an unbroken horse) is tamed by the forces of civilization.[28]

But their greatest differences emerge in the realm of religion and law. It has been remarked that Sophoclean heroes are more archaic, more Homeric in spirit, than those of Aeschylus.[29] This generalization applies with a vengeance to Antigone, whose cult of the dead remains unparalleled in world literature until Wagner's Isolde and whose reverence for the primal gods of the underworld amounts to a fetish that reverses the *Oresteia*'s defeat, or at least its co-option, of the chthonic deities. Creon believes in the Olympian gods: in his opening speech to the elders it is Zeus whom he calls to witness for the priority of city over friend; and in his late tirade against Teiresias it is again Zeus's eagles and Zeus's throne that he invokes. But it is to please the dead and to honor the laws of the infernal deities that Antigone chooses to defy Creon's law. It is an oversimplification to say that Creon represents law and Antigone religion. Rather, Creon is a more progressive figure than Antigone; he has reached a point in his thinking at which he is able to separate church and state, religion and law. His principles are initially correct, but circumstances eventually force him to abandon them as he degenerates into tyranny. In Antigone's more archaic mentality, in contrast, religion and law, *ethos* and *polis*, constitute an indivisible whole.[30]

It is to the "unwritten and steadfast traditions of the gods" (*agrapta k'asphalê theôn nomima*, 454–55) that Antigone appeals in her great dialogue with Creon—a theme that makes its first appearance in the Antigone myth here in Sophocles' treatment.[31] What is more, Sophocles' play contains the first occasion on which the term *nomos* has been so fully co-opted to designate *legislated* law that customary law must be distinguished from it by the retroformation "unwritten."[32] However, she opposes these unwritten traditions not to *written* law but rather to *man-made* law, which she designates most often with the vocable *kêrygma* ("proclamation" by a herald or *kêryx*).[33] This, not a conflict between law and justice, is the defining opposition of the drama; for both Antigone and Creon appeal in their arguments to *dikê*, which Sophocles regards less as an absolute value than as a neutral force that restores order when the physical or moral world has lost its balance[34]—or, in Heidegger's useful translation, *Fug*, a poetic-legal term signifying proper order or fitness (as a joint fits together in carpentry).[35] (It has frequently been noted that many important political terms in Greek, such as *nomos* and *kosmos*, go back etymologically to roots signifying good order or proper allocation.) In her opening conversation Antigone asks Ismene if she has yet heard of the *kêrygma* (8) proclaimed by the new commander of the city. And in the following verses she uses verbal forms of the same word three more times (27, 32, 34). In their subsequent exchange Creon demands to know (using the verbal form *kêrychthenta*, 447) if she was not aware of his proclamation, which he uses interchangeably with the normal word for "law" (*nomous*, 449). In her response Antigone stresses pointedly that it was not Zeus who "made this proclamation" nor Dike, who resides with the gods of the netherworld (*hê xynoikos tôn katô theôn Dikê*, 451), who imposed such laws (*nomous*, 452) on men. Indeed, she could not believe that any *kêrygma* proclaimed by a mere mortal could surpass or transcend the great unwritten commandments of the gods. For those traditional commandments live eternally, and no one knows when they first appeared. She goes on to say that she would never violate those eternal laws—not for fear of any human judgment but out of respect for divine justice. In the remarkable passage that we have already considered, to be sure, Antigone seems to undermine her own single-minded reverence for the unwritten laws. But that passage serves ultimately to make her seem, in the light of her death anguish, a more human, more compelling figure. She later goes to her death confident that she has defied no law of the chthonic deities (*daimonôn dikên*, 921).

Creon, until his final collapse, is utterly unable to comprehend this reverence for unwritten laws of the archaic deities. A progressive practitioner of realpolitik, he is committed to the laws of human society, whether written or proclaimed, and not to the obscure commandments dictated by custom or personal feeling. Indeed, as the only political ruler besides Oedipus depicted by Sophocles in his plays, he shares many characteristics with his brother-in-law, including a pronounced elevation of the state.[36] Creon, exemplifying the essence of political organization, embodies the claim of the *polis* on the individual.[37] He demands the subordination of the individual to the rules through which the community seeks to assure its welfare. His attitude, contrasting sharply with Antigone's *philia*, emerges from his first speech, in which he affirms his belief in the state and attests his own values by declaring a "nonentity" (*oudamou*, 183) anyone who regards a friend or relative (*philon*, 183) more highly than his country. For Creon the true test of a ruler's character is his wisdom in making laws (*nomoisin*, 177), and it is by such laws (again he uses a form of the word *nomos*, 191) that he intends to exalt the city. He makes almost no distinction between *kêrygma* and *nomos*, calling the proclamations that he has issued regarding Polynices "intimately related" (*adelpha*, 192) to the laws. (There is no doubt an irony in his use of the term *adelphos*, which Antigone employs so lovingly to characterize family relationships, to designate his laws.) And it is conspicuous that the chorus, speaking for the *polis*, supports Creon's view at every juncture until his collapse at the very end. Since he regards anarchy as the supreme wrong, he takes it as his sacred duty to punish anyone who violates the laws (*nomous*, 663) of the community.

YET FROM the very beginning the seeds of doubt are sown into the dialogue. Creon's principles may be correct, but they are vitiated by flaws in his character: his intractability, his paranoid suspiciousness, his blindness toward the claims of tradition. Inasmuch as he collapses into political tyranny and personal tragedy, his figure may be seen in part as a critique of the *polis*, which for Sophocles had been rendered problematic by political developments since Salamis[38]—and more generally of the entire rational optimism of the fifth-century enlightenment and specifically of Sophocles' ambivalence toward Pericles.[39] (Yet the fact that Creon becomes a bad ruler does not necessarily imply that all rule is bad;[40] we must guard against confusing the dramatic situation with political theory.) When Creon, overreacting to the sentry's report, blames the messenger himself, the sentry remarks that it is "terrible" (*deinon*, 323) when the person who is supposed to govern wisely makes false judgments. This remark anticipates Haemon's criticism of his father much later in the play. Similarly, in its Ode to Man the chorus praises lawmaking as the summit of human activity, but only that lawmaking which interweaves the laws of the land (*nomous chthonos*, 368) with divine justice (*theôn dikan*, 369). It is precisely his disregard of divine law that causes Creon's downfall and teaches him the importance of respecting the established laws (*kathestôtas nomous*, 1113), that requires him to learn too late the meaning of justice (*dikên idein*, 1270), and that forces him to the insight that he has himself become through his neglect a contemptible "nothing" (*mêdena*, 1325).

Yet even though Creon is compelled to succumb—to bury Polynices, to forgive (albeit too late) Antigone, to acknowledge the power of the chthonic deities, and to survive as a tragically broken figure—it is noteworthy that

Antigone is not saved by those gods whom she unswervingly venerates. While the gods force Creon to complete her work, "they do not condone her indifference to the claims of the *polis*."[41] (It is not likely that Sophocles intends to suggest that she is abandoned by the gods because of her own brief doubts.) This conclusion, aesthetically so satisfying in its dramatic balance, contains significant implications for the attitude toward law that informs Sophocles' great drama.

Sophocles and Athens

Sophocles, like Aeschylus, is dramatizing archaic and semimythical material, but he locates the action in a setting that is at least recognizably Athenian (not Homeric) so that, like Aeschylus, he can come to grips with contemporary political issues of the period (that is, of the years immediately before the play's first performance ca. 441 B.C.).[42] We know that the generations following Sophocles grasped the political implications of the text. Pericles, in his Funeral Oration (Thucydides 2.35–46) some ten years after the first performance of *Antigone*, includes allusions consistent both with Antigone's "unwritten laws" and with Creon's notion of civic duty.[43] Demosthenes had lines from Creon's opening speech on loyalty to the *polis* read out in court as an example to his political opponent Aeschines (who had himself played the part of Creon in performances).[44] Aristotle, as we shall see below, cited the drama in two key passages of the *Rhetoric*.

When Sophocles wrote his *Antigone*, Athens had just attained a position of political leadership in the Mediterranean world that was marked by equally spectacular advances in philosophy, scientific thought, and political philosophy. Many of these achievements were reflected at least indirectly in his text. The *nomos-physis* controversy, which played a central role in the development of Western thought, did not become a major factor in Athenian intellectual life until the 420s, more than a decade after *Antigone*, when the Sophists first began to distinguish between the forces that hitherto had been taken essentially as one.[45] The political implications of this controversy cannot be exaggerated: it gradually undermined the traditional Athenian respect for law by arguing that all *nomos* is essentially secondary, a man-made construct, in comparison to the primary and eternal forces of *physis*. According to the tract *On Truth* by the Sophist Antiphon, for instance, "the dictates of the laws (*ta tôn nomôn*) are adventitious, whereas the dictates of nature are inescapable; dictates of the laws, based on agreement as they are, are not natural growths, whereas the dictates of nature (*ta tês physeôs*), being natural growths, are not based on agreement."[46] Since the majority of things sanctioned as just in terms of the law are inimical (*polemiôs*) to nature, the Sophist concludes, a citizen is "likely to use justice to his own best advantage, if he stresses the importance of the laws in the presence of witnesses, but when he is alone and there are no witnesses (follows) the dictates of nature." Because Antiphon defines law as "based on agreement" it is likely that he has in mind the *nomoi* sanctioned by the Athenian democracy at a moment in history (427 B.C.) when Thucydides (3.37) could quote Cleon as remarking that a state is stronger when it enforces bad *nomoi* which are inviolable than when it has good laws which lack authority. The appeal to *physis* or the laws of nature, in contrast, was a characteristic of the Athenian upper classes who were becoming disenchanted with democratic processes and who still felt a loyalty to the ancient bonds summed up by the word *physis*.

Sophocles was writing some fifteen years before Antiphon's tract, but it seems obvious that *Antigone* reflects an early stage of the great controversy in the history of rationalism.[47] Creon is more than a vulgar demagogue, but his demand for absolute obedience to the law, no matter how irregular it may be, strikingly anticipates Cleon's position. And Antigone not only appeals for her authority to the immemorial laws of nature; she also uses forms of the cognate verb *phyo* in several notable passages. In her most famous statement, for instance, she justifies her behavior by saying that "I was born" (*ephyn*, 523) to love, not to hate. Earlier she told Ismene that she can now demonstrate through her actions whether she was "born" (*pephykas*, 38) noble or base. This early evidence for the *nomos-physis* controversy that we can sense in *Antigone* provides, as we shall see, an important clue to the subsequent popularity of the play as a philosophical reference point. We might almost say with calculated exaggeration that we can see in the respective positions of Antigone and Creon an anticipation of Platonic metaphysics and Aristotelian rationalism.[48]

It has been persuasively argued that the political views advanced by Creon accurately reflect the rationalist views of the Sophist enlightenment during the second half of the fifth century.[49] In addition, no doubt, his acquaintance with Pericles provided Sophocles with the ideal opportunity to observe the danger of tyranny inherent in any popular and powerful democratic leadership. As recently as 443 B.C., Pericles had succeeded in ostracizing his enemy Thucydides, who had organized the Attic nobility to oppose Pericles' misappropriation of moneys from the Delian League to support his building program on the Acropolis.[50] In any case, the new democracy required the fifth-century Athenian to assume for his political behavior a certain moral responsibility that had not been necessary or permitted under the tyrants.[51] Sophocles' acquaintance with such contrasting political models as Cimon and Pericles hints at his own ability to juggle and balance political extremes. Above all, the development of the *polis* and of Athenian democracy went hand in hand with the development of law, *nomos*:[52] each is inconceivable without the other, and this accounts for the authority that Creon's position enjoys in the eyes of the chorus.

At the same time, Sophocles was subject to other influences. Born around 495, he was old enough to have experienced the *polis* at its moment of greatest glory in the years immediately following Salamis. His political views were already well formed by the time the democratic impulse began to spread after Ephialtes' reforms, and from his stance of traditional conservatism he was keenly aware of the dangers of excessive freedom and, in particular, the liberation of the individual from the restraints of religion and custom.[53] Because he was born and spent his youth at Colonus, his religious views were shaped by the hero cults, which, unlike the more joyful Eleusinian Mysteries that bred Aeschylus, were dedicated to a celebration of death and the grave.[54] Initially exposed to the cult of Oedipus celebrated at Colonus, Sophocles was later associated with other hero cults: he was a priest of the (otherwise unknown) hero Halon; he established a shrine to the hero Herakles; and he served as the official welcomer of Asclepios in 420 B.C. when the subsequently popular cult of that hero was brought from Epidauros to Athens.[55]

As a social conservative he was more than merely ambivalent about the democratic reforms that, since Cleisthenes, tended to break down the old family units (*genê*) and ancient clan connections and, in particular, to bring about the fateful dissociation of the unity of religion and law that provided the moral basis for the ancient *polis*.[56] Hence Sophocles sympathized instinctively with Antigone, the member of a *genos* who is destroyed by the *polis*,[57] and her reverence for the "primeval gods" (*theoi progeneis*, 938) to whom she appeals in her final words.[58]

Dealing with archaic events from an essentially preliterate society, Sophocles did not frame his argument in terms of unwritten (*agraphoi*) versus *written* laws. Yet during the very years when he was writing his play, that conflict had emerged as a burning issue in Athenian politics. Athens had known written laws since Draco and Solon set up their wooden tablets of laws on *axones* in the Prytaneum. The Athenians had a long-standing reverence for the written laws that symbolized their liberation from tyranny.[59] But the very fact that they existed in written form meant that the laws were exposed—in Athens just as in any other society—to discussion and critique in a manner not applicable to words that exist only in an oral form. As a result, some Athenians, especially conservatives from the upper classes, began in moments of legal or political dissatisfaction to measure their positive written laws against the remembered ideal of unwritten laws. During the republican enthusiasm of the fifth century the people experienced such a euphoria of legislation that many (often ill-advised) statutes were promulgated (*psêphismata*) which came into conflict with older customary laws (*nomoi*), written or unwritten, to the end that a skepticism regarding all law was engendered.[60]

At the same time, the constant striving of the other city-states of the Delian League for autonomy (*autonomia*) and the validity of their own constitutions represented a threat to the hegemony and political authority of Athens.[61] Sophocles knew these tensions at first hand from his experience in 443–442 as chairman of the board of financial overseers (*Hellenotamiai*) of the Delian

League. (It can be no accident that the politically weighted term *autonomos* is used by the chorus to criticize Antigone's insubordination.) As a result, the Athenians pushed, at least in external affairs, for the authority of their own written law. Finally, one important aspect of the struggle against Sparta during the first Peloponnesian War was the circumstance that Sparta had remained legendary as the home of *unwritten* law while Athens was famous as the fountainhead of *written* law.[62] (This polarity was so renowned that it had become proverbial by the time of Justinian's *Institutes*, where we read [1.2.10] that civil law seems to be divided "not inelegantly" into two kinds whose origin stems from the institutes of the two states of Athens and Lacedaemon: *in his enim civitatibus ita agi solitum erat, ut Lacedaemonii quidem magis ea, quae pro legibus observarent, memoriae mandarent, Athenienses vero ea, quae in legibus scripta reprehendissent, custodirent.*)

In sum, through his dramatization of the conflict between man-made law and unwritten law Sophocles was thematizing a debate that would have been instantly evident to his audience. His drama involved forces and factors other than the individualized conflict between man and woman, between age and youth, between state and family, between law and religion. Although separated by fewer than twenty years from the *Oresteia*, *Antigone* stands at the end of a process whose beginnings constitute the climax of Aeschylus's great trilogy. *The Eumenides* looks back to the moment at which state and tradition, law and religion, were first unified as the spiritual basis of the new Athenian *polis*. *Antigone* amounts to a prescient commentary on the disintegration of the *polis* as law and religion begin to be articulated into wholly distinct functions, with all the implications entailed by that transformation: the emergence of the professional politician (like Creon, Pericles, and later Cleon) and, under the influence of rationalism, the disenfranchisement of religion through mythologization.[63] To that extent it became a debate on the very nature of Athenian law during the turmoil of the republic, on the claims of the ancient cults versus the Sophists, on the hegemony of Athens vis-à-vis its neighboring city-states, and on the *nomos-physis* controversy that was soon to dominate philosophical discussion in Athens. It was Sophocles who, by casting into dramatic form the discussion on the nature of law, succeeded in making accessible to the Athenian public the philosophical dimensions of a problem that, in the next century, was to vex Plato and Aristotle.[64]

From Unwritten Law to Epieikeia

It was precisely the *nomos-physis* dilemma that Aristotle sought to resolve in several of his writings. While the Areopagus continued in its limited way to represent the unwritten law of earlier aristocratic times, fifth-century democratic Athens displayed a reverence for written law that produced a veritable riot of legislation.[65] In his Funeral Oration (Thucydides 2.37.3) Pericles could praise the Athenians for their obedience to all law, both written and unwritten. Only half a century later Plato in the *Republic* (8.563d) concluded that it is one of the major flaws of democracy to arouse an untrammeled sense of liberty with the result that men "finally pay no heed even to the laws written or unwritten." It was this tension between written and unwritten, this extreme radicalization of *nomos* and *physis*, that Aristotle sought to reconcile through the notion of equity or *epieikeia*.

Although the adjectival form of the word occurs in Homer with the meaning "suitable," "fitting," or "meet," the term was rapidly claimed by Athenians to designate a special sense of justice distinct from *dikaion*.[66] (Vinogradoff has proposed the translation "fairness" in order to distinguish *epieikeia* from "equity," which, though "originally an equivalent," has subsequently assumed potentially misleading technical connotations as a branch of English law.)[67] The cultlike appeal of the notion in the rapidly evolving democracy can be estimated from the opposition that the term aroused among those who feared that an untrammeled equity could destroy the very fabric of the law: Euripides, Cleon, Isocrates, Demosthenes, Plato, and later the Stoics. It amounted therefore to an enormous philosophical challenge, not to say provocation, when Aristotle sought to co-opt the notion and to define it not as opposed to but within the parameters of justice. Toward the end of book 5 of his *Nicomachean Ethics*, following a strange mathematico-geometrical theory of distributive and corrective justice, Aristotle announces the need to discuss the relations of equity (*epieikeia*) and the equitable to justice (*dikaiosynê*) and the just (10.1137b) and the confusions that stem from their use.[68] The difficulty arises, he continues, because we sometimes praise an action as equitable even though it is distinct from what is legally just. This suggests that either the just is not good or the equitable is not just since they are by common usage different. Aristotle resolves the apparent dilemma by arguing that the equitable is just—not according to written law, but rather as a correction of legal justice (*epanorthôma nomimou dikaiou*). Every law aspires in general to be universal (*katholou pas*), but some things cannot be encompassed in a universal statement. The law rightly takes as its basis the generality of cases, even though it understands that not every case can be covered by its formulations. It is therefore proper, in cases that the lawgiver has omitted to cover, to set right the omission by ruling as the lawmaker himself would rule were he himself present. Thus, Aristotle concludes, the equitable is not superior to absolute justice, but it is better than any sort of limited law: it is "a rectification of law where law is defective because of its generality." Accordingly the equitable man is one who acts according to the principles of equity and, without insisting on the letter of the law, is content where appropriate to waive his claims though they are backed by the law.

In his *Rhetoric* Aristotle gives a more detailed analysis of that famous statement. First, in his discussion of juridical speech (1.10.1368b) he distinguishes sharply between two kinds of law (*nomos*): positive or particular (*idios*) law, that is, the written law by which cities are governed; and common (*koinos*) law, that is, the unwritten law that appears to be universally recognized. Later, when he is talking about guilt (1.13.1373b), he extends this preliminary definition. There are still two kinds of law, positive and general. But at this stage positive law (*idios*), which is determined by each people for its own benefit, can be either unwritten (*agraphos*) or written (*gegrammenos*); while common or general law is the law of nature (*kata physin*). For there exists inherent in nature a sense of justice and injustice (*physei koinon dikaion kai adikon*) that all men divine, even if they are not bound by any commonality or treaty. It is this justice, Aristotle continues, that Sophocles' Antigone apparently has in mind when she argues that it is just by nature (*physei dikaion*) to bury Polynices. At this point he quotes Antigone's words (456–57) to the effect that there is an eternal law whose source no one knows. In other words, Aristotle conflates the two controversies, the written-unwritten law and *nomos-physis*, and adduces *Antigone* as evidence for doing so. A few paragraphs later (1374a) he rephrases his statement to point out that there are two kinds of just and unjust actions: those defined by written law and those understood according to unwritten law. Those actions not defined by written law, in turn, fall into two classes: those that represent the highest degree of virtue and vice and that are recognized by public praise or reproaches; and those that correspond to a deficiency (*elleimma*) in the written or unwritten positive law. At this point he introduces the notion of equity: "The equitable [*to epieikes*] seems to be just, but it is a justice [*dikaion*] that goes beyond the written law." Explaining that some of the legal lacunae are unintentional (owing to oversights) and others intentional (in cases when the lawmakers are forced to a general formula that is not universal in its applicability), Aristotle provides a number of examples of relevant cases. "To be equitable," he concludes (1374b) "is to make allowances [*syggignôskein*] for human fallibility. It is to consider not the law, but the lawmaker, not the word but the spirit [*dianoian*] of the lawmaker, and not the deed but the intention [*proairesin*], not the part but the whole, not what is now but what always has been—at least most of the time." If we recall the good that has been done unto us rather than the bad, the benefits we have received rather than the services we have rendered; if we learn to tolerate injustice; if we prefer to settle disagreements by word rather than by action; if we prefer arbitration rather than a decision at court—this is equitable. "For the arbitrator sees equity, the judge sees the law."

Aristotle cites the same lines from *Antigone* a few paragraphs further on (1375a) in his discussion of the five types of proof: by law, deposition of witnesses, declarations under torture, agreements, and oaths. With respect to laws (*nomoi*) it is evident that, if the written law (*gegrammenos*) is unfavorable to the case, one should have recourse to common law (*koivos*)—that is, to laws that are more equitable (*epieikesterois*) and more just. It is not necessary, in the effort to preserve the spirit of the law, to apply written law: for the equitable, like the common law (that is, natural law) is eternal and unchanging, while written laws often change. Hence Antigone is able to justify her actions by saying that even though she acted in violation of Creon's law, her actions did not violate the unwritten law; and Aristotle cites again the appropriate lines.

The introduction of *epieikeia* constitutes Aristotle's most original contribution to legal theory, for "the concept of epieikeia as defined by Aristotle has no antecedent in the whole of pre-Aristotelean literature."[69] Aristotle recommends no anarchic liberation from the law. Indeed, he wants the law to be as complete and as detailed as possible. The judge should normally be able to reach his decision according to the properly framed rule. But since the laws cannot cover all possible cases, *epieikeia* is a safeguard against the inadequacies of positive law. "In this sense the Aristotelean epieikeia served as a model for the Roman aequum et bonum, aequitas and bona fides, notions which were bound up with the *arbitrium boni viri* (*eugnômosunê*); it was also the forerunner of English equity, of German *Treu und Glauben*, etc."[70] And through its repeated citation of Sophocles' great legal drama it introduced *Antigone* into the philosophical discussion of law and equity.

CHAPTER NINE

Law and Equity II

From Epieikeia to Equity

Justinian's *Digest* opens (1.1.1) with the statement by the second-century jurist Celsus that defines law explicitly in terms of equity: *Ius est ars boni et aequi*. There is no more troublesome set of phrases in Roman law than those involving *aequitas*, including specifically *ius aequum* and *bonum et aequum*—so problematic, indeed, that some modern historians of law have preferred to regard them as interpolations.[1] But two points should be noted. First, several other passages in the *Digest* that are attributed to Celsus show a pronounced Aristotelian tone.[2] In Celsus's maxim, for instance, Aristotle's injunction to consider not the words of the law but the spirit of the lawmaker becomes: *Scire leges, non hoc est verba earum tenere, sed vim ac potestatem* (*Digest* 1.3.17). Similarly he respects Aristotle's insight that the law must be written in such a manner as to apply to cases that occur frequently, not rarely: *nam ad ea potius debet aptari jus, quae et frequenter et facile, quam quae perraro eveniunt* (*Digest* 1.3.5). So it is plausibly assumed by many scholars that the influence of Aristotle is evident in the famous statement that "law is the art of the equitable," even if the notion itself was not unfamiliar to Roman thought.[3]

Second, in classical Latin from Cicero to the early-third-century jurist Paulus the phrase *bonum et aequum* was regularly used in ethical-political-legal writings virtually as a single concept. In *De oratore* (3.27.107), for instance, Cicero lists the topics upon which the trained orator should be able to expatiate both *pro* and *contra*: *de virtute enim, de officio, de aequo et bono, de dignitate, utilitate, honore, ignominia, praemio, poena similibusque de rebus*. The list, which otherwise contains only single vocables, suggests that *aequum et bonum* should also be taken as a unit meaning something like "the positive force of equity." Over two centuries later Paulus defines law—that is, natural law—as "equity": *id quod semper aequum et bonum est, jus dicitur, ut est jus naturale* (*Digest* 1.1.11). It is important to establish this linkage because the medieval Italian jurists sought to separate the two terms and to understand *aequum* alone as meaning nothing more than "just" (*iustum*).[4]

In sum, if *bonum et aequum* signifies the qualities that Aristotle associated with *epieikeia* and if *justitia* is the art of *bonum et aequum*, then it is reasonable to believe that the readers of the *Digest* understood *justitia* to be identical with *epieikeia*. But this does not mean that the concept played the same role in Roman legal thought as it did in the *Nicomachean Ethics*. For the Romans, to be sure, *justitia/aequitas* was the living spirit informing the formalized *ius*;[5] indeed, the etymological explanation at the beginning of the *Digest* perversely derives the vocable *ius* from *iustitia*. But their interest, their passion, lay almost exclusively with the formulation of the positive law, and not with the philosophy of law. Nor did Justitia play the same role in the allegorical vocabulary of the Romans as did Dike in that of the Greeks. Latin literature offers us no equivalent to Clytemnestra hovering over the body of Agamemnon with sword in hand, an image calculated to remind viewers of the figure of that Dike whose name had been evoked so often in the text of the play. And precisely the same principle applies to the figure of Aequitas, who along with Justitia led a peripheral existence in Rome: no major statues or monuments, but only the vague profile on the occasional coin.[6]

The rediscovery of Justinian's *Corpus Iuris Civilis* did not signify an immediate appreciation of the Aristotelian aspects of the Roman law or of the philosophical implications of *aequitas*. The early Italian commentators and glossators, concerned primarily with establishing the literal meaning of the words and the correctness of the texts, had no reason or inclination to come to grips with Aristotle's theory of *epieikeia*. In their minds *aequitas* was nothing but the quality of justness, fairness, righteousness in the application of existing law; it did not have the Aristotelian force of correcting or supplementing positive law.

The introduction of Aristotelian philosophy into scholastic thinking was one of the most influential events of the Middle Ages. Albertus Magnus appears to have been the first of the great medieval thinkers to pay attention to the Stagirite's definition of *epieikeia*,[7] but it was his protégé Thomas Aquinas who in his *Summa Theologiae* devoted himself extensively to the discussion of *epieikeia* in the *Nicomachean Ethics*.[8] By relating Aristotle to the most important passages on *aequitas* in Justinian's compilation he created a bridge between the classical Roman jurists and the moral theologians of the Middle Ages. His identification of the two concepts—for the first time in the Middle Ages—is stated clearly in *Quaestio 120* of the *Secunda Secundae*, which bears the title *de epieikeia*.[9] Weighing the point as to whether or not *epieikeia* can be regarded as a virtue, Saint Thomas first advances the thesis that inasmuch as it sometimes goes beyond the law, it cannot be a virtue. However, he then entertains the antithesis and concludes that in certain cases (for instance, returning a sword to a madman in the grip of his madness) it would be wrong to follow the positive law. But it is good, "setting aside the words of the law, to follow that which is demanded by the meaning of justice and the common good" (*praetermissis verbis legis, sequi id quod poscit justitiae ratio et communis utilitas*). To this end *epieikeia* is invoked, "which we call equity" (*quae apud nos dicitur aequitas*). From this it follows that *epieikeia* is a virtue.

Aquinas's understanding of *aequitas*, as we see in the phrase *communis utilitas* and later in such defining terms as modesty (*modestia*) and temperance (*temperantia*) in the observance of the letter of the law, lent a new dimension of meaning to the notion of *epieikeia*, a dimension that led easily in the following decades and centuries to the Christian caritative sense of *misericordia* and *benignitas*.[10] Saint Thomas, in other words, initiated the process that expanded the notion of *epieikeia* in moral theology to embrace the wholly un-Aristotelian notion of Christian "mercy." It is no accident that the figure of Justitia as we know it today—with her familiar attributes of sword and scales (but still without the blindfold!)—first emerges in the mid–thirteenth century during the lifetime of Saint Thomas. (The first known representation stems from the year 1247 on the sarcophagus of Pope Clement II in Bamberg.)[11] A symbolic image representing justice and equity became necessary and comprehensible only at the moment when the Christian notion of *misericordia* was introduced into the history of legal thought. In the recently rediscovered Roman law, we recall, "justice" plays virtually no role after the famous introductory definition.

Although *epieikeia* was familiar as a term of Christian moral theology from the thirteenth century forward, then, the term was not introduced into non-canonical legal thought on the Continent until the sixteenth century, when it became an important element in the controversy between the *mos italicus* and the *mos gallicus*. The early Italian jurists were for the most part legal positivists obsessed with the philological and historical understanding of Roman law; for them *aequitas* was little more than a synonym for *iustitia*, and their thinking was stuck essentially at the point where Aristotle began his discussion of *epieikeia*—that is, at the apparent dilemma that the just is not good since in common usage the two notions are distinguished (a distinction paralleled in Saint Thomas's dialectical reflections on the nature of *epieikeia*). It was only in the later fourteenth and early fifteenth centuries that certain postglossators began to create a philosophy of law based on a modified Aristotelianism and the Christian moral thought of Saint Thomas.[12] Many of the North European jurists, in particular, were interested in the philosophy of law, an enterprise fueled by the rediscovery of Aristotle's works and their translation into Latin.

The turn to Aristotle's notion of *epieikeia* specifically was motivated by the dilemma whose urgency we have already noted: the skepticism regarding all law, whether customary or Roman, summed up by the widely quoted proverb that characterizes the spirit of the times: *summum ius, summa iniuria*. Paradoxically Erasmus, who deals with the saying in his *Adagia*, makes no reference to Aristotle; he is concerned with the philology of the maxim and its history, from Terence by way of Cicero to the present, but not with its legal-philosophical implications.[13] However, Erasmus's French contemporary Budaeus (Guillaume Budé) placed Aristotle's discussion of *epieikeia* at the center of his *Annotationes in quattuor et viginti Pandectarum libros* (1508), one of the works that dominated European jurisprudence for the entire sixteenth century.[14] Attacking the Italian jurists for seeking to separate *aequum* from *bonum* in their explication of Celsus's famous definition, Budé begins by explaining that the quality called *aequum [et] bonum* by the Romans was designated by Aristotle by the adjective *epieikes* and that *aequitas* is therefore identical with *epieikeia*. Citing the *Nicomachean Ethics*, Budé goes on to define *epieikeia* as the freedom that judges use to emend the juristic concept of strict legislation (*ius strictum*). He thus restores to the classical Roman understanding of *aequitas* (= the spirit of justice) the original Aristotelian conception of *epieikeia* as a system of law supplementary to the positive law of the age.

Owing to the influence of Budé's *Annotationes* and his identification of *epieikeia* with *aequitas*, the Aristotelian concept dominated the lively sixteenth-century debate on the philosophy of law. In particular, it emerged as the principal liberating force opposed to the popularly suspect *ius strictum* or *summum ius*. During the first half of the century many of the most important thinkers in Europe devoted their energies to this legal-philosophical debate, which inevitably began with Budé's revolutionary idea. The French jurist Claude Chansonnette, known as Claudius Cantiuncula (1490–1549), dealt at length with the question of equity in his major work, *De officio iudicis* (1543). The Milanese jurist Andreas Alciatus (1492–1550) devoted the thirtieth chapter of his *Parerga iuris* (1538–54) to a defense of Budé's identification of *epieikeia/aequitas* against the mindless Italian *grammatici* who often ridiculed the philological abilities of the philosophers of law. The leading German jurist of the century, the South German Ulrich Zasius (1461–1535), wrote repeatedly and extensively on the topic, notably in his posthumously published commentary on several titles of Justinian's *Digest* (*In titulos aliquot Digesti Veteris commentaria*, 1537). The Swiss scholar Bonifacius Amerbach (1495–1562), in his initial lecture at the University of Basel (*Defensio interpretum iuris civilis*, 1525), sought to achieve a typically Swiss compromise between the *mos italicus* and the *mos gallicus* with specific reference to the problem of equity. The North German Johannes Oldendorf (1488–1567) was the first jurist to dedicate a monograph in the vernacular to the topic, *Wat byllick unn recht ys* (1529; Latin version under the title *De iure et aequitate*, 1541), a work that deserves particular notice as providing the basis for the Lutheran theory of natural law.

It is no exaggeration to say that the question of equity dominated jurisprudential thought of the entire century—from Melanchthon's orations *De aequitate et iure stricto* (1542) and *De stricto iure et aequitate* (1544)[15] down to Hugo Grotius's *De jure belli et pacis* (1625), the magisterial work in which the distinguished Dutch statesman (1583–1645) established the basis for modern international law. Grotius's work ends with an appended essay *De aequitate, indulgentia et facilitate*, which shows that the question of equity still vexed the mind. Since universal justice consists in the observance of the law, he begins, and since equity sometimes appears to be at odds with this observance, it is necessary for the good man as well as the jurisconsult to understand to what extent they agree and wherein they are distinguished.[16] Equity or the equitable is appropriate to all law (*aequitatem aut aequum de omni interdum jure dici*) inasmuch as—and here he cites Celsus—jurisprudence is the art of the good and the equitable. He goes on, however, to point out that the equitable is that sense by which the law is corrected (*Aequum autem est id ipsum, quo lex corrigitur*). Without mentioning Aristotle by name, he argues that the Latin word comes etymologically from the Greek word *eikos* (Doric *aikos*), and proceeds to repeat the argument from the *Nicomachean Ethics*: that since laws framed to be universal cannot cover every specific case, there is need for a virtue that can provide equality for unequal matters, *unde haec virtus aequitas latinis, graecis vero epieikeia dicitur*. He goes on to say that equity is a disposition of the will, not of the intellect (*voluntatis habitus, non intellectus*). Following the discussion of the related concepts *indulgentia* and *facilitas*, Grotius concludes his essay with the Aristotelian observation that equity is not at odds with justice because true justice follows the law not according to the words but according to the mind of the legislator and the true meaning of the law (*quia Justitia legi obsequitur, non secundum verba, sed mentem legislatoris, & secundum verum ordinem legum*).

It is not necessary for our purposes—indeed, it would be presumptuous for a nonspecialist in this hotly debated field—to trace in intricate detail the often enormously subtle distinctions pursued by these ingenious sixteenth-century jurists and philosophers of law. What matters is to demonstrate the intensity of the discourse on equity, accompanied by translations of the *Nicomachean Ethics* and commentaries on the tenth chapter of book 5, that pervaded jurisprudence during the century from Budé to Grotius. The discussion, which amounted to a conscious philosophical response to widespread public despair at the notion of *summum ius, summa iniuria* with which the fifteenth century ended, invoked Aristotle's notion of *epieikeia* in a manner quite distinct from the moral theology of the scholastics, where the term had moved ever closer to the Christian idea of *misericordia*.

Equity and Anomy in Elizabethan England

The situation in England took a somewhat different course of development owing mainly to the emergence there of the Court of Chancery. As early as 1300 King Edward I—known as the "English Justinian" because he "laboured carefully to reduce our *Law* into order, and writing"[17]—found himself overwhelmed by legal appeals from litigants whose cases could not be accommodated within the rather narrow framework of the courts of common law. Accordingly he delegated to his chancellor the authority to deal with a large number of them. By about 1330 Edward III, over the objections of the common-law judges, decided to permit his chancellor to adjudicate cases that the judges refused to hear and thereby formally established a Court of Chancery that was altogether separate from the courts of common law. As a result two entirely independent systems of jurisprudence existed side by side in English law. "The common law courts acted *in rem* on the property of the litigants; and equity courts acted *in personam* on the person of the litigants."[18] Typically the chancellor, who was not constrained by a jury, issued an injunction or decree that rendered invalid on grounds of equity the judgment or writ of the common-law courts. The ensuing conflict between these courts, revolving essentially around the authority of equity vis-à-vis the common law, lasted almost three centuries. Only in 1616, in the famous case of *Glanvill vs. Courtney* that pitted Sir Edward Coke, lord chief justice of the King's Bench, against Lord Chancellor Ellesmere, did James I resolve that in cases of irreconcilable difference of opinion the Court of Equity should prevail.[19]

The chancellors, who until the Reformation were ecclesiastics, were traditionally guided not by the letter or even the principles of the common law but by the doctrines of Christianity.[20] It was therefore through this agency that the ecclesiastical understanding of equity as Aristotelian *epieikeia* was introduced into English legal thought even before the sixteenth-century revival on the Continent. We can clearly see this development in one of the most influential sixteenth-century English works on law, Christopher St. German's *Doctor and Student* (1523).[21] St. German, in his effort to provide a simple guide to law and legal principles for the layman, became the first English author to attempt to describe and, in so doing, to prescribe the equitable jurisdiction of the chancellor,[22] and it is largely as a result of his influence that England formalized courts of legal equity after the model of Aristotle rather than of moral conscience in the fashion of the medieval theologians. (The "equity" according to which the chancellor was often said to proceed in the Middle Ages was canonical equity, with its implications of *misericordia*, rather than *epieikeia* in the Aristotelian sense.) Ordinarily the "equity" of canon law applied only to ecclesiastical cases. But when adherence to the civil law could cause a sin to result, canonical equity took precedence over civil law and was binding upon laymen even in civil cases. This meant not simply that the judge might refrain from applying the letter of the law; he might also decide to impose the rule of the Law of Nature as understood by the Church. *Epieikeia*, as we have seen, differs emphatically from this broad principle because it requires the judge to remain within the general context of the civil law.

Doctor and Student, according to the fiction explained in the introduction, amounts to an extended dialogue between a doctor of divinity (*doctor theologiae*, 6) and a student in the laws of England (*quodam studente in legibus anglie*, 6). The theologian wishes to understand the foundations of the law of England, but since it is written in French, a language he does not command, he implores the student of laws to come to his assistance. In the conversations that follow, each interlocutor, referring to his own field of specialization, poses questions to the other. Because the theologian has repeatedly invoked the term "equity" in their exchanges, the student asks him to explain it. The theologian replies (chap. 14 of the Latin original and chap. 16 of the English translation) that

> Equytye is a [ryghtwysenes] that consideryth all the pertyculer cyrcumstaunces of the dede the whiche also is temperyd with the swetnes of mercye. . . . And the wyse man sayth: be not ouer moch ryghtwyse for the extreme ryghtwysenes is extreme wronge. . . . It is not possyble to make any generall rewle of the lawe but that it shall fayle in some case. . . . & to that intent equytie is ordeyned that is to say to tempre and myttygate the rygoure of the lawe. And it is called also by some men epicaia. The whiche is no other thynge but an exepcyon of the lawe of god or of the lawe of reason from the generall rewles of the lawe of man.

> *Equitas est [iustitia] pensatis omnibus circumstantiis particularibus dulcore misericordie temperata. . . . Et sapiens dicit noli esse nimis iustus alioquin summa iustitia summa iniustitia fit. . . . non fuit possibile aliquam regulam generalem legis institui que in nullo casu deficeret. . . . et ad hoc ordinatur equitas que etiam dicitur Epikaya scilicet obtemperare legis rigorem. Que equitas nichil aliud est quam exceptio legis diuine siue legis rationis a regulis generalibus legis humane.*[23]

Although Aristotle is not cited specifically in this passage, he has been mentioned previously in *Doctor and Student*—as "the Philosopher" and also as the author of the *Ethics*. But this discussion clearly finds its proper niche in the context of the general European discussion taking place on the Continent. Equity is identified with *epieikeia* and understood as the exceptions to positive law that are made in the name of divine law or the law of reason in those cases when positive law is too rigorous for the case at hand. The passage is of particular interest for two further reasons. First, it is specifically linked to the saying *summa iustitia summa iniustitia*. Second, it is related to the Aquinian moral tradition of Christian *misericordia*, which is here called "the sweetness of mercy."

It is worth noting at this point that the chapter on equity is immediately followed by the law student's response to a question posed earlier by the theologian, who has heard it said that English law requires a man who has repaid a debt and lost his receipt to pay the debt again.[24] This law strikes the theologian as being inconsistent with the law of reason, whereupon the student explains that it is not the intent of the practice to oblige debtors to pay more than once but to preclude the great inconvenience that might occur should men seek to avoid their obligations by empty words (*nuda verba*). Accordingly "as the defendaunt is charged by a sufficyent wrytynge that so he must be discharged by suffycyent wrytyng or by some other thynge of as hygh auctorytie as the oblygacyon is." But, he concludes, if a man finds himself without remedy at common law, he may find recourse in equity—in cases of debt and "in many other cases where conscyence seruyth for hym." When the theologian inquires in which courts a man may be helped by conscience, the student asks in turn for an explanation of "the nature and qualytie of conscyence" (*de natura & qualitate conscientie*).

It is unnecessary to pursue the discussion any further. The point to be seized upon is this. *Doctor and Student*, and especially the first dialogue, was a representative and popular work that, reprinted twice in 1528 and again as late as 1604, enjoyed a considerable success among nonspecialist readers.[25] In this work the issue of equity is not only linked to Aristotelian *epieikeia* but, in contrast to Continental sources, related to the paradox of *summum ius*, to the Aquinian quality of mercy, and specifically to discussions of unsecured loans. This is not to suggest that the actual practice of civil law of the state was radically changed by the debate; but no less an authority than Holdsworth adduces *Doctor and Student* to make the point that "the minds of those who were framing a system of equity in the late fifteenth and sixteenth centuries were influenced by the current scholastic philosophy."[26] It would be going too far to suggest that *Doctor and Student* provided in any sense a direct source for Shakespeare. Indeed, the word "equity" occurs only four times in all his plays.[27] But the work can be regarded as exemplary for the special tone that the general sixteenth-century European discourse concerning *epieikeia* assumed in England, where equity was identified with "mercy," where it was opposed to "strict law," where people were concerned about the "quality of conscience," and where one of the primary examples was drawn from the field of moneylending.

At the same time, the presence of courts of equity in which strict law was tempered by the quality of mercy was not unstrained. Many people who sought more regularity and predictability in the law agreed with John Selden's bon mot that Chancery was "a roguish thing" because it had no measure more constant than the chancellor's foot.[28] Indeed, the conflict between the various courts of common law and the Court of Chancery, in the decades immediately before its resolution, was the great issue in legal justice in England.[29] The conflict is most clearly evident in William Lambarde's *Archeion, or, A Discourse Upon the High Courts of Iustice in England*, which was long the standard authority. (Although the work was first published in 1635, it was written before 1591, widely copied, circulated, and discussed among Lambarde's colleagues at Lincoln's Inn, and exerted its influence on the courts of the realm decades before its first publication.)[30] Lambarde's great work begins with a sketch of law in the Bible, among the Romans, and in the medieval ecclesiastical courts; outlines the history of courts in England; and then surveys the confusion of courts that have emerged in England by the end of the sixteenth century. Repeating a popular etymology that goes back at least to John of Salisbury, Lambarde explains that the chancellor "is said to *cancell*, *deface*, or *make void* a *Record*" (46)[31] by drawing lines through it. Lambarde traces the history of the office and the chief functions of the chancellor and then discusses the need for the Chancery Court of Equity with specific reference to Aristotle. "For *written Lawes* must needs bee made in a generalitie, and grounded upon that which happeneth for the most part, because no wisedome of man can fore-see every thing in particularitie, which Experience and Time doth beget" (69). The written law, he continues, has "need of Correction," an action known to Aristotle and the Greeks as *epieikia* (*sic*; 69). Normally, however, the common law should prevail and equity be invoked "only in rare and extraordinary matters" (71), for otherwise the Beast of "unruly affections" rules. A good chancellor will provide that "the Gate of *Mercie* may bee opened in all Calamitie of Suit: to the end, (where need shall be) the Rigour of *Law* may bee amended, and the short measure thereof extended by true consideration of *Iustice* and *Equitie*" (73). Yet no good chancellor will

> make this Proclamation, *Nullus recedat a Cancellaria sine remedio*, and thereby not onely abuse the Text of the Statute, which meant onely the making of *Writs* (that there might bee *in consimile casu remedium consimile*) but also arrogate authoritie in every complaint that shall bee brought before him, upon whatsoever suggestion, and thereby both overthrow the authoritie of the Courts of *Common Law*: Then to bring upon men such a confusion and uncertaintie, as hardly any man should know how, or how long to hold his owne assured to him. (72–73)

Lambarde, who displays a healthy fear of social confusion, repeatedly stresses the importance of seeking a mean or "golden mediocrity" between the majesty of the king and the authority of the common-law courts. The plaintiff requires the security of knowing where to take his complaint and needs certainty of knowing the law according to which his case will be adjudicated. Otherwise a state of legal anarchy prevails. "Shall the *King* and his *Councell* open a Court for all sorts of *Pleas* that be determinable by the course of *Common Law*? that were to set an *Anomy*, and to bring disorder, doubt, and incertaintie overall" (120).

Lambarde's *Archeion* provides the first documented use of the word "anomy" in English, but the term enjoyed a notable vogue in Renaissance England, especially in theological circles, where biblical commentators encountered the word in such key passages as 1 John 3.4: "Every one who commits sin is guilty of lawlessness; sin is lawlessness" (*Omnis qui facit peccatum, et iniquitatem facit: et peccatum est iniquitas*). In the Greek text, upon which the Renaissance began to write its commentaries, the term for *iniquitas* or "lawlessness" is *anomia*. "Lambarde's attempt to reconcile conflicting jurisprudential claims parallels the aims of English humanists in all areas of study, whether legal, Biblical, or moral."[32]

Shakespeare was almost certainly acquainted with Lambarde by 1596, if not before, and there is good reason to assume that he was familiar with *Archeion*; we know that he had in his library Lambarde's earlier work *Archaionomia* (1568).[33] Lambarde's great tract reflects the mood of the 1590s—the period of social upheaval and civil disorder following the defeat of the Armada in 1588, when thousands of demobilized and unemployed soldiers and sailors roamed the English countryside[34] and when, in 1593 and again in 1595, violent anti-alien riots took place. It was during these years that the conflict between the courts of common law and equity reached its greatest intensity. Indeed, during the reign of Elizabeth "hundreds of cases were recorded in which one litigant had a *judgment* in his favor and the other litigant had a *decree* in his favor, in the same controversy."[35] In the confusing variety of courts, moreover, litigants often did not know where to turn.[36] Ellesmere, who became lord keeper of the Great Seal in 1596, presumed to challenge the common-law judges more freely than any earlier chancellor and to grant injunctions against their actions. When Elizabeth convened Parliament in 1597, Ellesmere's speech before the two houses included the following symptomatic passage:

> And whereas the number of laws already made are very great, some also of them being obsolete and worn out of use; others idle and vain, serving to no purpose; some again over heavy and too severe for the offense; others too loose and slack for the faults they are to punish, and many of them so full of difficulties to be understood that they cause many controversies; you are therefore to enter into a due consideration of the said law, and where you find superfluity to prune, where defect to supply, and where ambiguity to explain, that they be not burthensome but profitable to the commonwealth.[37]

This is precisely the legal, social, and spiritual situation that Lambarde called "anomy"—a situation where norms have disappeared, where behavior has become unpredictable, where the law itself has become questionable. The term, with the spelling "anomie," was introduced into modern social science by Émile Durkheim in *Suicide* (1897) and has subsequently been defined, refined, and often discredited by other students of sociology.[38] But anomy, as "a condition in which both the social effectiveness and the cultural morality of norms tend towards zero,"[39] has been known in English since Lambarde, and, as Ralf Dahrendorf argues, "it would be a pity to abandon the word, . . . which is so strong and has been so close historically to the description of the opposite condition to social order." Surely it is no accident that the term was rediscovered in England precisely at the moment when social and legal anarchy seemed so close and when, furthermore, religious and philosophical thinkers were coming to grips with urgent ethical issues: "law, transgression, free will, and the role of human reason in the moral sphere."[40]

It is within this "climate of opinion" of the debate on equity and law, whose almost uninterrupted continuity can be traced by way of Budé and Aquinas through Celsus and Aristotle back to Sophocles, and the urgent Renaissance concern about order and anomy, I believe, that we need to locate *The Merchant of Venice* (1596 or 1597)—and not, of course, that work alone. Book 5 of Spenser's *Faerie Queene*, which appeared that same year (1596), is devoted to "The Legend of Artegall or of Iustice" and explains how Astraea teaches Artegall "to weigh both right and wrong / In equall ballance with due recompence, / And equitie to measure out along / According to the line of conscience" (bk. 5, canto 1, st. 7).

I am of course not suggesting that such specific cases as the many lawsuits in which his father was engaged (notably *Shakespeare vs. Lambert* with its analogies to *Shylock vs. Antonio*) or Shakespeare's view of Venice as an endangered civilization losing its positive values[41] do not play a role. And despite the provocative argument of the following pages I wish to complement rather than to displace many other discussions of the play. But we can make out hitherto unexposed dimensions of Shakespeare's work if we view it in the context of the sixteenth-century European debate on equity and *epieikeia*, which anticipates not only many of the ideas of the play but also the very vocabulary of the discourse.[42] And we can reconcile many of the critical controversies surrounding the play if we see it as an attempt to thematize the very anomy that Shakespeare and his contemporaries recognized in the society of the 1590s—a mood that stands in sharp contrast to the optimism characterizing Shakespeare's other "legal" play, *Measure for Measure* (1604), which was written in the spirit of hope attending the accession of a new monarch.

For well over a century *The Merchant of Venice* has provided an inexhaustible text for the ingenuity of scholars of law and literature, whose views of the play have been at least as radically polarized as those of the literary scholars.[43] The positions were staked out well over a century ago. In one of the most influential legal works of the nineteenth century, *The Struggle for Law* (1872), Rudolf von Jhering argued that from a jurist's standpoint Shylock is cheated out of his legal due and that, as he stumbles off the stage, "the law of Venice has been bent along with him."[44] Jhering's championing of individuals like Shylock was consistent with the theories of social utilitarianism that he represented, but it was at odds with the legal neo-Hegelianism then prevalent in Germany, which gave priority to the state and its institutions. Only a decade later, therefore, another great German legal thinker maintained in direct opposition to Jhering that "the trial scene . . . is a typical image of the legal development of all times: it contains the quintessence of the nature and progress of law; it contains a more profound jurisprudence than ten volumes of Pandects and opens up a deeper view into the history of law than all works of legal history from Savigny down to Ihering." Kohler dealt with the problem of Shylock, whom in any case he regarded as a scoundrel, by observing in proper dialectical fashion that "no progress in the world is possible without individual injustice."[45] And the debate surrounding the legal issues of *The Merchant of Venice* has continued virtually unabated down to the present, when we can recognize the principles underlying the controversy between Jhering and Kohler in the interpretations of two legal thinkers prominent in Law-and-Literature studies. Richard Weisberg refers explicitly to Jhering in his argument that Shylock is fully justified in expecting to be upheld by the law and that his rights are violated by Portia.[46] Richard A. Posner, while he gives no evidence of familiarity with the German tradition, echoes Kohler in his view that the play amounts to the defense of a legal system evolving law from strict liability to equity, and believes that Portia "personifies the spirit of equity."[47] The place of honor occupied by *The Merchant of Venice* among students of Law and Literature—next to Melville's *Billy Budd*—is attested by the fact that a special issue (vol. 5, no. 1) of the *Cardozo Studies in Law and Literature* was devoted to it in 1993.

The ambiguities of this perhaps most controversial of Shakespeare's plays have of course elicited the ingenuities not only of the Law-and-Literature critics.[48] The spectrum of interpretations among literary scholars ranges from those who perceive "fulfillment and reconciliation" in the ending of the play[49] to those who regard it as an "ironic comedy" in which the happiness of Belmont is exposed as an illusion masking the amorality of a varnished reality.[50]

But what if, to use Lambarde's phrase, "disorder, doubt, and uncertainty" were precisely the point of the play? What if it were Shakespeare's intention not to advocate either the need for strict liability or the appeal of equity but to expose the unpredictability of the legal system in which Shylock and Portia encounter each other? What if it were his aim not to contrast Venice and Belmont but to reveal the anomy governing the society that embraces them both? If we read the play in this way, in the legal and social context of the 1590s, we lose a romantic comedy, but we gain a remarkable commentary on Elizabethan England.[51]

The Merchant of Venice: Judicial Irregularities

Shortly after her "Mercy" speech, when Portia qua doctor of laws has acknowledged the validity of Shylock's claim, she orders Antonio to prepare his bosom for the knife that Shylock has been earnestly whetting (4.1). As Shylock approaches to claim his bond, Portia asks if he has balances in which to weigh the flesh, and Shylock assures her that they are at hand. Modern critics have made surprisingly little of this remarkable scenic configuration. But is it conceivable that the contemporary audiences for Shakespeare's play—at the end of the century that witnessed not only the agitated public debate on common law and Chancery, law and equity, but also the dramatic emergence all over Europe of the image of Justitia with her sword and scales—is it conceivable that this audience did not recognize in Shylock with his knife and balance a striking image of Justitia? (We know from the almost contemporaneous *Henry*

IV [pt. 2, 5.2.103] that the newly crowned Henry V endowed the chief justice with "the balance and the sword" as attributes of office as well as judicial impartiality.)

The scene is bewildering in more senses than one, for the attributes of Justitia are borne by a man who has been clamoring loudly for the full rigor of the law—a man, moreover, who during the trial calls repeatedly for law (six times) and the strict enforcement of his bond (seven times) but never mentions justice.[52] (This suggests that Shakespeare distinguishes more precisely between "law" and "justice" than do many of his commentators.)[53] At the same time, the young spokesperson of "mercy," who cites "justice" some eight times (= over half of the fifteen occurrences of the word in the play), is clad in the black garb identified customarily with courts of common law and their *summum ius*.[54] The uncertainties created by these visual images and linguistic usages are calculated to arouse in the audience a total sensation of confusion, of parodistic inversion, of—in a word—anomy.

We know that Shakespeare, as a citizen in a litigious society permeated by legalism, was fascinated by law and familiar with the legal terminology and procedures of his day.[55] (Even when his plays are set abroad, it is always the familiar common law of England that Shakespeare applies.)[56] The degree of his interest is indicated by the prominence of the trial scene in *The Merchant of Venice*. In Shakespeare's probable source, *Il Pecorone* (1558), the legal incident amounts to not much more than one episode among many, occupying roughly one-tenth of the narrative.[57] Indeed, it is not even a formal trial but a consultation with the lady posing as a lawyer (presumably at the inn where the lawyer has taken lodgings). The case is restricted exclusively to the annulment of the (nameless) Jew's bond when he is informed that he must spill no blood while taking his pound of flesh: there is no Alien Statute, no forced conversion, no deed of gift to a disinherited daughter. In Shakespeare's play, in contrast, the trial scene takes up the entire fourth act, constituting almost one-fifth of the action. Moreover, it is a proper trial that, in word and procedure, is fully consistent with the practice of English law as Shakespeare knew it in the 1590s.[58] Accordingly, it is appropriate to take the trial scene very seriously.

As the juxtaposition and confusion of the images of *Ius Strictum* and *Justitia* in the persons of Shylock and Portia has already suggested, the fourth act comes closer to a travesty than to a representation of a trial. It has often been pointed out that "any trained lawyer would find it difficult to commit the liberties with procedure of which Shakespeare was guilty in this trial."[59] But the irregularities go well beyond procedural inaccuracies. I am not referring here to the contract itself or its validity. Volumes have been written about the terms of Shylock's bond with Antonio, tracing the pound of flesh back to the Twelve Tables of Roman law and then forward again by way of Athens, India, Mosaic law, the Cherokee Indians, and primitive Germanic tribes.[60] But the question of whether such a bond would have been legal according to English law of the Elizabethan period or medieval Venetian law, no matter how fascinating it may be to legal historians, is completely beside the point, as is the fact pointed out by many lawyers from Jhering to Kornstein that the bond might have been declared illegal and void as *contra bonos mores* or against public policy.[61] For *within* the play the legality of the bond is never in the slightest doubt. Indeed, it is wholly consistent with Shakespeare's practice of using an irrational law as the catalyst for his plots.[62] And along with the validity of this specific instrument the sanctity of law in general is repeatedly confirmed. Antonio, as a businessman, recognizes early that

> The duke cannot deny the course of law:
> For the commodity that strangers have
> With us in Venice, if it be denied,
> Will much impeach the justice of the state,
> Since that the trade and profit of the city
> Consisteth of all nations.
>
> (3.3.26–31)

Shylock also knows that, if his bond is denied, the danger will light "Upon your charter and your city's freedom" (4.1.39).

> If you deny me, fie upon your law!
> There is no force in the decrees of Venice.
>
> (4.1.101–2)

Again at the beginning of the trial Antonio remarks that "no lawful means can carry me / Out of his envy's reach" (4.1.9–10); and the duke, by his appeal to Shylock's "pity" and "mercy," implicitly acknowledges the validity of the bond. Even Portia, in her capacity as *Doctor iuris*, acknowledges, despite the strange nature of Shylock's suit,

> Yet in such rule, that the Venetian law
> Cannot impugn you as you do proceed.
>
> (4.1.174–75)

And she repeats the concern regarding the implications of a broken contract:

> It must not be, there is no power in Venice
> Can alter a decree established:
> 'Twill be recorded for a precedent,
> And many an error by the same example
> Will rush into the state,—it cannot be.
>
> (4.1.214–18)

Similarly, Shylock's motives—no matter how unattractive we may find his lust for revenge against the Christian who "hates our sacred nation, and . . . rails / (Even there where merchants most do congregate) / On me, my bargains, and my well-won thrift" (1.3.43–45)—are no more a factor than are Antonio's reasons for "breaking a custom" by taking out a loan against interest or the Elizabethan prejudices against usury.[63] For the purposes of the play the bond is regarded as valid and its terms as legal by everyone concerned. As an alien, moreover, Shylock has every reason to distrust the broad discretion of the judge and to cling to a strict interpretation of the law.[64] (Traditionally, in the evolution of law, the institution of contract has been the essential means by which individuals have managed to free themselves from their inherited status.)[65] And even his revenge remains ultimately within the letter of the law.

The legal irregularities begin with the opening words—"What, is Antonio here?"—because they suggest a lack of impartiality on the part of the duke, not to say favoritism regarding a fellow Christian, a respected member of the Venetian business community. In contrast, he labels the plaintiff generically as "the Jew" and characterizes him as

> A stony adversary, an inhuman wretch,
> Uncapable of pity, void, and empty
> From any dram of mercy.
>
> (4.1.4–6)

Antonio has already heard that the duke, in pretrial motions, "hath ta'en great pains to qualify / His rigorous course" (4.1.8–9). As soon as Shylock enters, the duke, rather than hearing his case, begins to berate him for his "malice" and lack of "mercy," suggesting in no uncertain terms that he expects the Jew to change his tune and give a "gentle" (4.1.34)—that is, gentile or Christian—response and even to forgive half the principal of the loan. But Shylock repeats his vow "To have the due and forfeit of my bond" (37), which, as we have seen, is regarded as valid by everyone concerned, and he is not swayed by Bassanio's offer to double the amount of the loan in repayment. "What judgment shall I dread doing no wrong?" (4.1.89).

The duke has already sent to Padua for the advice of the learned doctor Bellario in this highly unusual matter and in his frustration and despair threatens to dismiss the court—in legal terms, to continue the case—until he has the benefit of that advice. Both these practices were quite legal. Continuation for a reasonable time was not uncommon during the reign of Elizabeth.[66] And since the early sixteenth century it had become an increasingly common practice in Europe for judges, especially lay judges without legal training (like the duke), to submit cases to law-faculty committees for adjudication. Indeed, on the Continent "imperial ordinances of 1570 and 1600 granted litigants the right to demand that law faculties hear their cases as an alternative to regular courts and offices of justice."[67] Even in the unlikely event that Shakespeare was not familiar with that widespread Continental practice, he would have known the custom in English law of the *amicus curiae*, who could appear on his own volition or at the request of the court to instruct or provide advice in unusual cases.[68] So there is nothing illegal or unusual in the fact that the duke has requested outside professional advice.

What is unusual to the point of impropriety and probably even illegality is the appearance of Portia in that role—a role that itself is never clearly defined: Is she a disinterested *amicus curiae*, Antonio's advocate, or the judge? Being married to a principal in the action, she can hardly be called disinterested; she has a pronounced interest in seeing the case come out in favor of her new husband's closest friend. In addition, she is guilty of harboring the plaintiff's daughter, an heiress whose abduction is a statutory felony.[69] Moreover, her appearance involves multiple perjuries. First, when Nerissa (herself posing as a lawyer's clerk) tells the duke that they have come from Padua as emissaries from Bellario, she is lying—and a lie in the context of a courtroom is implicitly perjury. For she and Portia have come directly from Belmont: they have neither been in Padua nor seen Bellario. Shylock, in contrast, explicitly refuses to perjure himself:

> An oath, an oath, I have an oath in heaven,—
> Shall I lay perjury upon my soul?
> No not for Venice.
>
> (4.1.224–26)

From that point on matters get progressively worse. The alleged letter from Bellario is either a forgery or itself perjury because it colludes in the deception that Portia is a Roman doctor of laws named Balthazar (a name apparently borrowed on the spur of the moment from the servant whom Portia had sent to her cousin Bellario). Portia then perjures herself: first, by appearing in the court under false pretences and, second, by lying about having come from Bellario (with whom she has communicated only by message). One wonders, in fact, if she appears in disguise precisely to conceal not her sex but her status: not that she is a woman but that she has no legal credentials or standing. The entire proceeding is technically invalidated by these multiple perjuries.

We should pause for a moment to consider the implications of Portia's action. And we are entitled to take them quite seriously because Shakespeare, knowing the law as well as he demonstrably did, would have been fully aware of all the procedural irregularities. We know from her earlier appearances that she is a young woman of quick intelligence and a ready tongue. But she is in no sense a trained lawyer, being in her own words "an unlesson'd girl, unschool'd, unpractised" (3.2.159). It is therefore rash to the point of irresponsibility for her to assume the awesome charge of defending Antonio, whose life is after all at stake. Even with the benefit of Bellario's written instructions, she would have been more prudent to spend her fortune on hiring a good lawyer rather than trusting recklessly and with a playful heedlessness to her own wits.

The issue of Bellario's written instructions brings us to the next important question: What did Portia know and when did she know it? For thereupon rests the issue of her "professional" ethics. First of all, from Bassanio, Salerio, and Antonio's letter she learns almost all the essentials of the case before her departure from Belmont. Antonio's ventures have failed, and his bond with its deadly consequences is forfeit because he failed to repay it on the appointed day. More important, she has been acquainted with the character of Shylock, who at this point would not take money to discharge the loan even if it were available and "plies the duke at morning and at night, / And doth impeach the freedom of the state / If they deny him justice" (3.2.276–78). His own daughter Jessica confides that she has heard him swear "That he would rather have Antonio's flesh / Than twenty times the value of the sum / That he did owe him" (3.2.285–87). Jessica warns Portia in her next lines that "If law, authority, and power deny not, / It will go hard with poor Antonio." Portia understands, finally, that paying the pound of flesh will cost Antonio his life. When she encounters Shylock in court, therefore, she is under no illusion that her appeal to mercy will be effective.

Bellario himself is fully informed about the case: even if the duke's summons mentioned at the beginning of the trial scene (4.1.105–6) did not outline the case, Portia has sent him a letter, which no doubt contains all the information she has just acquired (3.4.47–50). Bellario, in turn, has sent Portia the garments for her deception as well as his notes on the case. Since Portia is no lawyer, we must assume that her legal tactics are dictated in detail by Bellario—that she knows in advance, that is to say, exactly what she is going to do. (To this extent she follows the courtroom maxim that one should never ask a question to which one does not already know the answer.) Even before she sets eyes on Shylock, in short, she knows that she is going to introduce the two courtroom tactics announced each time by the word "tarry." She will first obtain an effective injunction against his cutting the pound of flesh by the laws of Venice according to which "Thou diest, and all thy goods are confiscate" (4.1.328) if he sheds a single drop of Christian blood (a restriction that is regarded as absurd, if not illegal, by many lawyers who have concerned themselves with the case). She will then cite the Alien Statute and bring a so-called cross action[70] in which Antonio (as a citizen) now himself becomes the plaintiff against the Jew (that is, the noncitizen alien) Shylock, who has allegedly contrived against his life. In sum, what begins as a civil case goes on to become a criminal action. This much, we are safe in assuming, is the advice of the learned jurist Bellario.

Accordingly, the pretty words about mercy are window dressing, hypocritical, and even sadistic:[71] Portia knows that Shylock will not be swayed and wishes merely to lure him into a false sense of confidence.[72] All the assertions that the bond is forfeit and that Antonio must prepare himself to pay the penalty amount to pettifoggery and, even worse, to Jew-baiting and unnecessary tormenting of the victim Antonio; for Portia knows in advance that it will never come to execution. In fact, if we accept the legality of the two laws that Portia invokes—and accept them we must in the same spirit in which we accept the legality of the bond—the whole matter could have been resolved without a trial, by a simple declaration from the duke. Bassanio's remarks about the malleability of the law seem to be coined with specific reference to her manipulations:

> In law, what pleas so tainted and corrupt,
> But being seasoned with a gracious voice,
> Obscures the show of evil?
>
> (3.2.75–77)

The way Portia plays with Bellario's legal advice reveals her character rather than her intelligence—and we recall that Grotius defined equity as a disposition of the will rather than the intellect. Portia's malicious behavior with Shylock is absolutely consistent with her earlier toying with the suitors and even her own betrothed. From her first appearance we get to know Portia as a young woman "curb'd by the will of a dead father" (1.2.24–25) who devised the lottery of the three chests for her suitors. Culturally and intellectually arrogant, and racist to boot (against blacks as well as Jews),[73] she is resentful and even a trifle self-pitying at being bound by this law, which might wed her to a man she regards as her inferior. Resolved to "die as chaste as Diana, unless I be obtained by the manner of my father's will" (1.2.102–3), she is nevertheless not above trying to influence the game. Her playful command for Nerissa to "set a deep glass of Rhenish wine on the contrary casket" (1.2.91–92) to sway the choice of a drunken German nobleman suggests that she gives thought to ways of improving her chances. Some critics have argued plausibly that the song she requests while Bassanio is deliberating tells him which casket he should choose.[74]

If Portia is not above playing fast and loose with the rules, she is also not above tormenting even those she is supposed to love. Her game with the rings falls little short of malicious. She knows the terms under which she gave Bassanio the ring,

> Which when you part from, lose, or give away,
> Let it presage the ruin of your love,
> And be my vantage to exclaim on you.
>
> (3.2.172–74)

It sounds almost as though she is setting him up for a trick that she intends eventually to play on him. Following the trial, when Bassanio offers her (disguised as the lawyer) a fee or a token of remembrance, it is she who insists upon having the ring and nothing but the ring, despite Bassanio's loyal pleas that he made a vow to his wife never to part with it. In the last act one must feel that her torment of Bassanio is unjust since it was she herself who tricked him into parting with the ring. If we stop to wonder why Portia behaves this way, it is not implausible to assume that she has transferred the resentment she felt toward her father for *his* rules to the man she has taken in his place as "her lord, her governor, her king" (3.2.165) and that she wants him to understand that she is capable of making the rules work to her own advantage.

In any case, Portia is wholly in character when she goes beyond Bellario's legal advice and torments Shylock even when she knows she has him in her power. For she has directed against him the full force not only of her anti-Semitic contempt but also her general hostility toward men. Shylock, as we saw, is quite precise in his vocabulary: "I stand here for law" (4.1.142), he says, and "I crave the law" (4.1.202). He charges Portia "by the law" (4.1.234) to proceed to judgment, and when he is informed that he cannot legally spill blood and satisfies himself that it is indeed the law (4.1.310), he is immediately prepared to drop his suit. It is Portia who in her "mercy" speech projects upon him the longing for justice:

> Though justice be thy plea, consider this,
> That in the course of justice, none of us
> Should see salvation: we do pray for mercy. . . .
>
> (4.1.195–97)

Her speech makes it clear that Portia is using her words in the evolving sixteenth-century sense that we traced at the beginning of this chapter. "Mercy" is a divine attribute ("an attribute to God himself") that, through natural law, becomes "enthroned in the hearts of kings" and "seasons" justice (4.1.189–93). Portia uses "justice," in contrast, to designate what in the strict Aristotelian sense is known as equity—a term never used in this play and, as I have noted, occurring only four times altogether in Shakespeare's works. As Lambarde defined equity, it is the quality applied to mitigate the rigor of the positive law when that law has "need of correction," the spirit informing the law but not coterminous with "law." Equity, or justice, is the sense by which *ius strictum* is altered to achieve what the judge regards as fairness. Hence Portia is able to state that

> I have spoke thus much
> To mitigate the justice of thy plea,
> Which if thou follow, this strict court of Venice
> Must needs give sentence 'gainst the merchant there.
>
> (4.1.198–201)

Yet her words amount to pure mockery when she tells him:

> For as thou urgest justice, be assur'd
> Thou shalt have justice more than thou desir'st.
>
> (4.1.311–12)

For justice is precisely what he does not receive. The *law*, as strict and written, cannot be manipulated; but *justice* or equity permits the interpretation and rectification of the law. It is symptomatic that all her talk of justice occurs in the first part of the trial: the part involving the bond and in which Shylock is the plaintiff. Here she uses "justice" against his claim for law. The young doctor of laws who has mouthed the virtue of mercy and justice—a "mouthpiece" in the worst sense of the word—turns out to be the most severe advocate of *ius strictum*. One might argue that justice would have been served if Portia had stopped, as did the source, with the forfeiture of Shylock's entire principal.

But in the second phase of the trial she goes on to tell him that "The law hath yet another hold on you" (4.1.343)—the Alien Statute that entitles Antonio to seize half his goods and the state the other half. Here, through the cross action whereby Shylock suddenly becomes the defendant in a criminal suit brought in compliance with the Alien Statute, the word "justice" disappears from Portia's vocabulary; for here, where Shylock is the defendant, she is interested not in "justice" (that is, equity), which would have taken into account the fact that no crime has actually been committed, but in the strictest possible construction of the law. The duke, alone among the participants, does show "mercy"—that divine attribute that seasons justice and the law—by reducing the state's claim to a simple fine. But Antonio compounds the sentence not only by taking half of Shylock's fortune in trust (to be rendered upon his death to Lorenzo, who eloped with Jessica) but by demanding of Shylock the greatest of indignities: his conversion to Christianity.

Shylock comes to court in a simple civil suit to get what is conceded by everyone involved to be his legal due. When he departs only half an hour later he has not only lost the principal of his bond in the civil suit; he has become the convicted defendant in a criminal suit that results in the forfeiture of half his fortune, a forced disposition against his will of the other half, and a humiliating conversion to Christianity. Some mercy! For all of this injustice is imposed on a man who has committed no offense: even if—and it is a big "if"—he is guilty of criminal intent (*mens rea*), there is no criminal act. Regardless of where our sympathies lie, with Portia or with Shylock, we cannot possibly come away from this scene still believing that we have witnessed an orderly legal procedure. An impostor, authorized through deception and perjury and arguing before a highly prejudiced court, has in the name of justice invalidated a perfectly legal bond and, through a string of tactics that can be called nothing better than pettifoggery, imposed a series of possibly illegal and certainly unjust sanctions on the initial plaintiff. If ever anyone needed a good lawyer, Shylock did![75]

The Merchant of Venice: The State of Anomy

If the brilliant fourth act amounts to an exposure of doubt and uncertainty regarding the Elizabethan legal system, it is by no means inconsistent with the rest of the play. For most of the principal characters—that is, the ones sensitive enough to be aware of it—are burdened by symptoms that can most precisely be defined as anomy, including the duke himself, whose perplexity is suggested by the fact that almost his first and last words in the play are "I am sorry" (4.1.3 and 401). We now see, for instance, that anomy can explain Antonio's mood, with which the play opens:[76]

> In sooth I know not why I am so sad,
> It wearies me, you say it wearies you;
> But how I caught it, found it, or came by it,
> What stuff 'tis made of, whereof it is born,
> I am to learn:
> And such a want-wit sadness makes of me,
> That I have much ado to know myself.
>
> (1.1.1–7)

In response to his friends Antonio protests that his mood stems neither from financial concerns ("Therefore my merchandise makes me not sad" [1.1.45]) nor from love. The normally imperceptive Gratiano probably comes closest when he tells Antonio:

> You have too much respect upon the world:
> They lose it that do buy it with much care. . . .
>
> (1.1.74–75)

These lines suggest that Antonio's sadness results not, as many critics believe, from any homoerotic attachment to Bassanio, but rather from his concerns regarding the state of the world and society—a state, as Lambarde characterized it, of "disorder, doubt, and uncertainty." It is this mood that causes him to "break a custom" and take out a loan on interest. When his friends report to Bassanio that he has lost his ships, they tell him that Antonio is "Not sick, my lord, unless it be in mind, / Nor well, unless in mind" (3.2.233–34). Later we learn that "griefs and losses have so bated me / That I shall hardly spare a pound of flesh" (3.3.32–33): a sense of indifference also characteristic of anomy. And this growing indifference carries over into the trial scene, where Antonio, calling himself "a tainted wether of the flock, / Meetest for death" (4.1.114–15), asks simply: "Let me have judgment, and the Jew his will!" (4.1.83).

The same world-weariness that characterizes Antonio marks Portia when we first meet her: "By my troth Nerissa, my little body is aweary of this great world" (1.2.1–2). When Nerissa tells her that she has much to be thankful for, she admits that they are "Good sentences, and well pronounc'd." But "If to do were as easy as to know what were good to do, chapels had been churches, and poor men's cottages princes' palaces" and other words to the same effect (1.2.10–26): the definition of anomy. Indeed, anomy defines very precisely the situation in which she finds herself, "curb'd by the will of a dead father" whose will she fails to understand and whose authority she resents and seeks at every turning to circumvent. It is her anomy, finally, that enables her to play fast and loose with the law, for she has no respect for or confidence in laws that can be so easily abused and manipulated as her father's caskets, her suitor's oath, and the laws of contract.

Another figure in this society depressed by anomy whose first words provide the clue to her behavior is Jessica, speaking to Launcelot:

> I am sorry thou wilt leave my father so,
> Our house is hell, and thou (a merry devil)
> Didst rob it of some taste of tediousness. . . .
>
> (2.3.1–3)

More than any other figure in the play, Jessica is torn asunder by doubts and uncertainties:

> Alack, what heinous sin is it in me
> To be ashamed to be my father's child!
> But though I am a daughter to his blood
> I am not to his manners: O Lorenzo
> If thou keep promise I shall end this strife,
> Become a Christian and thy loving wife!
>
> (2.3.16–21)

But her actions bring her no happiness. She betrays her father's trust when he leaves her with his keys and entrusts his house to her (2.5.11–16). She not only steals his money; she also takes a turquoise ring that he received from his dead wife, one of the few objects precious to him for human and emotional reasons. Yet despite the profligacies to which she is led by her spendthrift husband (they spend fourscore ducats at a single sitting in Genoa) she is still a melancholy outsider when they reach Belmont; Gratiano tells Nerissa to "cheer yond stranger" (3.2.236).

Few scenes in Shakespeare are more ironically ambivalent than the love duet between Lorenzo and Jessica at the beginning of act 5, for every figure that they adduce is an image of betrayed or unhappy love: Cressida, Thisbe, Dido, Medea. Indeed, the allusion to Medea has quite sinister overtones if we recall that on two earlier occasions Bassanio (1.1.169–72) and Gratiano (3.2.240) referred to the pursuit and conquest of the women of Belmont as the quest for the Golden Fleece. If we read the images with any consistency at all, then they hint at Bassanio's future betrayal of Portia and the Medea-like vengeance she might take.[77] It is possible, of course, to give the dialogue a happy twist, reading it as teasing.[78] Yet every word resonates with a bitter double entendre:

LORENZO: In such a night
Did Jessica steal from the wealthy Jew,
And with an unthrift love did run from Venice
As far as Belmont.
JESSICA: In such a night
Did young Lorenzo swear he loved her well,
Stealing her soul with many vows of faith,
And ne'er a true one.

(5.1.14–20)

After a messenger reports the impending arrival of Portia, Lorenzo continues his bland hymn to the beautiful night, unaware of the dejection that leads Jessica to utter her last words in the play: "I am never merry when I hear sweet music" (5.1.69). At the end, when Portia and Nerissa hand over the deed assuring the improvident couple of Shylock's fortune, they address themselves to Lorenzo: "How now Lorenzo? My clerk hath some good comfort too for you" (5.1.288–89). Jessica stands silent, no doubt aware that she has betrayed her father and her faith for nothing—that she is still an alien, like Shylock, among the broken oaths and mindless entertainments of the jeunesse dorée of Belmont. If Antonio is able to muster himself at the news of his own good fortune to say "I am dumb!" then Jessica exemplifies that state.

It takes a considerable act of faith to see in *The Merchant of Venice* the blissful resolution of a romantic comedy.[79] Its melancholy is not nearly exhausted by the conflict between Shylock and Portia or between a narrowly conceived "law" and "equity": it is about the unpredictability of an entire legal and social system. What the unbiased eye sees is a play that begins and ends with the extreme depression of two characters (Antonio and Jessica) who find themselves excluded as outsiders—just as fully as Shylock himself—from the frenetic gaiety of a group of mindless young people (notably Gratiano and Nerissa) who seek to lose themselves in carousing and sexual excitement. This society, which pays lip service but little actual respect to contracts (the caskets) and oaths (the rings), embraces a central action (the trial) in which the images of Law and Justice are satirically inverted, in which the law is abused by shrewd manipulation in the name of "justice" or equity but applied ruthlessly when it suits the needs of a biased court and a perjured jurisprudent, and in which "mercy" is applied with haughty benevolence to a convicted defendant who has committed no crime.

The play has proved the validity of Shylock's worst fear—that there is indeed "no force in the decrees of Venice" (4.1.102)—and virtually predicts the economic decline of a state whose justice and contracts have been so greatly impeached (3.3.29–30). A savage *ius strictum* has been undone by an irresponsible equity. *Summum ius, summa iniuria* is escalated into *summa justitia summa iniustitia*. The doubts and uncertainties pervade Venice and Belmont alike. If

Antonio and Shylock have good reason to wonder whether any future contract will be honored in Venice, then Portia and Nerissa and Jessica must be equally concerned about the oaths and fidelity of their fortune-seeking new husbands.[80] Far from a festival of reconciliation, *The Merchant of Venice* reveals itself as Shakespeare's brilliant contribution to the contemporary debate on jurisprudence: a legal parable portraying a society whose collective consciousness was pervaded by precisely that state of anomy that his contemporary and friend Lambarde had within the same decade diagnosed as the condition of Elizabethan England in the 1590s.[81]

CHAPTER TEN

The Attractions of Codification

The Age of the Great Codes

The urge to codify laws belongs among the most primal impulses of human civilization. We have already noted the incentive that prompted many early societies to engrave their laws on tablets of stone or bronze, which they set up in public places as a token of their order: the code of Hammurabi inscribed on a pillar of black stone in Babylon; the Ten Commandments allegedly etched on two tablets of stone by the hand of God; the code of Gortyn, chiseled into the walls of a law court in Crete; the codes of Draco and Solon displayed on wooden tablets in Athens; and the Twelve Tables, on which the Romans inscribed the common law of their earliest community. Other codes of more recent origin also record material of great antiquity: for example, the Hindu Code of Manu (ca. A.D. 400) or the code of the T'ang dynasty (A.D. 630), which provided the basis for the great "Manchu Code" of the seventeenth century.[1] The common denominator linking all these early examples was the general belief that the code embodied the people's sense of moral right.

A second wave of codifications took place early in the common era when the Germanic tribes encountered the Romans, who had just summarized a millennium of legal sophistication in Justinian's great compilations. Under the influence of the *Corpus Iuris Civilis* the peoples of the *Völkerwanderung* were inspired to record their own customary law in Latin. The most important of these *leges barbarorum* were the early-sixth-century *Lex Burgundionum*, in which King Gundobad and his son Sigismund sought to accomplish a compromise between Germanic law and the Roman law that they experienced in southeastern France; the *Lex Salica* prevailing in the territories of western Europe that came under Frankish domination; the Langobardic (Lombard) law of northern Italy; and the *Lex Visigothorum*, through which King Alaric II and his successors established a legal order that endured in Spain until the fourteenth century.[2] The rationalism of the thirteenth century produced, as we have already observed, a third wave of codifications that extended across western Europe: from Alfonso's *Siete partidas* and Philippe de Beaumanoir's *Coutumes de Beauvaisis* by way of Eike von Repgow's *Sachsenspiegel* and Henry de Bracton's *De legibus et consuetudinibus Angliae* to the Icelandic *Grágás*.

All these great codes, however, regardless of their scope and historical importance, amounted to little more than variously sophisticated compilations of existing statutes. Justinian's *Digest*, as a synthesizing repository of existing laws, comes closest to a modern code, although it conflates private, procedural, and penal law. None of the early codes fulfills the criteria that define any modern code: substantive completeness, logical systematization, and terminological clarity[3]—factors that came into play only during the Age of Reason, whose enlightened monarchs usually placed the codification of law near the top of their political agendas as a tool of territorial consolidation. Inspired by practical reforms in Prussia and philosophical initiatives in France, especially in Montesquieu's *De l'esprit des lois* (1748), the second half of the eighteenth century witnessed a broad movement toward codification in the modern sense although not all the projects were completed.[4]

The impulse toward codification emerged in Prussia under Friedrich Wilhelm I, who in 1714 ordered his law faculty at the University of Halle to consolidate the scattered laws in his territories—a project that remained fragmentary. In 1746 his son, Frederick the Great, again took up the initiative and ordered his chancellor, Samuel von Cocceji, to organize the constitutions of the various Prussian territories into a system based on natural reason. Cocceji's *Corpus Juris Fridericianum*, which was to comprise the existing Prussian common law arranged according to the categories of Justinian's *Institutes*, began to be published in 1749–51 but, because of Cocceji's death in 1755 and Frederick's preoccupation with the Seven Years' War, was never completed and put into effect.

Inspired by Frederick's cabinet order of 1746, the kingdom of Bavaria also sought in 1750 to rationalize and consolidate its existing *ius commune* according to the model of Justinian's *Institutes*. The next few years witnessed the publication of a code of criminal law (*Codex iuris Bavarici criminalis*, 1751), of procedural law (*Codex iuris Bavarici judicialis*, 1753), and of private law (*Codex Maximilianeus Bavaricus civilis*, 1756). Moved by the same pervasive spirit of the times, Catherine II of Russia (herself a German by birth and education) appointed in 1767 a legislative commission whose charge she outlined in a 119-page "Instruction," which she caused to be translated into the major Western languages. However, owing to a profound conflict between the ideal of liberty motivating the commission and the czarina's more absolutist notions, Catherine's ambitious project was never carried out.

Meanwhile, a new Prussian cabinet order in 1780 initiated the final thrust toward codification under a new commission directed by Heinrich Casimir von Carmer and Carl Gottlieb Svarez. This initiative resulted in an eight-volume draft for an *Allgemeines Gesetzbuch*, whose titles appeared individually from 1784 to 1788. The revision of this draft, incorporating suggestions for improvement solicited from jurists throughout Europe, was published in 1791 with the expectation that it would take effect in 1792. This did not occur.

After the death of Frederick the Great in 1786, his nephew Friedrich Wilhelm II had acceded to power along with his mistresses and his minister, Johann Rudolf von Bischoffwerder. As a result of their reactionary tendencies, the general public fears generated by the French Revolution, and the opposition of the nobility to this so-called equality code ("Gleichheitskodex") that threatened to diminish their privileges, the code was revised to tone down some of its more enlightened (and hence more objectionable) principles. The result, entitled *Allgemeines Landrecht für die Preußischen Staaten* (*ALR*) or General Territorial Law, was finally published in 1792 but did not take effect until 1794, when the addition of new lands to Prussia following the partition of Poland in 1793 necessitated a code appropriate for the enlarged kingdom.

Yet for all its conservatism this great document of the Prussian Enlightenment challenged customary provincial law simply by the fact of codification, which took the control and interpretation of law out of the hands of established authority and vested it in the people.[5] The *ALR* was therefore a highly ambivalent document, balancing modern theory against social and political constraints, looking both to the past and to the future, and embodying the generalizing tendencies of all enlightened modern codes.

The Prussian code of 1794, to which we shall return, constitutes the culmination of European legal culture in the eighteenth century—a general code embracing private, criminal, public, administrative, and commercial law based on and organized according to principles of natural law expounded in the introduction. Moreover, as the first stage in the great reforms that were enacted in the following decade, it functioned in practice as a constitution for the emerging state of Prussia. Yet, evolving as it did from the specific circumstances of the Prussian Enlightenment, it remained an isolated example, limited by its very wealth of specific detail (43 titles with 19,091 paragraphs consisting of one sentence each) and by its use of the German language, which was less well known in Europe than Latin or French.

Even in Prussia its effect was restricted and not immediate: indeed, the history of Germany in the nineteenth century is in no small measure the history of opposition to the *ALR* by the regional and local practices that it sought to displace (a tension reflected, as we shall see, in Kleist's comedy *The Broken Pitcher*). Initially regarded as a subsidiary law in cases not covered by provincial rights, statutory ordinances, and customary law, and qualified by concessions to such special interest groups as hunting, mining, and associations (such as the Freemasons and learned societies), the *ALR* served for several decades mainly as a guide for the bureaucracy and the courts—especially the superior courts whose officers were often not familiar with the complexities of the various local laws with which they had to contend.

Although the *ALR* was not a formal subject of instruction at universities until 1826, it became well known through the publicity attending its publication, through the great debate of the 1790s, through the "Crown Prince

Lectures" that Svarez delivered in 1792 for the legal edification of the crown prince, and through such public education as the "Instruction on the Laws for the Inhabitants of the Prussian States" (*Unterricht über die Gesetze für die Einwohner der Preußischen Staaten*) that Svarez published in 1793. A government order of January 1, 1797, required all law candidates to pursue the study of philosophy and natural law in order to obtain the premises for a proper understanding of the *ALR*.[6] That these requirements were not merely formal we know from the examinations for civil servants, in which the candidates were first examined on natural law and subsequently tested on German and Prussian law.[7]

The movement toward codification did not end with the eighteenth century. The French *Code civil* of 1804 was the product of a commission of four officials appointed by Napoleon in 1800, but its success was due to the circumstance that the commission was able to draw on sources going back to the *coutumes* of Paris, which had been reduced to writing in 1580,[8] as well as François Bourjon's *Le Droit commun de la France et la coutume de Paris reduits en principes* (1743).[9] Indeed, the *Code civil* amounted less to an act of original legislation than to a fusion of existing legal materials into a new product. Both shorter (only 2,281 paragraphs) and more abstract than the lengthy *Landrecht*, and based as it was on the familiar pattern of Roman law (though lacking the general introduction typical of codes based on the principles of natural law), it was easily accessible and readily applicable in other civil-law countries on the Continent and in territories of the New World. The Austrian code of 1811—the *Allgemeines Bürgerliches Gesetzbuch* (*ABGB*)—similarly retained the model of Justinian's *Institutes*. Going back by way of the Josephine codification of 1786 to initiatives of a commission established as early as 1753 by Empress Maria Theresa to unify the private law of Austrian territories, the legal reform was directed during the 1790s by Karl Anton von Martini, who sought to base the new legal code on constitutional principles guaranteeing human rights. However, the introduction spelling out these intentions (typical of such natural-law codes as the Prussian *ALR*) was subsequently eliminated for political reasons by Martini's student, Franz von Zeiller, who was responsible for the final form of the *ABGB*.

While the impulse toward codification was strongest in civil-law countries, it was not unknown in common-law lands. As early as 1789 Jeremy Bentham had published his *Introduction to the Principles of Morals and Legislation*, in which he developed views that he later specified in *A General View of a Complete Code of Laws*. However, despite his impact on British criminal law and procedure, Bentham's thoughts on codification enjoyed a greater success on the Continent, where codification was proceeding apace, and in the colonial codes of Anglo-India, than in England. Bentham also sent the draft of proposed legislation to the United States in the unrealized hope of persuading the American Congress to adopt a code for their new republic. Meanwhile, in the United States articulate advocates of codification emerged in the persons of Edward Livingston and David Dudley Field. Livingston, a New York lawyer who moved to New Orleans in 1804, became familiar with the *Code civil* when he was appointed to a commission to prepare a provisional code of judicial procedure in the newly purchased territory of Louisiana. The so-called Livingston Code of criminal law that he completed in 1824 was never adopted by the state of Louisiana; but it was widely reprinted in Europe, where Livingston became known as "the first legal genius of modern times."[10] Field, who visited Europe in 1836 to study the Continental legal systems, devoted the next forty years of his life to the codification of American law, which he advocated in his influential pamphlet *The Reorganization of the Judiciary* (1846). Indeed, his civil and criminal procedures provided the model for the codes now in force in many states. But in substance the United States, like England, resisted the general Continental impulse toward codification, preferring the flexibility and ease of amendment of common-law legislation.

The Codification Controversy in Germany

Around the turn of the century, then, three different conceptions of law were competing in Europe for authority: the tradition of Roman law with its inherent tendency toward codification; the philosophy of natural law with its claim to reason and order; and the practice of customary law with its appeal to familiarity. It goes without saying that the controversy stemmed from the conviction of all three parties that their version of law best expressed the sense of social and moral order. Nowhere was this strife more pronounced than in Germany. In France, as we have seen, the tradition of Roman law as adapted to the local *coutumes* was unimpeded; in England the common law maintained its undisputed authority despite Bentham's appeals to natural law; and in Prussia the *ALR* gradually achieved canonical status. But elsewhere in Germany all three modes were in a state of considerable tension.[11] Especially after 1806, when Franz II of Austria abdicated as ruler of the Holy Roman Empire and the apparatus of the Imperial Chancery was dismantled, the various principalities previously governed by Roman law had to decide whether to accept one of the existing codes, to create for themselves a new code based on natural law, or to fall back into a judicial chaos encompassing scores of local systems of customary law.

Ever since the Reception of the fifteenth and sixteenth centuries the various German territories of the Holy Roman Empire had been ruled by the so-called *usus modernus pandectarum*—that is to say, by the *Corpus Iuris Civilis* as interpreted by the *glossatores* and adapted to traditional Germanic customary law. After the middle of the seventeenth century a second element was added to this modernized Roman law: natural law.[12] There is of course no single "law of nature," which might most simply be understood as the ideological system on the basis of which an age seeks to justify its existing positive law. In antiquity and the Christian Middle Ages this legitimation was sought mainly in transcendental authorities. For classical Roman law, as Ulpian put it in the words that stand almost at the beginning of Justinian's *Institutes* (bk. I, title 2), the authority for natural law is nature itself: *Ius naturale est, quod natura omnia animalia docuit*. Thomas Aquinas and other Christian thinkers also perceived behind the secular laws of the thirteenth century a *lex aeterna*, one that expressed not nature but the will of God. With the rationalism of the seventeenth and eighteenth centuries, however, the emphasis was shifted: an anthropological natural law sought the basis of universal human rights not in God or in a divine nature but solely in human reason. Instead of regarding human rights as the secular expression of a higher will, Hugo Grotius and his successors in Germany—Samuel Pufendorf, Christian Thomasius, Christian Wolff, and others—sought to deduce their ideal law from pure reason alone. To the degree that natural law gradually liberated itself from the existing positive law (whether Roman or customary), natural law became less and less a juristic and increasingly a philosophical exercise. Fichte published a "Foundation of Natural Law" (*Grundlage des Naturrechts*) in 1796, and in the following years Kant brought out his "Metaphysical Rudiments of the Legal Theory" (*Metaphysische Anfangsgründe der Rechtslehre*) as the first part of his *Metaphysics of Morals*. This led to the circumstance that natural law became a widely discussed topic of intellectual discourse: in 1771 Goethe cited Ulpian's famous statement among the fifty-six theses that he proposed for debate when he was examined for his law degree at the University of Strassburg.[13] But it degenerated into a discourse in which everyone, even the juristically unskilled, felt qualified to participate. In 1791 the twenty-one-year-old Friedrich Hölderlin wrote to a friend that "I am having myself instructed about the rights of man by the great *Jean Jacques*"; and six years later he enthused to his brother that mathematics and natural law are "the only complete, pure sciences in the entire realm of the human spirit."[14]

Such popularization led to the gradual discrediting of natural law. Loosed from all restraints of positive law and historical reality, this untrammeled theorizing generated toward the end of the eighteenth century a flood of systems. People joked that every annual book fair produced a new theory of natural law.[15] In 1795 Friedrich Schiller poked fun at two of the most famous theorists of natural law in his satirical poem "The Universal Sages" ("Die Weltweisen"):

> "Der Mensch bedarf des Menschen sehr
> Zu seinem großen Ziele,
> Nur in dem Ganzen wirket er,
> Viel Tropfen geben erst das Meer,
> Viel Wasser treibt die Mühle.

Drum flieht der wilden Wölfe Stand
Und knüpft des Staates daurend Band."
So lehren vom Katheder
Herr Pufendorf und Feder.[16]

("Man needs his fellow man to achieve his great goal; he can be effective only as part of the whole; it takes many drops to make the sea: much water to move the mill. Therefore flee the condition of wild wolves and knot the lasting bond of the state." This is what Herr Pufendorf and Herr Feder teach from their lecterns.)

Three years later Friedrich Schlegel scoffed at the so-called philosophical jurists who "in addition to the other laws, which are often so unjust, also have a Natural Law, which not rarely is even more unjust."[17]

As a result of these developments, Germany of the Napoleonic age witnessed a series of legal controversies, which were followed knowledgeably by many contemporaries—and not just by the astonishing number of German writers who were also trained in law.[18] Despite the moderating efforts of Friedrich Wilhelm II the *ALR* could not deny its natural-law basis. This is clearly expressed in the introduction, under the heading "Sources of the Law": "The general rights of the individual are based on the natural freedom to seek and further his own welfare without infringing on the rights of another" (§83).[19] The principal opponents of natural law were the legal positivists and jurists of the Historical School. Legal positivism emphasized in contrast to natural law the reality of the existing laws and had as its goal a codification of positive law in a form that would be accessible to the people. The Historical School, as it developed under Friedrich Karl von Savigny in Berlin, rejected natural law for different reasons: out of the conviction that law cannot be discovered by reason but only given by history. The pronounced opposition of these two juristic schools led to the ridicule and decline of natural law in Germany, a result regarded by many historians as the main symptom of the differences between the legal system that emerged in Germany and those of the other Western countries.[20] The poet Joseph von Eichendorff recalled that, during his student years in Halle and Heidelberg during the first decade of the century, "the jurists were teaching a so-called Natural Law, which was valid nowhere and never could be valid."[21]

It was predictable that Savigny, the founder of the Historical School of law and the most influential jurist of his generation, would reject the *ALR* as a *Schweinerei*,[22] for it combined the codification that he regarded as artificial with the natural law that he detested as unhistorical. It was also in his opinion an antijuristic document to the extent that it ruled out as grounds for interpretation both legal history and judicial opinions: "In future decisions no regard shall be taken of views of the teachers of law or older opinions of judges" (intro., §6). Savigny's opposition, articulated in his powerful pamphlet on the unreadiness of his generation for the act of legislation and jurisprudence (*Vom Beruf unserer Zeit für Gesetzgebung und Rechtswissenschaft*, 1814), eventually carried the day in the great controversy that he waged against Anton von Thibaut, the leading advocate of codification.[23] As a result, the Prussian initiative was not adopted in other German-speaking territories, which therefore—unlike France, Austria, and other countries—had no comprehensive legal code until 1900, some thirty years after the consolidation of Germany under Bismarck. Yet Savigny's eloquent and powerful opposition should not blind us to the epoch-making impact of the *Allgemeines Landrecht*. Exemplifying the response of the average Prussian citizen is Achim von Arnim's defense of the code vis-à-vis his brother-in-law Savigny:

> The *Landrecht* possesses for our people from a legal point of view the same importance as in a religious context Luther's translation of the Bible. Previously there was a law, just as previously there were also Christians. Neither of them is an easily understandable chapbook. But both are consulted and compared with the statements of the judges and preachers.[24]

Arnim's evaluation has been repeatedly confirmed by the historians, who point to the great "unifying power" of the *ALR* in Prussia.[25]

Kleist and the Prussian Code

Scholars were long inclined in their reading of Heinrich von Kleist (1777–1811) to attribute insufficient weight to the historical context that shaped his thinking.[26] We know all too little about the life of this great Prussian individualist, the scion of a distinguished military family who at age fourteen entered the elite Guard Regiment in Potsdam as a corporal, served in 1793–94 as an ensign in the Rhineland campaign against the French revolutionary army, was promoted to second lieutenant in 1797, and then in 1799—to the dismay of his family and friends—resigned his commission. For the next twelve years, until his suicide in 1811, Kleist led a peripatetic life: for three semesters as a student in Frankfurt an der Oder, a few months in Berlin as an intern in government service, then years of wandering through France and Switzerland until, from 1805 to 1807, he again worked as a civil servant, only to give it up for a shaky career as a journalist in Dresden and Berlin. Yet during these years he wrote some of the greatest stories and dramas in the history of modern European literature. Despite the fact that Kleist, unlike so many writers among his contemporaries, had little formal legal training, the law plays a conspicuously central role in his thought and works. Indeed, he exemplifies paradigmatically the tension between law and moral conviction as he veers between the laws of reason and what he called the "laws of the heart" in his desperate search for stability.

Although we have only limited knowledge about Kleist's education during the formative years before his resignation from the military, a few conclusions can be deduced. It is essential, first of all, to keep in mind the fact that Kleist's education up to the age of twenty-one was military—that is to say, it lacked the background in classics and humanities that was the mainstay of the secondary education of almost all his literary contemporaries. For that reason, when Kleist left the army to attend the university, he was restricted in his choice of fields to the natural sciences and mathematics that had constituted the basis of his military training. Moreover, he had to attend special classes at the *Gymnasium* in Potsdam to compensate for educational deficiencies, and he was required to take a qualifying examination before he was admitted to the university in his hometown of Frankfurt an der Oder. Kleist was a variously talented young man: we hear, for instance, of his musical virtuosity on the flute and clarinet. But he was essentially self-taught and therefore untrained by systematic habits of thought to resist the enthusiasms or the disappointments that his often unsupervised reading thrust upon him. His friend Ludwig Tieck, in the introduction to his edition of Kleist's works, observed in this connection:

> It is natural that most autodidacts place far too much weight on what they have learned in their peculiar, random, and vehement manner; it is just as understandable that in other hours, when their knowledge and learning does not give them the calm satisfaction that gently expands and unobtrusively enriches our souls, they despise all knowledge, thinking, and learning, all information and erudition, and place an imagined and impossible state of nature higher than all culture—indeed, regard it as the truest and happiest state.[27]

We should keep this shrewd evaluation in mind as we review Kleist's agitated responses to the intellectual fashions of his day.

Official thought in late-eighteenth-century Prussia was profoundly informed by a natural-law anthropology as expounded by Pufendorf, and this impulse accordingly was fundamental in Kleist's thinking.[28] Samuel Pufendorf was the principal mediator of a moderate natural law, and in the second half of the eighteenth century his influence had reached its high point.[29] Locke, Blackstone, and Adam Smith in England; Montesquieu, Diderot, and Rousseau in France; Samuel Adams, Hamilton, and Jefferson in America—even Peter the Great in Russia—all admired his system of thought, whose elements played a formative role in the new constitutions. Above all in Frederick the Great's Prussia, Pufendorf's conception of natural law exerted a powerful attraction because of its emphasis on human duties and responsibilities along with the human rights that were otherwise so fashionable in the age of revolutions. Because his textbook of natural law, *De officio hominis et civis juxta legem naturalem* (1673), both in the Latin original and in various translations, provided a major component in European school instruction down to the early nineteenth century, Pufendorf figured not only among the professional philosophers but also in the popular consciousness. That Pufendorf's name meant something to Kleist we know from a casual reference in his comedy *The Broken Pitcher* (*Der zerbrochne Krug*, sc. 4, lines 311–12), where the village justice Adam tries to demonstrate his learning by telling the inspector that the world is growing steadily cleverer and everybody reads "Puffendorf":

> Die Welt, sagt unser Sprichwort, wird stets klüger,
> Und alles liest, ich weiß, den Puffendorf.
>
> (1:188)[30]

But also the letters of the twenty-two-year-old display the thoughts and in particular the vocabulary of natural law. Thus in the great letter of May 1799, where he is outlining his "life plan" for his sister Ulrike, we hear that *something* must be sacred to mankind:

> For the two of us, to whom the ceremonies of religion and the prescriptions of conventional society are not sacred, the laws of reason must be all the more so. The state demands from us nothing further than that we do not transgress the Ten Commandments. But who, if not reason, orders us to practice the virtues of love of humanity, of tolerance, of modesty, of morality? The state assures us of our property, our honor, and our life; but who assures us our inner happiness if reason does not do so? (2:491)

Already here the language betrays an acquaintance with the text and the principles of the *ALR*, which contained statutes governing not only the nobility (II 9) and the military (II 10 §§1–67) but even universities and students (II 12). For the moment, however, in the mind of the young man who only two months earlier was still in the Prussian army, the sentiments of a rapturous natural law, which Kleist identifies with virtue and morality, assert their priority.

Kleist's presumably early acquaintance with natural law was expanded at the university in Frankfurt an der Oder, where in addition to his studies in science and mathematics he attended the lectures of Professor Ludwig Gottfried Madihn (1748–1834). Madihn was a product of the school of Daniel Nettelbladt at the university of Halle, a school of law notorious for its disregard of historical source-study and its mindless use of natural-law commonplaces.[31] Madihn personified this school in exemplary fashion.[32] Continually plagued by financial difficulties, he hastily compiled compendiums for the use of his students in every field of legal science. To this end he published in 1794 a commentary on the *ALR* as well as "Principles of Natural Law for the Use of His Lectures" (*Grundsätze des Naturrechts zum Gebrauch seiner Vorlesungen*, 1774, 1789, and 1795), lectures for which Kleist intended to enroll in the autumn of 1800—for a tuition fee of ten *Reichsthaler*, as he wrote to his sister

Ulrike (2:533). From Madihn Kleist would have received at most a simplifying enthusiasm and least of all a critical attitude toward natural law. It was in all probability Madihn whose lectures brought Kleist to the decision that he did not want to study law, as his family advisers were urging him to do. "Ach, Wilhelmine," he lamented at the beginning of 1800 in a letter to his fiancée,

> I recently heard debated in Natural Law the question of whether the contracts of lovers could be valid because they are made in a state of passion—and what am I supposed to think about a discipline that racks its brains over the issue of whether there is such a thing in the world as property and which for that reason would only teach me to doubt whether I may ever justifiably call you *mine*? No, no, Wilhelmine, I don't want to study law [*die Rechte*], not the vacillating, uncertain, ambivalent laws of reason; I want to cling to the laws of my heart, and I want to practice them, whatever all the systems of philosophy may object. (2:503–4)

Here we see an early instance of the dissociation of law and moral conviction ("laws of my heart") that will later plague all of Kleist's heroes.

We should not take too seriously this emotional outburst of the despairing twenty-three-year-old—not at least outside its specific context. For Kleist, unlike 70 percent of the 220 students matriculated at the time in Frankfurt an der Oder, was not a proper jurist. In the first place, his Latin did not suffice for the mastery of Roman law. (To be sure, he did undertake the study of Latin at the university, and he later learned enough Greek to read Homer in the original.) And as far as we know, he attended no lectures by the most distinguished legal scholar of the day at Frankfurt an der Oder: Johann Friedrich Reitemeier (1755–1839), who published important books on legal reform in Germany as well as on international law.[33] (In a town as small as Frankfurt an der Oder, of course, with its total of nineteen professors it is unlikely that Kleist did not from time to time pick up various details in extracurricular settings.) In other words: the student Kleist was not shielded by any solid juristic learning against the errors of natural law. At the same time he possessed no systematic knowledge of positive law. For that reason his exclamation against "law" signifies a rejection at most of the excesses of natural law. His naive conception of natural law explains the disappointment that pervaded the idealistic young traveler when he came to the realization in Paris in the summer of 1801 that the French, for all their appeals to Rousseau, had not remained true to his principles. "Rousseau is every fourth word of the French," he wrote to a friend; "and how ashamed he would be if someone should tell him that this is *his* work?" (2:664–65).

Only in this light is it possible to understand the "legal crisis" that Kleist experienced in the summer of 1801, a few months after his so-called Kant crisis. This turning point in Kleist's intellectual development has been much discussed, and there is no need here to recapitulate the entire argument.[34] The essential points are laid out in the letter of March 22, 1801, that he wrote to his fiancée, in which he reports that he has recently become acquainted with "the new so-called Kantian philosophy." We must bear in mind the fact that the twenty-three-year-old recording this experience is a philosophical autodidact who has grown up in the naively rationalistic belief that, according to the title of an essay he had written two years earlier, it is possible "to find the sure way to happiness" ("Aufsatz, den sichern Weg des Glücks zu finden," 2:301–15). Now, suddenly, his entire faith in the rational access to knowledge and happiness has been undermined by Kant's theory of knowledge, according to which we can never know reality as such (*das Ding an sich*) but only the categories of human consciousness and our own perceptions. As Kleist puts it:

> If all people had green glass instead of eyes, then they would have to believe that the objects which they see through them *are* green—and they would never be able to decide whether their eye is showing them the things as they are or whether it is not adding something to them that belongs not to the objects but to the eye. So it is with human reason. We cannot decide whether what we call truth is truly truth or whether it only appears so to us. If the latter is the case, then the truth that we accumulate here no longer exists after death—and all our striving to acquire an [intellectual] possession that will accompany us even into the grave is in vain.
>
> Ach, Wilhelmine, if the point of this thought does not puncture your heart, then don't smile at another who feels wounded by it in his most sacred inner being. My single, my highest goal has fallen, and I have nothing more. (2:634)

His disenchantment with metaphysics and with rational understanding carries over to his former belief in natural law. Five months later he asserts, for instance, that "people still doubt after many millennia whether there is such a thing as law" (2:683; the German word *Recht* is ambiguous: it can mean either "law" or "right," legal authorization or moral entitlement). "Let it not be said," he continues, "that an inner voice secretly and clearly confides to us what is right. The same voice that urges the Christian to forgive his enemy urges the islander to roast him, and with reverence he gobbles him up" (2:683). This rejection of a shallow natural law does not have the least thing to do with Kleist's understanding of positive law, for in Kleist's mind natural law and positive law existed on separate tracks just as was the case at the universities of the age. It might even be claimed that it was a logical result of the Kant crisis, which after all undermined all intellectual certainty, that prompted Kleist to cling to the moral certainty of positive law. Accordingly Kleist, despite his rejection of "law," was able a few years later to return to jurisprudence when in 1805 he again sought a government position in the Department of Finance and was urged, in order to prepare himself, to study the law of demesnes as well as the Institutions and Pandects in Königsberg (2:753). The juristic mode of thought was not alien to him, as is clear in the essay "On the

Gradual Production of Thoughts While Speaking" ("Über die allmähliche Verfertigung der Gedanken beim Reden"). When he is seeking there to illustrate a typical examination question, an example from legal instruction immediately occurs to him: "What is the state? Or: what is property?" (2:323). We should not forget that many of his friends and acquaintances—from the close friend of his student years Ludwig von Brockes to Savigny, whom he later got to know socially in Berlin—were jurists. Adam Müller, his collaborator in various editorial enterprises in Dresden and Berlin, was also a jurist who compared himself as a philosopher of law to Montesquieu.[35] Despite the gaps in his irregular education Kleist was living in a juristic culture and always had the opportunity to inform himself about the most important developments in the field of legal science or the philosophy of law, in which he longed to find the embodiment of moral certainty and social order. It became, as it were, his passion to reconcile the two denotations expressed by the vocable *Recht* in German: "law" and "right."

Already in the cited letter of May 1799 Kleist distinguishes pedantically between the natural-law "laws of reason" and the positive laws of the state, which guarantee "our property, our honor, and our life." With this reference to property, honor, and life Kleist is recapitulating the first part of the *ALR* (titles 8–22 treat questions of property) as well as the last title of the second part, which deals with crimes against life and injuries to honor. Kleist was a civil servant precisely in the years when the *ALR* was being heatedly discussed and was gradually displacing regional customary law. As a "servant of the state in the military" (*Militairbedienter*) he was subject to the "articles of war and other relevant prescriptions" delineating the special obligations of the military (II 10 §4). It is unlikely that the young cadet was indifferent to the controversies surrounding the new legal code—above all on the part of the nobility, whose privileges appeared to be threatened by what was known contemptuously as the "equality codex" (*Gleichheitscodex*). But like Achim von Arnim, a member of the impoverished nobility living in a similarly precarious situation, Kleist had little reason to fear the loss of privileges. After his release from the military he entered the civil service, where according to the *ALR* he was still a servant of the state: "All officials of the state who do not belong to the military are included under the general heading of civil servants" (II 10 §68). During his months in Berlin, when he was serving as an intern in the technical delegation of the Office of Public Finance and Economic Affairs (1800–1801)—the only office for which he seemed remotely qualified on the basis of his previous education—he was expected to prepare himself for further government work by acquiring "a more general view of the territorial constitution" (that is, the *ALR*).[36] While he was subsequently working in the Office of Provincial Administration in Berlin and Königsberg (1805–7), he acquired considerable practical experience and, by attending lectures on law and public administration, a certain theoretical knowledge of the Prussian code.

His training left an indelible mark on his writing style as well. In Berlin and especially in Königsberg his responsibilities included the preparation of *Relationen*, or legal briefs, which were delivered orally to the members of the chamber of judges who made the decisions in various cases. In Prussia these *Relationen* had to be written according to a normalized outline. The first part amounted to a straightforward narrative, or *species facti*, in which all the relevant facts of the case were selected and presented from a point of view consistent with the statutes of the *ALR*. It has been demonstrated that Kleist's narratives, and especially the opening paragraphs regarded as typically "Kleistian," follow precisely the order specified by such manuals as Justus Claproth's *Grundsäze von Verfertigung der Relationen aus Gerichtsacten* (4th ed. Göttingen, 1789).[37] In addition to the organization, sequence, and presentation of the material, Kleist's literary style was determined by these judicial *Relationen*, which reflect the style of the *ALR* itself. Down to such details as sequence of tense, syntax, the typically Kleistian hypotaxis, and the preference for such conjunctions as "dergestalt, daß," Kleist's language is imbued with the style of Prussian legal bureaucracy. (This is consistent, by the way, with the fact that his style was developed under circumstances wholly different from those of his literary contemporaries. Most of them wrote a German shaped extensively by the classical languages through which they were educated. Kleist, lacking that background, developed a style that was determined by Prussian chancellery German.)

His experiences in the course of fifteen years in Prussian military and civil service also taught him another important fact: that in every state the ultimate power resides in the legal code. Accordingly he sought even in his career as a journalist to stay close to the law. In 1807 in Dresden, precisely at the time when his anti-French fervor was at its peak, he entertained the notion of establishing a publishing company that would obtain the rights to the German edition of the "Kodex Napoleon," and hoped that he would be selected by the French government "to spread its publications in Germany" (2:793). For our purposes it is beside the point that these unrealistic hopes did not materialize. What matters is Kleist's shrewd recognition of the great significance of the French codification and his calculating hope to profit from the dissemination of the *Code civil*, which was being imposed or adopted in various German principalities. The second important attempt was the subsequent founding of his journal, the *Berliner Abendblätter* (1810–11), which Kleist hoped would become a "semiministerial paper" (2:851). In the announcement Kleist promised as the journal's main attraction to evaluate "changes in the legislation of the fatherland" (2:458). Even though Kleist was more often critical about the Prussian reforms of Stein and Hardenberg, as for instance in his comments on the new financial measures ("Über die Finanzmaßregeln der Regierung," 2:405–7), for him legislation counted as "above all else the closest and most worthy object of general concern." So Kleist applauded Adam Müller's demand (in the *Berliner Abendblätter* of October 4, 1810) that, in the future, no one should be permitted to enter the judiciary or the general administration of Prussia who was not equipped "with a competent and complete experience of the national universe," under which rubric he of course included the *ALR*.

In sum, Kleist's intellectual biography from 1799 until his death in 1811, in its steady development away from natural law and toward an ever firmer relationship to positive law in the form of the *ALR*,[38] paralleled the history of Prussia itself. The early letters display a superficial acquaintance with a popularized natural law in the tradition of Pufendorf, in which he saw exemplified the moral sense of Prussia. But after his "legal crisis" in the summer of 1801 his attitude vis-à-vis natural law became steadily more critical as he detected a discrepancy between the laws of reason and the "laws of the heart." Accordingly he turned gradually to the positive law as it had been formulated in Prussia since 1794 as *ALR* and in France since 1804 as *Code civil*, documents in which he saw, if not absolute morality, then at least a basis for social order.

The Prussian Code in Kleist's Works

What significance do these facts and conjectures have for our understanding of Kleist's works? Formulating the effect of the law as precisely as possible, we can affirm first of all that in Kleist's oeuvre, with the exception of the anecdotal narrative "The Beggarwoman of Locarno," there is hardly a single literary text in which legal issues do not play a significant role.[39] This extends from the inheritance contract that triggers the action in *The Schroffenstein Family* (*Die Familie Schroffenstein*, 1803), the "law of marriage" in *Amphitryon* (1807), and the marriage contract in "The Marquise of O——" (1808)—indeed, contracts in general—to the complicated legal and court situations portrayed in great detail in *Michael Kohlhaas* (1810). Formally, moreover, Kleist displays (like Kafka a century later) a pronounced predilection for inquisitorial dialogues and a narrative that approaches the chancellery style of official documents with their strict causal sequence. In the dramas and stories alike we find a wealth of legal practices from the most varied times and places: German-speaking lands in the late Middle Ages, the sixteenth and seventeenth centuries; Italy in the Renaissance and the eighteenth century; Spanish colonies in the seventeenth and French colonies in the early nineteenth century—with Roman *ius gentium* and Germanic customary law, with the criminal tribunals of the *Vehmgericht* and with lay courts (*Schöffengericht*), with military law and trial by combat, with secular and ecclesiastical courts. In his fascination with the legal circumstances of the most varied cultures Kleist shows himself to be a true contemporary of the emerging Historical School in Germany.

From the jurists who have concerned themselves with his works we have learned that Kleist, while his capacity for empathy was often sensational, can in no way be considered a specialist in the history of law. One legal scholar has determined that in Kleist's medievalizing works, "whenever he presents past legal circumstances in an astonishingly precise manner, anachronisms can inevitably be exposed."[40] Another notes that in *The Prince von Homburg* various "deviations from the historical starting point" are evident, especially in connection with military legislation.[41] It should hardly surprise us that this notorious autodidact did not have at his disposal the knowledge of a legal historian. In 1801 he confided to his sister that he "always goes from one field of learning to the other and always only floats on the surface without ever penetrating the depths" (2:629–30). The wonder is, rather, that he succeeded to such an extent, despite his lack of systematic study, in grasping intuitively the legal situation of his various fictional settings.

How did Kleist help himself in those cases when he needed a specific legal point? A simple example is provided by the comedy *Amphitryon*, in which positive law plays a slighter role than in virtually any other play by Kleist. In the early scene in which Jupiter and Alkmene appear for the first time after their night of love, Jupiter wants to assure himself that Alkmene surrendered to him out of passion and not out of any (however mistaken) sense of marital obligation:

> Du weißt, daß ein Gesetz der Ehe ist,
> Und eine Pflicht, und daß wer Liebe nicht erwirbt,
> Noch Liebe vor dem Richter fordern kann.
>
> (Lines 446–48)

(You know that there is a law of matrimony and a duty, and that whoever fails to win love can demand it from the judge.)

Kleist had apparently forgotten—or, more likely, never known—that the mythological Amphitryon set out on his military expedition only because Alkmene had, according to ancient Greek law, legally denied him his marital rights until he had avenged the death of her brothers. The "law of marriage," therefore, had no precedent in either the classical source or the explicitly natural-law *Amphitryon* of Molière.[42] Kleist's Jupiter can most easily be understood as an enlightened despot relying on the *ALR*, which specifies in the section on rights and obligations of married couples: "Spouses may not persistently deny each other their matrimonial duty" (II 1 §178)—a conception that distinctly differs from the classical as well as the French situation.

Similar examples can be found in many other works. In general, whenever Kleist requires for his plot a legal fact, regardless of the historical period in which the work is set, he reaches to the source that lay most readily at hand: the *Allgemeines Landrecht* of 1794. Many readers have been surprised, for instance, that the Count F—— in the novella "The Marquise of O——" is not punished for his violation of the unconscious marquise, as were the five soldiers who had tried to rape her. But the matter can be easily clarified by the *ALR*. The execution of the five soldiers results from an explicit charge lodged by the commandant, the marquise's father, and under the military law that was in force at the time. Soon thereafter the army withdraws: "Everything now returned to the old order of things" (2:109), and in normal times "commissioned and noncommissioned officers of noble descent . . . are subject in their personal affairs, like the local nobility, to the laws of the province in which they are headquartered" (II 10 §5). By the time the marquise's pregnancy is discovered, therefore, civil law is again in effect, and specifically the paragraphs of the *ALR* that concern rape (*Nothzucht*): "Whoever deprives an innocent female of her senses by means of drink or other means in order to abuse her for lustful purposes, shall, even if he did not accomplish his purpose, be punished with three to six months imprisonment and, if the abominable deed was actually accomplished, with four to six years imprisonment" (II 20 §1048). It is self-evident, the *ALR* continues, that "the criminal is obligated to give the injured party private satisfaction" (II 20 §1059). But these ordinances are ultimately qualified by the last paragraph: "If the injured parties do not lodge a complaint regarding such crimes and if thereby no public nuisance has been created: then no judicial investigation takes place at official instigation" (II 20 §1060). Kleist is enabled by the legal circumstances to deal with what interests him most: not the legal technicalities, but the personal and psychological aspects of the extraordinary event—the seemingly inexplicable pregnancy of the marquise and her paradoxical response to the count, when she learns that he is the guilty party. (In several other works Kleist deals with the paradox of innocent women whose sexual guilt at first appears manifest but subsequently turns out to be illusory.)

Even when Kleist is dealing with older times and circumstances the *ALR* often offers an adequate analogy. In the historical drama *Käthchen von Heilbronn* (1810) the quarrel between Friedrich Count vom Strahl and Kunigunde von Thurneck concerns her claim to one of his properties:

> The Rhine count demands, in the name of Fräulein Kunigunde von Thurneck, the repurchase of your estate Stauffen—those three towns and seventeen villages and farms that were sold to your ancestor Otto by her ancestor Peter under the said stipulation. (1:456)

Later Kunigunde seeks to win the affection of the count by her alleged renunciation of those rights:

> Take them, take them, Count! The letters are ambiguous, I now realize, and the repurchase to which they entitle me has expired. But even if my right were as clear as the sun, I can no longer insist on its validity against you. (1:475)

But the count does not accept the document and recommends that she submit her case to the emperor and the imperial court so that "the law may decide who was mistaken." His mother seconds this sober recommendation: "Accept my son's advice and have the papers inspected at Wetzlar." The reference to Wetzlar alerts us to one of Kleist's famous anachronisms: he had forgotten that the imperial court was not transferred to that town until 1683. But Kleist needed neither the imperial court nor the "Swabian laws" to which there is an allusion in another place (1:456) in order to demonstrate the invalidity of Kunigunde's claims. For the *ALR* leaves no doubts in the section "On Prior Rights to Family Estates." Kunigunde's claim is invalid in the first place because it has expired: "If a property has once left the family and the prior right has expired under the statute of limitations: then the prior right is not revived" (II 4 §248). In the second place, Kunigunde has no claim to the estate because of the ancient provision of Salic law that "Female members of the family and their descendants, even if male, cannot exercise the prior claim" (II 4 §233).

In connection with *Michael Kohlhaas* the *ALR* explains at least as much as the imperial decree of 1495 or the determinations of specific articles of Emperor Charles V's great criminal code (the *Carolina* or *Peinliche Gerichtsordnung*) of 1532.[43] Kleist's most famous novella is in one sense a handbook of legal procedures as well as an exemplum for the philosophy of law: indeed, variants of the word *Recht* occur three times in the first paragraph. The action is triggered when two splendid horses of the horse dealer Michael Kohlhaas are impounded as security under trumped-up charges by a Junker's henchmen at a crossing-point on the border between Brandenburg and Saxony. Kohlhaas, who is introduced as an upstanding and law-abiding man with a fierce sense of right (his famous *Rechtgefühl*), first seeks to resolve the case through the normal legal channels: he lodges a simple civil claim for the return of his property in Dresden, the capital of Saxony, where the tort actually occurred. When nothing happens for a year (because two of the Junker's cousins are well-placed in Saxon officialdom), he appeals as a citizen of Brandenburg to the elector of his own state, who turns the case over to his chancellor; but since the chancellor is also related to the Junker the case is allowed to languish. When Kohlhaas threatens to sell his property and leave Brandenburg on the grounds that he does not wish to live in a land that will not protect his rights, his wife goes with a personal petition to Berlin, where she is accidentally but fatally injured by the elector's guards. Kohlhaas is driven by his offended *Rechtgefühl* to take matters into his own hands, and from this point forward the action intensifies steadily as his personal moral conviction drives him to violate the law of the land.

Kohlhaas attacks and burns the castle where his horses were initially misappropriated, and issues a general mandate to anyone giving shelter to the Junker. Raising a private army, he attacks the town of Wittenberg, which he burns and whose local forces he routs. He then defeats two territorial armies sent out against him and sets fire to the city of Leipzig, under the impression that the Junker is being sheltered there. When Martin Luther accuses Kohlhaas of injustice, Kohlhaas is distressed and visits the Reformation hero in Wittenberg, persuading him of his honest intentions and requesting safe-conduct to plead his case in Dresden. The elector of Saxony, after listening to various legal arguments, grants the safe-conduct; the Junker is summoned to appear; and the horses are located. But Kohlhaas with his strict sense of right refuses to accept his now decrepit animals until they have been restored to their original condition. Owing to a certain confusion—Kohlhaas's former mercenary troops are now looting the countryside on their own—public sympathy shifts against Kohlhaas. The amnesty is revoked, and after he is tricked into attempting to escape, he is found guilty and condemned to be drawn and quartered. At this point the elector of Brandenburg finally intervenes, and Saxony, under the threat of war from Poland, agrees to surrender Kohlhaas. Kohlhaas returns to Berlin, where he finally obtains his justice: his horses are returned to him in a fully restored condition. But Kohlhaas himself, who has breached the peace of the realm with his quest for private justice, is put to death to satisfy the imperial law.

In this steadily escalating case, which begins as a trivial civil suit and ends as a case involving not just two principalities but also the chancellery of the Holy Roman Empire, we seem to be dealing with sixteenth-century law. Yet not a single legal issue arises that cannot be explained by reference to the statutes and principles of the *ALR*. Moreover, several important issues cannot be explained by reference to the *usus modernus pandectarum*. In connection with the legal-philosophical question that is central to the story—the protective obligations of the state toward its subjects—the older status-based law of the sixteenth century protected its subjects only when they were acting as representatives of their class and not as individuals; it knew nothing yet of the social contract between ruler and subject that was developed only in the course of the next two centuries.[44] The *ALR*, in contrast, takes a natural-law position whose contractual attitude, under the heading "On the Rights and Duties of the State concerning the Special Protection of Its Subjects," is quite specific: "The state is obligated to care for the security of its subjects with respect to their persons, their honor, their rights, and their fortune" (II 17 §1). For this crucial principle, which determines the elector of Brandenburg's decision to assist Kohlhaas, Kleist relies on the modern Prussian law of the *ALR*.

Concerning another important principle—the right of the individual to self-help—both older law and the *ALR* are in accord. We have already observed in the various late-medieval versions of Reynard the Fox that the effort to ensure the peace of the realm was one of the earliest moves of rulers seeking to consolidate their realms. A general prohibition against private feud, breach of the peace, and self-help specifically lay at the heart of Emperor Maximilian's imperial peace of 1495. The *ALR* is equally clear on this point: "Whoever, circumventing the authorities, seeks to seize his own right without special permission of the laws, shall, if this occurs without force toward persons or things, be punished by a money fine or civil arrest . . ." (II 20 §157). In addition, the *ALR* makes it clear that further crimes committed in the pursuit of self-help, as is clearly the case in Kleist's story, will result in more severe punishment: "If in the exercise of self-help another crime is committed which involves a more severe penalty: then the punishment is always intensified because of the additional injury to the state" (II 20 §159). Kohlhaas, to be sure, never speaks of feud or self-help but of rights and revenge; and it has been pointed out that at least one contemporary source Kleist may have known—the Kantian philosopher Ludwig Heinrich Jakob—argued in his "philosophical ethics" (*Philosophische Sittenlehre*, 1794) and his "philosophical theory of law" (*Philosophische Rechtslehre*, 1795) that the individual has the right to secure his own rights when the state does not fulfill its obligations.[45] Generally speaking, however, the full weight of philosophical and legal authority argued against such action.

The determinations with regard to the rights of the individual to protection and the inviolable security of the state coincide wholly in intent and partially in their wording with the two main themes of *Michael Kohlhaas*. For at the end the elector of Brandenburg restores to his subject Kohlhaas "all that you forfeited at Tronkenburg as the result of violence and that I, as your ruler, was obligated to restore to you" (2:101). At the same time Kohlhaas must "reconcile the world on account of the all too hasty attempts to obtain within it his rights for himself" (2:100).

If we leaf further in the classic code, we encounter over and over passages that help to explain legal situations in Kleist's story. For instance, the title "On Impoundments" (I 14 §§413–65) makes it clear that the individual whose property (normally cattle) is impounded has the right to the restoration of his property as soon as he has applied for a hearing (§448)—that is, as soon as Kohlhaas lodges his complaint at Dresden. Kohlhaas is justified in his impatience and entitled to feel legally abused. The title "On the Duties and Rights That Arise from Unpermitted Actions" contains further principles that concern the illegal seizure of Kohlhaas's two black horses as a bond. It is made clear that Kohlhaas is in the right to hold the Junker Wenzel von Tronka responsible although the injury was actually inflicted by his servants. "Whoever knowingly permits his servants to inflict an injury on another, is regarded as a participant in the unallowed action of said servants" (I 6 §61). Moreover, according to the *ALR* Kohlhaas has every right "to demand the restoration of the horses in their earlier condition; and replacement of damages" (2:46). "If a damage has occurred, then everything, as much as possible, must again be put in the condition that existed before the damage occurred" (I 6 §79). As far as the severity of Kohlhaas's final punishment is concerned, we do not need to go back to the *Carolina* because the "enlightened" *ALR* specifies for "Crimes against the External Security of the State" a series of punishments ranging from the wheel, the rope and gallows, to fire and sword (II 20 §§102–14). If the legal context of Kleist's novella is provided by the *ALR*, the dramatic tension arises from Kohlhaas's offended sense of personal right and social order, when it is violated by the very representatives of the law. As soon as the two are reconciled, Kohlhaas can die in the conviction that justice has been restored in the world.

Many juristic details in other works can also be explained by extrapolation from the *ALR*. For instance, we know from the laws governing "Seduction" why Jeronimo is in jail at the beginning of "The Earthquake in Chile":

> Educators, preachers, and other teachers who abuse the persons entrusted to their education or their special instruction are forever disqualified for all public offices, honors, and honorary positions. In addition they have forfeited imprisonment in a fortress or penitentiary for two to four years. (II 20 §1031–32)

Similarly the section "On Adoption in Place of a Child" (II 2 §§666–716) and the section "Revocation of Gifts on Account of Ingratitude" (I 11 §§1151–61) contain all the provisions concerning adoption, inheritance rights of the adopted child, and revocation of those rights that are necessary to explain the legal situation in "The Foundling."[46] The terrible denouement takes place when Piachi's sense of right is violated by the abuse of those laws: unscrupulous churchmen help his morally corrupt adopted son to drive him out of his own house.

Let us formulate our conclusions cautiously. The possibility is obviously not excluded that Kleist became acquainted with older legal procedures from his sources or from his own research in legal history—above all, with respect to such historical institutions as trial by combat or the secret criminal tribunals known as vehmic courts. But it often appears that the specific legal formulations that are constitutive in the works are adequately articulated in the *ALR*. In any case we may certainly assume that the juristic expectations Kleist takes for granted in his readers are entirely consistent with the principles of the Prussian code of 1794.[47] Even when Kleist is ostensibly dealing with remote times and exotic places, his focus is inevitably on his own Prussia at the turn of the nineteenth century,[48] and the action is generated by the conflicts that arise when Prussian law, or its enactment, veers away from Kleist's own sense of right (*Rechtgefühl*).

Kleist's Critique of the Judicial System

Let us consider in this connection Kleist's most famous legal play, *The Broken Pitcher* (*Der zerbrochne Krug*, 1808), which was based on an engraving of a juridical scene by Le Veau (1782).[49] Kleist's courtroom drama has often been compared to *Oedipus Rex* because, as in Sophocles' analytic drama, all the action has taken place before the play begins: the denouement is devoted to the analysis and understanding of those actions. During the preceding night Adam, the justice of the peace in a seventeenth-century Dutch village, attempted to seduce the virtuous Eve by threatening to have her fiancée, Ruprecht, inducted for military service in the East Indies. Ruprecht, without recognizing him in the dark, caught Adam in Eve's chamber. In the attempt to seize the fleeing judge, he hit him on the head with a door handle and, in the process, broke a beautiful earthenware pitcher. On the following morning Eve's mother, Frau Marthe, appears in court to sue Ruprecht for having broken the pitcher, while Ruprecht in turn has become convinced that his fiancée is a common slut. (The broken pitcher becomes a symbol for Eve's alleged loss of innocence.) Just as the hearing is about to begin, Justice Adam's secretary, Licht, announces an impending inspection by Councillor Walter. The court session becomes a multiple comedy of deception as Adam and Eve, for their own separate reasons, he out of guilt and she out of shame, try to keep the truth from emerging even though all the clues—the prints of Adam's clubfoot in the snow, the gash on his head, his lost wig—point to the true culprit. As Adam exploits his considerable skill in local court procedures to hide the facts, Walter, astonished by the unorthodox proceedings, seeks to discover the truth and to carry out his official inspection of the court records and finances. The truth is ultimately exposed, along with the fact that Adam has also misused court moneys. The comedy ends when Adam takes flight and Walter appoints the toadying and ambitious Licht as his temporary replacement. Order is restored, in sum, when the abused law is once again reconciled with the characters' sense of right.

Earlier scholars have pointed to parallels between the reform efforts of Councillor Walter in *The Broken Pitcher* and the reform movement that led to the promulgation of the *ALR*.[50] But we can go even further: neither the juridical structure nor the juristic situation of the comedy requires any special acquaintance with Netherlandic jurisprudence at the end of the seventeenth century. It is known that Kleist used the official procedural handbook (*Allgemeine Gerichtsordnung für die Preußischen Staaten*, 1793) both to justify the inspection and as a source for much of the juridical terminology.[51] Moreover, all the bureaucratic relationships that exist among Walter, Adam, and Licht are summarized in the paragraphs "On Sheriffs and Village Justices of the Peace" (II 7 §§46–72) and "On Village Courts" (II 7 §§79–86). For example: "During visitations that are undertaken in the village at the request of the authorities or other persons legitimated by the police, tax, or other offices, [the village justice] must provide the necessary assistance." The anxieties of the justice of the peace are adequately explained by extensive provisions in other paragraphs. The general statutes covering rape (*Nothzucht*) make it clear that "anyone who seduces [an innocent woman] to lust by means of guile or deceitful means shall, in addition to any private satisfaction owing to her, suffer imprisonment of six months to a year in a fortress or penitentiary" (II 20 §1050). And the sanctions are even more severe in the case of "Officials of Justice Who Are in Breach of Their Duties" (II 20 §§366–408). Thus in the paragraph concerning injustices that result from passion: "Justice officials who out of animosity, private passions, or other secondary intentions are carried in their official capacity to actions contrary to their duties, shall be removed from office and in addition punished with two to five years of fortress arrest" (II 20 §371). The penalties for misuse of public funds (II 20 §§418–57) are enumerated in similar detail. In agreement with the generic norms of comedy, of course, the penalties are correspondingly reduced. When the councillor orders the fleeing justice of the peace to be seized and brought back, he states, "To be sure he is suspended from his office, and I command you [his secretary Licht] to exercise that office here in the village until further disposition; but if the accounts are correct, as I hope, I shall not compel him to resign" (lines 1862–66).

Clearly Kleist intends a critique of the judicial system—though not of the law itself. Adam shows how the law can be abused for personal (financial and sexual) gain. Licht exemplifies the ambitious careerist who uses the law for his own advancement. It has even been argued, perhaps too severely, that Councillor Walter is himself guilty of irresponsible leniency toward Adam, who has not only abused his office but also misused court funds. For Walter holds out the possibility that Adam may be reinstated in his office.[52] The plot exposes the tensions between the new *ALR* of 1794 and the local customary law that it gradually had to displace in many areas of Prussia—an enterprise undertaken as early as 1747 by Samuel Cocceji at the express order of Frederick the Great, who sent his chancellor on an inspection trip to the province of Pomerania to clear up the notoriously delayed court cases.[53]

The Affirmation of Positive Law

In his affirmation of the codified Prussian law Kleist distinguished himself from many of his contemporaries in other parts of Germany, who under the influence of Savigny and the Historical School wanted to return to the "good old law."[54] Friedrich Schlegel, for instance, wrote in 1807 in his patriotic poem "Freiheit":

> Wo nach altem Recht
> Fromme Sitte gilt,
> Da sind edle Mächte
> Noch der Freiheit Schild.[55]
>
> (Where according to the old law
> Pious custom prevails,
> There the noble powers
> Are still the shield of freedom.)

Immediately after Napoleon's defeat the lawyer-poet Ludwig Uhland composed a poem in which he celebrated the *usus modernus pandectarum*:

Wo je bei altem, gutem Wein
Der Württemberger zecht,
Da soll der erste Trinkspruch sein
"Das alte, gute Recht"![56]

(Wherever with a glass of good old wine
A citizen of Württemberg is drinking,
Let his first toast be:
"The good old law"!)

Similar sentiments can be found in the poems of Clemens Brentano and the writings of Jacob Grimm. In the case of Kleist we are dealing with a wholly different mentality. But it is not enough simply to ascertain that specific legal issues in his works are posed and answered in a manner consistent with the terms of the *ALR*. It can be argued that the affirmation of the positive law in whatever society is being depicted becomes a paradigm underlying all of Kleist's stories and dramas—a symbolic affirmation of order that Kleist opposes to the constant threat of disorder in a world undermined philosophically by Kant's epistemology and politically by the French Revolution.

Over and over again at the end of these literary works the legal system that prevailed at the beginning is reinstated: that is, law and the sense of right wrenched apart through the plot come together in a renewed sense of justice and social order. In "The Earthquake in Chile" Don Fernando and Donna Elvire remain in South America and continue to live with their adopted son under the same laws that at the beginning plunged his parents, Jeronimo and Donna Josephe, into misfortune.[57] In "The Engagement in St. Domingo" Herr Ströhmli and his family return to a Europe where the same laws are in place that prevailed in Haiti before "the ill-advised steps of the National Convention" (2:160) abolished them and made way for the inhuman "laws" of the rebellious slaves. (This point is not invalidated by the fact that Kleist protests the slave society that existed in prerevolutionary Haiti.) In "The Foundling" Piachi is ultimately protected against the death for which he longs by the same canon law that earlier robbed him of his possessions. "The Duel" results in a situation that confirms despite all contradictory appearances the validity of the divine trial by combat and the decrees of the imperial court. In *Michael Kohlhaas* the law is ultimately affirmed in two forms—the territorial law through which Kohlhaas obtains his satisfaction and the imperial law through which he is condemned. And the same paradigm obtains in the dramas. In *The Broken Pitcher* the law is fulfilled despite all the confusions and evasions of the wily magistrate Adam. Prince Friedrich von Homburg, who saved the life of the elector of Brandenburg by disobeying the rules of battle, reaches the summit of bliss at the end of the play when he arrives at the insight:

Ich will das heilige Gesetz des Kriegs,
Das ich verletzt', im Angesicht des Heers,
Durch einen freien Tod verherrlichen!

(1750–52)

(I desire to glorify the sacred law of war,
Which I violated, in view of the army
Through a freely accepted death.)

For the purposes of this argument it makes no difference that he is subsequently pardoned—that the elector exercises his privilege of mercy *after* the validity of the law has been affirmed by everyone. At this point Homburg's personal sense of right is wholly in harmony with the positive law.

Kleist was driven by the same longing, even passion, for order that was felt by many of his contemporaries at the time of the crisis in Prussia and the great Romantic revaluation of all values. In what he called "the monstrous disorder of the world" (in *Michael Kohlhaas*; 2:24) and "the fragile organization of the world" (in "The Marquise of O——"; 2:143), at least the law offered the solace of security. As a Prussian he believed that he could find this social order in the *ALR* and, by analogy, in the codifications of any society that he was depicting in his works. Accordingly the existing positive law is almost always affirmed again at the end: an affirmation that has been noted by several legal scholars who have concerned themselves with his works.[58] That this is emphatically not the case in most works of literary criticism can be attributed to two factors of literary reception. In the first place, Kleist scholarship for many years was under the influence of the public legal-philosophical discussion in Germany after 1945, which favored a new natural law and sought to discredit anything that smacked of legal positivism.[59] There was no desire to recognize in Kleist, who was heralded as a precursor of existential freedom, a venerator of Prussian law. In the second place, many scholars confused Kleist's intellectual crisis—the Kant crisis—with his subsequent moral crisis of law, assuming that his rejection of his early enthusiasm for natural law implied as well a repudiation of positive law.[60] As we have seen, however, Kleist's works, although they may begin with a disruption of law and right, invariably end with their reconciliation in a new confirmation of justice.

Kleist's affirmation of positive law does not signify, of course, that the law always functions exactly as it is supposed to. However, it is not the law itself but its human administrators who are at fault. The negative figures and powers in his stories and dramas are invariably those who seek to undermine the existing law or to distort it to their own advantage: the unscrupulous village magistrate or the Junker von Tronka and his scheming relatives. As far as the anticlerical Kleist is concerned, the representatives of the Church take first place among the corrupters of the law. In "The Foundling" there is no reason to doubt that Piachi would have been installed once more in possession of his fortune if the cunning Carmelite monks had not for their own purposes supported their unscrupulous ward Nicolo. For that reason "malice was victorious, and at the instigation of this spiritual gentleman the government pronounced a decree through which Nicolo was confirmed in his ownership and Piachi was ordered not to molest him therein" (2:214). In "The Earthquake in Chile" the Carmelites are once again involved since Donna Josephe at the time of her seduction has been placed in a Carmelite nunnery. Again it is the severity of monastic law, and not the civil law, that threatens Donna Josephe first with death by fire on account of her sinful pregnancy and then with the "milder" decapitation.[61] "The most severe case" (2:144) is brought against her at the command of the archbishop, not the secular court of law. And at the end it is again a representative of the Church—this time, to be sure, a Dominican monk—who stirs up the people against the young couple, despite the attempts of civil law in the person of a military officer to restore order.

Other forces can also undermine the justice of the law. It is not the law that precipitates the tragic events in St. Domingo, but rather the annulment of the laws by the "ill-considered steps of the National Convention." In the patriotic drama glorifying the battle of the Germanic tribes under Arminius against the Romans in the Teutoburg Forest (*Die Hermannsschlacht*) numerous legal issues emerge. We hear not only about property disputes among the Germans but also about treaties between the Germans and the Romans. Varus, who as a Roman understands the natural-law principles underlying the *ius gentium* (lines 1186–93), is also familiar with the laws of war, "Which no request can disarm, nor I" (1162). In this culture, both sides of which believe in law and justice, it is Hermann (Arminius, chief of the Cherussi) who contemptuously rejects "duty and law" as defined by Cicero (2208–2220) when he permits his Roman prisoner Septimius to be clubbed to death. And Kohlhaas is ultimately accorded his rights by the existing law; it is not the law but the human henchmen of the law who have injured him.

In general, then, the positive law in force from case to case is confirmed in Kleist's works, and he decisively rejects the "revolution of all conditions" ("Umsturz aller Verhältnisse") that unleashes furious energies in "The Earthquake" (2:153). That story reveals among other things that the dream of a paradisiacal community without law and order in Rousseau's sense—the community that exists for a few hours in the forest immediately following the earthquake—is ultimately an illusion, no matter how seductive it may appear at first. "The Engagement in St. Domingo" dramatizes in all vividness the dangers of the lawless society that results when the former slaves take over Haiti. Kohlhaas, who is introduced in the first sentence of the story as "one of the most upright [*rechtschaffensten*] and at the same time most terrible men of his time" (2:9), is not presented in any sense as an *imitandus*: he must be executed, to preserve the stability of society through the law, precisely because he is driven by his sense of right (*Rechtgefühl*) to become a robber and killer.[62] In Kohlhaas, to the extent that he knows "all the princely decrees that concerned his trade" (2:10), that he insists on his rights "according to the laws" (2:55), and that he is tormented by the "monstrous disorder" of the world (2:21), we recognize the Kleist who, following his disillusionment with a naively understood natural law, willingly accepted the reassuring security of the Prussian code. Kohlhaas's attempted "self-help" turns out to exemplify the impossibility of a state of nature without law, this time in the sense of Hobbes's *bellum omnium contra omnes*.

What is questioned in Kleist's writing—and this must be explicitly emphasized—is not the law that human society has devised to create order. It is the meaning of any transcendental world that he challenges.[63] Precisely as a response to the incomprehensibility of the world (as an intellectual fact), the reassuring validity of the existing law (as a moral fact) is again and again affirmed. As a man disenchanted with the philosophy of law and experienced in the practical workings of the Prussian legal system, Kleist understood that a society without laws is chaotic and that, given the ambivalent nature of man, it is best for the law to be accessible in the form of a straightforward legal code—not just to the experts, who seek to exploit it for their own ends, but to every citizen. We come closest to Kleist as a social being and writer if we seek to understand him in the juristic context of his own age and not from the legal-historical sources of earlier centuries or the legal-philosophical prejudices of our own problematic epoch.[64] Kleist is both a product of and an advocate for the great Prussian codification of 1794. "The age appears to want to bring about a new order of things," he wrote to a friend early in 1805, "and we shall experience nothing but the collapse of the old one" (2:761). In the meantime, the *ALR* was a bulwark against disorder and a tangible constitution of the new order to come.

ALTHOUGH MOST of his German contemporaries were advocates of the "good old law," Kleist was not the only writer of his age who supported codification. As a Jewish Francophile from the Rhineland, Heinrich Heine was an enthusiastic proponent of the code promulgated by his hero, Napoleon, and imposed in 1804 on German territories west of the Rhine.[65] Stendhal famously claimed that he liked to tune up ("prendre le ton") each morning while he was composing *La Chartreuse de Parme* by copying out two or three pages from the *Code civil*.[66] Dostoevsky was fascinated by the bold legal reforms of Alexander II that were formalized in the Codes of 1864.[67] And E.T.A. Hoffmann, who in one of his tales called the *ALR* "the lawbook of a highly enlightened state,"[68] was himself by training a lawyer who, like Kleist, had studied at Königsberg and ultimately went on to become a highly respected judge in the Prussian

Supreme Court. However, despite the brilliant legal satire of his last major work, the fairy tale *Master Flea* (1822), Hoffmann's tales are not so pervasively saturated with law, legal issues, and specifically the Prussian code as are the stories and dramas of Kleist, who remains the great literary representative of codification and the positive law of Prussia as the embodiment of right.

CHAPTER ELEVEN

The Modern Crisis of Law

The Legal Situation in Fin-de-Siècle Austria

At the beginning of the twentieth century, the philosophy of law was experiencing its greatest crisis since the codification controversy a century earlier.[1] In a widely circulated lecture that he delivered in 1907 as prorector at the University of Heidelberg, the distinguished philosopher of law Georg Jellinek spoke of the contemporary Battle of the Old and the New Law as yet another stage in a perennial struggle going back to Aeschylus's *Eumenides*.[2] It is not surprising, as we shall see, that thoughtful writers of the period were also engaged in the problematics of law.

Nineteenth-century legal thinking had been dominated in Europe and the United States by a legal positivism that denied the existence of absolute standards or moral norms and focused its attention instead on the rational analysis of existing systems of law.[3] Legal positivism eventually reached its radical extreme in the so-called Pure Law theory of the Viennese jurist Hans Kelsen, according to which the law is autonomous and self-contained, a formal pattern of pure logic distinct from political and social ideology.[4] The excesses of legal positivism inevitably produced a reaction in the form of sociological approaches that sought to understand the law as an expression of society and its values. Legal sociology, associated in Europe with the names of Rudolf von Jhering and Max Weber and in the United States with the legal realism of Oliver Wendell Holmes and Roscoe Pound,[5] rejected the pure rationalism of positivism in favor of a realism grounded in experience. Jhering maintained, in the conclusion of his *The Spirit of Roman Law* (*Der Geist des römischen Rechts*, 1852–65), and after his famous "conversion" from conceptual jurisprudence, that "Life does not exist for concepts, but the concepts exist for life. It is not logic that should postulate what happens, but life, contact, the sense of right, whether it is logically deducible or impossible."[6] Holmes echoed that sentiment in the statement that opened his classic work *The Common Law* (1881): "The life of the law has not been logic: it has been experience." This tendency reached its extreme in the so-called Free Law school (*Freirechtsbewegung*) of Hermann Kantorowicz, Ernst Fuchs, and Eugen Ehrlich, who argued that the particular circumstances in any given case were more important than written legal norms and that the judge should feel free to ignore positive law altogether, or to fill in its gaps, by applying his sense of right and wrong (Jhering's *Rechtsgefühl*) to the realities of the case (*Natur der Sache*) before him.[7]

That a controversy with such direct public implications kindled broad interest is suggested by the contemporary literary response. A typical embodiment of the conflict is evident in the popular (and widely translated) novels by the Austrian writer Karl Emil Franzos (1849–1904). Franzos, who studied law at Vienna during Jhering's tenure there (1868–72), paid homage to Jhering's great pamphlet *The Struggle for the Right* (*Der Kampf um's Recht*, 1872) in the title of his best-known novel, *For the Right* (*Ein Kampf ums Recht*, 1882). Set in Galicia in the late 1830s, the novel portrays, in specific analogy to Kleist's *Michael Kohlhaas* (which had recently been eulogized by Jhering), the career of a rural judge with an infinite faith in justice, who is so grievously offended by an injustice perpetrated on his community that he leaves wife and home and, with a band of renegades, takes to the mountains as "the great avenger." Ultimately his blind love of justice leads him to commit what he recognizes to be a crime. Like Kohlhaas, he submits to the laws of the realm once the emperor has restored the wrongfully seized property that initially triggered his crusade. Franzos's next novel, *The Chief Justice* (*Der Präsident*, 1884), takes place in Bohemia during the repressions of 1852–53 that followed the 1848 revolution and exposes the inadequacies of an antiquated legal system to deal with modern conflicts of social classes. Specifically, it depicts the spiritual turmoil of an outstanding judge who is caught in a dilemma between law and personal morality. Rather than commit the judicial murder that would result if he should apply the letter of the law in the case of a young woman who has killed her illegitimate infant, he helps the woman, who turns out to be his long-lost daughter, to escape to a new life—and then, again like Kohlhaas, returns home to demand the full penalty for his actions.

The opposition of legal positivism and juristic sociology, with their extremes of "pure law" and "free law," was simply one form in which the crisis of law manifested itself at the turn of the century. In addition to the spirited controversy over such specific issues as the death penalty,[8] deportation,[9] and the jury system, the larger debate over the relationship between law and ethics had attained its perhaps most radical polarization among leading thinkers of Western jurisprudence. At the dedication of a new hall of the Boston University School of Law in 1897, Justice Holmes warned his listeners of a great pitfall situated perilously near the narrow path of legal doctrine: "the danger, both to speculation and to practice, of confounding morality with law."[10] Holmes pointed out with his accustomed good sense that "a bad man has as much reason as a good one for wishing to avoid an encounter with the public force": a very practical reason for distinguishing between law and morality. The worst confusions arise from taking words common in legal jargon—rights, duties, malice, intent, negligence—in their everyday moral connotation.

> When we speak of the rights of man in a moral sense, we mean to mark the limits of interference with individual freedom which we think are prescribed by conscience, or by our ideal, however reached. Yet it is certain that many laws have been enforced in the past, and it is likely that some are enforced now, which are condemned by the most enlightened opinion of the time, or which at all events pass the limit of interference as many consciences would draw it. Manifestly, therefore, nothing but confusion of thought can result from assuming that the rights of man in a moral sense are equally rights in the sense of the Constitution and the law.

Holmes observed that the word "malice" as it is used in the law of civil liability means something quite different from its usage in morals. His own experience had persuaded him that it would be "a gain if every word of moral significance could be banished from the law altogether, and other words adopted which should convey legal ideas uncolored by anything outside the law."

Fifteen years later Hans Kelsen, expressing the view of the Viennese school of "pure law," argued that the fact that certain legal norms happen to specify the same aims as moral laws is no reason to attribute to them a higher validity than to any other laws. "For the legal binding force of legal doctrines, their normative character, derives from a wholly different source than the binding force of moral laws. In their normative nature each is wholly independent of the other."[11] Whatever the origin of moral commandments may be, he continues, the source of binding laws is "exclusively and solely the will of the state." Legal doctrines have authority only because they represent that will, which is enforced by the state's factive power, "and for this legal binding force it makes no difference whether or not they are consistent with moral commandments." The criminal is punished not because he has transgressed the moral code but because a legal statute has imposed a penalty on his behavior.

The separation of law and morality in fin-de-siècle legal positivism reflected the growing recognition among social thinkers that the modern Western world itself was shifting away from traditional communities, in which law, religion, and morality were fully integrated, toward modern societies, in which those functions had become largely dissociated. In the work that defined for sociology the modern concepts of "community" and "society" Ferdinand Tönnies postulated two fundamental types of social order: one based on a harmony arising from the agreement of individual wills and authorized by an ethical code and religion; and another based on the convention of coinciding elective wills and deriving its security from political legislation and its justification from public opinion.[12] The contrast is further exemplified by two forms of positive law: "a common and binding positive law as a system of enforceable norms with reference to the reciprocal relationship of the individual wills, which, rooted in family life and deriving its most significant content from the facts of land ownership, receives its forms as essentially determined by custom consecrated by religion"; and "a similar positive law that, intent upon keeping disentangled the elective wills through all their ties and knots, has its natural premises in the conventional order of trade and similar relations; but which acquires its validity and regulatory authority through the sovereign elective will and the power of the state, as the most important tool of its policy."

Law, however, as one of the most conservative institutions, tends in every age to lag behind the most advanced social and legal thought. This was nowhere more evident than in the Habsburg monarchy, which was proudly conscious of its history and traditions, especially vis-à-vis what it regarded as its upstart neighbors to the north. In 1917 Hugo von Hofmannsthal drew up a scheme contrasting Prussia and Austria in terms remarkably similar to those of Tönnies.[13] Prussia is a "loose social fabric" with classes that are culturally different, while Austria is a "tight social fabric" with culturally unified classes. The Prussian lacks a sense of history but possesses a talent for abstraction, while the Austrian, with little gift for theorizing, has a powerful historical instinct. More specifically, while the Prussian is motivated by the "struggle for his rights" (Jhering's *Kampf um's Recht*), the Austrian takes a more casual attitude (*Lässigkeit*) toward these matters. Hofmannsthal's scheme reflects a certain reality. At the turn of the century the Austro-Hungarian empire was ruled by the oldest criminal code still in force anywhere on the Continent: the *Strafgesetz* of 1852, based on the criminal code of 1803, which in turn went back by way of Emperor Joseph's 1787 code to the *Constitutio Criminalis Theresiana* of 1768. The urgent need for reform was obvious not only to jurists of the Free Law movement but to the thoughtful laity as well. "The severity of the punishments, the relative valuation of legal interests, and the scope given by the law to juridically punishable wrong, is inconsistent with the views and needs of our age"—this was the conclusion of the commission appointed in 1912 to propose a thoroughgoing revision of the criminal code.[14]

> Stemming from the Age of Absolutism, the criminal law has been only externally and incompletely adapted to the demands arising from the nature of the constitutional state and from the basic laws of the state; it has remained the criminal law of the absolute state. If a law stands in contradiction to society's sense of right and wrong and the requirements of the age in which it is supposed to prevail, then it is pushed aside more and more in actual practice.

The extent to which this debate on reform of the criminal law code dominated the public consciousness is suggested by the role that it plays in Robert Musil's novel *The Man without Qualities* (*Der Mann ohne Eigenschaften*, bk. 1, 1930), a panoramic work portraying Viennese society as experienced by Ulrich, the "man without qualities," in the immediate prewar year 1913. In chapter 111 we are informed that Ulrich's father is a member of the commission appointed by the Ministry of Justice for the revision of the criminal law code. "It is difficult in a short time to do justice to justice" is Musil's ironic commentary on the workings of the group.

> The commission consisted of approximately twenty scholars, who were capable of assuming some thousand standpoints vis-à-vis one another, as can be easily calculated. The laws that were supposed to be improved had been in effect since the year 1852; so they were dealing in addition with a very long-lasting state of affairs, which should not be lightly replaced by another one. And in general the stationary institution of the law cannot follow all the leaps of thought of the intellectual fashion prevailing at any given moment.[15]

The specific issue that interests Musil, along with the principals of his novel, is the commission's attitude in the matter of legal responsibility and insanity. One of the dominant figures in the first half of the vast work is the good-natured carpenter Christian Moosbrugger, who stands accused of the brutal murder of a prostitute. His trial becomes a cause célèbre occupying the attention of all the characters of the novel and providing occasion for much speculation on the subject of criminal law and on the ambiguities involved in law and psychiatry: specifically, was Moosbrugger in possession of his faculties when he committed the murder?

Austria was a leader in the development of modern criminal psychology. The interest in the criminal mind evident from time to time among Viennese psychiatrists is certainly not a factor to be ignored. But Freud and his colleagues were concerned primarily with the psychiatric aspects of their cases, not the legal ones. (For instance, the case of Daniel Paul Schreber, whose *Memoirs of My Nervous Illness* [*Denkwürdigkeiten eines Nervenkranken*, 1903] aroused considerable attention in psychoanalytical circles and prompted important writings by Freud and Bleuler in 1910 and 1911, was of interest not because Schreber was a leading figure in the legal system of the neighboring Kingdom of Saxony—president of the Judges Panel at the Supreme Court—but because he depicted in such detail, with such analytical intelligence, and so coherently a classic case of acute paranoia.)[16] More significant is the controversy between two schools of legal liberalism, which was fiercely raging at the end of the nineteenth century but whose conclusions, owing to the conservatism of criminal justice, were not incorporated into law until the last third of the twentieth century.[17] The so-called classical school began with the assumption of human free will: the criminal is an individual who has freely decided to break the law; therefore he deserves the punishment specified for his crime, which he can foresee and take into account. One of its most radical statements is evident in Kant's *Metaphysics of Morals* (*Metaphysik der Sitten*, 1797), which is based on the conviction that "if justice perishes, there is no further point in men living on earth." Accordingly, Kant continues: "If [a man] has committed a murder, he must die. In this case no surrogate can satisfy justice." Kant goes on, notoriously, to argue that even in an island society that has agreed to disperse, "the last murderer still in jail would have to be executed so that everyone should receive his just deserts for his deed and so that no blood guilt should cling to the people for failing to insist upon the punishment."[18] Kant's severe position was adopted by the neo-Kantian school of jurisprudence in Germany.

Many Austrian criminologists, in contrast, were associated with the "modern school," which derived from Franz von Liszt and was not concerned exclusively with the majesty of the law, but also took into account the social background of the criminal. In particular Hans Gross (1847–1915)—from 1898 on the editor of the *Archiv für Kriminalanthropologie und Kriminalistik* and in 1912 the founder at the University of Graz of the first Kriminalistisches Institut in Europe—became known as the father of criminal psychology.[19] In his standard work on the subject (*Criminal Psychology* [*Criminalpsychologie*, 1897; 2d enl. ed. 1905]) Gross argued that psychology has a major role to play in the understanding of any crime: not just the mental state of the criminal, but also the psychology of the judge, experts, witnesses, jury—in short, of every agent in the judicial process.

Precisely this activity is reflected in *The Man without Qualities*. We know from his journals that Musil, in preparation for the legal sections of his novel, studied many works on criminal law and the philosophy of law, including Pufendorf's classic *De jure naturae et gentium*, Hans Kelsen's theory of "pure law," and contemporary newspaper reports.[20] Here we learn that the question of the individual's moral freedom—"in a word, the good old question of freedom of the will" (chap. 111)—provided the center that generated all the differences of opinion in the commission for revision of the criminal code. "To be sure, the psychological knowledge of these jurists had remained about fifty years behind the times"; so the members are almost prepared to agree on the standard old circular definition: that a criminal is legally responsible if he is intellectually and morally capable of committing a crime. At this point Ulrich's father undergoes what he terms a "momentous turn to the social school"—to the view, namely, that the criminally "degenerate" individual should not be judged in a moralizing way but only with respect to his potential to do harm to society. His ideological enemy on the commission pounces eagerly on the word "social," which he accuses of being "materialistic" and even—the supreme insult in the 1913 Austro-Hungarian monarchy—of displaying a "Prussian state mentality."

Gross, who unlike many German academic jurisprudents had twenty-three years of practical judicial experience, was also the author of an influential and widely translated handbook for examining magistrates (*Handbuch für Untersuchungsrichter*, 1893), which established his reputation as one of the principal founders of modern scientific-inductive criminal investigation. Gross's career is representative of the intimate reciprocal connection between legal theory and practice in Austria,[21] which is captured brilliantly in *The Class Reunion* (*Der Abiturientenlag*, 1928) by the Prague author Franz Werfel, perhaps the finest portrayal in German literature of the problematics of the examining magistrate.[22] The novel is the firsthand account of a magistrate in an Austrian provincial capital, who finds his own emotions engaged when he conducts the preliminary investigation concerning a man accused of murdering a prostitute. Believing the man to be a former classmate whom he had led astray in their youth, the magistrate is forced, precisely in Gross's sense, to scrutinize his own subjective standpoint and to wonder if he himself could ultimately be the guilty party in this case. (We note a striking resemblance to Tolstoy's *Resurrection* [1899], in which a nobleman who once seduced an innocent young woman finds himself years later on the jury that must decide a case charging her, now a prostitute, with poisoning a client.) It turns out that the accused man is not his classmate after all and that he is in any case not guilty. But the reassessment of his own career and function, triggered by the release of his repressed memories, changes the examining magistrate presumably forever. It would be hard to find a better literary embodiment of Gross's writings on criminal theory and the role of the examining magistrate. (The Swiss popular novelist John Knittel provides a Swiss analogy in his best-known novel *Via Mala* [1934], in which a young examining magistrate accidentally uncovers a murder committed by his wife's family. Torn between his respect for the law and his liberal sociological principles, he finally buries the case and then commits suicide.) Werfel's typical Austrian emphasis on the preliminary investigation emerges vividly when it is contrasted with the German literary preference for the later stages of the proceedings, which is strikingly evident in Leonhard Frank's *The Cause* (*Die Ursache*, 1916) and Ricarda Huch's *The Deruga Case* (*Der Fall Deruga*, 1917). In both novels, which deal respectively with cases of murder and euthanasia in pre-1914 Germany, the focus is on the accused, not the investigator(s), and the scene is restricted almost entirely to the courtroom.

The novels by Musil and Werfel, exemplifying the Austrian literary fascination with law, record accurately the activities of the commission to reform the antiquated criminal law and the public discussion regarding certain issues: specifically the conflict between the classical and the modern or social schools of jurisprudence, the contrast between subjective and objective law, and finally the opposition between morality and law. However, the importance of the debate was not appreciated by writers only in retrospect. One of the severest literary indictments of the Austro-Hungarian legal system appeared in 1908: Karl Kraus's *Morality and Criminal Justice* (*Sittlichkeit und Kriminalität*), a gathering of forty-one articles that Kraus, perhaps the sharpest observer and critic of law in fin-de-siècle Vienna, had published from 1902 to 1907 in his influential one-man journal *Die Fackel*. Kraus, who had studied law in Vienna without taking a degree, was concerned—indeed, obsessed—with the decriminalization of all behavior that is not socially harmful. His particular obsession, beyond the anachronisms of the 1873 code of criminal procedure, was the hypocrisy of a legal system that insisted on condemning in public law what it condoned in private practice, especially in cases involving such sexual matters as adultery, pornography, and prostitution. Appropriately, therefore, the book begins with several quotations from Shakespeare's *Measure for Measure*, and notably the duke's speech (5.1.318–24):

> My business in this state
> Made me a looker on here in Vienna,
> Where I have seen corruption boil and bubble
> Till it o'er-run the stew; laws for all faults,
> But faults so countenanced, that the strong statutes
> Stand like the forfeits in a barber's shop,
> As much in mock as mark.

On the celebration in 1903 of one hundred years of the criminal code, Kraus writes in the title-piece: "For the imminent hundredth anniversary of the Austrian paragraph-thicket, it would be instructive to have a compilation of the crimes, offenses, and misdemeanors of which the law and its strict constructionists have made themselves guilty."[23] The best opportunity to expose the incompatibility of morality and criminality, he continues, is in adultery trials. "German philosophers, who have thought at the most ideal heights of morality, have spoken out in favor of eliminating adultery from criminal law and of making divorce easier for the wife." Instead, "a textbook case of legally supported immorality has recently been brought before the horrified gaze of the Viennese public": a notorious adultery trial in which the press spared its readers not a single intimate detail of the marriage and its disintegration. In a piece linking "Eros and Themis" Kraus portrays the perverse scene in closed court "when men in the dignity of office are enthralled by a woman's letters, stare with glazed eyes at every detail of a night of love, and share this bliss of the imagination with twelve excited husbands from the people."[24] According to Kraus, the closed hearings in which these indecencies occur are the secret sins of justice. His comments on the salaciousness of press and public in celebrity trials remain shockingly relevant today.[25]

In another piece, concerning a notorious case of child pornography—a university professor was sentenced to three months imprisonment for photographing two naked boys, inciting them to masturbation, and "touching indecently"—Kraus concludes that "Austrian statecraft in its entirety is a product of mutual onanism" in a country where investigations against the purveyors of obscene photographs are dropped because they name highly placed personalities among their customers and where procuresses are jailed only if they cannot call on the protection of an important clientele.[26] The judges should not forget that without their gowns they are themselves ordinary men. Kraus takes delight in imagining a scene in which a woman accused of prostitution might say to the judge, "You spoke to me quite differently that day when you were watching me in the park near the Votive Church." "Not a day passes," Kraus summarizes in a piece bitterly entitled "Nulla dies . . . ," "without a legal case that preaches recognition of the true purpose of all legality and bureaucracy: to be a derision of its purpose, and payment for its ridicule."[27] It has long been suspected, but it will be known as a certainty when finally a new criminal law puts an end to the present disgrace, that "this brazen playing-at-judge of grown-up schoolboys, whom one has sought by means of ministerial edicts to disabuse of their alienation from real life, has not worked." "The crime begins with the court proceedings themselves. All the evil urges are assembled for the hearing, all *dolus* of the world is summoned up to create a *culpa*. Mankind is bleeding to death under the desolate acuity of a science that operates and does not bind up the wounds. How long will we stand for it? How long will the judges be permitted to punish with impunity?" Elsewhere Kraus points out that, however unpleasant a verdict of guilty may be, someone who has been deemed guilty by a century-old paragraph is troubled more by his embarrassment than by his conscience. "The thunder of justice has long since lost its terror in this country, and anyone entering the district court will take home with him not so much the tremor of the Last Judgment as the disgusting pissoir-stench of Austrian bureaucracy."[28]

It is hardly surprising that Kraus frequently adduces the image of a despoiled Justitia to hammer home his point about an Austrian justice suborned by the lechery of the judges themselves. At the beginning of the piece involving child pornography he wrote:

> We shall never forget the impression. We unspoiled children of the age have seen how they groped under the skirts of Justice incarnate. She had her eyes bound and didn't know what was happening to her. If she were a virgin, if we didn't know that she had already often succumbed to the wishes of powerful men, often gone back to the chambre privée, the culprits and their henchmen would have to be punished for their deeds.[29]

Elsewhere we hear that "The goddess of Justice is blind, stops up her ears, and puts on a chastity belt. Thus attired, she has nothing to fear from new revelations."[30] In an allusion to the lecherous judiciary, he suggests that "a delirious Justitia is more ridiculous when she gets herself worked up morally than politically. In her eagerness to see what is most secret she tears the blindfold from her eyes in order to conceal her private parts [*Scham*] with it."[31]

A telling image of the apocalyptic sense of law and judgment that obsessed thoughtful Austrians of the prewar years can be seen in Hugo von Hofmannsthal's *Everyman* (*Jedermann*, 1911), an adaptation of the late-medieval morality play in which the Lord God, angered by mankind's blatant disregard of its agreement with him, determines to hold judgment (*Gerichtstag*) and accordingly summons Everyman to his final reckoning. That Hofmannsthal's work touched a sensitive public nerve is suggested by the enormous success it enjoyed following its performance in 1920 at the first of the Salzburg Festivals. The enduring national obsession with law, crime, and punishment is evident in a statement by the late-twentieth-century Austrian writer Thomas Bernhard, who began his literary career in the early 1950s as a court reporter for the Salzburg socialist newspaper *Demokratisches Volksblatt*: "The whole world is nothing but jurisprudence."[32]

Kafka and the Law

The statement in Bernhard's story, uttered by a man driven half-mad by guilt over the murder of his wife twenty-two years earlier, sounds very much like the remark by the painter Titorelli, made "half in jest, half in explanation" in Kafka's novel *The Trial* (*Der Prozeß*): "Everything belongs to the Court."[33] Readers have long been aware of the centrality in Kafka's works of "the Law," which is conspicuous not only in frequent metaphors in his diaries[34] but also in the titles of many stories, such as "The Judgment," "In the Penal Colony," "The New Advocate," "Before the Law," "On the Question of our Laws," and "The Advocates" (Kafka uses the archaic German term *Fürsprecher*). For many decades it was widely assumed that "the Law," whenever it occurs in Kafka's works, is nothing but an image for concerns that are theological, metaphysical, psychological, or generally sociological in their meaning.[35] Even readers with an informed interest in law and literature, such as the editors of the *Yale Journal of Law and the Humanities*, recently cited Kafka as representative of "the humanist's vision of the law" still unmindful of "both the coercive and the constitutive power of law"—apparently unmindful themselves that Kafka was a professional lawyer keenly aware of the legal debates of his day.[36]

Only recently have scholars begun to realize that the frequent legal allusions also have a more specifically jurisprudential significance in the works of a writer who was himself a trained lawyer and involved professionally with law for over twenty years—from his enrollment in 1901 as a law student at the Ferdinand Karl (German-speaking) University of Prague until his retirement, for medical reasons, in 1922 from his position as legal specialist in the Workers' Accident Insurance Corporation, a semiofficial institution established by the Austrian Ministry of the Interior.[37] After all, Kafka studied and practiced law during a period that, as we have just seen, was one of the most exciting in the history of modern jurisprudence.

We know in detail what Kafka studied in the course of the eight-semester law curriculum leading to his doctorate of jurisprudence.[38] Unlike the universities in the recently unified German Empire, whose code of criminal law dated back only to 1871 and whose thoroughly modern constitution had taken effect as recently as 1900, universities in the Habsburg monarchy still expected their students to have a thorough grounding in the Roman law upon which Austro-Hungarian law was still essentially based. Accordingly Kafka, who entered the university with a good command of Latin and with adequate Greek, spent most of his first two years studying civil law and canon law, along with the history of German and Austrian law. The intermediate examination, which he passed in July of 1903 "with good success," dealt with Roman law. In the second half of the curriculum Kafka was concerned principally with contemporary law: Austrian civil law and procedure (seven courses), general and Austrian constitutional law, economics and trade law, administrative law, and, most relevant for our purposes, four courses with Hans Gross, who was a professor in Prague from 1902 until 1905—three in criminal law and one on the history of the philosophy of law. We can safely assume that Kafka was familiar at first hand with Gross's ideas on criminal psychology—notably, that it is not the crime but the criminal who is the proper object of punishment—and judicial procedure, and that he was exposed through his studies in the philosophy of law to the lively legal controversies prevailing at the time in Germany and Austria.[39]

It was not only in his courses that Kafka encountered these ideas. From 1902 until 1905 he attended irregularly the biweekly meetings of the so-called Philosophers' Circle at the Café Louvre, where one of the liveliest participants was Oskar Kraus (1872–1942), a lecturer in philosophy at the university, who was active especially in the field of law and ethics and regarded himself as a mediator in the dispute between Pure Law and Free Law.[40] Moreover, Kafka avidly perused the detailed court reports that filled the German-language Prague newspapers of the day.[41] We also know from his letters that Kafka was an occasional reader of *Die Fackel* and that in March 1911 he attended a reading by Kraus in Prague.[42] So there is every likelihood that Kafka was aware of Kraus's crusade against the contamination of law with morality. A year later, in May 1912, Kafka attended a performance of Hofmannsthal's *Everyman*. In the absence of documentary evidence we can also make an educated guess that Kafka was acquainted with the legal fictions of Karl Emil Franzos, who like Kafka himself was a legally trained Jew from the Austro-Hungarian provinces. Finally, we must assume that Kafka kept abreast of developments in his field. For a year following the completion of his degree (1906–7) Kafka acquired personal experience of the criminal justice system as an intern in the provincial criminal court in Prague. In May 1908 he attended a special course on workers' insurance at the Prague Trade Academy,[43] and that same year his first major legal brief, on insurance obligations in the building trades ("Umfang der Versicherungspflicht der Baugewerbe und der baulichen Nebengewerbe"), impressed his supervisors with its "excellent conceptual power."[44] His success as a practicing lawyer with special competence in administrative law earned him in 1913 (shortly before he wrote *The Trial*) promotion to the responsible position of vice-secretary in his firm. Is it conceivable that a legally trained writer like Kafka, any more than Heinrich von Kleist, could deny in his own work the lawyer's mentality or what Germans call the "juristic style of thought" (*juristischer Denkstil*)? Indeed, it has been shown that in many of his works Kafka displays a fondness for scenes built around courtlike interrogations and that his vocabulary shows a pronounced proclivity for such legal terms as hearing (*Verhör*), court (*Gericht*), judge (*Richter*), right (*Recht*), wrong (*Unrecht*), justice (*Gerechtigkeit*), justification (*Rechtfertigung*), and judgment or verdict (*Urteil*).[45]

The Trial: A Burlesque of Legal Procedure

For these reasons it has recently come to be recognized that *The Trial*, which Kafka wrote from August 1914 to January 1915 (but which was not published until 1925, a year after his death), constitutes in one sense a burlesque of the very legal procedures of which Kafka himself was a master[46]—and not simply a generalized satire of the dysfunctional Danube monarchy or the corrupt bureaucracy of modern capitalism.[47] This is not to deny, of course, that the richly multivalent work has other implications.[48] But the legal view enables us to understand why, when Kafka read the first chapter of *The Trial* to a group of friends including other young lawyers like his friend Max Brod, he "laughed so much that there were moments when he could not read any further."[49]

"The Trial" is actually a mistranslation of the German title. *Prozeß* in German legal terminology designates the entire proceeding that may or may not culminate in a formal trial. In the German and Austrian system of justice a process begins when the state attorney (*Staatsanwalt*) notifies the examining magistrate (*Untersuchungsrichter*) that there is reason to believe that a crime has been committed and to suspect an individual of a particular crime.[50] The examining magistrate, a lower court official with legal training for his specific role (as outlined by Hans Gross), thereupon undertakes a series of preliminary interviews with full powers of investigation, including search and seizure. Only if his inquisitorial investigation concludes that the suspected individual (at this point still known as *der Beschuldigte*) is actually guilty does the examining magistrate recommend a formal indictment and turn his dossier over to the prosecuting attorney, whereupon *der Beschuldigte* becomes *der Angeklagte* and the actual trial, now an accusatory rather than an inquisitorial process, takes place. It is important to understand that up to this point the procedures are essentially secret. The suspect is permitted only limited access to an attorney since, according to the Continental theory of justice, the examining magistrate in his inquisitorial role is interested not in proving the guilt of the suspect but in establishing truth and is therefore sympathetic to the suspect. (This function is brought out clearly in Werfel's novel *The Class Reunion*. In contrast, Jakob Wassermann's *The Maurizius Case* [*Der Fall Maurizius*, 1928], probably the finest fictional portrayal of the German criminal justice system, concerns a distinguished state's attorney and an advocate of Pure Law, who sends an innocent man to prison for murder and is devastated when he learns the truth many years later.) In the Austro-Hungarian system, moreover, the examining magistrate has a considerably more extensive authority and latitude than in Germany—a result in part of popular suspicion of the relatively recently established office and role of the prosecutor.[51] When Josef K. learns that he has been arrested, the normal methodology to be anticipated in a legal proceeding would consist of four clearly articulated stages: investigation (*Vernehmung*), accusation (*Anklage*), defense (*Verteidigung*), and verdict (*Urteilsfindung*).[52] (We know from the late story "Advocates" that Kafka was precisely aware of this sequence: there he speaks of accusation [*Anklage*], defense [using the archaic term *Fürspruch*], and judgment [*Urteil*].[53] Similarly, in the story "In the Penal Colony" the explorer is shocked to learn that accused criminals go directly from crime to execution with no intervening trial procedures.) But Josef K.'s *Prozeß* turns out differently.

The Trial has a definite beginning and end: Josef K. is arrested on the morning of his thirtieth birthday, and he is executed exactly a year later, on the eve of his thirty-first birthday.[54] But everything that comes in between, including the completed chapters as well as several unfinished ones and other deleted passages, was left in a state of confusion: it is not certain either what precise order of sections Kafka had in mind or what episodes he might have intended still to add to his unfinished manuscript.[55] Yet in broad outline the plot is clear. Following his "arrest," K. is left free to go about his business as usual. Returning home later on that first day from his job as chief clerk at the bank, he makes elaborate apologies to his landlady, Frau Grubach, and to a fellow tenant in the rooming house, Fräulein Bürstner, for any inconvenience caused them by the intrusion earlier that day of the arresting officers (chap. 1). Several days later he is notified by phone that he must appear on the following Sunday for a preliminary investigation of his case, which takes place in a distant suburb in the crowded attic rooms of a tenement house—an unruly occasion that suggests to Josef K. a political assembly rather than a court hearing and "the worst corruption of the bureaucracy" (61). He leaves the proceedings indignantly, telling the examining magistrate and those in attendance that he wants nothing further to do with their hearings (chap. 2).

Nevertheless, though he receives no further summons, he returns the following Sunday at the same time, only to find the premises empty. He tries to elicit information from the various people he encounters there and in the chancellery rooms: the wife of the court usher, a law student, the court usher himself, and the information giver; but he gets no real clarification (chap. 3). Back in the rooming house, Fräulein Bürstner's friend, Fräulein Montag, informs K. that Fräulein Bürstner has no wish to continue their casual acquaintance (chap. 4). As he leaves the bank one evening, he hears a noise in a closet and opens the door to find, to his astonishment, two of the arresting wardens being whipped because, as they tell him, he complained of their behavior to the examining magistrate. He tries unsuccessfully to bribe the whipper to spare the two men, but on the following day he finds all three men in the same place again going through precisely the same exertions (chap. 5).

Several weeks later K.'s uncle arrives from the country and tries to help his nephew by taking him to see his old school-friend, the lawyer Huld, who lives in the remote suburb where the court chancelleries are located and who is reputed to be versed in their legal practices. During the interview, which is also attended by the administrative director of the courts, K. is sexually diverted by the lawyer's housekeeper Leni and leaves the room with her to engage in an almost animal act of copulation (chap. 6). In the following months K. visits lawyer Huld several times and acquires bits and pieces of information about the court. Distracted at work by the case, he is urged by one of his clients to look up the painter Titorelli, who through his portraits has good connections to the court and is able to provide K. with still further insights into its workings (chap. 7).

Frustrated by the delays in his case, which has still not advanced beyond the preliminary stages, K. determines to discharge Huld, but at the lawyer's house he is engaged by another client, the merchant Block, who tells him about his own long-standing case; the uncompleted chapter ends inconclusively (chap. 8). At the bank, K. is asked one day to accompany a visiting Italian businessman to the cathedral. Waiting for the visitor, who fails to show up, K. hears from the pulpit a parable about a man from the country who spends his life before the door of the Law, talking to the gatekeeper and even imploring the fleas in his greatcoat; as he dies, having made no effort to get past the gatekeeper and to enter the premises of the Law, he learns that the door has been there only for him and that now it will be closed. K. falls into conversation with the preacher, who turns out to be the prison chaplain, and learns from him that his case has taken a turn for the worse—that he is considered guilty (chap. 9). On the eve of his thirty-first birthday, finally, K. is fetched from his room by two men, who look to him like second-rate actors. They lead him to an abandoned quarry on the outskirts of the city, where they remove his coat, vest, and shirt and then stab him to death with a butcher knife (chap. 10).

We are told in one of the uncompleted chapters that K. is fully aware of his legal rights (275). He lives in a constitutional state (*Rechtsstaat*, 12) where "all the laws were in force" (12). He possesses the requisite legal documents although, in his agitation, he can lay his hands only on his birth certificate. One of his close friends is the state prosecuting attorney; he has conducted long conversations on legal matters with the attorney who represents the bank at which he works; and he himself is regarded among his friends as an expert in trade law (*Handelsrecht*, 283). His clients at the bank consider him as "virtually a lawyer" (164). So K. has every reason to expect that his case will proceed as specified in the 1873 Austrian code of criminal procedure (*Strafprozeßordnung*).

But it soon becomes apparent that K. has been caught up in a different jurisdiction altogether. As he remarks to the student in the empty interrogation rooms, "I do not yet understand your court system very precisely" (74). And he is not alone; as he learns a little later from the information giver: "since the nature of our court is not very familiar among the populace, much information is requested" (88). He later tells his uncle, "Above all, uncle, it does not involve a case before the normal court" (117). When he meets Huld, he is astonished to learn that the lawyer is associated with the court "in the attic" and not in the palace of justice (127). Huld explains to him the difference between "normal legal affairs" and "these legal affairs" (226). Leni is also aware of the difference: "against this court one cannot defend oneself; one must make a confession" (132). It is unclear, moreover, where the Law is actually written down: the alleged "law books" that K. sees in the interrogation rooms turn out to be pornographic novels (67), and even Huld confesses that he has never actually read the Law (185). All the self-proclaimed experts in the secret Law—Huld, Leni, Block, Titorelli, the priest—know it only by hearsay. Even in the final moments of his life (according to a passage cut from the novel), K. recognizes the difference between the official state legal system and the one that has condemned him. As he is being dragged off to his death, he sees a policeman and thinks: "The state is offering me its help . . . What if I shifted my case over to the jurisdiction of the state laws?" (311).

The parallel existence of dual legal systems is not in itself unusual. As Kafka knew from his studies, Roman civil law and Church canon law functioned side by side effectively throughout centuries of European history. He was also aware that the two systems, deriving as they did from a common source in Justinian's *Corpus Iuris Civilis*, shared procedures that often betrayed their kinship. In his novel, accordingly, Kafka stresses the existence of the familiar legal system because the procedures of the paralegal court invariably depend for their effect upon our knowledge of that system. (His story "In the Penal Colony," written in October 1914 during the composition of *The Trial*, also depends for its alienating effect on the fact that the explorer comes from a European country governed by a legal system utterly different from the one in force on the penal island he is visiting.) In a few cases, familiar civil rights established by Emperor Franz Joseph I in his so-called December constitution of 1867 are violated, as in the opening scene when the basic article concerning the inviolability of the home (Article 9) is infringed by the three men who invade K.'s bedroom to arrest him without a warrant.[56] A few other incidents involve a violation of the prevailing Austrian code of criminal procedure.[57] For instance, the arresting officials do not give him the reason for his arrest, as stipulated by Section 209 of the code, nor does the examining magistrate inform him of the nature of his crime, as required by Section 199 of the code, or warn him, as provided in Section 203 of the code, that his refusal to participate in the hearing could deprive him of the grounds for defense.

In most cases, however, Kafka achieves his effect simply by alienating what is legally obvious.[58] For instance, on the morning of his arrest K. is instructed that the authorities are "attracted by guilt and must send out the wardens" (15). K. tells the arresting officials that he is unaware of that law and suggests that it exists only in their heads. Yet this statement, as metaphysical as it may sound, is nothing more than routine procedure: when the state has reason to suspect a crime or criminal, it is required to instruct the examining magistrate to undertake an investigation: to this extent it is "attracted by guilt." The wardens joke with each other that "he concedes that he doesn't know the Law and at the same time claims to be innocent." But again they are simply stating a principle inherent in all civilized law, as in §3 of the Austrian criminal code (*Strafgesetz*) of 1852: "No one can claim innocence on the basis of ignorance of the existing criminal law." Yet their behavior along with Josef's astonished reaction has the effect of making this fundamental legal principle seem somehow absurd, as does his reaction to the announcement that he is free to go about his business: pretrial detention is rare in the Austrian system (although, to be sure, the student subsequently reminds K. [74] that the magistrate has the right, as he does also under Austrian law, to confine the individual being investigated between hearings if there are grounds for believing that he might flee).

Similarly, when K. announces that the state prosecutor is his good friend and asks if he may phone him, the arresting official says he may—"but I don't know what sense it would have unless you have some private matter to discuss with him" (22). K.'s consternation at this response distracts us from the obvious: once the state prosecutor has turned a case over to the examining magistrate for investigation, he has no further role whatsoever until a recommendation is made either to pursue or to drop the case.[59] The same applies to the role of the defense attorney. Josef is frustrated at what he regards as the inadequacy of Huld's efforts on his behalf; but in the Austrian system the defending attorney has no active role until the examining magistrate has actually recommended an indictment and handed the case over to the prosecution. To this extent, then, as Huld tells K.: "The defense is not actually permitted by the Law, but only tolerated" (139–40).

The same technique of estrangement is evident with respect to the secrecy of the proceedings. Huld tells K. to bear in mind, as though it were something unusual, "that the proceedings are not public. They can become public if the court regards it as necessary, but the Law does not prescribe an open court" (139). But he is describing the normal procedures of civil-law courts, where the investigation remains private and confidential as long as it is in the hands of the examining magistrate, and becomes public only when that official turns it over to the prosecutor with the recommendation of a trial. Not until this point does the defense become formally involved. All these matters, which may well strike the reader from such common-law states as England or the United States as odd or unusual, should seem perfectly straightforward to the reader from civil-law countries. It is only through the reactions of defendants new to the system, like K. or the merchant Block, that we are persuaded to regard as absurd procedures that are perfectly normal according to Austrian law. The same applies to the attorneys of varying qualifications—from the hacks (*Winkeladvokaten*) through the merely competent attorneys to the major lawyers that Block categorizes for K. (214–15)—who are to be found in any legal system, whether civil- or common-law. And the same is true of the petitions submitted by the attorneys on behalf of the defendants, with much Latin, many formulas of courteous address, and "investigations of legal cases from olden times that are supposed to be similar to mine" (213): namely, arguments from precedent. It is nothing but the attitude of the defendants that distances these perfectly normal practices, making them seem strange and even absurd.

THE ACTUAL preliminary investigation (chap. 2), in contrast, amounts in every sense to a burlesque of a normal investigation as specified in the code of criminal procedure and as portrayed, for instance, in Werfel's *The Class Reunion*. The location of the interrogation room in the attic of a tenement building in a remote suburb, rather than in the palace of justice familiar to K., sets the tone for the occasion. The hearing itself, rather than being a private inquisition, takes place in a room crowded with people in a manner that suggests a political assembly rather than a court of law. The examining magistrate—Kafka uses the official term *Untersuchungsrichter* (54)—sits at a small table on the crowded podium, joshing with his cronies. He chides K. for being over an hour late, although no time for the hearing was specified, and points out that he has no obligation under the circumstances to interrogate K. However, he agrees to undertake the interrogation as an exception and, reaching for his small notebook, which looks like a school exercise book, begins by asking if K. is a house painter. These are his last words until K. is about to leave the room, at which point he tells K. that through his behavior he has deprived himself of any advantage the hearing might have for the accused (63). The remainder of the "interrogation" amounts to K.'s indignant rehearsal of the incidents at the time of his arrest, his refusal to take the proceedings seriously, and his denunciation of the entire organization, whose sole purpose seems to be "to arrest innocent persons and initiate against them a senseless and mostly, as in my case, fruitless procedure" (61).

It can be argued that Kafka is using this scene to exemplify Hans Gross's criticism of the jury system, which had been restored in Austria in 1873 and which was not generally approved by legal scholars.[60] Indeed, the controversy surrounding the jury led to the subsequent drastic modification of its function in both Austria and Germany. Gross in particular believed that the task of the judge had been made more problematic by a jury of laymen "who perhaps for the first time in their lives are involved in a court of law, who perhaps are seeing a criminal for the first time, and are under these circumstances the arbiters of a man's fate."[61] But there may be another implication as well. When K. goes back to the interrogation rooms a week later, the court attendant's wife shows him the old, worn books that are still lying on the magistrate's table. Opening the top volume, he sees a crudely drawn pornographic picture of a naked man and woman. When he looks at the title page of a second volume, he reads: "The Miseries That Grete Had to Endure from Her Husband Hans." Moreover, the law student who carries off the usher's wife embodies the sexual energies represented in the books. It has been suggested that Kafka is making use here of a tradition that goes back to Dottore Graziano in the commedia dell'arte and associates lawyers and judges with lechery.[62] But another analogy lies closer to hand. K.'s indignation at the thought that he is supposed to be judged by men who peruse legal texts of that sort (67) and behave in that manner suggests nothing more strongly than Karl Kraus's campaign in *Die Fackel* against a judiciary, as well as a public constantly incited by the tabloids, that takes private pleasure in prostitution and pornography while publicly and legally opposing and punishing it.

The novel, then, amounts in several senses to a burlesque of familiar legal procedures. Indeed, Kafka's constant implicit references to the code of criminal procedure have persuaded one scholar that "whatever structure the novel has is provided by that world or a parody of it,"[63] while another goes so far as to suggest that "this mirror-image design of the fictional court helped Kafka to plot the narrative's triallike progression in advance."[64] Moreover, the burlesque is suggested by the very title of the work, which was the working title that Kafka used from the beginning in his letters, journals, and conversations with his friends.[65] Properly understood, the title draws our attention to the legal proceedings themselves and not to any such dramatic culmination as suggested by the English word "trial." Indeed, as in the legal system described in "In the Penal Colony," K. is executed summarily without a trial or defense. The case moves directly from the preliminary hearing to execution, with nothing more than a hint in the cathedral scene (the penultimate chapter) that a finding of guilt is being contemplated by the examining magistracy, which, if handed down, would normally lead at most to a formal indictment with defense and trial yet to come. In fact, only a single misbegotten preliminary investigation takes place. K. hears rumors, to be sure, about other court activity. But throughout the work the rumors refer only to judicial activity at the level of examining magistrates. As late as the cathedral scene, the prison chaplain tells K. that his case "will perhaps never get beyond a lower court" (252).

Even the portraits that K. sees in Huld's rooms (chap. 6) and Titorelli's studio (chap. 7), Josef complains, represent nothing but the lowliest preliminary judges.

In addition, in the preliminary investigation that does take place, the procedures are presented in such a manner as to appear comical and even absurd, even when they are perfectly routine according to the Austrian Code of Criminal Procedure. The effect of absurdity and alienation is produced in part by the clownish behavior of various representatives of the court system: for instance, the arresting wardens in the first chapter and their reappearance in another triad of figures in the whipping chapter. It is heightened by the contrast between the shabby setting and irregular conduct of the interrogation and the elaborate proceedings that take place in the elegant palaces of justice in the Habsburg monarchy. And lest the reader miss the none too subtle hints at procedural irregularities, Kafka draws our attention to them through the astonished reactions of K. himself. However, Kafka's critique of Austrian legal procedure, no matter how comical it may be and consistent with the attacks by Karl Kraus and other contemporaries, would be in itself a superficial response to the crisis that was wracking legal thought at the precise time Kafka was writing his novel. Despite the considerable procedural detail required for the burlesque, this aspect of the novel does not hint at the substantive issues that were causing the pressures for legal reform in Austria during the prewar years.

Kafka's Critique of the Law

Kafka's awareness of these tensions is suggested vividly by the pastel painting of the judge—again only a lowly examining magistrate—that K. sees when he visits Titorelli. It is not the image of the judge that is relevant but the large figure visible on the back panel of the judge's chair, which the painter identifies as Justice (*die Gerechtigkeit*).[66] At that point K. recognizes her from the bandage around her eyes and the scales that she holds in her hand. But he is surprised to make out wings on her heels and to see that she is running. Titorelli explains that he was commissioned to depict the figure exactly that way, as Justice and the goddess of victory in one. "'That is not a good conjunction,' said K., smiling, 'Justice must be at rest, otherwise the scales sway and a just verdict is not possible'" (176). As they talk, the painter continues to work on the figure, which gradually emerges more sharply from the background until "it scarcely still resembled the goddess of justice, nor also of victory, but looked rather exactly like the goddess of the hunt" (177). This image is absolutely consistent with the principles of the legal system K. has encountered—a justice that pursues its quarry without remorse until it achieves victory. But does it have implications that extend beyond the text?

We know from the first paragraph of his novel *Amerika* that Kafka enjoyed playing with familiar cultural icons: there the Statue of Liberty that Karl Rossmann sees as his ship approaches New York City is holding aloft a sword, and not the usual torch. What suggested to Kafka the notion of portraying Justice without her customary sword, but with the distinguishing blindfold and scales as well as winged feet that enable her to pursue her victims with greater nimbleness? We have already noted that Karl Kraus made frequent parodic use of the figure of Justice in his attacks on contemporary Austrian law: for example, the prurient Justice who tears the blindfold from her own eyes in order to see the secrets of others, while concealing her own private parts with the bandage. But there may well be more to it than this.

In January 1907 the minister of public works for the German Empire, in conjunction with the minister of justice, issued an edict ruling that henceforth all paintings and sculptures of Justitia on new public buildings should be unblindfolded.[67] Now this act was no doubt intended to reflect a difference between Germany, which had just recently adopted a thoroughly modern legal code, and Austria, which still adhered to its traditional laws and procedures—and to the traditional blindfolded Justitia. The lawyer who reported this radical break with tradition in the *Deutsche Juristen-Zeitung* (12 [1907]: 1130) first noted that the blindfold, though introduced four centuries earlier for satirical purposes in Sebastian Brant's *The Ship of Fools*, had subsequently come to be regarded as a venerable symbol of impartiality. But he went on to conclude: "Shall in the near future her scales and sword be taken from Themis, or shall she herself be banned from the courthouses? Art, we believe, should not be hemmed in by bureaucratic prescriptions." It is implausible that Kafka was unaware of this episode. The edict itself was an extraordinary one; and the case was reported, during the year while Kafka was serving his internship in the Prague provincial courts, in the leading German-language professional newspaper for the legal profession. If, indeed, Kafka had that episode in the back of his mind, then his description of the wingèd Justitia may well have been intended to embody the situation of legal turmoil that existed in Germany and Austria after the turn of the century: the conflict, that is, between a classical positivistic law intent simply on pursuing and punishing the guilty and the modern sociological law that wanted to weigh more carefully the elements involving both the crime and the criminal.

It has been noted by several scholars that the duality of legal systems in the novel is reflected in Kafka's consistent use of the forms "laws" (*Gesetze*) and "Law" (*Gesetz*).[68] On the only two occasions when he uses the plural form he is clearly referring to the positive laws of the constitutional state in which K. is a citizen. "All the laws were in force" (12) is his first thought when he assumes that some mistake has been made in his arrest. The same form occurs again at the end, when he contemplates the implications of shifting his case to the jurisdiction of "the laws of the state" (311). But whenever reference is made to the other system, the speakers consistently use the singular: "the Law." When the arresting agents tell K. that the Law is attracted by guilt, they repeat: "That is the Law" (15). When K. claims not to know that law, they observe triumphantly: "He concedes that he doesn't know the Law and at the same time claims to be innocent." These passages manifest a certain ambiguity. At the outset the reader tends to assume along with K. that "the law" here simply refers to a specific statute; but it gradually becomes clear that it adumbrates another legal realm altogether in which, as K. is told, "everything belongs to the court" (181). In sum, the realm of "the laws" is everyday society, in which the legal system with its palace of justice constitutes simply one among many social institutions. "The Law," in contrast, denotes in Tönnies's terms a more wholly integrated community to which every member is totally committed all the time. In one sense, then, Kafka's novel depicts the struggle going on in fin-de-siècle Europe between the conservative values of the past and the progressive forces of modern society or, even more specifically as Hofmannsthal suggested, between Austria and Prussia—and, ultimately, between the antiquated laws of the Habsburg monarchy and the more modern legal system represented by the 1871 code of the German Empire.

That this is more than mere speculation is suggested by a careful reading of the novel's first sentence: "Someone must have slandered [*verleumdet*] Josef K., for without his having done anything wrong, he was arrested one morning."[69] Kafka is not making a loose general statement; he is referring clearly and specifically to the Austrian Criminal Code of 1852, the version in effect when he was a student and beginning the practice of law. The Austrian code uses the word *Verleumdung* for slander (chap. 25, §§209–10), in contrast to the prevailing German criminal code (*Strafgesetzbuch für das Deutsche Reich* of 1871), which uses the term "false accusation" (*falsche Anschuldigung*, sec. 10, §§164–65). In the words of the Austrian code: "Whoever reports someone to the authorities because of an imputed crime, or accuses him in such a way that his accusation could serve as the cause of an official investigation, or of inquiries against the accused, makes himself guilty of the crime of slander." In other words, Kafka is using the term "slander" in a very precise and technical sense: Josef K. assumes that someone has reported him to the authorities because of an imputed crime, and that report does indeed precipitate the official investigation and inquiries that constitute the plot of the novel. It is also worth noting that slander was punished more severely in Austria (by imprisonment from one to five years) than was "false accusation" in Germany (jail for not less than a month and the possible loss of civic rights).

This point leads us well beyond terminology and directly into the heart of the two legal codes and their conception of justice. In general, the content of the substantive criminal law of most civilized countries is remarkably similar, especially with respect to major crimes against persons, property, and the state. For instance, the terminology, definition, and punishment for robbery and dueling are essentially identical in the Austrian and German codes of 1852 and 1871. But the superficial similarity conceals a profound conceptual difference between the two codes, a difference implicit in the first sentence of *The Trial*. Josef K. is arrested "without his having done anything wrong" ("ohne daß er etwas Böses getan hätte"), and the vocable *Böses*—inadequately rendered by the English word "wrong" (*Unrecht*)—adumbrates a concept that, while nonexistent in the German criminal code of 1871, has resided at the heart of the Austrian criminal law ever since the *Josephina* of 1787.[70]

The German penal code of 1871, which was long regarded as the model of modern criminal law and the most perfect product of the liberal constitutional state, aspired to absolute rational clarity in the definition of crime (in which it emulated the French penal code of 1808) and justified punishment in the Kantian sense solely on the grounds of retribution. Accordingly, the brief introductory provisions of the German code begin (§1) with the definition of offenses—felonies (*Verbrechen*), gross misdemeanors (*Vergehen*), and petty misdemeanors (*Übertretung*)—according to their penalties (length of confinement and/or amount of fine). For instance, "A felony is any act punishable by confinement in a penitentiary or by incarceration for more than five years."[71] The second paragraph introduces the famous Enlightenment principle of *nulla poena sine lege*: "A deed can be punished only if the punishment has been lawfully determined before the deed was committed." The short first section of the code goes on to specify the legal punishments and various doctrines and principles (attempt, complicity, mitigating circumstances). The major second section consists entirely of the rules defining crimes and specifying their penalties. An example is §80 on high treason: "The murder or attempted murder, carried out against the kaiser, or one's own provincial ruler, or during a stay in another state against the ruler of that state, is punished as high treason by death."

Now although we have already seen that many crimes and punishments are treated similarly in Austria and Germany, the organization of the Austrian code is so wholly different as to suggest an altogether different conception of law. It consists of two roughly equal parts: the first devoted to felonies (*Verbrechen*) and the second to misdemeanors (*Vergehen und Übertretungen*). Unlike the German code, which began with a definition of crimes and misdemeanors according to the severity of their punishment—that is, purely external and rational criteria—the Austrian code begins with a paragraph defining crime according to an inner criterion: "evil intent" (*böser Vorsatz*).[72] In other words, we are plunged directly into a moral universe that is absent in the German code: "For a crime [to occur], evil intent is required" ("Zu einem Verbrechen wird böser Vorsatz erfordert").[73] The code goes on to discuss the reasons for excluding "evil intent" (§2) and to deny impunity on the grounds of ignorance of the law (§3). But it returns in §4 to stress the moral responsibility of the criminal: "The crime arises from the malice (*Bosheit*) of the perpetrator, not from the character (*Beschaffenheit*) of the person against whom it is committed." The word *Böses* in the first sentence of Kafka's novel, in other words, points directly to the basis of the criminal code prevailing in Prague in 1914: K. is not protesting that he has committed no "wrong" or illegal act; he is denying that he has done anything with malice or evil intent. The term, in short, points to the subjective element, the motivation, and not to the objective element or any actual delict. Along with the technical term *verleumdet*, in other words, it suggests unmistakably the mentality of the lawyer trained specifically in the criminal law of the Austro-Hungarian monarchy.

Young lawyers in the civil-law tradition, whether German or Austrian, are trained, when confronted with a possibly criminal act (*Handlung*), to analyze it according to three criteria: the actual facts of the case (*Tatbestand*), the nature of its illegality (*Rechtswidrigkeit*), and the degree of guilt of the perpetrator (*Schuld*).[74] To put it most simply: an act must have taken place; the act must correspond to a crime as defined in the penal code; it must not be excluded for some such legitimate reason as self-defense; and the accused individual must be capable of legal responsibility (*mens rea*). This entire process of analysis takes place, needless to say, during the first stage of any criminal process, and depending on the results of his inquiry the *Untersuchungsrichter* decides whether or not to pass his dossier along to the prosecutor for a formal indictment. In actuality, matters are far more complex. The changing definition of these components and the shifting relationship among them has produced in the past two centuries a vast library of commentary.[75] For our purposes it will suffice to note that the young German lawyer of the fin de siècle was trained, as the code suggests, to look first of all for the occurrence of a punishable act (*strafbare Handlung*) without extenuating circumstances—to focus, that is to say, on the first two of the three components. Indeed, the concept of guilt (*Schuld*), at least in its moral dimension, does not occur in the German criminal code. This does not mean, of course, that German lawyers are not concerned with guilt; but it is not so much a moral concept as a legal definition: the failure to take the law into account.[76] This attitude is made explicit in Alfred Döblin's fictionalization of a notorious murder trial in Berlin (*Die beiden Freundinnen und ihr Giftmord*, 1924), which gives a detailed account of the public trial as well as the deliberations in the jury room. (The jury system was not abolished in Germany until 1924.) The jury is instructed not to concern itself with questions of motive or "guilt" but only with the facts of the case and the possibility of mitigating circumstances.[77]

Kafka's contemporaries, in contrast, especially as trained by Gross and others, tended to concentrate more on the criminal than on the criminal act. (This is evident in Werfel's *The Class Reunion*, where the examining magistrate barely registers the facts of the crime—the murder of a prostitute—and spends all his energies investigating the character of the alleged perpetrator.) According to the first sentence of their criminal code, as we have just remarked, the crime is defined by the presence or absence of "evil intent"; and the word "guilt" occurs in the second sentence.

We know that Kafka was familiar with this mode of legal thought, of which he was after all a product. The term *Tatbestand* occurs in one of the uncompleted chapters of *The Trial* (283), and the examining magistrate of the preliminary investigation is designated several times by his proper title, *Untersuchungsrichter*. It is plausible to conclude, therefore, that the first sentence of the novel points, just like the first sentence of the Austrian criminal code, at the notion of evil intent and, thereby, at the motivation of the accused criminal rather than at any act he may have committed. Given this premise, the remainder of the novel falls into place as an extension, albeit to absurd extremes, of the Austrian theory of criminal law.

The Austrian understanding of crime (*Verbrechen*), which traces its philosophical heritage back to Pufendorf's theory of natural law, is essentially subjective.[78] It is concerned with the person who commits the crime (*täterbezogenes Strafrecht*) more than was the essentially deed-oriented positivistic German penal code of 1871 (*Tatstrafrecht*).[79] This tendency goes so far that it has become an axiom of Austrian law that there can be guilt without illegality (*Schuld ohne Rechtswidrigkeit*)[80]—in cases where, for instance, the attempted crime can be punished even if it is not successfully committed. Thus the Austrian code (§8) explains:

> To have a crime it is not necessary that the deed be actually carried out. Even the attempt at a wicked deed [note the moralizing term *Übeltat*] is a crime as soon as the person with evil intent [*der Bösgesinnte*] has undertaken an action leading to its actual execution, but the completion of the crime has failed only because of incapacity, because of the intercession of an alien obstacle, or because of chance.

The German code contains the same provision without the moralizing words, but with an important difference: in the Austrian code the law applies to all attempted crimes unless an exception is specifically mentioned; in the German code, in contrast, it applies only when specifically stated. Several scholars have pointed to an analogy in the 1913 case, well-known to Kafka, in which his former professor, Hans Gross, caused his son to be arrested in Berlin and returned to a mental institution in Vienna—not for any crime he had actually committed but simply because of the possibility that, under the influence of drugs, he might do so.[81]

In line with his training in Austrian law, Kafka has constructed an absurd paradigm of the legal system that believes in a theoretical "guilt without illegality" and that concentrates on the criminal rather than on the criminal act. In Kafka's fictional world the legal system focuses wholly on the accused and never specifies the nature of the alleged crime—or, for that matter, whether any crime was actually committed. In the absence of any deed whose facts correspond to the criminal code (*Tatbestand*) or whose illegality (*Rechtswidrigkeit*) can be determined, the procedure is perforce restricted to the third of the analytical criteria, the determination of guilt (*Schuld*) and of the evil intent (*böser Vorsatz*) of the accused. This shift of emphasis, in turn, reflects the typical "subjectivism" of Austrian criminal law in contrast to the rational objectivism of the neo-Kantian German law.

Kafka's novel is of course more than a parodistic paradigm of fin-de-siècle legal controversies: it makes a moving statement about the nature of human guilt and responsibility altogether—our tendency to deny the guilt into which we are inevitably plunged by existence and our reluctance to accept responsibility for the unforeseen consequences of our actions. In the course of his year of trial, Josef K. discovers, and refuses to accept, reasons enough for his guilt.[82] And this guilt need not be understood in any narrowly criminal sense: it can be read as theological, metaphysical, existential, or social guilt. At the same time, we have seen that the organization and terminology of the novel are heavily indebted to the legal system in which Kafka was trained and in which he functioned effectively. But more: it is unreasonable to assume—and only literary critics who rarely emerge from their libraries would do so—that a writer as responsive as was Kafka to the intellectual currents of his time could witness the disruptions of the philosophical bases of his own profession, one of the most urgent and exciting issues of the day, without coming to grips with them. As Josef K. puts it at one point: "I would never have interfered in these matters of my own free will, and the need of this judicial system for reform [*die Verbesserungsbedürftigkeit dieses Gerichtswesens*] would never have disturbed my sleep. But by the fact that I was allegedly arrested, I am forced to intercede here, and specifically for my own sake" (66). So too Kafka felt obliged to take a stand. As Walter Müller-Seidel has eloquently demonstrated,[83] in the story "In the Penal Colony," which was written precisely during the months of the novel's composition, Kafka came to grips with one set of issues: deportation, the death penalty, and generally the problems of penology and the execution of justice. In *The Trial* he dealt with another aspect of the Habsburg criminal justice system.

In sum, the novel goes beyond its obvious burlesque to substantive critique. Kafka cannot be pinned down to a simple position. Nor has he made our task easier by expressing himself on matters of legal philosophy. Like Hofmannsthal, he recognizes the differences between Austrian traditionalism and Prussian modernism, but as a citizen of Prague, situated midway between Vienna and Berlin, he characteristically takes an intermediate position on the various legal issues. He does not equate the duality dividing the community of the Law from the society of laws as an opposition between tradition and modernity. The statue of Justitia pursues wrongdoers with neo-Kantian vigilance, but it is also blindfolded, as in Austria. However, we can draw some cautious conclusions on the basis of textual evidence.

The Trial portrays the injustices of a subjective law as practiced in the Habsburg fin de siècle and carried to its absurd extremes: a system in which the preliminary investigation has displaced the other stages of the procedure with its guaranteed protection for the rights of the individual. The preliminary investigation, in turn, goes to the extreme in ignoring the objective facts of the case and focusing on the guilt of the accused. It carries out its activities, moreover, in an atmosphere that abuses the rights of the accused both by violating privacy and discretion in its hearings and by concealing from the accused and his advisers the information needed for his defense. Finally, the system moves from inquiry to execution without defense, trial, or notification. In the intellectual context of the times, these episodes suggest a variety of responses. On the one hand, Kafka's account of the whimsicality of the *Untersuchungsrichter* implies a degree of discomfort with the Free Law movement that sought to liberate judges from the narrow constraints of the codified law. On the other hand, the conclusion of the novel, where K. is summarily executed "like a dog" with no understanding or clarification of his guilt, suggests an equal dissatisfaction with any theory of Pure Law with its severe notion of punishment as retribution and its faith in law as an autonomous absolute. The opposition of the constitutional state of laws and the total, even totalitarian system of the Law suggests that Kafka, contemplating the shift from community to society that characterized the modern bourgeois world, was firmly on the side of society with its codified laws and safeguards for the rights of the individual. At the same time, the portrayal of K.'s obsession with the vagaries of his "guilt" and with "malicious intent" lets us surmise that Kafka, along with Karl Kraus, was less than sanguine about a legal system that conflated law and morality and stressed modern subjective concerns with the doer over the objective definition of the deed according to the classical *nullum crimen sine lege*. Precisely the same ambivalence is evident in Kafka's other great legal fiction, "In the Penal Colony," where the explorer hastily departs from the island, equally dissatisfied with the Old Law of the officer and the former commandant and with the New Law of the present governor; it is his sense that, despite any changes, it remains essentially the same system.[84]

Kafka's attitude vis-à-vis the legal issues of the day is symbolized by a Justitia who would remove her blindfold for greater clarity of vision but also forsake the wings on her ankles in order to hold her balances steady. *The Trial* reflects the views of a legally trained mind that refused to dissociate itself from the legal-philosophical crisis of the age. To that extent Kafka's novel can be productively compared, as exemplary rather than exceptional, with a group of other contemporary literary works whose authors were also struggling with the urgent jurisprudential issues of classical and modern, of objective and subjective, of pure and free, of law and morality, of community and society. Kafka's *The Trial* exemplifies to that extent the continuing process of evolution that has characterized the history of Western law since its earliest beginnings.

CHAPTER TWELVE

Twentieth-Century Legal Evolutions

THE WORKS REVIEWED in the preceding chapters mirror crucial stages in the evolution of Western law, from the earliest emergence of legal societies out of the blood vengeance of primitive tribes to the great codes conceived in the eighteenth and nineteenth centuries as the judicial expression of the modern state. The literary documents show us how early Germanic law was first exposed to the softening influence of Christianity and how it was shaped by its contact with Roman law into the customary law that governed most of Europe during the Middle Ages. Time and again writers have reflected in their works the tensions that inevitably emerge as changing social values come into conflict with the positive law of any society, from Periclean Athens through medieval Iceland and Elizabethan England to fin-de-siècle Europe.

At the same time, we have witnessed a grand historical evolution moving from the primal unity of law and religion evident in the Early Codes (and still effective today in certain Islamic fundamentalist societies) through the gradual dissociation of those forces down to the radical polarization of law and morality in the minds of many American and European jurisprudents at the end of the nineteenth century. This disjuncture took such various forms as the opposition of divine and man-made laws in Greek antiquity, the anomy stemming from the conflict between the common-law and equity courts in late-sixteenth-century England, the controversy surrounding codification in the eighteenth century, and the disputes between Pure Law and Free Law in early-twentieth-century Germany and Austria.

Brook Thomas has argued that the lack of a historical perspective in modern American legal education produces a conservative drag that tends to preserve the status quo as lawyers uninformed by historical understanding come to accept as legitimate and, so to speak, eternally valid the laws they are trained and paid to administer.[1] Precisely the same argument can be applied to the general educated public. If we are limited temporally and spatially, if we know only the present legal system, or only the American legal system, if we do not understand that the law has been engaged in a continual process of evolution since its beginnings, then we do not adequately appreciate that it is natural and inevitable for the law to change in response to shifting social values. Similarly, if we do not grasp the complex tensions linking law and morality, we run the risk of mistaking strong conviction for right and of confusing passion with justice. The literary works that we have considered, which in almost every case (with Kleist as the major exception) have challenged the legal status quo, exemplify the fact that "canonical" works do not necessarily serve the hegemonic function often attributed to them by Marxist critics and deconstructionist theorists. These works provide, rather, a reassuring mirror for the constant evolution of justice under the pressure of social change.

The evolution of law did not of course cease in the early twentieth century at the stage reflected in Kafka's *The Trial*. World War I and the disintegration of traditional systems of order produced in Europe an enormous social, economic, and political chaos. The ensuing legal confusions in the Weimar Republic were registered in the novels of Alfred Döblin, Jakob Wassermann, and Franz Werfel.[2] The total disaffection with the existing legal system in Germany is manifested in Ferdinand Bruckner's *The Criminals* (*Die Verbrecher*, 1928), a drama making use of Expressionist techniques and a "simultaneous stage" to expose various flagrant miscarriages of justice involving the inhabitants of a tenement house in Berlin.[3] The real criminals—embezzlers, homosexual seducers, blackmailers, even a murderess—go free while innocent people guilty of trivial delicts or forced by circumstances to crimes of despair are condemned without sympathy or understanding by unfeeling judges to the harshest penalties. At the end a student, the fiancé of a young secretary sentenced to three years for a failed suicide attempt through which her pregnancy was aborted, sums up the theme of the play in the title of the book he is writing: "There Are No Criminals." In his novel *Success* (*Erfolg*, 1930), finally, Lion Feuchtwanger expands his fictional horizons to encompass the world. As the subtitle indicates, the panoramic narrative covers essentially "Three Years of History of a Province" (Bavaria in the years 1921–24). The multilineal action is catalyzed by a trial in which a controversial left-wing museum director in Munich is found guilty on trumped-up charges of perjury by reactionary political forces. Early in the novel, however, Feuchtwanger makes it clear that the situation in Bavaria stands for the corruption of law in every country after World War I. A "Brief Retrospective View of Justice in Those Years" (bk. 1, chap. 1) catalogs the politicization of law across the globe—from China and India by way of eastern and western Europe to England and the United States. "This happened either in the name of the republic or of the people or of the king—in every case, in the name of right."

Totalitarian Law

The pluralism of completing and conflicting ideologies arising out of this spiritual vacuum generated a profound longing for security and order that prepared the way for the totalitarian systems, notably Nazi Germany and the Soviet Union under Stalin, as well as the nontotalitarian dictatorships that characterized the early twentieth century in Italy, Spain, Hungary, and other countries around the world. This is not the place to pursue the controversial issue of the origins and causes of totalitarianism.[4] It is widely agreed that the most distinctive feature of modern totalitarian states can be seen in their relentless pursuit of a single stated goal—racial hegemony, for example, in Nazi Germany or the dictatorship of the proletariat in the Soviet Union—that is ruthlessly achieved through the forced participation of all citizens in a univeral one-party system imposed by the organized violence of the state.[5] To accomplish this end by means that have at least the appearance of legitimacy, both Hitler and Stalin, for all the antagonistic differences between National Socialism and communism, embraced similar techniques: justice was moralized; the law was instrumentalized; and the judiciary was politicized.[6] As a result, the radical polarization of law and morality at the turn of the century was followed, in Nazi Germany and the Soviet Union, by a new identification of the two forces that was as compelling as in the Early Codes, although in this modern hypostasis morality was based not upon religion but upon politics.

The emergence of this politicized justice that became known as *Gesinnungsjustiz* is clearly evident in the history of National Socialism. As early as 1920 Hitler was proclaiming the need for a "German law" as a particularly important plank in the party platform. Referring to a case in which a plaintiff sympathetic to the Nazis was rejected and forced to pay the court costs, Hitler said: "This blow against the sound sense of the people ["das gesunde Empfinden des Volkes"] must pass. We don't want a Mirror of Saxons or of Swabians, but a law adapted to economic and modern requirements, based upon Germanic and not upon Jewish feeling."[7] Two years later Hitler, who was notoriously ill-disposed toward lawyers, was complaining about

> enraptured legal scholars [who] groveled around in medieval laws, devoured the Mirrors of Saxons and Swabians, and believed that they could without further ado shift an entire people back by a thousand years. In their inner estrangement from the world they did not understand that it was not a question of the rebirth of outlived forms but the creation of a new Germanic law, adapted rigorously to the economic conditions of our time and corresponding intimately to the feeling of our blood, the instincts of our race.[8]

At the heart of National Socialism lay the conception of a people's collective (*Volksgemeinschaft*) or, to use the term that Hitler employed ritually in *Mein Kampf*, the "folkish organism" (*völkischer Organismus*).[9] Nazi law was not the instantiation of some eternal ideal but the expression of the feeling of this German organism of the people. In a memorandum of 1932 concerning the establishment of a National Socialist Party jurisdiction Hitler wrote:

> The purpose of justice is the maintainance of human collective life. It is therefore limited by the nature and the extent of the social organization that affects it. It is only a means to the end and is accordingly determined by that

> end. The justice system in the National Socialist state bears the responsibility of protecting the collective life of our people, carried out in the sense of the National Socialist idea, from destructive phenomena that harm or even threaten this community.[10]

It is hardly surprising that this principle was rapidly put into effect following the Nazi parliamentary victory of 1933. The draft for the new German Penal Code stated baldly: "The sound sense of the people for right and wrong determines the content and application of the penal law."[11] Through an amendment of July 28, 1935, which was heralded as a "revolution in penal law,"[12] judges were given the authority to punish acts not specifically prohibited by law if they offended "the sound sense of the people." Specifically, according to §2 of the National Socialist Penal Code (*Reichsstrafgesetzbuch*):

> Any person shall be punished who commits an act that the law declares punishable or that according to the basic principles of a penal code and according to the sound sense of the people deserves punishment. If no specific penal law is directly applicable to the act, then the act is punished according to the law whose basic principle best applies to it.[13]

It is obvious that this new legal principle (the so-called doctrine of analogy), which incorporated the racial hegemony motivating Nazi ideology, undermined the sacred Enlightenment principle of *nullum crimen sine lege*. Kafka's worst nightmares had come true: no law is required for a crime to take place if the deed violates the sensibility of the German people. As explained by Dr. Roland Freisler, the most fanatical expositor of Nazi law, that outmoded "palladium of bourgeois freedom" preserved nothing but "the 'freedom' for indecent behavior" and protected no one but "the citizen who wants to build his life in the broad swamp between respectability and what is explicitly prohibited."[14] According to Nazi legal theory, "the antithesis of law and politics is just as false as the antithesis of law and morality."[15] For—and here Freisler italicizes for emphasis—"*There is no other ultimate source of law than the conscience of the people itself.*"[16] Accordingly the legal order cannot be neutral: "Right is what serves the interests of the German people, and wrong is what harms it."[17] The sense of right inherent in the legal consciousness of the German people, the people's will to law (*das Rechtswollen des Volkes*), finds its authoritative expression in the pronouncements of the "volition bearer of the people" (*Willensträger des Volkes*), the Führer himself,[18] who has become the "supreme legal authority" (*der höchste Gerichtsherr*).[19]

The Nazis were able to accomplish these dramatic changes in a constitutionally legal manner by means of the so-called Enabling Act (*Ermächtigungsgesetz*) of 1933.[20] Following their seizure of power in 1933, the Nazi majority did not abolish the parliamentary assembly. Instead, claiming a national emergency, the party simply transferred to the executive all legislative power, which originally was the exclusive prerogative of Parliament. Even though this transfer was nominally subject to temporal limitations and was ostensibly carried out under parliamentary supervision, it opened the way in fact for a total dictatorship that was accomplished with the eager collaboration of a rapidly co-opted judiciary. Meanwhile, many professors of law at German universities provided a philosophical justification for the Nazis' arbitrary acts.[21] Chief among these was Carl Schmitt, who had the dubious distinction of being "theorist for the Reich."[22] In his notorious essay "The Führer as the Guardian of Justice"[23] Schmitt ingratiated himself with the Nazis by justifying on legal and moral grounds the murders committed after the elimination of former party accomplices in the Röhm Putsch.

Although Hitler through the "revolution in penal law" was quickly able to introduce his theory of the people's will and feeling, the courts were at least initially still occupied by judges appointed during the Weimar Republic, who did not always act according to party principles. While the Nazis were perfectly content to permit many civil legal matters to proceed according to existing laws, they became impatient in matters involving political issues. In 1934, accordingly, Hitler established the so-called People's Court (*Volksgerichtshof*), which became, especially under Roland Freisler (1943–45), the feared executor of the "people's will." This moralized justice and instrumentalized law evidently required a judiciary that had been politicized into the system, and this function too is stated explicitly by Freisler, who approvingly cites the new German code: "The officer [of the court] is the executor [*Vollstrecker*] of the will of the state borne by the National Socialist Workers Party."[24] Freisler himself, who had learned fluent Russian as a prisoner of war during the First World War and had for a time sympathized with the communists, became known as the Nazi Vyshinsky because he had mastered so effectively the techniques of the Moscow purge trials and applied them in the proceedings of the *Volksgericht*.

ALTHOUGH under these circumstances it was dangerous to criticize directly the party or Nazi law, writers managed to come to grips with the new legal situation that was in effect after 1933. Within Germany writers resorted to indirection, and the most powerful allegorical representation of totalitarian law—which managed even under the Nazis to sell over half a million copies—was Werner Bergengruen's novel *The Prince and the Court* (*Der Großtyrann und das Gericht*, 1935), which is set in northern Italy during the late Middle Ages.[25] Bergengruen (1892–1962), a poet and novelist with a strong religious orientation (and a convert to Catholicism in 1936), was prompted to write this novel in 1926, when he came across an Oriental fairy tale about a sultan who orders his vizier, on pain of death, to solve a complicated murder case within three days.[26] Although he worked on the material sporadically during the next few years, settling on the place (a fictitious walled town in northern Italy named

Cassano) and the time ("no later than the fifteenth century"), he had completed only the first of its five parts by the spring of 1931. He wrote the remainder of the book in 1933 and 1934 under the direct impact of current events, which provided the compelling focus for his tale.

> An entire nation was faced with the questions with which I intended to confront the figures of my book. On every side was exposed the easy seducibility of powerless and threatened people. All human freedom was suspended, over everyone hung danger, and almost all sharers of power, right down to the least of them, succumbed to the temptation of wanting to be godlike. I found myself in a condition of despair and outrage at what was taking place before my eyes and of burning concern about what had to be expected from the immediate future.[27]

Under these circumstances Bergengruen wrote his novel about the early Renaissance prince who orders his chief of security, Nespoli, to determine within three days who murdered within the castle precincts a monk whom the prince had often employed for diplomatic missions. To anticipate the conclusion: the prince had himself killed the monk, whom he had found guilty of treason. Bergengruen uses this device as the basis for a profound study of absolute power and its corrupting influence. (Lord Acton's famous quip would have been a suitable epigraph for the novel.) Under the threat of the prince's capricious authority, the entire city-state is morally and spiritually poisoned. First, Nespoli in his desperation tries to pin the murder on a simpleminded girl who, seduced allegedly by a monk, had recently drowned herself. When that fails—and of course every subterfuge fails since the prince already knows who is guilty—Nespoli's mistress, Vittoria, attempts to intervene on his behalf: when her elderly husband suddenly dies, she causes a forged confession to be found in his bedclothes. But when the prince threatens to confiscate all her husband's wealth and property if he is found to be guilty of murder, she looks to her own welfare and is willing to betray Nespoli. Meanwhile, her husband's son from an earlier marriage, Diomede, in the effort to save his own inheritance and his father's good name, bribes a prostitute to state that the old man had been with her at the time of the murder. Finally, the dyer Sperone, a local lay-preacher, dismayed at the corrupting influence that the affair is having on the entire city-state, surrenders himself to the prince claiming that he is the murderer.

> "Hasn't the condition of this city become evident? Is it not poisoned unto death? There was a time when it was no more sinful than all other places where people carry on their lives together. But now there will soon not be a single person in Cassano who has not become involved. Temptation, suspicion, and betrayal abound. Lies and perjury take place between brothers and spouses. Acts of violence are carried out, bodies and souls are corrupted. Are you not overcome by horror at the despicableness of your city?"[28]

Matters are resolved when the prince summons the affected persons and confesses his deed. The simple priest-confessor thereupon accuses him of the greatest sacrilege of all: of daring to play God with the destiny of human beings and of sitting in judgment over them. Overwhelmed with remorse, the prince begs forgiveness and asks the others to come to terms with their own consciences. He reinstates Nespoli as his chief of security; proposes to make Diomede the representative of justice in the city as soon as he has completed his studies; and invites Sperone to become his confessor—an invitation that the dyer refuses.

In the allegorical setting of his novel Bergengruen is able to contrive a reasonably peaceful solution to his plot. But as a study of power and its corrupting force the work leaves many questions unanswered. The prince, for all his good qualities, belongs recognizably—so recognizably, indeed, that it is astonishing the censors permitted the book to appear in Nazi Germany—to a political tradition extending from Machiavelli to Hitler and Stalin. He is incapable of hate, he tells Nespoli, because he regards his subjects simply as means to an end: "Who hates his own tools, which after all serve him to the ends that he needs to reach?" (126). In conversation with Diomede, a law student with whom he conducts several long dialogues on law and justice and statecraft, he points out: "You no doubt understand more about the nature of the law than I do, for I am one of those who make laws, not those who explain them. . . . Insofar as law has an earthly source in addition to its divine one, I am the source of law in this city and its environs and hence also the master of its exposition" (193). Like the dictator of any totalitarian state, he regards the health of the whole as the single most important goal and places the good of the community above the rights of any individual. "Will you not concede to me the right to cultivate justice in such a way that it serves as its highest goal the continuing existence of the mighty and thriving communal state of Cassano, even if perchance the trivial claim to justice of some market-pedlar from time to time is violated?" (195). He knows what is best for the people because he regards himself—and Hitler could not have said it better—as "the hidden will of the people" (237). As he tells Diomede: "There is nothing on earth more magnificent and worthy of a man than power! We are created for power, to seize it and to exercise it!" (235). And in this exercise of power and law his rule is totally autonomous. "I want to tell you something else that is a mystery to many, even the rulers of many cities and lands: just as a proper ruler amidst all constraints of the human condition is still an image of God, so too he resembles Him in that he has to act solely according to the principles of *his* being, but not according to standards that have arisen outside of him, no matter where they may originate" (243).

In many of his works Bergengruen was obsessed with the problem of justice. "The question of justice has preoccupied me as long as I can remember," he wrote in his literary memoir.

> I don't mean by that the way, inherent to every man, of being outraged at injustices that occur, a tendency that sometimes causes us to lose all sense of measure. I am no malcontent, no Kohlhaas and no innkeeper Hahn. But it was always my way to wonder about the tension between right and might, justice and the needs of the state, justice and the claims of life, and to inquire into the insoluble connection, but also the insoluble conflict between divine and human justice. The old Roman saying, according to which the highest justice is at the same time the greatest injustice, made on me even in my childhood a compelling impression demanding reflection.[29]

The theme of law and justice plays an important role in many of his other works, but most often the discussion takes place within the context of Bergengruen's Christian humanism.[30] Only in his great novel of 1935 does he come to grips, albeit allegorically, with the legal implications of contemporary political developments—with the jurisprudence of totalitarianism.

Writers living outside Nazi Germany were free to deal with Nazi law more directly. Bertolt Brecht, in the twenty-four satirical sketches on Nazi Germany that he produced during his Danish exile under the title *Furcht und Elend des Dritten Reichs* (Fear and misery of the Third Reich, written 1935–38),[31] included an exposé of Nazi law entitled "Legal Finding" ("Rechtsfindung").[32] A judge in Augsburg in January 1934 has been given a case involving three Nazis (members of the SA) who entered the jewelry store of a Jewish merchant, beat him up, and caused over eleven thousand marks' worth of damages. The seemingly straightforward case turns out to be politically complicated. The police inspector in charge of the investigation—a man worried about the welfare of his family—points out that the building's owner, who wants to get rid of the Jewish tenant, has complained about violations of the racial purity laws by the Jew's beautiful daughter. Reminding the judge that he too has a family, the inspector suggests that the Nazis were provoked by the Jew and therefore need not be charged with any crime. Moreover, the Jew has an Aryan partner with close connections to the SS who may have encouraged the Nazis to vandalize the shop so that he could demand restitution for his losses from his Jewish partner and then dissolve the partnership.

No sooner has the policeman left than the state attorney appears and insists that a Jew can still get justice in a court of the Third Reich: it was not he but an unemployed Marxist, shoveling snow in front of the shop, who provoked the three Nazis; indeed, witnesses attest that the Jew was not even present at the time. If the Jew goes free, he will hardly bring charges against three members of the SA, and the Marxist agitator has already been put into a concentration camp. When the judge sighs that it is no longer a simple matter to determine justice, the state attorney reminds him that "Right is whatever serves the interests of the people." The judge recalls the police inspector, only to learn that the Marxist is a war veteran with a throat injury that renders him incapable of shouting any loud provocations—and, in any case, is the state attorney's advice purely disinterested? Or is he angling for the judge's job? The judge becomes more and more agitated as the building begins to resound with the shouts of SA rowdies, who have filled his courtroom.

Just at this point a servant girl appears with the judge's morning snack and assures him that all the decent people in the neighborhood are on his side—that is, on the side of the Jew and the unemployed Marxist: the three SA men are former criminals who broke into the shop to steal an engagement ring for a girlfriend. In desperation the judge confers with a more experienced superior, who tells him that he alone can decide whether he wants to be at odds with the commissioner of justice or with the SA. The judge, now thoroughly confused, pleads that someone must advise him which decision is in the higher interest of the people. As the noise outside in the courtroom gets louder and the judge's wife phones to tell him that friends are canceling engagements with them, the bailiff summons him to his destiny. In a few pages Brecht succeeds deftly in conveying the dilemma of the judge and the confusions of a legal system caught between the Weimar Republic and Nazi Germany. Justice is whatever serves the people's interests; but, even setting aside the Jew and the Marxist, who are the people? the SA or the residents of the neighborhood? the policeman fearful for his family, the careerist attorney, or the Pilate-like superior judge?

While Brecht depicted from his Danish outpost the early contaminations of law in Nazi Germany, Alfred Neumann, writing from American exile a decade later, exposed to the world one of the most notorious cases of full-fledged Nazi "justice" within Germany. His novel *Six of Them* (*Es waren ihrer sechs*, 1944) was inspired by the story of the student resistance group in Munich known as the "White Rose." From brief news accounts Neumann learned about the fate of Hans and Sophie Scholl and their associates, who were arrested on February 18, 1943, for distributing anti-Nazi leaflets at the University of Munich, and executed four days later after a show trial conducted by none other than Roland Freisler, the head of the *Volksgericht*, who flew down from Berlin specifically for the occasion. Neumann's work is not a fictionalized account of the actual events: he had too little information at his disposal. His novel, written from September 1943 to June 1944, is a free reworking of the situation, based upon Neumann's firsthand knowledge of circumstances in Nazi Germany. The actual action concerns the brief period between the arrest of the group and their execution forty-eight hours later: their interrogation by the examining magistrate, the trial, and the execution by ax. But through flashbacks—in the thoughts of the six during their incarceration, and during the interrogations and trial as well—Neumann succeeds in providing a detailed depiction not simply of Nazi legal procedures and the *Volksgericht*, but also of six representative destinies in Nazi Germany. The legal aspects are highlighted by the fact that the professor is a professor of criminal psychology rather than (as in the case of the actual Professor Kurt Huber) of musicology and philosophy. Since two of the defendants are former soldiers, Neumann is able to introduce images of the German military and other Nazi institutions, such as the Hitlerjugend. What emerges is a vivid portrayal of life under Nazi totalitarianism.

It is unnecessary for our purposes to recapitulate the lives of the six conspirators, which are related in parallel strands: we hear the details of the six arrests, six separate interrogations, six statements before the court, six scenes in the prison when their heads are shaved for execution, six scenes with the chaplain, and finally the beheadings. The interrogation by the examining magistrate takes place more or less as we have encountered it in other works (such as Wassermann's *The Maurizius Case*), and the trial itself—conducted by a court consisting of two professional judges plus three lay judges—offers an opportunity not only to depict the operation of the *Volksgericht* under Freisler but also to characterize the personalities and motivations of the judges. Thus the president, Dr. Fritz Behn, was a minor district judge in 1932; but by finding SA rowdies "not guilty" by reason of self-defense (shades of Brecht!), he endeared himself to the Nazis and advanced rapidly in the judicial system to become presiding judge of a superior court and also a passionate believer in Hitler's law.

The trial, conducted in accordance with "the accelerated proceedings of the People's Court, which according to Article III, Paragraph 3, of the law of April 24, 1934, has taken over jurisdiction from the Reich's Supreme Court" (88),[33] is portrayed in considerable detail, beginning with a description of the courtroom itself, the arrangement of the tribunal, the president's throne, and the judges' red robes. For his own fictional purposes Neumann alters the prevailing court procedures to enable the prisoners to speak much more extensively in their own justification than was normally the case in Freisler's notorious trials (which amounted to interminable tirades by Freisler himself, who barely permitted the defendants to speak). But the theory of justice by which the trial is conducted accords perfectly with Nazi law. As the presiding judge informs the six:

> "The People's Court is not bound to the procedure prescribed by the penal code. It is responsible only to the Führer, is guided by, and renders its judgment in accordance with, the principle on which he has founded this court, to wit: A man is to be judged guilty or innocent according to whether or not he constitutes a danger to the security of the State. The procedure of the People's Court serves solely to render this decision; it is not impeded by any formality nor constrained to any legalistic cliché. The Court may even revoke its admittance of the officially appointed counsel for the defense if it should consider his activities injurious to or interfering with the judgment of the Court." (114)

The presiding judge anticipates that Professor von Hennings, as a teacher of law, will be disposed to favor the procedures prescribed by the penal code and to be prejudiced against the new methods of inquiry. But von Hennings is pleased to have an opportunity to express his own views, even if by so doing he in effect convicts himself. He has perceived, namely, "the sinister significance of the ingenious trick of the National Socialists not to permit any martyrs to arise" (127) and to emasculate martyrdom through the principle of concentration camps: "medieval oubliettes, abodes of oblivion, refurbished with a new and cheaper name and colossally intensified in number of occupants as well as concentration of effect: mass production of oblivion." This principle does not merely emasculate the dispensation of justice:

> "It is the strangulation of justice through the restoration of the Vehmic courts of the Middle Ages under the cheaper, though mendaciously blasphemous name of the People's Court as the highest tribunal of judicial secrecy and secret strangulation, with judges and judged swathed in invisibility and with the noiseless punching machine stamping out the inevitable double sentence: death and oblivion."

While the self-incrimination afforded by the statements of the six accused enables Neumann to unroll a broad panorama of life in Nazi Germany, it has the inevitable effect that Professor von Hennings anticipates. The chief judge, who (like Freisler) pounds the table and shouts at everyone, has through his own accusations stolen all the thunder from the prosecuting attorney, who can only compliment "the brilliant conduct of the trial" and ask for the sentence that the six have already passed on themselves through their confessions. "The defendants Hennings and Associates are guilty of the crime of high treason according to Paragraph 83, Section 3, of the Penal Code" (281). Accordingly he asks for the death penalty. The counsel for the defense, a timid and plaintive man, does not even try to question or minimize the defendants' guilt. In his brief statement he simply asks the court to consider the possibility of invoking the Führer's mercy for one or the other of the defendants in view of their youth. Thereupon the People's Court adjourns for deliberation, with a sequence of voting that is legally prescribed, beginning with the court reporter (one of the two professional judges), followed by the three lay judges, and concluded by the presiding judge. The decisions regarding guilt and punishment are nominally made by a majority, but the president demands a unanimous vote. "No, not he, but the dignity and sovereignty of this People's Court responsible only to the Führer demand it" (282). Neumann takes the occasion to offer insight into the motivations of the five judges, but the result is the inevitable penalty of death by the ax for high treason. "The People's Court declines to invoke the Führer's mercy for the condemned men and women. The verdict of the People's Court is final and beyond appeal, and is to be executed without delay" (291).

The last chapter, which introduces the barber and the chaplain in the prison, is anticlimactic from a legal standpoint. The novel ends with a brief account of the assembly at the university at which the punishment of the conspirators is announced, and during which hundreds of leaflets come flying down through the airshafts and from the roof of the building. "The Security Department, prepared for every eventuality, succeeded in arresting the students active on the roof. There were six of them."

While Brecht and Neumann were concerned with the impact of Nazi law on German citizens, a wholly different view of the Nazi judiciary was offered by Louis Aragon—the one-time surrealist poet who later became a dedicated communist and resistance fighter—in his story "Roman Law No Longer Exists" ("Le Droit romain n'est plus").[34] The story, told in alternating monologues and narrative passages, concerns a judge, Commandant von Lüttwitz-Randau, at the German Military Tribunal in occupied France near Grenoble. While on an excursion in the countryside he and his secretary, a rather stupid young woman named Lotte Müller, are captured by partisans. Fräulein Müller purchases her life by blabbing freely. The partisans try to educate and co-opt Lüttwitz-Randau by driving him around to the sites of various German atrocities, but he is convinced of the rectitude of the German cause. Finally the partisans slaughter him "like a chicken" ("comme une poule") and leave his body in a ditch.

The story interests mainly for its shrewd portrayal, primarily through flashbacks, of the German military judge and his intellectual development. We learn that, as a student, he wrote his thesis on Germanic law (*De jure germanico*) and then joined the party in 1933 to assist in the Nazi renewal of German law. "Our tribunals were still infected by Roman law, the Code Napoléon, the Jewish laws" (238). The renewal was the responsibility of jurists like himself: those trained in the old school but open to the new ideas and capable of working out a juridical terminology enabling Germans to apply laws favorable to the fatherland. The Führer, he insists, is legally inspired by an ancient conception of justice that can be traced back to the legendary time of Siegmund and Sieglinde. "Le droit germanique," which suppresses any laws that do not further German national interests, functions as a "war machine against the enemy" (206–7).

All these works, then, expose the dilemma of the individual caught within a system in which the law has become nothing more than the expression of the political will of the leader or "the people." Their only possible responses are either abject surrender of conscience and identification with the whole or futile resistance.

The Soviet Venue

Although we have focused, for reasons of continuity, mainly on German examples, very precise analogies exist in the literary response to totalitarian law in the Soviet Union. Without going into detail, let me suggest several examples that are readily accessible to further analysis. Even before he was confronted by history with Nazi law, Bertolt Brecht came to grips with totalitarian law in its communist form in one of his finest works, *The Measures Taken* (*Die Maßnahme*, 1930). In this didactic play the legal system is represented by a "control chorus" of workers constituting a paralegal comrades' court, who must pass judgment on the actions of four party agitators who have returned from a covert mission in China. They report that a fifth member endangered the project—to produce revolutionary conditions by exacerbating the hardship of various workers—by alleviating their plight out of human concern and pity. When the agitators' security is threatened by their comrade's all too human behavior, they convince him of his errors; he makes a confession and asks to be liquidated. He is shot and thrown into a lime pit, where his body disappears without a trace. The chorus, after listening to this report, acquits the remaining agitators of any guilt and approves the measures they have taken (hence the title) in the interests of the party.

While Brecht's play was written several years before the notorious purge trials of 1936–38, it displays a shrewd understanding of the implications of totalitarian law. As described in a classic document by A. Y. Vyshinsky, who served as prosecutor in the trials, "law is, of course, a political category. At the foundation of soviet law lie the political and economic interests of workers and peasants."[35]

> The most fundamental task confronting all scientific workers in the field of the science of law and state at the present time is the final extirpation—the complete and conclusive liquidation—of all the remnants of these provocateur fabrications: that is to say, the complete and final purging of the Augean stables of our legal science from the mud and all the filth of hostile "theories," from all the trash which unfortunately has accumulated among us over the years.

Not only must the goal of the party be put ahead of individual interests (as in Nazi law), but—and this was uniquely characteristic of Stalinist law, in contrast to Hitler's legal system—it was important for the health of the party that the accused individual confess his guilt and responsibility. (Kafka anticipated this development in *The Trial*, in whose court of the Law one may not defend oneself but may only make a confession.) Indeed, such confessions had evidentiary validity on the theory that no one would confess to counterrevolutionary crimes unless one were actually guilty.[36]

This acknowledgment constitutes the theme of Arthur Koestler's novel *Darkness at Noon* (1940), whose central character, N. S. Rubashov, is "a synthesis of the lives of a number of men who were victims of the so-called Moscow Trials."[37] As Koestler recounts in his classic document of disenchantment with communism, both his brother-in-law and two of his closest friends were arrested during Stalin's mass purges. One friend's experiences in Russian prisons and with the GPU's methods of obtaining confessions provided part of the material for *Darkness at Noon*.[38] Not unlike Neumann's novel, Koestler's work begins when the cell door slams shut on Rubashov following his arrest, and it ends with his execution by a pistol shot behind his ear. Similarly, too, the three "hearings" that constitute the bulk of the narrative contain flashbacks covering Rubashov's earlier life and career. Unlike the conspirators in *Six of Them*, Koestler's hero is not an enemy of the regime: "For forty years he had lived strictly in accordance with the vows of his order, the Party" (258). At the beginning of the novel Rubashov has been jailed because he has been accused of an attempt on the life of "No. 1"—a charge that not only he but also his prosecutors know to be patently absurd. In a deeper sense, however, Rubashov comes to realize that he is guilty in principle: for a man who even in theory concedes the fallibility of the State is capable of acting against it.[39] Rather, therefore, than depicting the murder of six innocent people by an evil legal system, Koestler is intent upon exposing the mentality of the Moscow purge trials: trials in which faithful party members were finally brought to confess publicly their guilt. Rubashov's earlier interrogations are conducted in a negligent manner by the first examining magistrate, Ivanov, who expresses "cynical doubts as to the well-foundedness of the accusation" (219). As a result, he is himself arrested and replaced by Gletkin, a right-thinking party member who points out to Rubashov that "Your task is simple. You have set it yourself: to gild the Right, to blacken the Wrong"—in sum, "to make the masses understand that opposition is a crime" (237–38). The trial itself, which is conducted by the president of the court, is a much briefer and more ceremonial occasion than the extended interrogations. Following the public prosecutor's demands that "all these mad dogs be shot" (250), Rubashov makes a simple declaration:

> "Citizen President," the accused Rubashov declared, "I speak here for the last time in my life. The opposition is beaten and destroyed. If I ask myself to-day, 'For what am I dying?' I am confronted by absolute nothingness. There is nothing for which one could die, if one died without having repented and unreconciled with the Party and the Movement. Therefore, on the threshold of my last hour, I bend my knees to the country, to the masses and to the whole people." (251)

If Koestler's novel provides a close analogy to Neumann's work, we can detect a fascinating parallel to Bergengruen's allegory in Aleksandr Solzhenitsyn's novel *The First Circle* (written 1955–64). In this otherwise sardonically realistic account of life in the Mavrino Special Prison on the outskirts of Moscow, Solzhenitsyn includes a remarkable scene (chap. 50) in which the inmates or "zeks" entertain themselves by staging a trial, according to the principles and procedures of Soviet law, of none other than I. S. Olgovich, the "Prince Igor" of Alexander Borodin's opera (which was completed in 1890 by

Nikolai Rimsky-Korsakov and Alexander Glazunov). According to the medieval classic upon which the libretto is based, *The Lay of Igor's Campaign*, in the twelfth century the Tartars captured Prince Igor and his son Vladimir. Khan Konchak, the leader of the Tartars, offers Igor his freedom if he will agree not to fight the Tartars. Rejecting the offer, Igor escapes and returns to his people, but his son, who has fallen in love with the khan's daughter, remains among the Tartars. At the trial it is reported that

> Organs of State Security have arrested the accused in the said case, Olgovich, I.S. The investigation has established that Olgovich, who was a military leader of the brilliant Russian Army, with the rank of prince, in the post of troop commander, turned out to be a foul traitor to his country. His traitorous activities consisted of voluntarily surrendering and becoming a prisoner of the accursed enemy of our people, Khan Konchak. In addition, he surrendered his own son, Vladimir Igoryevich, as well as his brother and his nephew, and the whole troop with all its men, armaments, and inventoried material property.[40]

Following a complete report, documented with quotations from Borodin's text, Olgovich is accused of "vile treason against his country, combined with sabotage, espionage, and collaboration," and found guilty of "crimes provided for in Sections 15-1B, 58-6, 58-9, and 58-11 of the Criminal Code of the Russian Socialist Federated Soviet Republic. . . . Guided by Section 268 of the Criminal Procedural Code of the Russian Socialist Federated Soviet Republic, the said case has been sent to the prosecutor for trial of the accused" (351). Following a discussion of whether or not there was any Soviet authority in Russia some 765 years earlier, secondary charges are brought against Borodin, A. P., "who must be arrested as a preventive measure," as well as the aristocrats (1) Rimsky and (2) Korsakov (353–54). Another prosecutor notes that Prince Igor would have been exposed as a security risk the first time he filled out a special security questionnaire because he was through his mother a half-Tartar. The defending attorney concurs in all the conclusions of the prosecutor, adding that Prince Igor should be not only hanged but also quartered. Indeed, he suggests that the prosecutor ought to be investigated himself for being so suspiciously lenient and settling for only twenty-five years of hard labor. After all, he remarks, "there is a punishment in our Criminal Code which is the final penalty, a punishment far more dreadful than twenty-five years of hard labor" (355): spiritual castration. "Section 20-Z, Paragraph a, provides that one is declared an enemy of the workers and expelled from the boundaries of the U.S.S.R.!" With this final joke the trial ends.

We might recall, in conclusion, Abram Tertz's (pseudonym of A. D. Siniavskii) satirical novel *The Trial Begins*, which takes place in Moscow in 1953, the year of Stalin's death. Public Prosecutor Globov is to prosecute a Jewish gynecologist, Rabinovich, for having performed an illegal abortion. Globov, a dedicated communist, believes in the righteousness of his cause and in victory at any cost for the party. His watchword amounts to the final perversion of the ancient adage *pereat mundus, fiat justitia*: "Let scores, let hundreds of innocents be condemned rather than allow one enemy to go free."[41] In the course of the brief action, however, his young wife deceives him and also undergoes an abortion; his teenage son is arrested for Trotskyism (that is, an idealistic view of society), and his revolutionary mother rejects him for his behavior and attitudes. Yet although his whole world is shattered, Globov feels vindicated at the end: "Our goal is reached. We have conquered" (114): the gynecologist, his son, and the author of the narrative all end up in the same prison camp.

The Theory of Universal Guilt

The collapse of Nazi Germany and the end of World War II left the Western world in a legal shambles. In Germany the occupation powers seized absolute control of the law and the courts. The network of the *Volksgericht* was abolished, the entire legal system with its procedures and judiciary organization was overhauled, and the laws themselves were in part annulled and generally revised. Not until 1949, when the new constitution (*Grundgesetz*) was put into effect under the supervision of the federal constitutional court (*Bundesverfassungsgericht*), was legal administration returned to the various *Länder*. Yet, as Milan Kundera shrewdly observed, "The totalitarian empires and their bloody trials have disappeared, but the *spirit of the trial* lingers as a legacy, and that is what is now settling scores."[42]

German legal thinkers, dismayed by the utter capitulation of law before the Nazis, sought the fault in the leading legal philosophies of the past, both positivism and the Free Law movement.[43] Their speculations resulted in Germany in a conspicuous turn to natural law colored by Christian humanism. Such prominent and politically uncontaminated legal thinkers as Gustav Radbruch and Helmut Coing sought by this turn to what was known as "supralegal law" to regain a legitimate basis in philosophy of law.[44] Radbruch, the first German law professor to be suspended from his position when the Nazis seized power in 1933, enjoyed particular esteem in Germany and abroad; and his turn from neo-Kantian positivism to natural law exerted an enormous influence on postwar generations. In particular, his theory of "wrong law" (*unrichtiges Recht*) affected important decisions of the German constitutional court as well as the Swiss supreme court.[45] Even before the war's end Radbruch had begun thinking about the reeducation of German jurists. As he put it in his notes for the revision of his magisterial introduction to the science of law: "Special care must be taken to work in the restoration or renovation of law with respect to the period of the Nazi regime. In a period of fluctuating legal conditions the legal-positivistic sections should be omitted in order to maintain the matters of principle."[46] This widespread suspicion of law corresponded to the more general distrust of ideology that characterized intellectual and cultural life in Germany during the postwar era.[47]

In France, meanwhile, a public *crise de conscience* was unfolding as efforts were made to explain the alacrity with which French jurisprudence had embraced Nazi policies and collaborated in the persecution of the Jews.[48] In England and the United States, at the same time, philosophers of law were seeking a legal justification for the Nuremberg trials, at which the Nazi judges were being tried. On what basis, it was asked, could judges be tried and punished if in fact they were doing their legal duty by enforcing legitimate albeit monstrous Nazi laws?[49] By what principle of law did one justify the retroactive legislation by which the Nazi judges were now being tried—especially since, according to the legal positivism current in the Anglo-American legal world, jurists at least since Holmes had been arguing for the separation of law and morality?[50] In sum, the war left a number of legal questions unanswered even for the victors and produced a state of controversy and anomy as unsettling as the one experienced in Elizabethan England or fin-de-siècle Austria, a situation characterized by one legal historian as a depletion (*Entleerung*) of the very concept of law and right.[51]

It was this situation to which Albert Camus responded in his philosophical essay *L'Homme révolté* (1951). In the chapter on state terrorism, Camus defines the totalitarian age as an era in which the universe of free men has given way to "the only universe in which history and expediency can in fact be elevated to the position of supreme judges: the universe of the trial."[52] He concludes the chapter by arguing that the universe of the trial has finally come full circle. "At the end of this long insurrection in the name of human innocence, there arises, by an inevitable perversion of fact, the affirmation of general culpability." In 1956, Camus and the Swiss dramatist Friedrich Dürrenmatt published remarkably similar and unusually ambiguous fictions in which former jurists come to grips with the issue of universal guilt that seemed to preoccupy thinking men and women in the decades following the war.

Camus had long been concerned with questions of justice and guilt.[53] In his early novel, *L'Étranger* (1942), written just at the beginning of World War II, he had undertaken what amounted to an attack on law and the legal system for its condemnation of an "innocent" man. It is perhaps possible to understand Camus's intention, which is quite similar to that of Bruckner's *The Criminals*, in the political context of the times. But in hindsight, for all the significance of the text as an existentialist document, one can also see that it is juridically flawed. Meursault is not only a totally unsympathetic figure; he is also, when all is said and done, guilty at the very least of second-degree murder. Regardless of the social prejudice that Camus depicts as a major factor in the verdict, which may be too harsh, he has killed a man.[54] (There is no question of innocence, as there is, for instance, in Faulkner's *Intruder in the Dust* [1948], or Harper Lee's *To Kill a Mockingbird* [1960], each of which deals more successfully with an innocent man indicted and, in one case, condemned simply because he represents an offense in the eyes of the community.)

Fifteen years later, after the war and the German occupation, Camus saw matters differently. Already in *L'Homme révolté* he had displayed a fascination with the Nuremberg trials, and in *The Fall* (*La Chute*, 1956) his narrator calls the destruction of the Amsterdam ghetto "one of the greatest crimes in history."[55] *The Fall* is in one sense a fictional essay on the problems of guilt and innocence exposed by the war years.[56] The religious dimension of the work has been frequently noted:[57] the title suggests man's fall from innocence (indeed, one of the preliminary titles was even more specific: "Le Jugement dernier");[58] the narrator has assumed the name Jean-Baptiste Clamence, a clear allusion to John the Baptist, the voice of one crying in the wilderness (*vox clamans in deserto*); Amsterdam's concentric canals are described in terms of Dante's circles of Hell; other biblical, religious, and theological references abound. But the legal aspect is equally pronounced.

Clamence is a former Parisian lawyer, who made his fame as an advocate for those—widows and orphans, among others—who seemed to obtain no justice from the courts. His profession is evident not only in his general command and love of language but more specifically in the legal terminology that colors his discourse. Within the first few lines he offers to "plead the case" ("plaider votre cause") in an Amsterdam bar for a Frenchman who is trying to order a glass of ginevre without knowing any Dutch. At the high point of his career, however, Clamence was made aware of his own hypocrisy, which consisted of grandiloquent words and sentiments accompanied by no human commitment: he failed one evening, out of indifference and cowardice, to make any attempt to rescue or aid a young woman who had leapt from a bridge into the Seine and drowned. For some time afterwards he was tormented by a sneering laughter that ridiculed his pretensions. At first he tried to drown out the secret laughter with the seductions of debauchery. Finally, his career in ruins, he moved to Amsterdam where he now serves as an advocate for the pimps and thieves who frequent the shabby bar he favors, seeking to silence the laughter with the interminable stream of words with which he overwhelms the unsuspecting tourists who stray into the bar.

While he was still in Paris, Clamence's disenchantment with the law as he successfully practiced it began to emerge on such occasions as a lecture before a group of young lawyers. In a rhetorical gesture worthy of Karl Kraus, he suddenly turns the tables and defends the criminal by exposing the crimes of the lawyer. He asks his audience to imagine the defense of a man who murdered a woman out of jealousy.

> Gentlemen of the Jury, consider, I should say, how venial it is to get angry when one sees one's natural goodness put to the test by the malignity of the fair sex. Is it not more serious, on the contrary, to be by chance on this side of the bar, on my own bench, without ever having been good or suffered from being duped? I am free, shielded from your severities, yet who am I? A Louis XIV in pride, a billy goat for lust, a Pharaoh for wrath, a king of laziness. I haven't killed anyone? Not yet, to be sure! But have I not let deserving creatures die? Maybe. And maybe I am ready to do so again. Whereas this man—just look at him—will not do so again. (94–95)

The very word "justice" causes him "strange fits of rage" (92). In Amsterdam, where his disenchantment with law and justice only increases, he gradually comes to believe in universal guilt: "Every man testifies to the crime of all the others—that is my faith and my hope" (110). His very definition of democracy is a situation in which we are all guilty (136). Indeed, he arrives at least implicitly at the point of accepting the burden of a collective guilt created by "our Hitlerian brethren" (11; "nos frères hitlériens," 16). In a statement reminiscent of Camus's admired model Kafka, Clamence observes that "the keenest of human torments is to be judged without a law. Yet we are in that torment" (117). His failure to act to save the drowning woman is generalized in a manner suggestive of the feeling of guilt that overwhelms survivors of such catastrophes as the Holocaust. "Knowing what he knew, familiar with everything about man—ah, who would have believed that crime consists less in making others die than in not dying oneself" (113). At this point, late in the book, we finally come to understand what Clamence means when he calls himself a *juge-penitent*. "I had to find another means of extending judgment to everybody in order to make it weigh less heavily on my own shoulders" (137). Universal guilt becomes the solution to individual guilt in a world that has gone through the crucible of totalitarianism. The Camus who earlier turned his indignation on the judges of the world for their condemnation of innocence now presents us with a world in which innocence has given way to universal guilt and the accused has become the judge.

The dilemma of the contemporary writer concerned with questions of law and justice in the face of postwar legal anomy is expressed by the utter ambiguity of Camus's late work. For it would be a mistake, despite a number of autobiographical elements, to identify Camus with Clamence, just as it would be an error to assume that Camus has forsworn his humanism for an abject nihilism.[59] Yet the very fact that Camus is capable of imagining such a figure as Clamence and of sustaining our fascination for so many pages indicates, at the same time, that he is no longer capable of looking at issues of right and wrong, guilt and innocence, law and justice, with the simplistic righteous indignation of the twenty-nine-year-old author of *L'Étranger*. Hitler, the Holocaust, the Vichy collaboration, the trials at Nuremberg had intervened to change the entire legal landscape.

WE ENCOUNTER precisely the same ambiguity when we turn to the other great legal fiction published that year, Friedrich Dürrenmatt's *The Breakdown* (*Die Panne*, 1956; also translated under the title *Traps*). Like Camus, Dürrenmatt was drawn by temperament and forced by history to the theme of justice, and especially justice perverted, throughout his entire literary career—from his early absurd story "The Sausage" ("Die Wurst," 1943), in which the judge absentmindedly consumes the evidence during the trial of a butcher for murdering and "sausaging" his wife, to the late novel *The Execution of Justice* (*Justiz*, 1985), in which a young attorney proves the innocence of a man convicted twenty years earlier of murder, only to discover that he has unwittingly created a legal conundrum in which justice can be restored only through another crime.

The Breakdown, which bears the subtitle *A Still Possible Story*, begins with a brief theoretical prologue in which the author speculates on whether real stories are still possible in an age in which destiny has left the stage, in which it is no longer God and Justice and Fate that threaten mankind, but traffic accidents, dike breaches resulting from construction flaws, and explosions in atomic-bomb factories produced by distracted lab workers. Dürrenmatt proposes to lead us into this modern world of mechanical breakdowns in search of a "still possible story," in which humanity can be glimpsed in the face of an average citizen, accident is generalized, and justice is reflected in the monocle of a drunk. In the phrase that Hannah Arendt had not yet coined, Dürrenmatt sets out to expose to his audience the banality of evil amidst the general guilt of humankind.

The "hero" of Dürrenmatt's banal tragedy is Alfredo Traps, the forty-five-year-old European sales manager for a firm marketing a successful artificial fabric called Hephaiston. One evening in the middle of June, on his way back home from a sales trip, Traps's car—a glitzy Studebaker—breaks down about an hour's drive from the city. Traps, who entertains himself with thoughts of his extramarital affairs and whose notorious conquests have earned him in his club the sobriquet "Marquis de Casanova," finds that the village inns are full; but he is invited to stay the night in the villa of an elderly pensioner and to take dinner that evening with his host's guests. It turns out that three of the four gentleman, all in their eighties, are retired jurists: his host is himself a former judge, the monocled Herr Zorn ("Mr. Wrath") a former prosecutor, Herr Kummer ("Mr. Worry") a former defense attorney; the fourth guest, Pilet, is a former hangman. These four gentlemen, Traps learns, gather for dinner every evening and reenact for their own amusement famous trials from the past—Socrates, Jesus, Joan of Arc, Dreyfus, among others; on occasions when they have guests, they invite the visitor to play the role of the defendant in trials "liberated from the unnecessary welter of formulas, protocols, scribblings, laws, and the other junk that burdens our courts" (58). As Herr Zorn assures Traps, "a crime can always be found" (47).[60] Their game is unique and intense because, in contrast to the official system of Swiss law, where it has been abolished, they have retained the death penalty. Traps, in the bland confidence of his own innocence, agrees delightedly to act as the defendant, and in the course of the long summer evening, over an opulent multicourse dinner featuring choice wines, his interrogation takes place. The defense attorney takes him aside at the outset and urges him to confess his crime, warning that "the way from guilt to innocence is difficult but not impossible, whereas it is hopeless to try to preserve one's innocence" (49). But Traps, whom we have come to know as an almost totally amoral man, protests his innocence and responds cockily to the prosecutor's first casual questions.

To make a long story short, the skillful prosecutor begins to construct a story of guilt from a few simple facts: Traps's expensive new automobile; the circumstance that he has only recently assumed his present position following the unexpected death of his former boss, Gygax; the boastful confession that Traps has had an affair with Gygax's wife. The four old men are jubilant to be on the trail of a murder, for murders, the prosecutor tells Traps, are the most painful of crimes to confess: the defendant is ashamed and represses the memory of his crime. Traps, who still does not understand what is going on, listens uncomprehendingly to a technical discussion about *dolus* (intention) and *dolus malus* (with evil intent). As a bottle of Château Pavie 1921 is uncorked, he is subtly led to confess how he wittingly caused Gygax's death: aware of his boss's severe heart condition, he arranged to have an intermediary tell Gygax about his wife's infidelity, whereupon Gygax collapsed and died of a heart attack. As soon as they have determined that they have a clear case of *dolus malus*, the old men celebrate by opening a bottle of Château Margaux 1914.

Traps is momentarily offended to discover that he is actually being accused of a murder, but the prosecutor makes a speech on the joy of discovering a murder, "an event that causes our hearts to beat more loftily and that poses new responsibilities, decisions, duties" (70). He congratulates Traps "because it is not easily possible to discover a murder, to carry out justice, without a culprit," and goes on to contrast the present circumstances with the days when, in the service of the state, their profession was gloomy and the accused stood before them not as a friend but as an enemy. They have now attained a lofty standpoint from which they no longer regard crime as something ugly but rather as the necessary and lovely precondition of justice. In jubilation the four old men embrace Traps and assure him that "a crime can lurk behind every incident, behind every person" (73). Traps is transported by the euphoria of the moment to make a full confession. "Remarkable! I feel that I am understood and am also beginning to understand myself as though I were making acquaintance with a person who I am but whom I formerly knew only vaguely . . ." (79). In his exalted mood Traps gradually is overcome by "a premonition of higher things, of justice, of guilt and expiation" (82). The prosecutor begins his summation, demanding the death sentence "for a crime that deserves admiration, wonder, respect and has a claim to be called one of the most extraordinary of the century" (84).

As they consume pastry and cognac, the defense attorney tries to justify Traps's action on the grounds that he is "not a criminal, but a victim of the epoch, of the West, of civilization, which, alas, has lost its faith, its Christianity" (87). But by this point Traps will have none of it: so overcome is he by the evening's proceedings that he insists it was a conscious murder on his part, which made him feel truly alive for the first time in his life. The judge pronounces the sentence of death, happy to be able to deliver a verdict that the accused so totally embraces. Accepting the judgment, Traps receives the "knighthood of justice" ("Ritterschlag der Gerechtigkeit," 92), than which nothing is loftier, nobler, greater. As dawn breaks outside, Traps staggers drunkenly up the stairs to his room, accompanied only by Pilet the hangman, who collapses in a stupor. But when the three totally inebriated old men arrive a few minutes later to deliver to Traps the written verdict, handsomely inscribed on parchment with Latin and Old German phrases, they discover to their consternation that Traps has taken their game seriously, has mistaken aesthetics for reality, and has hanged himself in the window frame. "Alfredo, dear Alfredo," the prosecutor with the glittering monocle cries in the last line, "What were you thinking, for heaven's sake? You have ruined the finest evening we've ever had!"

Dürrenmatt has exposed not only the banality of evil but also, in the aesthetic game of the four old men, the fate and criminal intentionality underlying a series of seemingly trivial events. Like Camus, Dürrenmatt has used his satirical fiction as the occasion for reflections on the most profound issues of justice and responsibility. Like Kafka before him, he has also played ironically with the device of parallel legal systems: the laws of the land, where the death penalty has been abolished, and the "law" preserved in the game of the four retired jurists, where legalisms give way to morality. Yet like Camus and others of his generation, Dürrenmatt is highly ambivalent—not only about the law, but even about his own responses. In the same year (1956) he produced a radio-play version of *The Breakdown*, which is identical to the novella in almost every important respect until the very end. But in the radio play, Alfredo Traps gets up the next morning, collects his repaired Studebaker, and drives back home utterly unmoved by the events of the preceding evening and feeling in his banality no sense of guilt for the death he had caused.[61]

Two decades later and still unable to let the material go, Dürrenmatt rewrote *The Breakdown* yet again, this time for the stage and exaggerating the familiar story into the grotesque.[62] In the end two verdicts are rendered: a "metaphysical" verdict of guilt and a "juristic" one of innocence; Traps is free to choose the one he prefers. Although it is made clear that he is actually innocent of his boss's death, he is so elated by the thought of his own guilt that he executes the penalty by shooting and hanging himself. The juristic chaos to which Dürrenmatt is responding is signaled by the fact that the aged judge, prosecutor, and defense attorney are exposed as having been utterly corrupt while in office. And the judge now has a granddaughter, a sex-crazed widow, both an embezzler and a murderess, whose symbolic role as Justitia is suggested not only by her name, Justine, but also by the shears with which she clips roses. In no uncertain terms the judge explains to Traps that the whole drunken evening has been nothing but "a parody of something that doesn't exist and by which the world continues to be taken in, a parody of Justice, the cruelest of the *idées fixes* in whose name man slaughters his fellowman" (164–65). Nothing could reflect more clearly than this late version of Dürrenmatt's *The Breakdown* the changes that were about to take place in attitudes toward law and justice.

The Lure of Anarchism

In the 1960s the situation changed drastically. Camus and Dürrenmatt represented the attitudes of thoughtful members of a generation that had grown up under the shadow of totalitarianism and now not only questioned the system of justice that had permitted those developments to take place but also entertained potentially upsetting second thoughts about the personal responsibility of "innocent" individuals for what had happened. The activists of the 1960s, in contrast, came to maturity, and in many cases were born, after World War II. Disclaiming any responsibility for events that they regarded as past history, they were concerned principally with issues of social injustice and personal liberty: notably the war in Vietnam, the unfulfilled promises of civil rights, and restrictions on individual rights. Convinced that these injustices were not only condoned but even actively supported by the existing political system, including the courts, they set out actively to expose inequities and inconsistencies by direct action. The decade witnessed, both in Europe and the United States, a rapid escalation of disruptive tactics and deliberate provocations that challenged the very legitimacy of the existing government and its laws. It is no accident that these actions were accompanied among political thinkers by a pronounced resurgence of interest in anarchism. In many countries writers rehearsed the history and theory of anarchism: George Woodcock (*Anarchism: A History of Libertarian Ideas and Movements*, 1962), James Joll (*The Anarchists*, 1964), Daniel Guérin (*L'Anarchisme. De la doctrine à l'action*, 1965), Erwin Oberländer (ed., *Der Anarchismus*, 1972). Meanwhile, such libertarian political activists as Herbert Marcuse, Noam Chomsky, and Michel Foucault proposed anarchism as a possible alternative to the authoritarian hegemony of the modern state.[63]

In the United States the sixties began rather benignly because the hippies and the student rebels at the beginning of the decade—the Students for a Democratic Society (SDS), the Berkeley Free Speech Movement—tended at least initially to challenge society and the law in demonstrative but nonviolent ways.[64] But the decade witnessed a gradual shift in tactics following the assassination of John F. Kennedy in 1963 and U.S. involvement in Vietnam in 1964: political activism within the framework of law gave way to anarchistic rejection of the law, only to be displaced finally by violent attacks on the system. The year 1967 saw burgeoning antiwar activities on many campuses with protests against military recruitment and classified research. The spring of 1968 marked a major culmination of the violence with the assassinations of Martin Luther King Jr. and Robert F. Kennedy.

Events in Europe paralleled those in the United States. During the early and mid-sixties such countercultural groups as the Provos in Amsterdam and their imitators elsewhere sought to disrupt the system—by which they meant bourgeois life as regulated by government rules and laws—by nonviolent and essentially anarchistic activities: disruptive demonstrations, street theater, traffic disturbances. However, in conjunction with the escalation of the Vietnam War the protests began to intensify. In June 1967, during a demonstration protesting a visit of the shah of Iran to West Berlin, the student Benno Ohnesorg was shot and killed by a policeman, an incident that radicalized many hitherto uncommitted students. In April 1968 the popular German student leader Rudi Dutschke was shot and wounded by an unidentified assailant; this attack provoked serious disturbances in German university towns and, in Berlin, a massive demonstration. The student protesters elicited statements of solidarity from prominent intellectuals and writers. A few weeks later in France, the turbulence extended beyond the universities to encompass young workers, whose boycotts and strikes paralyzed Paris and most of the nation for the month of May.

An event symbolizing the turmoil of the late 1960s, the anarchistic cusp of the development leading from nonviolence to terrorism, can be recognized in the so-called Conspiracy Trial of the Chicago Seven.[65] The Yippies (Youth International Party) of Abbie Hoffman and Jerry Rubin had come to Chicago with the stated purpose of disrupting the Democratic National Convention in August 1968 and opposing the nomination of Hubert Humphrey as the Democratic presidential candidate. Through their tactics—outrageous, but essentially nonviolent—the Yippies along with other groups succeeded in provoking the Chicago police into a confrontation in Lincoln Park, which resulted in substantial injuries on both sides. Eight leaders of the Yippies and other participating groups were charged with conspiracy to provoke a riot, and the Yippies had their day in court.

Hubert Humphrey was simply the symbol for the entire political and legal system that the Yippies considered corrupt. It was their hope to undermine the system not by violence but by anarchism and guerilla theater. When they were summoned following the convention to testify before the House Un-American Activities Committee, Jerry Rubin turned up "naked to the waist, face painted, and carrying a toy machine gun with a bandolier of live ammunition. Abbie [Hoffman] came in a shirt designed after the American flag. The cops tore the shirt off and discovered that he had a Vietcong flag painted on his back."[66]

Along with Congress, it was mainly the courts that the Yippies were bent on attacking. After the fall elections Jerry Rubin wrote an article in which he called the courts "the nation's toilets."[67] The Yippie party platform that Abbie Hoffman read in the plaza before the Chicago Federal Building at the time of the Democratic National Convention included among its eighteen points, in addition to an immediate end to the war in Vietnam, the legalization of marijuana and the abolition of money: "A judicial system which works toward the abolition of all laws related to crimes without victims—that is, retention only of laws relating to crimes in which there is an unwilling or injured party, i.e., murder, rape, assault."[68] By the time their trial approached, in the fall of 1969, the legal system had become a central object of concern for the defendants. As one of the defendants, Tom Hayden, a cofounder of the SDS, wrote: "We need to expand our struggle to include a total attack on the courts. The court system is just another part of this apparatus that is passed off as 'open and impartial.' This is no reason for us to become submissive at the courtroom door."[69] Later Hayden sought to provide a philosophical basis for protest when he told reporters that he and his fellow radicals saw themselves as "participants in the creation of a new society in the streets . . . with its own natural laws, structures, language and symbols."[70]

Accordingly the trial of the Chicago Seven turned into an anarchistic theatrical event in which the defendants systematically disrupted the court of Judge Julius Hoffman through their antics and violated the dignity of the law: they refused to rise when the judge entered the courtroom, they greeted the jurors with raised fists or Nazi salutes, they used profanity and abused the (Jewish) judge by comparing him to Hitler, they compared the proceedings in "Amerika" to Nazi courts, their witnesses recited poetry and sang folk ballads. In a compromise verdict, five of the defendants were found guilty of the reduced charge of crossing state lines with the intention to incite a riot and released pending appeal; all seven were charged by Judge Hoffman with contempt of court.

It has not been the purpose of these few paragraphs to write yet again the social history of the 1960s. It was their aim simply to suggest how a new and, especially among the young, utterly cynical attitude toward the law emerged in response to the events of the decade—a cynicism to which the only adequate response seemed, to many young people, to be anarchism. In this charged atmosphere the thoughtful and subtle ruminations of Camus and Dürrenmatt carried little weight.

PERHAPS the representative legal fiction of that anarchistic decade was Heinrich Böll's novel *End of a Mission* (*Ende einer Dienstfahrt*, 1966), which, written before the turn of events that led to the violence of the late 1960s, captures the more playful attitude of the Provos, the Yippies, and other groups that challenged the law as the symbol of what they perceived as a thoroughly corrupt system. Böll was engaged during much of his career in political protest of a leftist tendency, and his social protest—for example, against retrogressive tendencies in German politics, in support of various minority or other groups marginalized by the economic miracle of the Federal Republic, against U.S. military installations in Germany—is reflected in his literary works. But for all his Rhenish anarchism, whose genealogy in his own family he proudly attests, he rarely addressed the German legal system, as he did in this novel.

Böll has explained that the incident underlying his novel stemmed from an anecdote he heard from a friend, who had been told by a soldier—"contrary to regulations" (*protokollwidrigerweise*)—that, as a military chauffeur, he was sometimes sent off to drive his vehicle aimlessly until it reached the kilometer count required for its routine inspection.[71] In the fall of 1965 Böll wrote a fifteen-page story based on the incident; half a year and six drafts later the story had grown into the 250-page narrative that it now constitutes. Along the way the author combined the incident, which he initially regarded simply as an example of the absurd and wasteful practices of the German military, with his thoughts on the social role of art, which were shaped in part by the "happenings" staged in the early 1960s by such avant-garde artists as his friend Joseph Beuys. These happenings, which often involved the demolition of such symbols of traditional bourgeois art as concert grand pianos, sought in contrast to popularize art by tearing down the artificial boundaries cutting it off from reality and to create instantaneous art involving the audience in the act of creation.

The novel revolves around a happening staged by Johann Gruhl, a fifty-year-old master carpenter of antique furniture, and his son Georg, a trained carpenter with pronounced artistic inclinations. In June 1965, shortly before his release from military service, Gruhl Jr. was sent out to clock up kilometers on an army Jeep so that it could be taken for its routine 5,000-kilometer inspection at the specified time. Instead the young soldier drove home with the vehicle. Four days later he and his father took the Jeep to a field path just off a main highway near their village, punctured its gas tank (so that it would not explode), doused it with gasoline brought along in canisters, and set it on fire. Filling the empty canisters with hard candies, they placed them in the Jeep, where the heated candies burst with a tympany-like sound. As the vehicle slowly burned, they sat nearby on a stone, singing the *ora pro nobis* from the All Saints' litany, and rhythmically knocking their pipes together. Meanwhile, some hundred onlookers gathered: passing field workers, schoolchildren on their way home, rubbernecking automobilists attracted by the happening, and local gendarmes.

An art expert subsequently testifies that the happening constituted a "pentamuseal" event, involving elements of architecture, sculpture, literature, music, and dance.[72] As we learn in the course of the story, the Gruhls were provoked to their deed by their hostility to a government that they considered corrupt. The elder Gruhl has been forced for the past ten years into bankruptcy and constant legal difficulties as a result of German tax laws that disadvantage independently employed artisans (and writers like Böll!).[73] The younger Gruhl is profoundly disturbed by the senseless waste of time, materials, energy, and patience required by the military. He has spent his term of duty building bars for officers' clubs and clocking twenty thousand kilometers on the autobahn—"that is, half the distance around the world"—for inspection purposes. Father and son decide to incinerate the Jeep as an aesthetic-anarchic act and, like the Yippies in Judge Hoffman's court, to publicize their protest and draw public attention to government waste and legal inequities.

To this extent the plot—the burning of a military vehicle as an artistic happening—incorporates the aforementioned themes of social protest and the social role of art: aspects that have been fully discussed by critics of Böll's work.[74] But in its final published version the novel encompasses far more: it amounts, first of all, to an affectionate portrayal of an entire small Rhine-Catholic community in an "aesthetics of the humane" of the sort that Böll envisaged in his 1964 lectures at the University of Frankfurt.[75] The story is presented in the form of a report on the one-day trial of the Gruhls that takes place some ten weeks after the event in the local magistrate's court in the small town of Birglar. Böll tells us, in his "introduction" to the novel, that he made a systematic study of the German laws governing criminal procedure and, for his setting, explored two small towns in the vicinity of Cologne that featured local magistrate's courts. (Birglar is a fictional composite.) For additional information on legal matters Böll also consulted a lawyer friend.[76]

The result amounts to a detailed depiction of a trial in a German local district court for the charges of destruction of property and public nuisance. In the course of one long day—from 9:00 A.M. until after midnight—the entire procedure, which takes place before a tiny group of local onlookers in the smallest of the town's three courtrooms, is unrolled before our eyes: the initial recording of personal information (even though the accused are well-known to everyone involved and related to several of them); the interrogation by the presiding judge with interjections by the conservative prosecutor and the liberal defense attorney, along with the occasional silent ruminations of the bailiff and the court stenographer; the interviewing of witnesses, ranging from the arresting officers and passersby at the scene of the happening to character witnesses (the village priest, a local prostitute, the head of the Carpenters Guild) and various specialists—a tax consultant, an art expert, four psychiatrists, and three representatives from Gruhl's army base. In the course of the proceedings, and especially during the noon break when the narrator follows the various officers and witnesses and visitors to their separate midday meals, an engaging portrait of the entire community emerges along with the small-town system of justice, which is so informal that one of the visitors calls the judge by his first name and the elder Gruhl absentmindedly lights up his pipe. We sense the tension between the villagers and the prosecutor, who has only recently been transferred to the Rhine village from his native Bavaria. (Böll slips in a number of asides hinting at the conservatism of Bavaria in contrast to the traditional Rhenish anarchism: the prosecutor, for instance, not only objects to any reference to the German Democratic Republic as a state; he also unwittingly uses the old Nazi phrase "the sound sense of the people" ["das gesunde Volksempfinden," 35] to characterize what he regards as the proper public indignation at the Gruhls' act of sabotage.)

However, the novel amounts to far more than a charming account of cunning villagers. It also constitutes a critique of the German legal system in a form that has often been compared to Kleist's *The Broken Pitcher*: that is to say, its narrative corresponds closely to the exposition of the play, in which the delict and the culprit(s) are known from the beginning but the motivation and the details are only gradually exposed in the course of the trial, which is observed by a representative from the superior courts. Gruhl is skeptical at the outset about the court and cannot believe that "even a kernel of truth would be ground out of the prayer-mills of justice" (20). Utterly indifferent to law and legality, he participates in the proceedings, he says, only out of personal regard for the presiding judge, the police inspector, and the various witnesses. And all his fears turn out to be confirmed even though—or rather, precisely because—he and his son are ultimately punished mildly with a jail term of six weeks (already fulfilled by the ten weeks of interrogation confinement) and a fine that is paid by a wealthy member of the community.

The entire trial turns out to be a setup rigorously controlled by political powers embodied in the mysterious President Grellber, presumably the head of the federal or at least provincial ministry of justice. Grellber, who appears in person only in the last pages of the book, communicates throughout by phone with various of the participants: Judge Stollfuß, who is trying his last case before retirement; Dr. Bergnolte, whom he has sent to the trial as an observer; Dr. Hermes, the defense attorney; Dr. Kugl-Egger, the prosecutor; as well as the editors of local newspapers and representatives to the German Parliament who have influence with the military. The government has no wish to permit the Gruhls to exploit their auto-da-fé for a political statement, and so it hushes up the entire affair in a conspiracy of silence. For that reason the case is tried in the local magistrate's court (*Amtsgericht*) rather than, as might have been expected, in a higher *Schöffengericht* (a court with professional and lay judges) in the nearby city. The brief newspaper account with which the narrative opens is notable because it never specifies the crime or misdemeanor for which the Gruhls are being so mildly punished. We learn later that Grellber has brought pressure to bear on the editors not to cover the trial, so no reporters are present. We also learn that the army has chosen not to charge the younger Gruhl before a court-martial on the (patently phony) grounds that, through a bookkeeping error, he had actually already returned to civilian status by the time the Jeep was burned. The new district attorney, unfamiliar with local politics, comes only slowly to the realization that he has been been used by the "higher powers" in their effort to avoid all publicity. The presiding judge, a worthy man who venerates "the dignity of the law" (232), acknowledges in his summation that he has been handed, as his final case, a case in which it is impossible to achieve real justice. For, more than any of the other participants, Judge Stollfuß is aware of the conflict here between law and morality, between the legal standards and the righteousness of the Gruhls' protest. But, paradoxically, he turns this aporia into a triumph, which he celebrates with a postmodern invocation of Justitia.

> That he declared himself helpless here as a judge, that for his last case a case was given to him which so clearly expresses the helplessness of human administration of justice: *that* is for him the loveliest farewell-present of that goddess with the blindfolded eyes, who had had so many faces for him, Stollfuß: sometimes the face of a whore, now and then that of an entangled woman, never that of a saint, in most cases that of a tormented, groaning creature receiving a voice through him, the judge—a creature that was animal, human, and a tiny, tiny bit goddess. (238)

Since the wise and kindly old judge, who fully understands the motives of the Gruhls, cannot resist the commands of authority—there are hints of a reward in the form of an order of merit—he sentences them to the mildest punishment and orders the army to restore the incinerated Jeep as an "instrument of art" (239). Even the Gruhls, it turns out, have been co-opted by the system because, contrary to their initial desire for a public scandal, they rationalize their act of protest as an aesthetic event, a happening, and accept the mild judgment that defeats their purposes and, in fact, has brought them additional benefits. (While in jail the younger Gruhl has found and impregnated a beautiful young fiancée; both men have come into an inheritance from a wealthy local woman, who has taken their case to heart.) In short, while they aspire to achieve the public attention of the Yippies in Chicago, their case is silenced as effectively as that of the student protesters in Neumann's *Six of Them*.

In his "introduction" Böll spoke of his novel as a "time bomb" that might destroy the padded cell through which society disarms by co-option: rather than permitting happenings to serve their political aim, government and society entomb them in museums (as happened conspicuously in the case of Beuys!), where they become part of establishment culture. It was Böll's hope that, by depicting this process of co-option, he could counteract it. But he was disappointed: reviewers and readers alike were charmed by the roguish humor and the endearing characters of the little masterpiece, and therefore, ironically, the novel was itself co-opted by the prevailing culture and lost its explosive effect.[77]

Justitia rediviva

End of a Mission sought to change the law by mirroring it in its sinister co-option by the state in pursuit of political goals. Again we note the tension between law and social values that has been characteristic of almost every first-rate work of legal literature. Böll, writing at the juncture between the innocent antics of the Provos and the urban terrorism of the Red Army Faction, was still able to maintain a playful and ironic attitude toward governmental abuse of power. Within a few years governments everywhere were using the law to discipline political opposition, especially among young protesters. As a result, the opposition was radicalized into the violence that characterized the early 1970s in Germany and the United States.

Yet in a larger sense a change was generated—if not by literature, then by the social pressures reflected in that literature. For the 1970s also witnessed a striking renewal of thinking about the law, thinking that reintroduced the notion of justice into law and that was directly influenced by the social upheavals and violence of the sixties.[78] From Plato and Aristotle down to Kant and Hegel, most of the thinking about law and justice had been accomplished by philosophers, in whose eyes the law constituted a natural facet of their work.[79] But in the nineteenth century, as philosophers turned away from metaphysics and toward hermeneutics, phenomenology, and epistemology, the study of law was left, as we have observed, more and more exclusively to (often brilliant) jurists and legal thinkers, such as Maine, Jhering, Holmes, Kelsen, Radbruch, and others. It was not until the 1970s that philosophers once again turned their attention systematically to the question of justice—primarily under the influence of John Rawls's *A Theory of Justice* (1971).[80] This attention has produced a new public awareness of issues of justice in fields ranging from politics and economics to sociology, psychology, and anthropology. And this interest has continued unabated in widely discussed works by

Walter Kaufmann (*Without Guilt and Justice*, 1973), Robert Nozick (*Anarchy, State, and Utopia*, 1974), Michael Walzer (*Spheres of Justice*, 1983), Alasdair MacIntyre (*Whose Justice? Which Rationality?* 1988), and others.

Rawls and the many thinkers stimulated by him have been more centrally concerned with social or distributive justice, and less with criminal or retributive justice. And it is understood by philosophers and political theorists alike that "the criteria of justice are not necessarily the same in the two areas."[81] Yet for all the differences, certain moral considerations, as we have repeatedly seen, provide a common ground on which social values and the law meet and often come into conflict. The past two decades have experienced a powerful revival of "legal moralism"[82] and brought to light many legal issues on which community opinion is sharply, and often violently, divided: abortion, affirmative action, the death penalty, drugs, euthanasia, gay rights, and gun control, to mention only a few that have received publicity and sometimes generated violence. In addition, technological developments in many new areas—notably astronomical space and cyberspace—along with concerns raised by the internationalization of business and industry have produced issues and problems of which jurisprudence and the philosophy of law could not have dreamed only a quarter-century ago.

The new foregrounding of law has produced a corresponding flood of literary works, films, and television programs seeking to capitalize on public interest. But most of these recent works, for all their sensationalism and popular success, are concerned less with the law and issues of legal philosophy than with lawyers and their careers or, at best, with the technicalities of legal procedure. To date, no work corresponding to *The Fall*, *The Breakdown*, or *End of a Mission* has appeared to reflect the tensions between law and morality in the 1980s or 1990s. Yet if there is any single lesson implicit in the evidence of the literary works considered in the preceding pages, it is this: that law continues to evolve in response to the tension between law and morality and that, as it evolves, writers are inevitably drawn at crucial moments to capture in their works those grand and often tragic events. There is every reason to believe that literature will continue in the future to serve in its traditional capacity as the mirror of justice.

AT AN exhibition of his works in 1994 the young German graphic artist Berndt Pfeifer displayed a striking triptych entitled *Justitia*.[83] Pfeifer, born in 1953 in the (then) East German town of Freiberg (Saxony) and trained in the West German city of Cologne, created the dramatic woodcut in 1991 to commemorate the reunification of the long-divided parts of Germany. All three panels depict Justitia: the two side panels show figures in white-on-black flanking the black-on-white Justitia seated in the center panel. All three figures hold the traditional sword and scales; all three, as clear-eyed as Maat or Dike, gaze out gravely at the viewer. The inscription underneath reads: "Vous avez encore une petite chance." The artist leaves it to the viewer to decide whether it is justice, or the people of Germany, or both who still have that slender chance. At the end of a century that began with the polarization of law and morality and then evolved through totalitarianism, radical skepticism, and irresponsible anarchism to reach the delicate equilibrium of the 1990s, we can perhaps expect no mode more appropriate than this guarded optimism of the postwar generation in which to contemplate the outlook for Justitia in the coming century. In any case, her eyes are once again open in case she should venture to take her mirror in hand.

NOTES

Chapter One
Introduction

1. *The Common Law*, ed. Mark DeWolfe Howe (Cambridge: Harvard University Press, 1963; reprint, Boston: Little, Brown, n.d.), 5.
2. *Der Untergang des Abendlandes: Umrisse einer Morphologie der Weltgeschichte* (Munich: Beck, 1963), 630 (= vol. 2, chap. 1, pt. 3): "Jedes Recht enthält in abgezogener Form das Weltbild seiner Urheber. . . ."
3. *The Evolution of Law and Order* (London: Watts, 1951), 303.
4. *Sachsenspiegel I. Landrecht*, ed. Karl August Eckhardt (Aalen: Scientia Verlag, 1973), 43 (lines 178–82).
5. Jacob Grimm, *Kleinere Schriften*, vol. 6 (Berlin, 1882), 152–91; here 153–54.
6. Henry Sumner Maine, *Ancient Law: Its Connection with the Early History of Society, and Its Relation to Modern Ideas* (New York: Holt, 1864; reprint, Tucson: University of Arizona Press, 1986), 2.
7. Rudolf von Jhering, *Der Kampf um's Recht*, 13th ed. (Vienna: Manz, 1897), 58–65.
8. Georg Müller, *Das Recht in Goethes Faust: Juristische Streifzüge durch das Land der Dichtung* (Berlin: Heymann, 1912).
9. Jay Watson, *Forensic Fictions: The Lawyer Figure in Faulkner* (Athens: University of Georgia Press, 1993).
10. Hans Fehr, *Das Recht in der Dichtung* (Bern: Francke [1931]); and *The Law in Literature*, vol. 1 of *The World of Law*, ed. Ephraim London (New York: Simon and Schuster, 1960).
11. E.g., James Boyd White, *Heracles' Bow: Essays on the Rhetoric and Poetics of the Law* (Madison: University of Wisconsin Press, 1985); and Eberhard Schmidhäuser, *Verbrechen und Strafe* (Munich: Beck, 1995), whose subtitle designates his work as "an excursion through world literature" ("Ein Streifzug durch die Weltliteratur von Sophokles bis Dürrenmatt"). Both books include excellent essays, but neither seeks to display connections between the works discussed or any historical development.
12. Friedrich Schiller, "Die Gesetzgebung des Lykurgus und Solon," in his *Sämtliche Werke*, ed. Gerhart Fricke and Herbert G. Göpfert, 4th ed. (Munich: Hanser, 1966), 4:805–36; here 831.
13. For a survey of possible meanings see A. Arthur Schiller, *Roman Law: Mechanisms of Development* (The Hague: Mouton, 1978), 367–68.
14. Ibid., 527–30.
15. Peter Stein, *Legal Evolution: The Story of an Idea* (Cambridge: Cambridge University Press, 1980).
16. Theodore Ziolkowski, *German Romanticism and Its Institutions* (Princeton, NJ: Princeton University Press, 1990), esp. 78–109.

17. See Gerd Kleinheyer and Jan Schröder, *Deutsche Juristen aus fünf Jahrhunderten: Eine biographische Einführung in die Geschichte der Rechtswissenschaft*, 3d ed. (Heidelberg: Müller Juristischer Verlag, 1989), 131–34.
18. Okko Behrends, "Rudolf von Jhering und die Evolutionstheorie des Rechts," in *Der Evolutionsgedanke in den Wissenschaften*, ed. Günther Patzig, Nachrichten der Akademie der Wissenschaften in Göttingen, I. Philologisch-Historische Klasse (1991), 290–311.
19. Maine, *Ancient Law*, 165.
20. *The Victorian Achievement of Sir Henry Maine: A Centennial Reappraisal*, ed. Alan Diamond (Cambridge: Cambridge University Press, 1991.
21. *The Common Law*, 5.
22. Dennis Lloyd, *The Idea of Law* (Baltimore: Penguin, 1964), 327.
23. E. Donald Elliott, "The Evolutionary Tradition in Jurisprudence," *Columbia Law Review* 85 (1985): 38–94. See also Uwe Wesel, "Bemerkungen zu einer evolutionistischen Theorie des Rechts," in *Gedächtnisschrift für Wolfgang Kunkel*, ed. Dieter Nörr and Dieter Simon (Frankfurt am Main: Klostermann, 1984), 523–62.
24. David Miller, *Social Justice* (Oxford: Clarendon, 1976), 253–335.
25. See *Justice: Views from the Social Sciences*, ed. Ronald L. Cohen (New York: Plenum, 1986), 117–51, 215–33.
26. Emile Durkheim, *De la division du travail social*, 2d ed. (Paris: Félix Alcan, 1902), 28.
27. *Max Weber on Law in Economy and Society*, trans. Max Rheinstein and Edward Shils (Cambridge: Harvard University Press, 1966), 198–225.
28. In the following paragraphs I recapitulate Diamond's theory as expounded in his more recent *The Evolution of Law and Order* (London: Watts, 1951).
29. Ibid., 115.
30. Cited according to the translation by Theophile J. Meek in *The Ancient Near East*, ed. James B. Pritchard (Princeton, NJ: Princeton University Press, 1958), 138–67; here 161.
31. Diamond, *Evolution*, 293.
32. *Das Zwölftafelgesetz*, ed. Rudolf Düll (Munich: Artemis, 1989), 46 (= Tabula VIII, 2).
33. See, for instance, the comment in *The New Oxford Annotated Bible*, ed. Herbert G. May and Bruce M. Metzger (New York: Oxford University Press, 1973), 94 n.
34. *The Papers of Thomas Jefferson*, ed. Julian Boyd, vol. 2 (Princeton, NJ: Princeton University Press, 1950), 492–93.
35. See Leopold Pospisil's thoughtful review of the 1971 revision of *Primitive Law* (*American Anthropologist* 77 [1975]: 631–34). Pospisil rejects several of the economic findings while welcoming the comparative typology and the historical dimension of Diamond's work.
36. Arthur Schiller, *Roman Law*, 23.
37. Miller, *Social Justice*, 326–28.
38. H. I. Marrou, *A History of Education in Antiquity*, trans. George Lamb (1956; reprint, Madison: University of Wisconsin Press, 1982), 4 and 39.
39. Uwe Wesel, *Juristische Weltkunde. Eine Einführung in das Recht* (1984; Frankfurt am Main: suhrkamp taschenbuch, 1993), 194–202; Heinrich Geddert, *Recht und Moral. Zum Sinn eines alten Problems* (Berlin: Duncker & Humblot, 1984).

40. Hans Hattenhauer, *Europäische Rechtsgeschichte* (Heidelberg: Müller Juristischer Verlag, 1992), 47–49 and 776–78.
41. Henry Sumner Maine, *Dissertations on Early Law and Custom* (New York: Henry Holt, 1886), 5.
42. Ibid., 26.
43. Lloyd, *The Idea of Law*, 46–47.
44. Hattenhauer, *Europäische Rechtsgeschichte*, 248–54.
45. Pt. 3 of the introduction to *Die Metaphysik der Sitten*; in Immanuel Kant, *Werke in zehn Bänden*, ed. Wilhelm Weischedel (Darmstadt: Wissenschaftliche Buchgesellschaft, 1968), 7:324.
46. O. W. Holmes, "The Path of the Law," in his *Collected Legal Papers* (New York: Harcourt, Brace, 1920), 167–202; here 179.
47. This image is frequently employed: see Lloyd, *The Idea of Law*, 57; and Robert von Hippel, *Lehrbuch des Strafrechts* (Berlin: Julius Springer, 1932), 1 n. 3.
48. Lloyd, *The Idea of Law*, 329–31.
49. Cozzens, *The Just and the Unjust* (New York: Harcourt/Harvest, 1970), 427–28.
50. Wesel, *Juristische Weltkunde*, 199.
51. Kant, *Werke in zehn Bänden*, 4:625 n.
52. See the essays collected in the volume *Begriff und Wesen des Rechts*, ed. Werner Maihofer, Wege der Forschung 79 (Darmstadt: Wissenschaftliche Buchgesellschaft, 1973), esp. 421–56 (Felix Somló, "Der Begriff des Rechts"); and *What Is Justice? Classic and Contemporary Readings*, ed. Robert C. Solomon and Mark C. Murphy (New York: Oxford University Press, 1990), esp. 3–8.
53. Alasdair MacIntyre, *Whose Justice? Which Rationality?* (Notre Dame, IN: University of Notre Dame Press, 1988), 9 and 1.
54. Lloyd, *The Idea of Law*, 130–31.
55. Cohen's introduction to *Justice: Views from the Social Sciences*, 2.
56. Hattenhauer, *Europäische Rechtsgeschichte*, 66. The word *iustitia* occurs only ten times in the entire *Corpus Iuris Civilis*, and five of the occurrences date from late antiquity.
57. Otto Rudolf Kissel, *Die Justitia. Reflexionen über ein Symbol und seine Darstellung in der bildenden Kunst* (Munich: Beck, 1984) is the authoritative treatment. See also Walter Ullmann, *The Medieval Idea of Law* (London: Methuen, 1946), 1–4 and 35–41; and Dennis E. Curtis and Judith Resnick, "Images of Justice," *Yale Law Journal* 96 (1987): 1727–72.

Chapter Two
The Birth of Justice from the Spirit of Tragedy

1. Johann Jakob Bachofen, *Das Mutterrecht* (1861), in *Mutterrecht und Urreligion*, ed. Rudolf Marx (Stuttgart: Kröner, 1954), 190–98.
2. Erich Neumann, *The Origins and History of Consciousness*, trans. R.F.C. Hull, Bollingen Series 42 (1954; reprint, Princeton, NJ: Princeton University Press, 1970), 168–69.
3. Esp. in chaps. 3–4 of *The Birth of Tragedy*; cf. Friedrich Nietzsche, *Werke in drei Bänden*, ed. Karl Schlechta (Munich: Hanser, 1954), 1:30, 35, and 134.
4. Heinrich Weinstock, *Die Tragödie des Humanismus: Wahrheit und Trug im*

abendländischen Menschbild (Heidelberg: Quelle & Meyer, 1953), 11. The humanist interpretation is not vitiated by such an oddity as the co-option of the trilogy (in the translation by Wilamowitz) by the National Socialists on the occasion of the 1936 Olympics to glorify the New Order in Germany; see Hellmut Flashar, *Inszenierung der Antike. Das griechische Drama auf der Bühne der Neuzeit 1585–1990* (Munich: Beck, 1991), 164–68.

5. E. R. Dodds, *The Greeks and the Irrational* (1951; reprint, Berkeley and Los Angeles: University of California Press, 1973), 28–63 ("From Shame-Culture to Guilt-Culture").
6. See *Max Weber on Law in Economy and Society*, ed. and trans. Max Rheinstein and Edward Shils (Cambridge: Harvard University Press, 1966), l–li. Although Weber does not cite the *Oresteia* specifically, he alludes to the conditions of Greek law reflected in that work; see esp. 89–91 and 232–34.
7. Richard A. Posner, *The Economics of Justice* (Cambridge: Harvard University Press, 1981), 226–27.
8. Sigmund Freud, *Das Unbehagen in der Kultur* (1930), in *Studienausgabe*, ed. Alexander Mitscherlich, Angela Richards, and James Strachey (Frankfurt am Main: S. Fischer, 1974), 225.
9. Weinstock, *Die Tragödie des Humanismus*, 8 and passim ("Weltgedicht").
10. Robert Fagles and W. B. Stanford, "A Reading of 'The Oresteia': The Serpent and the Eagle," in Aeschylus, *The Oresteia*, trans. Robert Fagles (New York: Penguin, 1979), 19.
11. Weinstock, *Die Tragödie des Humanismus*, 8.
12. Hugh Lloyd-Jones, *The Justice of Zeus* (Berkeley and Los Angeles: University of California Press, 1971), 94.
13. Richard Thurnwald, "Blood Vengeance Feud," in *Encyclopaedia of the Social Sciences*, ed. Elwin R. A. Seligman (New York: Macmillan, 1930), 2:598–99; Leopold Pospisil, "Feud," in *International Encyclopedia of the Social Sciences*, ed. David L. Sills (New York: Macmillan and the Free Press, 1968), 5:389–93; Elmer Klinger, "Revenge and Retribution," in *The Encyclopedia of Religion*, ed. Mircea Eliade (New York: Macmillan, 1987), 12:362–68; Susan Jacoby, *Wild Justice* (New York: Harper & Row, 1983); and Robert C. Solomon, *A Passion for Justice* (Reading, MA: Addison Wesley, 1989).
14. David Daube, "*Lex Talionis*," in his *Studies in Biblical Law* (Cambridge: Cambridge University Press, 1947), 102–53.
15. A. S. Diamond, *Primitive Law* (London: Longmans, Green, 1935), 151–59; and Robert J. Bonner, *Lawyers and Litigants in Ancient Athens* (Chicago: University of Chicago Press, 1927), 29–30.
16. Rudolf Köstler, *Homerisches Recht: Gesammelte Aufsätze* (Vienna: Österreichischer Bundesverlag, 1950), 7–25 ("Die Homerische Rechts- und Staatsordnung").
17. Cited here and below according to Robert Fagles's translation of *The Iliad* (New York: Viking Penguin, 1990).
18. Köstler, *Homerisches Recht*, 65–77 ("Die Gerichtsszene auf dem Achilleusschild").
19. Ulrich von Wilamowitz-Moellendorff, *Aischylos Orestie*, Zweites Stück: *Das Opfer am Grabe* (Berlin: Weidmann, 1896), 9.
20. Werner Jaeger, *Paideia: The Ideals of Greek Culture*, trans. Gilbert Highet (New York: Oxford University Press, 1939), 354.

21. *Aischylos Orestie*, 24–25 and 246–56.
22. Hesiod, *The Homeric Hymns and Homerica*, trans. Hugh G. Evelyn-White, new ed., Loeb Classical Library (Cambridge: Harvard University Press, 1936), 526–27.
23. J. Vürtheim, *Stesichoros' Fragmente und Biographie* (Leiden: Sijthoff, 1919), 45–56.
24. On the history of the term *dikê*, and in particular its shift from the general sense of natural order to the particular meaning of vengeance, see Jane Ellen Harrison, *Themis: A Study of the Social Origins of Greek Religion*, 2d ed. (Cambridge: Cambridge University Press, 1927), 514–35; and Eric Wolf, *Griechisches Rechtsdenken* (Frankfurt am Main: Klostermann, 1950–52), 1:22–45. For a summary of more recent bibliographical references see Lloyd-Jones, *The Justice of Zeus*, 166–67 n. 23; and Mihai I. Spariosu, *God of Many Faces: Play, Poetry, and Power in Hellenic Thought from Homer to Aristotle* (Durham, NC: Duke University Press, 1991), 45–46 n. 71 and 47 n. 72.
25. H.D.F. Kitto, *Sophocles, Dramatist and Philosopher* (London: Oxford University Press, 1958), 47–59, argues that the only adequate translation for *dikê* is often "retribution"—that is, restoring the general balance in human affairs as well as nature. On the development of the concept of *dikê* in the *Oresteia*, see also Wolf, *Griechisches Rechtsdenken*, 1:379–424.
26. I cite the Greek text by line according to Gilbert Murray's edition of Aeschylus's works in the Oxford edition (1938; reprint, 1952). It will frequently be necessary for my purposes to cite the Greek text in order to demonstrate consistency in the usage of specific vocables that cannot always be preserved even in the finest translations.
27. Harrison, *Themis*, 520–22.
28. For an analysis, "Four 'Electra' Plays," see Brian Vickers, *Towards Greek Tragedy: Drama, Myth, Society* (London: Longman, 1973), 553–91.
29. For the extension of these figures into the twentieth century see Käte Hamburger, *Von Sophokles zu Sartre: Griechische Dramenfiguren antik und modern* (Stuttgart: Kohlhammer, 1962), 65–93 ("Elektra"); see also Fagles and Stanford, "A Reading," 69–70.
30. George Thomson, *Aeschylus and Athens: A Study in the Social Origins of Drama* (1940; reprint, New York: Haskell House, 1967), 248; for bibliographical details see *The Oresteia of Aeschylus*, ed. George Thomson (Cambridge: Cambridge University Press, 1938), 2:355.
31. See Hamburger, *Von Sophokles zu Sartre*; and Elisabeth Frenzel, *Stoffe der Weltliteratur: Ein Lexikon dichtungsgeschichtlicher Längsschnitte*, 8th ed. (Stuttgart: Kröner, 1992), 13–16, 361–67, and 598–603.
32. Hauptmann's tetralogy reveals a certain internal inconsistency: the concluding piece, *Iphigenie in Delphi*, which was actually first in order of composition, assumes that Orestes, maddened by the Erinyes, has come to Delphi in search of redemption. But the thematically preceding *Elektra*, written subsequently, ends with a liberated Orestes. See Theodore Ziolkowski, "Hauptmann's *Iphigenie in Delphi*: A Travesty?" *Germanic Review* 34 (1959): 105–23; and Hubert Razinger's afterword to his edition of Hauptmann's *Die Atriden-Tetralogie* (Gütersloh: Bertelsmann, 1956), 243–337.
33. H. G. Robertson, "Legal Expressions and Ideas of Justice in Aeschylus," *Classical Philology* 34 (1939): 209–19; here 217.
34. See Thomson, *Aeschylus and Athens*, 245–97.
35. On the history of the Council of the Areopagus see Bonner, *Lawyers and Litigants in Ancient Athens*, 26–43; and Robert J. Bonner and Gertrude Smith, *The Administra-*

tion of Justice from Homer to Aristotle, vol. 1 (Chicago: University of Chicago Press, 1938; reprint, New York: Greenwood, 1968), 251–78.

36. See the notes and commentary in *Aristotle's Constitution of Athens*, ed. John Edwin Sandys, rev. ed. (London: Macmillan, 1893); and the extensive commentary accompanying *Staat der Athener*, trans. Mortimer Chambers, Aristoteles Werke in deutscher Übersetzung 10/1 (Berlin: Akademie-Verlag, 1990). On Aristotle's discussion of the Areopagus see also Bonner and Smith, *The Administration of Justice*, 88–97.

37. Christian Meier, *Die politische Kunst der griechischen Tragödie* (Munich: Beck, 1988), 113–17, 178–85. See also Meier's earlier work, *Die Entstehung des Politischen bei den Griechen* (Frankfurt am Main: Suhrkamp, 1980), 275–325, on the conceptual shift in political-social thought in fifth-century Athens.

38. Thomson, *Aeschylus and Athens*, 286.

39. See the appendix on this issue in Hugh Lloyd-Jones's translation of *The Eumenides* (Englewood Cliffs, NJ: Prentice-Hall, 1970), 75–77; see also his note, 54–55, *ad* 693f.

40. See Fagles and Stanford, "A Reading," 95. A. M. Bowie, "Religion and Politics in Aeschylus' *Oresteia*," *Classical Quarterly* 43 (1991): 10–31, surveys the conflicting views and gives a balanced assessment: while we cannot confidently extract Aeschylus's position, the text itself displays a pattern reflecting recent changes in the Athenian political scene.

41. Meier, *Die politische Kunst*, 132; and Meier, *Entstehung*, 144–246.

42. This count leaves out Euripides' satyr play *Cyclops* as well as the problematic *Rhesus*, a dramatization of *Iliad* 10 sometimes attributed to Euripides.

43. George Steiner, *The Death of Tragedy* (New York: Knopf, 1961), 8: "Tragedies end badly."

44. Some manuscripts have the masculine ending for the participle (*praunas*) rather than the feminine (*praunasa*), requiring a less satisfactory reading according to which it is Orestes, or even Aeschylus himself, who soothes and renames the Erinyes. See *The "Eumenides" of Aeschylus*, ed. A. W. Verrall (London: Macmillan, 1908), xxxvii.

45. On the use of pigs in rites of purification see Jane Ellen Harrison, *Prolegomena to the Study of Greek Religion*, 2d ed. (Cambridge: Cambridge University Press, 1908), 152–54. This famous scene was frequently depicted in Attic vase-paintings; see *Prolegomena*, 228–31.

46. Ibid., esp. chap. 1.

47. On the primitive origins of Greek binding spells see ibid., 141–43. Similar spells are also common in primitive Germanic societies.

48. E.g., Verrall in his edition, *The "Eumenides" of Aeschylus*, lv and 100, *ad* 568; and Lloyd-Jones in his translation, *The Eumenides*, 45, *ad* 566.

49. See Thomson, *The Oresteia*, 2:288, *ad* 573.

50. Thomson, *Aeschylus and Athens*, 297.

51. For a sympathetic discussion of the patrilinear theory of procreation see Vickers, *Towards Greek Tragedy*, 414–16 and 636–43.

52. For a summary see Thomson, *The Oresteia*, 2:298, *ad* 737–46.

53. We need not engage ourselves in the avidly debated question as to whether Athena's vote *broke* a tie or *made* a tie. As important as this issue may be for the history of Athenian law, it is irrelevant for our purposes.

54. Paul Gewirtz, "Aeschylus' Law," *Harvard Law Review* 101 (1988): 1043–55, draws on modern legal debates to make the persuasive point that the inclusion of the Erinyes in the new legal system represents Aeschylus's acknowledgment of the emotional or even irrational element in law and, at the same time, the inclusion of the female in the predominantly male system.

55. Verrall, *The "Eumenides" of Aeschylus*, xxxv–xxxvii.

56. Here I differ from Lloyd-Jones, *The Justice of Zeus*, 95, who believes that the new court "is not to replace, but to assist the Erinyes." In my view the text implies precisely the opposite. However, Lloyd-Jones, 93–94, properly emphasizes the fact that the punitive function of the Erinyes continues under the new arrangement.

57. Hermann Diehls, *Die Fragmente der Vorsokratiker* (Berlin: Weidmann, 1903), 79–80 (Frg. 94).

58. See Verrall, *The "Eumenides" of Aeschylus*, xl–xlv. On the origins of the Erinyes—Semnai Theai—Eumenides see Harrison, *Prolegomena*, 213–56.

59. On legal procedures in Athens see Bonner, *Lawyers and Litigants in Ancient Athens*, 44–58. On the use of these legal procedures in *The Eumenides* see Verrall's introduction, Thomson's notes, and Fagles and Stanford, "A Reading," 78–82.

60. William Arrowsmith, "The Criticism of Greek Tragedy," *Tulane Drama Review* 3 (1959): 31–57; here 37.

61. Verrall, *The "Eumenides" of Aeschylus*, xlvi.

62. In his *Sonnets to Orpheus* 2:4 Rilke speaks of "the beast that does not exist"; but because the people believed in it and left room in their imaginations, it came into being:

> Zwar *war* es nicht. Doch weil sie's liebten, ward
> ein reines Tier. Sie ließen immer Raum.
> Und in dem Raume, klar und ausgespart,
> erhob es leicht sein Haupt und brauchte kaum
> zu sein.

63. Paragraph 9 of Murray's (unpaginated) edition.

64. Harrison, *Prolegomena*, 223–24.

65. On the animal imagery see Fagles and Stanford, "Notes," 319–20, *ad* 94 and 116.

66. On the history of the Erinyes see Harrison, *Prolegomena*, 213–39.

67. On the function of fear in Greek religion see esp. ibid., chap. 1.

68. Arrowsmith, "The Criticism of Greek Tragedy," 49.

69. Lloyd-Jones, *The Justice of Zeus*, 1–2.

70. Thomson, *Aeschylus and Athens*, 291.

71. Ibid., 289.

72. Ibid., 302–5.

73. J. Peter Euben, introduction to *Greek Tragedy and Political Theory*, ed. J. Peter Euben (Berkeley and Los Angeles: University of California Press, 1986), 1–42; here 24.

74. Werner Jaeger, "Praise of Law: The Origin of Legal Philosophy and the Greeks," in *Interpretations of Modern Legal Philosophies: Essays in Honor of Roscoe Pound*, ed. Paul Sayre (New York: Oxford University Press, 1947), 352–75; here 361.

75. In a lecture delivered in Athens in 1955, "The Future of Tragedy"; in Albert Camus, *Lyrical and Critical*, trans. Philip Thody (London: Hamish Hamilton, 1967), 183–84.

76. For an analogous reading see Weinstock, *Die Tragödie des Humanismus*, whose impressive chapter on the *Oresteia* (7–66) focuses particularly on the birth of the *polis* in the context of Greek tragedy.

Chapter Three
The Ambivalence toward Pagan law

1. W. P. Ker, *Epic and Romance: Essays on Medieval Literature* (1897; reprint, New York: Dover, 1957), 57.
2. Given the temporal difference of a millennium plus the idealizing and generalizing nature of Tacitus's propagandistic tract, it should not be necessary to warn against any oversimplifying identification. At the same time, many scholars have stressed the relatively primitive state of Germanic society as it existed in Iceland. See Andreas Heusler, *Das Strafrecht der Isländersagas* (Leipzig: Duncker & Humblot, 1911), 4; Jan De Vries, *Die geistige Welt der Germanen* (Darmstadt: Wissenschaftliche Buchgesellschaft, 1963), 5.
3. Ker, *Epic and Romance*, 6–9; Ulrich von Wilamowitz-Moellendorff, *Aischylos Orestie*, Zweites Stück: *Das Opfer am Grabe* (Berlin: Weidmann, 1896), 3–4; and A. S. Diamond, *Primitive Law* (London: Longmans, Green, 1935), 147–49.
4. The basic facts and essential outlines of early Icelandic history are fairly well established: see G. Turville-Petre, *Origins of Icelandic Literature* (Oxford: Clarendon, 1953); Paul Schach, *Icelandic Sagas* (Boston: Twayne, 1984); William Ian Miller, "The Social Historical Setting," in *Law and Literature in Medieval Iceland*, by Theodore M. Andersson and William Ian Miller (Stanford: Stanford University Press, 1989), 3–62; and William Ian Miller, *Bloodtaking and Peacemaking: Feud, Law, and Society in Saga Iceland* (Chicago: University of Chicago Press, 1990).
5. *Max Weber on Law in Economy and Society*, ed. and trans. Max Rheinstein and Edward Shils (Cambridge: Harvard University Press, 1966), 86–97.
6. Miller, *Bloodtaking and Peacemaking*, 223.
7. Heusler, *Strafrecht*, 108.
8. Magnus Magnusson's introduction to *Njal's Saga*, trans. Magnus Magnusson and Hermann Pálsson (Harmondsworth: Penguin, 1960), 16.
9. Richard F. Allen, *Fire and Iron: Critical Approaches to Njáls saga* (Pittsburgh: University of Pittsburgh Press, 1971), 139.
10. Heusler, *Strafrecht*, 26.
11. Miller, *Bloodtaking and Peacemaking*, 267–70.
12. Schach, *Icelandic Sagas*, 117.
13. Magnusson, "Introduction," 9.
14. Turville-Petre, *Origins of Icelandic Literature*, 253.
15. Ker, *Epic and Romance*, 69.
16. Sigurdur Nordal, "Sagalitteraturen," *Nordisk Kultur*, 8 B (1953): 180–273; here 259. Cited by Lars Lönnroth, *Njáls Saga: A Critical Introduction* (Berkeley and Los Angeles: University of California Press, 1976), 205.
17. Gudbrand Vigfusson, in the prolegomena to his edition of *Sturlunga Saga* (Oxford: Clarendon, 1878), 1:xlii.
18. Theodore M. Andersson, *The Icelandic Family Saga: An Analytic Reading* (Cambridge: Harvard University Press, 1967), 304.

19. Schach, *Icelandic Sagas*, 117 ("trilogy with a preface"); Magnusson, "Introduction," 17 ("tripartite construction"); Einar Ól. Sveinsson, *Njáls Saga: A Literary Masterpiece*, trans. Paul Schach (Lincoln: University of Nebraska Press, 1971), 52–53 (trilogy with two preludes).
20. I quote the text by chapter number or, where appropriate, by page number from the translation of Magnusson and Pálsson and from the standard edition by Einar Ól. Sveinsson: *Brennu-Njáls Saga*, Íslenzk Fornrit 12 (Reykjavik: Íslenzka Fornitafélag, 1954).
21. Each chieftain maintained at Thingvellir a hereditary "booth" (*búð*)—that is, a temporary abode that was outfitted for lodging and entertainment at the time of the annual assemblies.
22. Burning, to which a special paragraph is devoted in *Grágás*, was penalized by outlawry; see *Laws of Early Iceland*, trans. Andrew Dennis, Peter Foote, and Richard Perkins (Winnipeg: University of Manitoba Press, 1980), 87 (*Koningsbók* §109).
23. Henry Ordower, "Exploring the Literary Function of Law and Litigation in *Njal's Saga*," *Cardoza Studies in Law and Literature* 3 (1991): 41–61, esp. 45–51.
24. *Laws of Early Iceland*, 23 (*Konungsbók* §1).
25. For a survey of legal studies of *Njála* see Lönnroth's *Critical Introduction*, 241–43; Carola L. Gottzmann, *Njáls saga: Rechtsproblematik im Dienste sozio-kultureller Deutung* (Frankfurt am Main and Bern: Peter Lang, 1982), 5–8; and Ordower, "Exploring the Literary Function," 42–45.
26. Vigfusson, "Prolegomena," 1:xlii.
27. Heusler, *Strafrecht*, 13.
28. Lönnroth, *A Critical Introduction*, 241.
29. Karl Lehmann and Hans Schnorr von Carolsfeld, *Die Njálssage insbesondere in ihren juristischen Bestandtheilen: Ein kritischer Beitrag zur altnordischen Rechts- und Literaturgeschichte* (Berlin, 1883).
30. Heusler, *Strafrecht*, 14.
31. *A Literary Masterpiece*, 158.
32. Lönnroth, *A Critical Introduction*, 192.
33. *Laws of Early Iceland*, 87 (*Konungsbók* §47).
34. Lönnroth, *A Critical Introduction*, 241–48.
35. *A Literary Masterpiece*, 26 and 34.
36. In the introduction to their translation of *Laxdaela Saga* (Harmondsworth: Penguin, 1978), 26–27.
37. Denton Fox, "*Njáls Saga* and the Western Literary Tradition," *Comparative Literature* 15 (1963): 289–310; here 301. See also Allen, *Fire and Iron*, 137.
38. Miller, *Bloodtaking and Peacemaking*, 224.
39. See especially Lönnroth, *A Critical Introduction*, 242.
40. Heusler, *Strafrecht*, 13.
41. See Sveinsson, *A Literary Masterpiece*, 164–66.
42. Heusler, *Strafrecht*, 109.
43. Miller, *Bloodtaking and Peacemaking*, 236. Miller provides a clear and concise recapitulation of the material presented by Heusler in his *Strafrecht*, 40–41.
44. *Laws of Early Iceland*, 3.
45. Heusler, *Strafrecht*, 215.
46. Schach, *Icelandic Sagas*, 123.

47. *Strafrecht*, 239.
48. See Andreas Heusler's "Einleitung" to his translation, *Die Geschichte vom weisen Njal*, Thule 4 (Jena: Diederichs, 1922), 10–11.
49. Ibid., 4.
50. See Gottzmann, *Rechtsproblematik*, 309–13; and Fox, "The Western Literary Tradition," 301.
51. Peter Sawyer, "The Bloodfeud in Fact and Fiction," *Tradition og Historie-Skrivning, Acta Jutlandica* 63:2 (Aarhus, 1984): 27–38.
52. Sveinsson, *A Literary Masterpiece*, 182.
53. Ibid., 16, mentions these four sources, which are generally acknowledged by most recent scholars.
54. Fox, "The Western Literary Tradition," 290–91.
55. Heusler, "Einleitung," 6.
56. Lönnroth, *A Critical Introduction*, 136–37.
57. See Einar Ól. Sveinsson, *The Age of the Sturlungs: Icelandic Civilization in the Thirteenth Century*, trans. Jóhann S. Hannesson, Islandica 36 (Ithaca, NY: Cornell University Press, 1953); Schach, *Icelandic Sagas*, 18–22; and Lönnroth, *A Critical Introduction*, 165–214.
58. Fox, "The Western Literary Tradition," 310 n. 30.
59. Gottzmann, *Rechtsproblematik*, 339.
60. Robert Fagles and W. B. Stanford, "The Serpent and the Eagle," in *The Oresteia*, trans. Robert Fagles (New York: Penguin, 1979), 80.

Chapter Four
The Role of Rome

1. *Institutiones*, ed. Paul Krüger, in *Corpus Iuris Civilis* (Berlin: Weidmann, 1902), 1:1.
2. Paul Vinogradoff, *Roman Law in Medieval Europe*, 2d ed. (Oxford: Clarendon, 1929), 11. The history has been written many times since Friedrich Carl von Savigny's six-volume *Geschichte des römischen Rechts im Mittelalter* (1815–31). See especially Hastings Rashdall, *The Universities of Europe in the Middle Ages*, ed. F. M. Powicke and A. B. Emden, 3 vols. (Oxford: Clarendon, 1936), 1:87–175 ("Bologna"); and Walter Ullmann, *Law and Politics in the Middle Ages: An Introduction to the Sources of Medieval Political Ideas* (Ithaca, NY: Cornell University Press, 1975), 81–117. A brief recapitulation is available in Charles Homer Haskins, *The Rise of Universities* (1923; reprint, Ithaca: Cornell University Press, 1979), 1–12.
3. See Katherine Fischer Drew's informative introduction to her translation of *The Lombard Laws* (Philadelphia: University of Pennsylvania Press, 1973).
4. See Rashdall, *The Universities of Europe in the Middle Ages*, 1:87–176 and 254–68.
5. Ibid., 254.
6. Gerald Strauss, *Law, Resistance, and the State: The Opposition to Roman Law in Reformation Germany* (Princeton, NJ: Princeton University Press, 1986), 67.
7. Cited by Jean Plattard, *The Life of François Rabelais*, trans. Louis P. Roche (New York: Knopf, 1931), 133 n. 1.
8. Alan Watson, *The Making of the Civil Law* (Cambridge: Harvard University Press, 1981), 7.

9. Vinogradoff, *Roman Law in Medieval Europe*, 93.
10. Otto Brunner, as cited by Heinrich Mitteis, "Geschichte der Rechtswissenschaft im Rahmen der allgemeinen Kulturgeschichte," in his *Die Rechtsidee in der Geschichte: Gesammelte Abhandlungen und Vorträge* (Weimar: Böhlau, 1957), 668–80; here 553.
11. On the *mos gallicus*, see Paul Koschaker, *Europa und das Römische Recht* (Berlin: Biederstein, 1947), 105–16; and Mitteis, "Geschichte der Rechtswissenschaft im Rahmen der allgemeinen Kulturgeschichte."
12. On English law and the reception, see especially William Holdsworth, *A History of English Law*, 3d ed., vol. 4 (London: Methuen & Co., Sweet and Maxwell, 1945), 217–93; on the differences among Germany, England, and France see Heinrich Mitteis, "Renaissance, Humanismus und Rezeption der fremden Rechte in Deutschland," in his *Die Rechtsidee in der Geschichte*, 552–63.
13. Holdsworth, *A History of English Law*, 4th ed., vol. 2 (1936), 147–49.
14. On the influence of Roman law on Glanvil, see ibid., 202–6.
15. Ibid., 267–82; here 282.
16. Ibid., 4:285–89.
17. Strauss, *Law, Resistance, and the State*, 74–75.
18. For a survey of nineteenth-century thinking on this issue, see Georg von Below, *Die Ursachen der Rezeption des Römischen Rechts in Deutschland* (Munich and Berlin: Oldenbourg, 1905), 1–34.
19. See Koschaker, *Europa und das Römische Recht*, 148–49.
20. Georg Dahm, "On the Reception of Roman and Italian Law in Germany," in *Pre-Reformation Germany*, ed. Gerald Strauss (London: Macmillan, 1972), 282–315; here 282–83.
21. For works on the problems in all countries see John A. Alford and Dennis P. Seniff, *Literature and Law in the Middle Ages: A Bibliography of Scholarship* (New York: Garland, 1984).
22. Wolfgang Kunkel, "The Reception of Roman Law in Germany: An Interpretation," in *Pre-Reformation Germany*, ed. Gerald Strauss (London: Macmillan, 1972), 263–81; here 265.
23. Fritz Hartung, "Imperial Reform, 1485–1495: Its Course and Its Character," in *Pre-Reformation Germany*, ed. Gerald Strauss (London: Macmillan, 1972), 73–135.
24. Strauss, *Law, Resistance, and the State*, esp. 65–95.
25. See O. Stobbe, *Geschichte der deutschen Rechtsquellen*, vol. 2 (Leipzig: Duncker & Humblot, 1864), 1–142.
26. See Strauss, *Law, Resistance, and the State*, esp. 3–30; and the documents reproduced by Strauss in his *Manifestations of Discontent in Germany on the Eve of the Reformation* (Bloomington: Indiana University Press, 1971), esp. 196–201.
27. These are the principal reasons summarized by Below, *Die Ursachen der Rezeption des Römischen Rechts in Deutschland*.
28. Kunkel, "The Reception of Roman Law in Germany," 268.
29. Roderich Stintzing, *Geschichte der populären Literatur des römisch-kanonischen Rechts in Deutschland am Ende des fünfzehnten und im Anfang des sechszehnten Jahrhunderts* (Leipzig: Hirzel, 1867).
30. This is the principal conclusion reached by Kunkel, "The Reception of Roman Law in Germany," 280.

31. Ibid., 278–79.
32. Holdsworth, *A History of English Law*, 4:243–44.
33. Guido Kisch, *Erasmus und die Jurisprudenz seiner Zeit: Studien zum humanistischen Rechtsdenken* (Basel: Helbing & Lichtenhahn, 1960), 3 n. 3.

Chapter Five
The Disenchantment with Customary Law

1. See the discussion and bibliography under the rubric "Ordeal," *Encyclopaedia Britannica* (1957), 16:850–52.
2. Jacob Grimm, *Deutsche Rechtsalterthümer*, 4th ed., 2 vols. (Leipzig: Dieterich'sche Verlagsbuchhandlung, 1899), 2:563–604. For a survey of early Germanic legal codes, see O. Stobbe, *Geschichte der deutschen Rechtsquellen*, 2 vols. (Leipzig: Duncker & Humblot, 1860), 1:4–208.
3. *The Burgundian Code*, trans. Katherine Fischer Drew (1949; reprint, Philadelphia: University of Pennsylvania Press, 1972), 52.
4. Ibid., 8.
5. *The Lombard Laws*, trans. with an introduction by Katherine Fischer Drew (Philadelphia: University of Pennsylvania Press, 1973), 81–82.
6. Ibid., 174.
7. Ibid., 195.
8. Johan Huizinga, *The Waning of the Middle Ages*, English adaptation (1924; reprint, New York: Doubleday Anchor, 1954), 101–2.
9. R. Howard Bloch, *Medieval French Literature and Law* (Berkeley and Los Angeles: University of California Press, 1977), 4. Bloch's first chapter (13–62) is "Trial by Combat and Capture."
10. Here I follow the more recent view of the British legal historian Paul R. Hyams, "Henry II and Ganelon," *Syracuse Scholar* 4 (1983): 23–35. Older scholars—notably Ruggero M. Ruggieri, *Il processo di Gano nella "Chanson de Roland"* (Firenze: Sansoni, 1936)—believed that the trial reflected archaic procedures (in the constitution of the tribunal and the substitution of a champion for the accused) more characteristic of the late ninth century.
11. *La Chanson de Roland*, ed. Gérard Moignet (Paris: Bordas, 1969).
12. Hyams, "Henry II and Ganelon," 30.
13. Erich Klibansky, *Gerichtsszene und Prozeßform in erzählenden deutschen Dichtungen des 12.–14. Jahrhunderts*, Germanische Studien 40 (Berlin: Emil Ebering, 1925), 59–63.
14. For legal details I rely on the thorough discussion in Rosemary Norah Combridge, *Das Recht im "Tristan" Gottfrieds von Strassburg*, 2d ed., Philologische Studien und Quellen 15 (Berlin: Erich Schmidt, 1964), 83–120. See also Vickie Ziegler, "The Burning Issue: Isolde's Oath in Its Historical Context," in *The Germanic Mosaic: Cultural and Linguistic Diversity in Society*, ed. Carol Blackshire-Belay (Westport, CT: Greenwood, 1994), 73–82; and Helaine Newstead, "The Equivocal Oath in the Tristan Legend," *Mélanges offerts à Rita Lejeune* (Gembloux: Dirculot, 1969), 2:1077–85.
15. Bloch, *Medieval French Literature and Law*, 54–57 ("Captured in the Act").
16. Gottfried von Strassburg, *Tristan*, ed. Rüdiger Krohn, 3 vols. (Stuttgart: Reclam, 1981), vol. 2.

17. See Grimm, *Deutsche Rechtsalterthümer*, 569–78, for details from many sources.
18. This commentary, which exists only in Gottfried's treatment of the story, has been subject to extensive interpretation: Is Gottfried making a theological or a social criticism? See the discussion and bibliography in the commentary volume of Krohn's edition, 3:148–50.
19. Combridge, *Das Recht im "Tristan,"* 112, stresses this point.
20. Krohn, *Tristan*, 3:148–49.
21. Elisabeth Frenzel, *Motive der Weltliteratur: Ein Lexikon dichtungsgeschichtlicher Längsschnitte*, 4th ed. (Stuttgart: Kröner, 1992), 296–311 ("Gottesurteil"); and John W. Baldwin, "The Crisis of the Ordeal: Literature, Law, and Religion around 1200," *Journal of Medieval and Renaissance Studies* 24 (1994): 327–53.
22. *Encyclopaedia Britannica*, 16:851.
23. *Deutsche Dichtung des Mittelalters*, ed. Michael Curschmann and Ingeborg Glier, 3 vols. (Munich: Hanser, 1981), 2:576–87.
24. Hans Sachs, *Werke in zwei Bänden*, ed. Karl Martin Schiller (Berlin and Weimar: Aufbau, 1966), 2:349–59; here 349.
25. In the *Xenien* published jointly with Schiller (1796); Goethe's *Werke*, Hamburger Ausgabe, 14 vols. (Hamburg: Wegner, 1948–60), 1:217.
26. See the notes in the Hamburger Ausgabe, 2:596–98.
27. Goethe, *Werke*, Hamburger Ausgabe, 10:359.
28. Hans Gerhard Gräf, *Goethe über seine Dichtungen* (Frankfurt am Main: Rütten & Loening, 1901), I. Teil, 1:275.
29. Thomas Carlyle, *Critical and Miscellaneous Essays* (New York: Alden, 1885), 5.
30. Jacob Grimm, *Reinhart Fuchs* (Berlin: Reimer, 1834), cclix. Grimm's classic study consists of a 296-page introduction on beast fable, followed by many of the most important Latin, Middle High German, and Netherlandic texts.
31. Adolf Glassbrenner, *Neuer Reineke Fuchs* (Leipzig, 1846), 3.
32. See the discussion and bibliography by Hubertus Menke, "Populäre 'Gelehrtendichtung' im Dienste der reformatorischen Lehre: Zur Sinndeutung und Rezeption der Rostocker Überlieferung des 'Reineke Fuchs,'" in *Reynaert, Reynard, Reynke: Studien zu einem mittelalterlichen Tierepos*, ed. Jan Goossens and Timothy Sodmann (Cologne and Vienna: Böhlau, 1980), 249–81; here 280.
33. J. C. Gottsched, *Heinrichs von Alkmar Reineke Fuchs* (Leipzig and Amsterdam, 1752).
34. Menke, "Populäre 'Gelehrtendichtung' im Dienste der reformatorischen Lehre," 262, makes a convincing case for the impact of the Rostock edition.
35. Grimm, *Reinhart Fuchs*, 291–442.
36. Jan M. Ziolkowski, *Talking Animals: Medieval Latin Beast Poetry, 750–1150* (Philadelphia: University of Pennsylvania Press, 1993), 153–97 (on *Ecbasis captivi*) and 210–34 (on *Ysengrimus*).
37. Ibid., 212.
38. Ibid.; see also Thomas W. Best, *Reynard the Fox* (Boston: Twayne, 1983), 1–32.
39. The basic work on the filiation of the several variants is still Lucien Foulet, *Le Roman de Renard* (Paris: Champion, 1914). See also John Flinn, *Le Roman de Renart dans la littérature française et dans les littératures étrangères au Moyen Age* (Toronto: University of Toronto Press, 1963).
40. For convenience I use the edition, with German translation, by Helga Jauss-Meyer,

Le Roman de Renart, Klassische Texte des romanischen Mittelalters 5 (Munich: Fink, 1965). This edition contains the *branches* (II, Va, III, IV, and I) that provided the source for the Middle High German *Reinhart Fuchs*. *Branches* II, Va, I, and VIII are available in a vigorous English verse translation by Patricia Terry: *Renard the Fox* (Boston: Northeastern University Press, 1983); and *branches* I–X and XIV–XVI in a prose translation by D.D.R. Owen: *The Romance of Reynard the Fox* (Oxford: Oxford University Press, 1994).

41. Jauss-Meyer, in the introduction to her edition, 7.

42. These collections have all been edited and published. The most recent of the three was published by M.D.-M. Méon, *Le Roman de Renart*, 4 vols. (Paris, 1826), the edition used by Jacob Grimm; the oldest and shortest of the collections was published by Ernest Martin, *Le Roman de Renart*, 3 vols. (Strassburg, 1882–87), in the order that is still used as the standard for identification of the *branches*; and the middle collection has been edited by Mario Roques, *Le Roman de Renart*, 5 vols. (Paris: Champion, 1948–60).

43. Foulet, *Le Roman de Renard*, 218–26, has convincingly identified the camel as a caricature of Cardinal Pierre of Pavia, the legate from Pope Alexander III to Louis VII of France.

44. Paulin Paris, in the introduction to bk. 2 of his edition, *Les Aventures de Maître Renart et d'Ysengrin son compère* (Paris: Éditions Crès, 1921), 177–78.

45. Jean Graven, *Le Procès criminel du Roman de Renart: Étude du droit criminel féodal au XIIe siècle* (Geneva: Librairie de l'Université, 1950), 15–16. Unfortunately Graven bases his analysis upon the modern retelling of the story by Paulin Paris and upon Paris's arrangement of the episodes.

46. Foulet, *Le Roman de Renard*, 207 and 331.

47. Ibid., and Flinn, *Le Roman de Renart*, 38–42.

48. This is one of the main themes of Bloch's *Medieval French Literature and Law*, 129–30.

49. Ibid., 136.

50. Kathryn Gravdal, "Law and Literature in the French Middle Ages: Rape Law on Trial in *Le Roman de Renart*," *Romanic Review* 82 (1991): 1–24, points out that the work, by transforming an alleged love affair into rape, also satirizes the literary conventions of courtly romances.

51. The text, known in its entirety only from a fourteenth-century manuscript, has a complicated history. See *Der Reinhart Fuchs des Elsässers Heinrich*, ed. Klaus Düwel, Altdeutsche Textbibliothek 96 (Tübingen: Niemeyer, 1984), IX–XXI.

52. Ibid., XXII–XXV.

53. See esp. Klibansky, *Gerichtsszene und Prozeßform*, 41–56. *Reinhart Fuchs* is so detailed, and sometimes unique, in its description of medieval German legal procedures that it has earned a rubric in the *Handwörterbuch zur deutschen Rechtsgeschichte* (Berlin: Erich Schmidt, 1971–), 4:835–37. See also the discussion by Klaus Kanzog, "Literatur und Recht," in *Reallexikon der deutschen Literaturgeschichte*, 2d ed. (Berlin: De Gruyter, 1965), 2:164–95; here 172. The fullest and most balanced discussion of legal aspects in the work is now available in Sigrid Widmaier, *Das Recht im "Reinhart Fuchs"* (Berlin: De Gruyter, 1993). Widmaier reads the work as a legal satire in which the old law is opposed ambivalently to the new: the German author defends a conservative structure and measures the present against the past while criticizing archaic aspects of the legal system (234–35).

54. *Handwörterbuch zur deutschen Rechtsgeschichte*, 3:582–87; see Düwel's introduction, XXX–XXXI.
55. *Handwörterbuch zur deutschen Rechtsgeschichte*, 1:1333–37 ("Fürsprecher").
56. This point is stressed in ibid., 4:836.
57. See Flinn, *Le Roman de Renart*, 549–97 and esp. 595–97, for the dark reading of the Middle High German *Reinhart*.
58. Klibansky, *Gerichtsszene und Prozeßform*, 55–56.
59. See, for instance, Flinn, *Le Roman de Renart*, 598–608, and Best, *Reynard the Fox*, 70–71.
60. B.H.D. Hermesdorf, "Van den Vos Reinaerde. Rechtshistorische aantekeningen," in his *Recht en taal te hoofde. Opstellen over de ontmoeting tussen Middelnederlandse letteren en Oudvaderlands recht*, Zwolse Reeks van Taal- en Letterkundige Studies 1 (Zwolle, 1955), 106–61.
61. K. Heeroma, "De Reinaert en het recht," *Tijdschrift voor Nederlandse Taal- en Letterkunde* 87 (1971): 260–74.
62. Frank Rainer Jacoby, *Van den Vos Reinaerde: Legal Elements in a Netherlands Epic of the Thirteenth Century* (Munich: Fink, 1970).
63. Ibid., 89–93; here 91.
64. *Reinaert*, ed. Ernst Martin (Paderborn: Schöningh, 1874). This edition contains both Willem's *Van den Vos Reinaerde* and its continuation, *Reinaerts Historie*. Willem's poem has been agreeably translated into English by Adriaan J. Barnouw in the anthology *Reynard the Fox and Other Mediaeval Netherlands Secular Literature*, ed. E. Colledge, Bibliotheca Neerlandica 2 (New York: London House and Maxwell, 1967), 45–164.
65. Jacoby, *Legal Elements*, 49 and 106.
66. Ibid., 106.
67. Ibid., 39–40.
68. E.g., Peter Schneider, "*. . . ein einzig Volk von Brüdern*": *Recht und Staat in der Literatur* (Frankfurt am Main: Athenäum, 1987), 35–80, bases his discussion of the legal issues on Goethe's 1794 adaptation of the 1498 Low German revision of the Flemish version.
69. Cited by Grimm, *Reinhart Fuchs*, CCXII. For this reason passages of the work are also cited in the chapter on political oppression and exploitation in Gerald Strauss's edition of documents, *Manifestations of Discontent in Germany on the Eve of the Reformation* (Bloomington: Indiana University Press, 1971), 89–96.
70. Hermann Heimpel, "Characteristics of the Late Middle Ages in Germany," in *Pre-Reformation Germany*, ed. Gerald Strauss (London: Macmillan, 1972), 43–72; here 65.

Chapter Six
The Reception of Roman Law in Germany

1. Klaus Manger, *Das Narrenschiff: Entstehung, Wirkung und Deutung*, Erträge der Forschung 186 (Darmstadt: Wissenschaftliche Buchgesellschaft, 1983), 29–31.
2. This analogy is cited frequently by German scholars, e.g., Manger (ibid., 18); or Hans-Joachim Mähl in his afterword to the modernizing edition of *Das Narrenschiff* by H. A. Junghans (Stuttgart: Reclam, 1964), 461.
3. The publishing history of *Das Narrenschiff* is outlined in Manger, *Entstehung*,

Wirkung und Deutung, 66–81; and in Edwin H. Zeydel, *Sebastian Brant* (New York: Twayne, 1967), 90–105.

4. Michel Foucault, *Madness and Civilization: A History of Insanity in the Age of Reason*, trans. Richard Howard (New York: Pantheon-Random House, 1965), 7–9. Foucault generalizes from two or three individual cases to conclude that "Frequently they were handed over to boatmen" and that "Often the cities of Europe must have seen these 'ships of fools' approaching their harbors."
5. Katherine Anne Porter, *Ship of Fools* (Boston and Toronto: Little, Brown, 1962), vii.
6. John Van Cleve, *Sebastian Brant's "The Ship of Fools" in Critical Perspective 1800–1991* (Columbia, SC: Camden House, 1993).
7. *Sebastian Brants Narrenschiff*, ed. Friedrich Zarncke (Leipzig: Georg Wigand, 1854), 1 and 115. Here and throughout, I cite the German text from Zarncke's still standard—and, indeed, exemplary—edition.
8. We now have a thorough evaluation of Brant's career and accomplishments as a jurist: Joachim Knape, *Dichtung, Recht und Freiheit. Studien zu Leben und Werk Sebastian Brants 1457–1521*, Saecula Spiritalia 23 (Baden-Baden: Valentin Koerner, 1992). Unfortunately Knape does not extend his investigations to include *Das Narrenschiff*.
9. Letter of January 4, 1484, cited by Knape, *Studien*, 32.
10. Knape, *Studien*, 78–82, presents evidence indicating that Brant's degree was technically in canon law.
11. Ibid., 93–97.
12. Ibid., 48–55.
13. Ibid., 97–126, provides a full description of Brant's editions of canonic works, including Gratian's *Decretum* as well as the Decretals of various popes.
14. Knape, *Studien*, 128–30; the poem is reproduced by Zarncke, *Narrenschiff*, 169–71. The practice of introducing legal works with rhymed prefaces goes back to Eike von Repgow's early-thirteenth-century *Sachsenspiegel* and was subsequently widely imitated; see the rubric "Reimvorreden" in *Handwörterbuch zur deutschen Rechtsgeschichte*, ed. Adalbert Erler and Ekkehard Kaufmann, vol. 4 (Berlin: Erich Schmidt, 1988–90), 823–29.
15. Knape, *Studien*, 130–33; Zarncke, *Narrenschiff*, 171–72. On the significance of the two works see also O. Stobbe, *Geschichte der deutschen Rechtsquellen* (Leipzig: Duncker & Humblot, 1864), 2:167–74.
16. Zarncke, *Narrenschiff*, 142–47; here 145–46.
17. Ibid., 187–88. This poem was subsequently included in Brant's *Varia Carmina* (1498); and an approximate German paraphrase is included in a manuscript collection of his epigrams and satires; Zarncke, xxxvii–xxxviii.
18. On the interpretation of *Das Narrenschiff* in general see Zeydel, *Sebastian Brant*, 74–89; and Manger, *Entstehung, Wirkung und Deutung*, 36–65.
19. Zarncke, *Narrenschiff*, 484, enumerates the relevant passages.
20. Gudrun Aker, *Narrenschiff: Literatur und Kultur in Deutschland an der Wende zur Neuzeit*, Stuttgarter Arbeiten zur Germanistik 216 (Stuttgart: Hans-Dieter Heinz Akademischer Verlag, 1990), 167.
21. The Susanna theme produced many treatments in sixteenth-century Germany; Paul F. Casey, *The Susanna Theme in German Literature* (Bonn: Bouvier, 1976). The extraordinary popularity of the theme is no doubt due at least in part to the role of the corrupt judges as villains—a role that confirmed popular opinion regarding the law.

22. Zarncke, *Narrenschiff*, 405, cites the relevant passages from *Sachsenspiegel*, *Schwabenspiegel*, and other sources.
23. Zarncke, *Narrenschiff*, 437.
24. It seems likely that Brant's drastic image may have been suggested by the view attributed to the Roman legal moralist Cato, who in a similarly cynical mood exclaimed that the law courts should be paved with caltrops: *Catonis censori, qui sternendum quoque forum muricibus censuerat* (as quoted by Pliny the Elder, *Hist. Nat.* 19.6.24).
25. Otto Rudolf Kissel, *Die Justitia. Reflexionen über ein Symbol und seine Darstellung in der bildenden Kunst* (Munich: Beck, 1984), 88.
26. For the text of the plays, as well as information regarding them, I have relied on Hugo Holstein, *Johann Reuchlins Komödien: Ein Beitrag zur Geschichte des lateinischen Schuldramas* (Halle: Verlag der Buchhandlung des Waisenhauses, 1888; reprint, Leipzig: Zentralantiquariat der DDR, 1973).
27. Ibid., 48–67.
28. Ibid., 73–95.
29. Ibid., 40–48.
30. *La Farce de maistre Pathelin*, ed. Guillaume Picot (Paris: Librairie Larousse, 1972).
31. Holstein, *Reuchlins Komödien*, 24–26.
32. Ibid., 97–106.
33. Reuchlin explains in his commentary that *valeat* means *pereat. in peiorem accipitur hic partem*. Ibid., 104.
34. "Ein comedi, mit 10 personen zu recidiern, doctor Reuchlins im Latein gemacht, der Henno," in *Hans Sachs*, ed. Adelbert von Keller, vol. 7 (Tübingen: Litterarischer Verein in Stuttgart, 1873): 124–53; here 139.
35. Ulrich von Hutten, *Schriften*, ed. Eduard Böcking, 5 vols. (Leipzig: Teubner, 1859–62), 1:195–217; here 217.
36. Hajo Holborn, *Ulrich von Hutten and the German Reformation*, trans. Roland H. Bainton (New Haven: Yale University Press, 1937). The English translation is a thoroughly revised and expanded, and hence more authoritative, version of Holborn's original German biography (1929). See also the classic biography by David Friedrich Strauss, *Ulrich von Hutten* (1858–60; reprint, Bonn: Strauss, 1895).
37. See the "Complaints of the Knights of Franconia as Presented to the Estates of the Empire" (1522), in *Manifestations of Discontent in Germany on the Eve of the Reformation: A Collection of Documents*, ed. and trans. Gerald Strauss (Bloomington: Indiana University Press, 1971), 179–92; esp. 184–89.
38. *Schriften*, 3:107–18.
39. Holborn, *Ulrich von Hutten*, 52.
40. *Schriften*, 1:175–84; see also Strauss, *Ulrich von Hutten*, 104–8.
41. *Schriften*, 1:195–217; here 211.
42. Ibid., 4:363–406.
43. Strauss, *Ulrich von Hutten*, 386–93, regards this rapprochement as the central theme of the work and plays down the legal satire.
44. See the proclamation of feud in Ulrich von Hutten, *Deutsche Schriften*, ed. Heinz Mettke (Leipzig: Bibliographisches Institut, 1974), 2:183–84.
45. Holborn, *Ulrich von Hutten*, 107; see also 59–50 and 183–87 for other observations on Hutten and Roman law.

46. Guido Kisch, *Melanchthons Rechts- und Soziallehre* (Berlin: De Gruyter, 1967), 23–24.
47. I cite the *Declamationes* according to the complete collection reprinted in vols. 11 and 12 of the *Opera*, ed. Bretschneider (Halle, 1843): *Philippi Melanthonis Opera Quae Supersunt Omnia edidit Carolus Gottlieb Bretschneider* (Halis Saxonum apud C. A. Schwetschke et Filium). Fourteen of the most important ones are reprinted in Kisch, *Melanchthons Rechts- und Soziallehre*, 185–298, and for the reader's convenience I have also noted wherever possible the relevant page from that edition.
48. Kisch, *Melanchthons Rechts- und Soziallehre*, 44–56.
49. Holstein, *Reuchlin's Komödien*, 54.
50. See Richard Nürnberger's introduction to his selection of *declamationes* in vol. 3 of *Melanchthons Werke in Auswahl*, ed. Robert Stupperich (Gütersloh: Gütersloher Verlagshaus Gerd Mohn, 1961), 15–16. This *Studienausgabe* contains only one of the orations on law: *De dignitate legum* (1543).
51. *Werke in Auswahl*, vol. 2, pt. 1, 55–56.

Chapter Seven
European Variations

1. This fact is generally acknowledged in studies of Erasmus and editions of his work, but the degree of influence is variously evaluated.
2. *Moriae Encomium: id est Stultitiae Laus*, ed. Clarence H. Miller, in Desiderius Erasmus, *Opera Omnia*, vol. 4, pt. 3 (Amsterdam and Oxford: North-Holland Publishing Company, 1979), 110 (lines 732–33).
3. It is symptomatic that Guido Kisch, in the collection of monographs that he published under the title *Erasmus und die Jurisprudenz seiner Zeit: Studien zum humanistischen Rechtsdenken* (Basel: Helbing & Lichtenhahn, 1960), mentions the *Moriae Encomium* only once (131) fleetingly in the course of some 550 pages.
4. Kisch, *Erasmus*, 55–68.
5. Ibid., 108–32.
6. *Institutiones Principis Christiani*, ed. O. Herding, in *Opera Omnia*, vol. 4, pt. 1 (1974), 194–204; here 204.
7. E.g., Paul Koschaker, *Europa und das römische Recht* (Berlin: Biederstein, 1947), 225. Kisch, *Erasmus*, 381–403, summarizing the views of such historians, disagrees and argues that the humanist return to the sources, along with their new emphasis on the principle of equity, constituted an important contribution to the development of modern law.
8. *Utopia*, ed. Edward Surtz, S.J., and J. H. Hexter, vol. 4 of *The Complete Works of Sir Thomas More*, The Yale Edition (New Haven and London: Yale University Press, 1965), 194, lines 6–24.
9. On More's view of law and lawyers, see the introduction by Hexter and Surtz to their edition of *Utopia*, liv–lvii and cxliv–cxlv.
10. M. A. Screech, *Rabelais* (London: Duckworth, 1979), 17. See also Jean Plattard, *The Life of François Rabelais*, trans. Louis P. Roche (New York: Knopf, 1931), 16–23.
11. Plattard, *Life of Rabelais*, 23 n. 2.
12. Screech, *Rabelais*, 17.

13. Plattard, *Life of Rabelais*, 24–25.
14. Ibid., 46–52.
15. Ibid., 68.
16. Screech, *Rabelais*, 24.
17. I cite the original text according to the *Oeuvres complètes*, ed. Guy Demerson (Paris: Seuil, 1973). The English translations and French modernizations are often misleading because they expand and translate the abbreviations used by Rabelais.
18. I refer to the *Digesta* as edited by Theodor Mommsen in the *Corpus Iuris Civilis*, vol. 1 (Berlin: Weidmann, 1902), 57–873.
19. Plattard, *Life of Rabelais*, 21–18.
20. Screech, *Rabelais*, 24 and passim.
21. Ibid., 82–84.
22. See Demerson's comment on this passage, *Oeuvres complètes*, 821 n. 2.
23. Erich Auerbach, *Mimesis: The Representation of Reality in Western Literature*, trans. Willard Trask (1953; reprint, Garden City, NY: Doubleday-Anchor, 1957), 240.
24. This is the view advanced by Screech, *Rabelais*, 265–72. Earlier scholars tended to emphasize the satirical aspect of the episode: e.g., Marcel Teitel, *Rabelais* (New York: Twayne, 1967), 55–56, who regards Bridoye as a "deformation of professional traits." The recent revision by Elizabeth Chesney Zegura and Marcel Teitel, *Rabelais Revisited* (New York: Twayne, 1993), 11, shows greater appreciation for the ambivalence of the episode as "an example of Christian folly" as well as "satire of the legal system."
25. I use here the translation, with its clarifying expansions, by Jacques LeClercq (New York: Random House–The Modern Library), 440.
26. Ibid., 444.
27. See Theodore Ziolkowski, "Judge Bridoye's Ursine Litigations," *Modern Philology* 92 (1995): 346–50.
28. LeClerq trans., 449.
29. Screech, *Rabelais*, 268–72.
30. Guy Demerson, *François Rabelais* (Paris: Fayard, 1991), 233–37, represents the current view, influenced by Screech, according to which Rabelais shares the humanists' toleration of the shabbiness of legal procedures because he believes so passionately in the spirit of law, which embodies the essence of humanity.
31. J.D.M. Derrett, "Rabelais' Legal Learning and the Trial of Bridoye," *Bibliothèque d'Humanisme et Renaissance* 25 (1963): 111–71.
32. Ibid., 123.
33. M.-A. Screech, "The Legal Comedy of Rabelais in the Trial of Bridoye in the 'Tiers Livre' de Pantagruel," in *Études Rabelaisiennes* 5 (= Travaux d'Humanisme et Renaissance 65) (Geneva: Librairie Droz, 1964), 175–95; here 192.
34. The dozens of handbooks, *summae*, *flores*, and other popular works produced during this period for the benefit of the German public are surveyed in Roderick Stintzing, *Geschichte der populären Literatur des römisch-kanonischen Rechts in Deutschland am Ende des fünfzehnten und am Anfang des sechzehnten Jahrhunderts* (Leipzig: Hirzel, 1867).
35. Screech, "Legal Comedy," 176.
36. Ibid.
37. Edwin H. Zeydel, *Sebastian Brant* (New York: Twayne, 1967), 100–101.
38. Plattard, *Life of Rabelais*, 283 n.

39. Screech, *Rabelais*, 271–72.
40. Plattard, *Life of Rabelais*, 113 n.
41. Paul Koschaker, *Europa und das römische Recht* (Berlin: Biederstein, 1947), 221–23.

Chapter Eight
Law and Equity I

1. A. S. Diamond, *The Evolution of Law and Order* (London: Watts, 1951), 304.
2. Richard A. Posner, *Law and Literature: A Misunderstood Relation* (Cambridge: Harvard University Press, 1988), 54–62; and Daniel J. Kornstein, *Kill All the Lawyers? Shakespeare's Legal Appeal* (Princeton, NJ: Princeton University Press, 1994), 91–96.
3. Marty Roth, "'The Blood That Fury Breathed': The Shape of Justice in Aeschylus and Shakespeare," *Comparative Literature Studies* 29 (1992): 141–56, compares *The Merchant of Venice* and *The Eumenides*; he sees a parallel between Portia and Athena as spokespersons for justice and argues that both works expose society's need to exclude "the fearsome other": in Athens the female and in London the Jew (154–55). My interpretations come to a wholly different conclusion.
4. Christiane Zimmermann, *Der Antigone-Mythos in der antiken Literatur und Kunst*, Classica Monacensia: Münchner Studien zur Klassischen Philologie 5 (Tübingen: Gunter Narr, 1993).
5. George Steiner, *Antigones* (Oxford: Clarendon, 1986), 103.
6. G.W.F. Hegel, *Phänomenologie des Geistes*, ed. Johannes Hoffmeister, Philosophische Bibliothek 114 (Hamburg: Felix Meiner, 1952), 337. Steiner in *Antigones* has given a thorough and nuanced treatment of Hegel's obsession with Sophocles' tragedy, which has been often remarked and analyzed. See also Brian Vickers, *Towards Greek Tragedy: Drama, Myth, Society* (London: Longman, 1973), 526–46.
7. Zimmermann, *Antigone-Mythos*, 309.
8. Hellmut Flashar, *Inszenierung der Antike: Das griechische Drama auf der Bühne der Neuzeit 1585–1990* (Munich: Beck, 1991), 169–73.
9. Dürrenmatt, "Theaterprobleme" (1954), in his *Werkausgabe in dreißig Bänden* (Zurich: Diogenes, 1984), 24:60.
10. Heinrich Böll, "Die verschobene Antigone," in his *Werke: Hörspiele, Theaterstücke, Drehbücher, Gedichte 1*, ed. Bernd Balzer (Cologne: Kiepenheuer & Witsch, 1978), 609–15. Böll's text was written as the scenario for Völker Schlöndorff's segment of the film *Deutschland im Herbst* (1978).
11. Bernard-Henri Lévy, *The Testament of God*, trans. George Holoch (New York: Harper, 1980), 70–71. I am indebted for this reference to George Steiner's *Antigones*.
12. Flashar, *Inszenierung der Antike*, 295–98.
13. The locus classicus is the chapter "Pflege und Verehrung der Todten" in Erwin Rohde, *Psyche: Seelencult und Unsterblichkeits-Glaube der Griechen*, 9–10th ed. (Tübingen: Mohr, 1925), 1:216–58; here 216 n. 1. See also Zimmermann, *Antigone-Mythos*, 302–8, for a bibliography and summary of recent scholarship.
14. Rohde, *Psyche*, 1:217–18.
15. Zimmermann, *Antigone-Mythos*, 3 and 115–20.
16. Victor Ehrenberg, *Sophokles und Perikles*, revised German version of 1954 English original (Munich: Beck, 1956), 35.

17. Christian Meier, *Die politische Kunst der griechischen Tragödie* (Munich: Beck, 1988), 208.
18. Goethe discusses the passage in his conversations with Eckermann (March 28, 1827). The fact that Aristotle cites these very lines in his *Rhetoric* only a century later gives them an authenticity that can be claimed by few other lines in Greek drama. For the *pros* see Bernard M. W. Knox, *The Heroic Temper: Studies in Sophoclean Tragedy* (Berkeley and Los Angeles: University of California Press, 1964), 104–6, who surveys the arguments for and against. For the *contras* see R. P. Winnington-Ingram, *Sophocles: An Interpretation* (Cambridge: Cambridge University Press, 1980), 145. Hermann Rohdich takes the controversy as the starting point for his *Antigone: Beitrag zu einer Theorie des Sophokleischen Helden* (Heidelberg: Carl Winter, 1980).
19. See C. M. Bowra, *Sophoclean Tragedy* (Oxford: Clarendon, 1944), 93–96.
20. Walter Jens, "Antigone-Interpretationen," in *Sophokles*, ed. Hans Diller, Wege der Forschung 95 (Darmstadt: Wissenschaftliche Buchgesellschaft, 1967), 295–310; here 310.
21. Steiner, *Antigones*, 177. Winnington-Ingram, *Sophocles*, 117–49, entitles his fine chapter on the play "Creon and Antigone."
22. Winnington-Ingram, *Sophocles*, 118–19, presents the case for viewing Creon as the hero of the play. George Steiner, "Variations sur Créon," in *Sophocle*, ed. Jacqueline de Romilly, Entretiens sur l'antiquité classique 29 (Geneva: Fondation Hardt, 1983), 77–96, surveys the works in which popular fascination with the figure of Creon himself has been expressed.
23. Knox, *The Heroic Temper*, esp. 67–75. My understanding has also been helped by Bowra, *Sophoclean Tragedy*, 63–115; Ehrenberg, *Sophokles und Perikles*, 67–75 and passim; Charles Paul Segal, "Sophocles' Praise of Man and the Conflicts of the *Antigone*," *Arion* 3 (1964): 46–66; and G. H. Gellie, *Sophocles: A Reading* (Carlton, Victoria: Melbourne University Press, 1972), 29–52.
24. Knox, *The Heroic Temper*, 103.
25. Winnington-Ingram, *Sophocles*, 147.
26. Warren J. Lane and Ann M. Lane, "The Politics of *Antigone*," in *Greek Tragedy and Political Theory*, ed. J. Peter Euben (Berkeley and Los Angeles: University of California Press), 162–82, discuss Antigone (171–77) as a champion of *philia*, which involves a loyalty to others rather than to the state. For further aspects of *philia* see Winnington-Ingram, *Sophocles*, 128–36.
27. See Lane and Lane, "The Politics of *Antigone*," 162–82. This feminist critique makes the plausible point that Antigone, though herself unconcerned with her role as a woman, is constantly measured against that role by others—notably Ismene, the chorus, and Creon. On Sophocles' treatment of women generally see Winnington-Ingram, *Sophocles*, 233–49.
28. Robert F. Goheen, *The Imagery of Sophocles' Antigone: A Study of Poetic Language and Structure* (Princeton, NJ: Princeton University Press, 1951), 26–35.
29. Knox, *The Heroic Temper*, 5.
30. Rudolf Bultmann, "Polis und Hades in der Antigone des Sophokles," in his *Glauben und Verstehen* (Tübingen: Mohr, 1952), 2:20–31; reprinted in *Sophokles*, ed. Hans Diller, 311–24. See also Ehrenberg, *Sophokles und Perikles*, 202–3; and Bernard Knox, "Sophocles and the *Polis*," in *Sophocle*, ed. Romilly, 1–27.

31. Zimmermann, *Antigone-Mythos*, 119.
32. Meier, *Die politische Kunst*, 219.
33. On this frequently discussed term see Ehrenberg, *Sophokles und Perikles*, 25–62; and Knox, *The Heroic Temper*, 95–87.
34. See H.D.F. Kitto, *Sophocles: Dramatist and Philosopher* (London: Oxford University Press, 1958), 47–50. Vickers, *Towards Greek Tragedy*, 23–29, objects to the view of *dikê* as cosmic order; but he cites various scholars who stress the opposing notions of *dikê* to which both Creon and Antigone appeal. Erik Wolf, *Griechisches Rechtsdenken*, vol. 2 (Frankfurt am Main: Klostermann, 1952), 248–80, understands the entire play as a contest over *dikê*, in which both Creon and Antigone are driven by *hubris* to excesses of self-righteousness.
35. In his interpretation of the first stasimon (= 52 of his *Einführung in die Metaphysik*, 1935), in Martin Heidegger, *Gesamtausgabe*, vol. 40 (Frankfurt am Main: Klostermann, 1983), 169.
36. Ehrenberg, *Sophokles und Perikles*, 90–91.
37. Rohdich, *Antigone: Beitrag zu einer Theorie des sophokleischen Helden*, 228–29.
38. Knox, "Sophocles and the *Polis*," 27.
39. Ehrenberg, *Sophokles und Perikles*, 129–43.
40. Gellie, *Sophocles*, 34.
41. Knox, *The Heroic Temper*, 115–16. See also Gellie, *Sophocles*, 254–55. who shares this view.
42. *Pace* Bowra, *Sophoclean Tragedy*, 63, who—in contrast to most recent scholars—begins his chapter on *Antigone* with the assertion that "It has no word about Athens, no political propaganda, no contemporary allusions, no appeal to patriotism." See in contrast Wolf, *Griechisches Rechtsdenken*, 2:198–203.
43. Knox, *The Heroic Temper*, 86 and 94–96. Ehrenberg, *Sophokles und Perikles*, 46–47, stresses the fact that Pericles, when he uses the phrase "unwritten laws," is referring not to universal laws but to customs localized to Athens and punished at most by the shame (*aischynê*) of the community.
44. Knox, *The Heroic Temper*, 181 n. 52.
45. Ehrenberg, *Sophokles und Perikles*, 43.
46. Martin Ostwald, "*Nomos* and *Physis* in Antiphon's *Peri Alêtheias*," in *Cabinet of the Muses: Essays on Classical and Comparative Literature in Honor of Thomas G. Rosenmeyer*, ed. Mark Griffith and Donald J. Mastronarde (Atlanta, GA: Scholars Press, 1990), 293–306; here 294. I take the further quotations in this paragraph from Ostwald's discussion.
47. Goheen, *The Imagery of Sophocles' Antigone*, 86–93.
48. Hans Kelsen, "The Metamorphoses of the Idea of Justice," in *Interpretations of Modern Legal Philosophies: Essays in Honor of Roscoe Pound*, ed. Paul Sayre (New York: Oxford University Press, 1947), 390–418. Kelsen does not draw this analogy, but he develops the Aristotelian and Platonic ideas of justice in such a manner that the conclusion seems inevitable to the reader of *Antigone*.
49. See Ehrenberg, *Sophokles und Perikles*, 129–43; Goheen, *The Imagery of Sophocles' Antigone*, 90–91 and 152 n. 28; and Segal, "Sophocles' Praise of Man," 63.
50. Meier, *Die politische Kunst*, 220.
51. This is one of the theses underlying Max Pohlenz, *Die griechische Tragödie* (Leipzig and Berlin: Teubner, 1930), see esp. 14–16.
52. Werner Jaeger, "Praise of Law: The Origin of Legal Philosophy and the Greeks," in

Interpretations of Modern Legal Philosophies: Essays in Honor of Roscoe Pound, ed. Paul Sayre (New York: Oxford University Press, 1947), 352–75; esp. 360–63.

53. Pohlenz, *Die griechische Tragödie*, 160.
54. On hero cults see Rohde, *Psyche*, 1:146–99.
55. Knox, *The Heroic Temper*, 53–55.
56. See Jennifer Tolbert Roberts, *Athens on Trial: The Antidemocratic Tradition in Western Thought* (Princeton, NJ: Princeton University Press, 1994), 48–70, on the early (fifth-century) attacks on democracy.
57. See Winnington-Ingram, *Sophocles*, 120.
58. The long conflict between *genos* and *polis* in Athens is analyzed in Aristotle's *Politics*. See Knox, *The Heroic Temper*, 76–79.
59. Werner Jaeger, *Paideia: The Ideals of Greek Culture*, trans. Gilbert Highet (New York: Oxford University Press, 1939), 99. See "The City-State and Its Ideal of Justice" (96–111) on Athenian thought more generally.
60. Rudolf Hirzel, *Agraphos Nomos*, Abhandlungen der philologisch-historischen Classe der Königl. Sächsischen Gesellschaft der Wissenschaften 20 (Leipzig: Teubner, 1900), 38–39, 41–42 and 62–63.
61. Ibid., 54.
62. Ibid., 71–72.
63. Ehrenberg, *Sophokles und Perikles*, 202–3.
64. Bowra, *Sophoclean Tragedy*, 97. Knox, *The Heroic Temper*, 95–96, argues reasonably that Sophocles would have formulated the issues more clearly had he been interested in the philosophical aspects of the problem. However, I am suggesting not that he was contributing to a philosophical debate but, rather, that his work anticipated—by depicting tensions already in the air—the debate that was to take shape in the next decade.
65. Hirzel, *Agraphos Nomos*, 40–42.
66. Ibid., 59–60, for citations. See esp. Francesco D'Agostino, *Epieikeia: il tema dell'equità nell'antichità greca* (Milan: Dott. A. Giuffre Editore, 1973), 1–21, for the etymology, history, and definition of the term.
67. Paul Vinogradoff, *Outlines of Historical Jurisprudence*, vol. 2 (Oxford: Oxford University Press, 1922), 63.
68. This corresponds to 5.10–11 of the text as published in the Loeb Classics edition, to which I refer here. See the discussion in D'Agostino, *Epieikeia*, 65–100.
69. Max Hamburger, *Morals and Law: The Growth of Aristotle's Legal Theory* (New Haven: Yale University Press, 1951), 89–93; here 82. See also J. Zepos, "Equity in Greek Law," in *Equity in the World's Legal Systems: A Comparative Study*, ed. Ralph A. Newman, California Western School of Law, U.S.I.U. Studies in Jurisprudence 1 (Brussels: Établissements Émile Bruylant, 1973), 433–41.
70. Hamburger, *Morals and Law*, 104–5.

Chapter Nine
Law and Equity II

1. Max Hamburger, *Morals and Law: The Growth of Aristotle's Legal Theory* (New Haven: Yale University Press, 1951), 108 n. 3. See also Guido Kisch, *Erasmus und die Jurisprudenz seiner Zeit: Studien zum humanistischen Rechtsdenken* (Basel: Helbing & Lichtenhahn, 1960), 26–36. The title provides little indication of the true subject of

Kisch's monumental work, which amounts to a history of the Aristotelian concept of *epieikeia* from classical antiquity through the Middle Ages and, especially, in sixteenth-century humanism. The volume, upon which I rely heavily in these introductory paragraphs, contains rich bibliographical citations and also reproduces in its appendix a number of the most important sources.

2. Hamburger, *Morals and Law*, 109–10.
3. Kisch, *Erasmus*, 32–33, makes the important qualification that the ancient Roman concept of *bona fides* resembled in many respects the Aristotelian *epieikeia*.
4. Ibid., 36–48.
5. Ibid., 16–17.
6. Otto Rudolf Kissel, *Die Justitia. Reflexionen über ein Symbol und seine Darstellung in der bildenden Kunst* (Munich: Beck, 1984), 23–24.
7. Kisch, *Erasmus*, 40–41.
8. Ibid., 203–219. See also the appendix "Epieikeia" in vol. 41 of the Blackfriars edition of the *Summa Theologiae*, with Latin text and English translation: *Virtues of Justice in the Human Community (2a2ae.101–22)*, ed. T. C. O'Brien (London: Eyre and Spottiswoode, 1972), 321–23.
9. *Summa Theologiae* 41:276–83.
10. Kisch, *Erasmus*, 39, 212. See also L. J. Riley, *The History, Nature and Use of Epikeia in Moral Theology* (Washington, DC: Catholic University Press, 1948).
11. Kissel, *Die Justitia*, 35–36.
12. Walter Ullmann, *The Medieval Idea of Law as Represented by Lucas de Penna: A Study in Fourteenth-Century Legal Scholarship* (London: Methuen, 1946).
13. Kisch, *Erasmus*, 55–68.
14. Ibid., 177–93.
15. Guido Kisch, *Melanchthons Rechts- und Soziallehre* (Berlin: Walter de Gruyter, 1967), esp. 168–84. In his appendix Kisch reproduces the full text of these two orations.
16. I refer to the edition published in Amsterdam in 1712, 940–43.
17. William Lambarde, *Archeion or, A Discourse upon the High Courts of Justice in England* (1635), ed. Charles H. McIlwain and Paul L. Ward (Cambridge: Harvard University Press, 1957), 36 (= p. 55).
18. Mark Edwin Andrews, *Law versus Equity in "The Merchant of Venice"* (Boulder: University of Colorado Press, 1965), xi.
19. For a full account see William S. Holdsworth, *A History of English Law*, vol. 1, 3d ed. (London: Methuen, 1922), 459–63.
20. Andrews, *Law versus Equity*, 29–31.
21. *St. German's Doctor and Student*, ed. T.F.T. Plucknett and J. L. Barton, Publications of the Selden Society 91 (London, 1974). The "First Dialogue," to which I refer, was published in Latin, anonymously, in 1523; a "Second Dialogue" in English followed in 1530; and an English translation of the "First Dialogue" by 1532.
22. For a discussion of St. German's doctrine of equity see the introduction to *Doctor and Student*, xliv–li.
23. *Doctor and Student*, 94–97.
24. This passage follows immediately (chap. 15) in the Latin original (p. 98), but in the English translation it has been moved forward into chap. 12 (pp. 77–79).
25. Holdsworth, *A History of English Law*, 3d ed., vol. 4 (1945), 279–82.
26. Ibid., 275–78; here 276.

27. *A Complete and Systematic Concordance to the Works of Shakespeare*, ed. Marvin Spevack, 9 vols. (Hildesheim: Olms, 1968–80), vol. 5 under "equity."
28. Quoted by Andrews, *Law versus Equity*, 30.
29. Wilbur Dunkel, *William Lambarde, Elizabethan Jurist 1536–1601* (New Brunswick, NJ: Rutgers University Press, 1965), 5. For an account of the court system in England during Shakespeare's times see E. W. Ives, "The Law and the Lawyers," *Shakespeare Survey* 17 (1964): 73–86.
30. Dunkel, *William Lambarde*, 133–34.
31. I cite the original page numbers according the text of the authorized edition (London, 1635) as reproduced in *Archeion*, ed. McIlwain and Ward.
32. Marco Orrù, *Anomie: History and Meanings* (Boston: Allen & Unwin, 1987), 64–93; here 71.
33. W. Nicholas Knight, "Equity, 'The Merchant of Venice' and William Lambarde," *Shakespeare Survey* 27 (1974): 93–104.
34. Dunkel, *William Lambarde*, 115–17.
35. Andrews, *Law versus Equity*, xi.
36. See George W. Keeton, *Shakespeare's Legal and Political Background* (London: Pitman, 1967), 3–10.
37. John Lord Campbell, *Lives of the Lord Chancellors*, vol. 2 (Boston: Estes & Lauriat, 1874), 341; cited by Andrews, *Law versus Equity*, pt. 2, 34.
38. Orrù, *Anomie*, 94–153.
39. Ralf Dahrendorf, *Law and Order* (London: Stevens, 1985), 26 and, in the following quotation, 24.
40. Orrù, *Anomie*, 80.
41. J. R. Mulryne, "History and Myth in *The Merchant of Venice*," in *Shakespeare's Italy: Functions of Italian Locations in Renaissance Drama*, ed. Michele Marrapodi et al. (Manchester: Manchester University, Press, 1993), 87–99.
42. Maxine MacKay, "*The Merchant of Venice*: A Reflection of the Early Conflict between Courts of Law and Courts of Equity," *Shakespeare Quarterly* 15 (1964): 371–75, discusses the play within the specific English context with no reference to the larger issues that concerned European jurisprudence.
43. For a survey of some fifty studies of law in *The Merchant of Venice* see O. Hood Phillips, *Shakespeare and the Lawyers* (London: Methuen, 1972), 91–118.
44. Rudolf von Jhering, *Der Kampf um's Recht*, 13th ed. (Vienna, 1897), 59–60. Jhering's famous essay was translated fifteen times within the first decade of its initial publication.
45. Josef Kohler, *Shakespeare vor dem Forum der Jurisprudenz* (Würzburg, 1883), 6 and 95.
46. Richard Weisberg, *Poethics and Other Strategies of Law and Literature* (New York: Columbia University Press, 1992), 206–10.
47. Richard A. Posner, *Law and Literature: A Misunderstood Relation* (Cambridge: Harvard University Press, 1988), 91–99; here 96.
48. See Thomas Wheeler's introduction to his edition of *The Merchant of Venice: Critical Essays* (New York: Garland, 1991), ix–xvi. Dietrich Schwanitz, *Shylock: Von Shakespeare bis zum Nürnberger Prozeß* (Hamburg: Krämer, 1989), uses the play as a paradigm for German history of the nineteenth and twentieth centuries, in which the Nuremberg trials constitute "Shylock's Revenge" and his "second trial."

49. Lawrence Danson, *The Harmonies of "The Merchant of Venice"* (New Haven: Yale University Press, 1978).
50. A. D. Moody, *Shakespeare: The Merchant of Venice*, Barron's Studies in English Literature 21 (Woodbury, NY: Barron, 1964). For a more recent "ironic" reading see René Girard, "'To Entrap the Wisest': A Reading of *The Merchant of Venice*," *Literature and Society*, Selected Papers from the English Institute 1978 (Baltimore: Johns Hopkins University Press, 1980), 100–119.
51. This approach is analogous to the Marxian reading of Walter Cohen, "*The Merchant of Venice* and the Possibilities of Historical Criticism," *ELH* 49 (1982): 765–89, who sees the play as a "symptom of a problem in the life of late sixteenth-century England" and as a critique of the worst aspects of the emerging economic system.
52. Shylock himself utters the word "justice" only one time in the entire play (3.3.8), when he expresses his confidence that "The Duke shall grant me justice." On two other occasions he is quoted by Solanio (2.8.17 and 21) and Salerio (3.2.278 and 282) as crying for justice; but that is hearsay evidence, and there is no guarantee that the two Christians are quoting him accurately. "Justice" is not an active word in Shylock's vocabulary.
53. Andrews, *Law versus Equity*, 52, claims that in Portia's speech "justice" is synonymous with the strict common law of England, but for reasons still to be shown I disagree.
54. I have come across no discussion of this image in the scholarly-critical literature. However, a photograph of the scene as staged in the 1938 London performance with John Gielgud as Shylock and Peggy Ashcroft as Portia suggests that the director of that production wittingly exploited the associations with Justitia. Cf. the illustration as reproduced in John Gross, *Shylock: Four Hundred Years in the Life of a Legend* (London: Chatto & Windus, 1992), between pages 152 and 153, number 9.
55. See among many works George W. Keeton, *Shakespeare's Legal and Political Background* (London: Pitman, 1967); O. Hood Phillips, *Shakespeare and the Lawyers* (London: Methuen, 1972); and Daniel J. Kornstein, *Kill All the Lawyers? Shakespeare's Legal Appeal* (Princeton, NJ: Princeton University Press, 1994). In contrast to the two earlier studies, which sought to locate Shakespeare's works in the legal context of their times, it is Kornstein's goal to identify the legal themes in the plays and to expose their relevance for the present.
56. Keeton, *Shakespeare's Legal and Political Background*, 140.
57. I am aware of the problems concerning this source, notably the absence of any known English translation available to Shakespeare. But in view of the remarkable similarity between the story and the play, I am convinced by the prevailing opinion that "It is highly probable that Shakespeare based his play on the Italian *Il Pecorone*, or on a lost English version, closer to its original than any now known." See John Russell Brown's introduction to the Arden Edition of *The Merchant of Venice* (London: Methuen, 1959), xxix. This generally accepted view is also held by Gross, *Shylock*, 5–8.
58. While I believe that Andrews, *Law versus Equity*, goes too far in his reconstruction of the trial scene—notably by dividing it into two sections, one set in a court of common law and the other in a court of equity, and by adding legal passages and then interpreting them as though they had textual authority—I also believe that he

makes a compelling case for Shakespeare's familiarity with the terminology and procedures of English law and with the contemporary dispute between the courts of common law and Chancery.

59. Keeton, *Shakespeare's Legal and Political Background*, 150; see also E.F.J. Tucker, "The Letter of the Law in *The Merchant of Venice*," *Shakespeare Survey* 29 (1976): 93–101, who asserts that "nothing remotely resembling this trial ever took place at Westminster Hall"; and William Chester Jordan, "Approaches to the Court Scene in the Bond Story: Equity and Mercy or Reason and Nature," *Shakespeare Quarterly* 33 (1982): 49–59, where it is stated that the court scene "has little claim to reality" (58).
60. For two of the most exhaustive studies see Kohler's *Shakespeare vor dem Forum der Jurisprudenz*, 7–72; and Berta Viktoria Wenger, "Shylocks Pfund Fleisch. Eine stoffgeschichtliche Untersuchung," *Shakespeare-Jahrbuch* 65 (1929): 92–174. There have been many subsequent additions to the bibliography on this subject.
61. Kornstein, *Shakepeare's Legal Appeal*, 70–71. Keeton, *Shakespeare's Legal and Political Background*, 132–33, points out that Antonio had as an additional valid defense the fact that his friends have also tendered on his behalf the owed sum.
62. Kornstein, *Shakespeare's Legal Appeal*, 127, refers specifically to *The Comedy of Errors*, *Measure for Measure*, and *A Midsummer Night's Dream*.
63. There is a vast bibliography on this subject: see, for instance, E. C. Pettet, "*The Merchant of Venice* and the Problem of Usury," *Essays and Studies by Members of the English Association* 31 (1945); W. H. Auden, "Brothers and Others," in his *The Dyer's Hand and Other Essays* (New York: Random House, 1962), 218–37; and Danson, *Harmonies*, 139–57.
64. Posner, *Law and Literature*, 97.
65. Kornstein, *Shakespeare's Legal Appeal*, 68.
66. Andrews, *Law versus Equity*, 43.
67. James Q. Whitman, *The Legacy of Roman Law in the German Romantic Era: Historical Vision and Legal Change* (Princeton, NJ: Princeton University Press, 1990), 34–35.
68. Andrews, *Law versus Equity*, 43.
69. Tucker, "The Letter of the Law," 98.
70. See Andrews, *Law versus Equity*, xiv.
71. Kornstein, *Shakespeare's Legal Appeal*, 76–77; see also John Lyon, *The Merchant of Venice*, Harvester New Critical Introductions to Shakespeare (New York: Harvester-Wheatsheaf, 1988), 109–11 and 116, for a particularly troubled ambivalence about Portia's character.
72. Kornstein, *Shakespeare's Legal Appeal*, 52–54, points out that the set piece on mercy is subsequently rendered hypocritical by Portia's actions in a manner that contrasts blatantly with the consistency of word and deed in Isabella's two pleas for mercy in *Measure for Measure*.
73. On Portia's racism see Weisberg, *Poethics*, 209; and Kornstein, *Shakespeare's Legal Appeal*, 76–77.
74. Arden Edition, 80 n. 63.
75. Kornstein, *Shakespeare's Legal Appeal*, 83–84, lists the various grounds that he would cite as counsel on appeal. See also David B. Saxe, "Shylock, Portia and a Case of Literary Oppression," *Cardozo Studies in Law and Literature* 5 (1993): 115–23.
76. Terry Eagleton, *William Shakespeare* (Oxford: Blackwell, 1986), 40–41, suggests

"melancholy" as the explanation for Antonio's condition; but melancholy is an effect rather than a cause. (It is worth mentioning that anomy is not one of the causes cited by Robert Burton in *The Anatomy of Melancholy* [1621].)

77. Moody, *The Merchant of Venice*, 46, finds such a reading congenial to his ironic interpretation of the play.

78. See Alice N. Benston, "Portia, the Law, and the Tripartite Structure of *The Merchant of Venice*," in *The Merchant of Venice: Critical Essays*, ed. Thomas Wheeler (New York: Garland, 1991), 163–94; here 181–82. Benston, while troubled by the ambiguities in Portia's nature, ultimately resolves the play into a festive celebration of law and love.

79. Weisberg, *Poethics*, 101–2, is among the most recent critics who have stressed the disharmonies of act 5.

80. Bentson, "Portia, the Law, and the Tripartite Structure," 189, belongs among those readers who believe that "Civil law has been reaffirmed in Venice and natural law in Belmont."

81. I take my interpretation to be consistent with Kornstein, *Shakespeare's Legal Appeal*, 22–23, who reads the notorious line in the earlier play, *2 Henry VI* (4.2.78)—"The first thing we do, let's kill all the lawyers"—as an expression of Shakespeare's ambivalence vis-à-vis the legal situation at the beginning of the 1590s.

Chapter Ten
The Attractions of Codification

1. Charles Sumner Lobingier, "Codification," in *Encyclopaedia of the Social Sciences*, ed. Edwin R. A. Seligmann, vol. 3 (New York: Macmillan, 1930), 606–13; here 606.

2. Hans Hattenhauer, *Europäische Rechtsgeschichte* (Heidelberg: C. F. Müller Juristischer Verlag, 1992), 89–103.

3. Lobingier, "Codification," 609–10.

4. See in this connection Hattenhauer, *Europäische Rechtsgeschichte*, 447–515; and Alan Watson, *The Making of the Civil Law* (Cambridge: Harvard University Press, 1981), 99–130.

5. On the nature and effect of the *ALR* see Hans Hattenhauer's introduction to his text edition of the *Allgemeines Landrecht* (Frankfurt am Main and Berlin: Alfred Metzner, 1970); and Reinhart Koselleck, *Preußen zwischen Reform und Revolution. Allgemeines Landrecht, Verwaltung und soziale Bewegung von 1791 bis 1848* (Stuttgart: Klett, 1967), 23–51.

6. Koselleck, *Preußen zwischen Reform und Revolution*, 26 n. 12.

7. Brunschwig, *La Crise de l'état prussien à la fin du XVIIIe siècle et la genèse de la mentalité romantique* (Paris: Presses universitaires de France, 1947), 20.

8. Charles Sumner Lobingier, "Code Civil," in *Encyclopaedia of the Social Sciences*, 3:604–6.

9. Watson, *The Making of the Civil Law*, 111–12.

10. H. S. Maine, "Roman Law and Legal Education," in *Cambridge Essays* (London: John W. Parker, 1856), 1–29; here 17.

11. See Theodore Ziolkowski, "The Law: Text of Society," in *German Romanticism and Its Institutions* (Princeton, NJ: Princeton University Press, 1990), 64–137.

12. Otto Gierke, *Natural Law and the Theory of Society 1500 to 1800*, trans. Ernest Barker (Cambridge: Cambridge University Press, 1950).

13. Gertrud Schubart-Fikentscher, *Goethes sechsundfünfzig Strassburger Thesen vom 6. August 1771. Ein Beitrag zur Geschichte der Deutschen Rechtswissenschaft* (Weimar: Böhlau, 1949), 3.
14. Letters of November 28, 1791, and January 10, 1797; in Hölderlin, *Sämtliche Werke*, vol. 6 (Stuttgart: Kohlhammer, 1959), 78 and 249.
15. Hans Dombois, "Das Problem des Naturrechts. Versuch eines Grundrisses," in *Naturrecht oder Rechtspositivismus*, ed. Werner Maihofer, 3d ed. (Darmstadt: Wissenschaftliche Buchgesellschaft, 1981), 444.
16. Friedrich Schiller, *Sämtliche Werke*, ed. Gerhard Fricke and Herbert G. Göpfert, vol. 1 (Munich: Hanser, 1965), 222.
17. In his "Athenaeum-Fragmente" (1798); in Friedrich Schlegel, *Kritische Schriften*, ed. Wolfdietrich Rasch (Munich: Hanser, 1956), 83.
18. For a discussion of the many legally trained writers see Eugen Wohlhaupter, *Dichterjuristen*, ed. H. G. Seifert, 3 vols. (Tübingen: Mohr, 1953–55).
19. I cite the *Allgemeines Landrecht* here and elsewhere in my own translation from the Hattenhauer edition.
20. See Gierke, *Natural Law*, and in particular the lecture by Ernst Troeltsch (1922) that is reprinted in that volume as an appendix. The pronounced return to natural law in Germany after World War II was a consequence of what legal thinkers regarded as the total failure of their existing system to oppose the Nazis. See chap. 12 below.
21. Eichendorff, *Werke und Schriften*, ed. Gerhart Baumann, vol. 2 (Stuttgart: Cott, 1957–58), 1047.
22. Cited in a letter from Achim von Arnim of December 1816; in *Arnims Briefe an Savigny 1803–1831*, ed. Heinz Hartl (Weimar: Böhlau, 1982), 143.
23. The documents relevant to the controversy are all reprinted in *Thibaut und Savigny: Ihre programmatischen Schriften*, ed. Jacques Stern (Munich: Vahlen, 1973). For a discussion of the controversy see Ziolkowski, *German Romanticism and Its Institutions*, 78–86.
24. Letter of October 29, 1814; in *Briefe an Savigny*, 108.
25. Koselleck, *Preußen zwischen Reform und Revolution*, 23–51.
26. Rudolf Vierhaus, "Heinrich von Kleist und die Krise des preußischen Staates um 1800," in *Kleist-Jahrbuch 1980*, 10.
27. Heinrich von Kleist, *Gesammelte Schriften*, ed. Ludwig Tieck, vol. 1 (Berlin: Reimer, 1826), 6–7.
28. Hans Joachim Kreutzer, "Über Gesellschaft und Geschichte im Werk Kleists," in *Kleist-Jahrbuch 1980*, 69.
29. See Leonard Krieger, *The Politics of Discretion: Pufendorf and the Acceptance of Natural Law* (Chicago: University of Chicago Press, 1965), 255–69; Sieglinde C. Othmer, *Berlin und die Verbreitung des Naturrechts in Europa. Kultur- und sozialgeschichtliche Studien zu Jean Barbeyracs Pufendorf-Übersetzungen und eine Analyse seiner Leserschaft*, Veröffentlichungen der Historischen Kommission zu Berlin 30 (Berlin, 1970); and *Humanismus und Naturrecht in Berlin-Brandenburg-Preußen. Ein Tagungsbericht*, ed. Hans Thieme, Veröffentlichungen der Historischen Kommission zu Berlin 48 (Berlin, 1979).
30. Kleist's works are cited here and elsewhere according to the two-volume edition of his *Sämtliche Werke und Briefe*, ed. Helmut Sembdner, 2d ed.(Munich: Hanser, 1961).

31. Ernst Landsberg, *Geschichte der deutschen Rechtswissenschaft*, I. Halbband (Munich and Leipzig, 1898), 439.
32. On Madihn see ibid., 440; Gerd Heinrich, "Die Geisteswissenschaften an der brandenburgischen Landesuniversität Frankfurt/Oder um 1800," in *Kleist-Jahrbuch 1983*, 80–81; and *Allgemeine Deutsche Biographie*, 20:36–37.
33. *Heinrich von Kleists Lebensspuren. Dokumente und Berichte der Zeitgenossen*, ed. Helmut Sembdner, 2d ed. (Bremen: Schünemann, 1964), 81–82.
34. See, for instance, Ernst Cassirer, *Heinrich von Kleist und die Kantische Philosophie*, Philosophische Vorträge 22 (Berlin: Reuther, 1919); Ludwig Muth, *Kleist und Kant. Versuch einer neuen Interpretation*, Kant-Studien 68 (Cologne: Universitäts-Verlag, 1954); and Robert Helbling, *The Major Works of Heinrich von Kleist* (New York: New Directions, 1975), 23–34.
35. In the afterword to his *Elemente der Staatskunst* (1808–9) Müller states explicitly: "I am dealing with the spirit of the laws" ("Vom Geiste der Gesetze handle ich")—an allusion of course to the title of Montesquieu's *De l'Esprit des lois*.
36. Official report of November 4, 1800, from Kleist's protector, Councillor Kunth, to Minister von Struensee; in *Heinrich von Kleists Lebensspuren*, 36.
37. Hans Kiefner, "Species Facti: Geschichtserzählung bei Kleist und in Relationen bei preußischen Kollegialbehörden um 1800," in *Kleist-Jahrbuch 1988–89*, 13–39; here 14.
38. Johann Karl-Heinz Müller, *Die Rechts- und Staatsauffassung Heinrich von Kleists* (Bonn: Bouvier, 1962), 57, also assumes on the basis of the early letters an affirmation of positive law; see also Joachim Rückert, "'. . . der Welt in der Pflicht verfallen . . .' Kleists 'Kohlhaas' als moral- und rechtsphilosophische Stellungnahme," in *Kleist-Jahrbuch 1988–89*, 375–403; here 403.
39. See A. Fink, "Heinrich von Kleist," in *Handwörterbuch zur deutschen Rechtsgeschichte*, ed. Adelbert Erler and Ekkehard Kaufmann, vol. 2 (Berlin: Erich Schmidt, 1978), 870–75.
40. Hartmut Boockmann, "Mittelalterliches Recht bei Kleist. Ein Beitrag zum Verständnis des 'Michael Kohlhaas,'" in *Kleist-Jahrbuch 1985*, 84.
41. Klaus Lüderssen, "Recht als Verständigung unter Gleichen in Kleists 'Prinz von Homburg'—ein aristokratisches oder ein demokratisches Prinzip?" in *Kleist-Jahrbuch 1985*, 66–67.
42. Hans Höller, *Der "Amphitryon" von Molière und der von Kleist. eine sozialgeschichtliche Studie*, Germanisch-Romanische Monatsschrift, Beiheft 3 (Heidelberg, 1982), 28 and 60–61.
43. Earlier legal interpretations of *Michael Kohlhaas* are recapitulated by Paul Michael Lützeler, "Heinrich von Kleist. Michael Kohlhaas," in *Romane und Erzählungen der deutschen Romantik. Neue Interpretationen*, ed. P. M. Lützeler (Stuttgart: Reclam, 1981), 213–39.
44. Rückert, "'. . . der Welt in der Pflicht verfallen . . . ,'" 390–91. See also Eberhard Schmidhäuser, *Verbrechen und Strafe: Ein Streifzug durch die Weltliteratur von Sophokles bis Dürrenmatt* (Munich: Beck, 1995), 26, who points out that Rousseau's thoughts on the social contract are put into Kohlhaas's mouth.
45. Rückert, "'. . . der Welt in der Pflicht verfallen . . .,'" 396–400.
46. See in this connection Hans-Jürgen Becker, "Adoption—Verlöbnis—Ehe. Die zi-

vilrechtliche Einbindung des Individuums bei Kleist," in *Kleist-Jahrbuch 1993*, 75–88; here 87–88.

47. Ernst Schubert, "Der Zweikampf. Ein mittelalterliches Ordal und seine Vergegenwärtigung bei Heinrich von Kleist," in *Kleist-Jahrbuch 1988–89*, 280–304, coins the term "Vergegenwärtigung" to designate the process through which Kleist "recalls" or "realizes" past law for the present audience.
48. Herbert Uerlings, "Preußen in Haiti? Zur interkulturellen Begegnung in Kleists 'Verlobung in St. Domingo,'" in *Kleist-Jahrbuch 1991*, 185–201; and Klaus Peter, "Für ein anderes Preußen. Romantik und Politik in Kleists 'Prinz Friedrich von Homburg,'"in *Kleist-Jahrbuch 1992*, 95–125.
49. For the most complete discussion of the visual sources see E. Theodor Voss, "Kleists 'Zerbrochner Krug' im Lichte alter und neuer Quellen," in *Wissen aus Erfahrungen. Werkbegriff und Interpretation heute. Festschrift für Herman Meyer*, ed. Alexander von Bormann (Tübingen: Niemeyer, 1976), 338–70.
50. Ulrich Vohland, *Bürgerliche Emanzipation in Heinrich von Kleists Dramen und theoretischen Schriften* (Bern and Frankfurt am Main: Lang, 1976), 187–88.
51. Hans-Peter Schneider, "Justizkritik im 'Zerbrochnen Krug,'" in *Kleist-Jahrbuch 1988–89*, 309–26; here 313.
52. Ibid., 321–26.
53. Ibid., 312.
54. Klaus Kanzog, "Literatur und Recht," in *Reallexikon der deutschen Literaturgeschichte*, 2d ed., vol. 2 (Berlin: De Gruyter, 1965), 187–89; and Ziolkowski, *German Romanticism and Its Institutions*, 94–114.
55. Friedrich Schlegel, *Dichtungen*, ed. Hans Eichner, Kritische Friedrich-Schlegel-Ausgabe, vol. 5 (Munich: Thomas-Verlag, 1962), 399–400.
56. Uhland, *Werke*, ed. Ludwig Holthof (Stuttgart, n.d.), 17.
57. Marjorie Gelus, "Josephe und die Männer. Klassen- und Geschlechteridentität in Kleists 'Erdbeben in Chili,'" in *Kleist-Jahrbuch 1994*, 118–40; here 140.
58. Joachim Bohnert, "Positivität des Rechts und Konflikt bei Kleist," in *Kleist-Jahrbuch 1985*, 46.
59. See the various contributions to the volume *Naturrecht oder Rechtspositivismus*, ed. Werner Maihofer, 3d ed. (Darmstadt: Wissenschaftliche Buchgesellschaft, 1981).
60. See, for instance, Diether Huhn and Jurgen Behrens, "Über die Idee des Rechts im Werk Heinrich von Kleists," in *Jahrbuch des Wiener Goethe-Vereins* 69 (1965): 179–81.
61. Even in the eighteenth century the hard provisions of the *Carolina* of 1532 were still in effect, providing for burial alive or impalement for such crimes as infanticide by an unwed mother. Drowning was regarded as a milder punishment and beheading by sword (which became increasingly common) virtually as an act of mercy. See Albrecht Schöne's commentary to his edition of Goethe's *Faust*, vol. 2 (Frankfurt am Main: Deutscher Klassiker Verlag, 1994), 196.
62. It is for this reason that most recent critics have rejected the unqualifiedly approving view of Kohlhaas advanced by Jhering in his *Der Kampf um's Recht* (1872). See, for instance, Joachim Bohnert, "Kohlhaas der Entsetzliche," in *Kleist-Jahrbuch 1988–89*, 404–31.
63. Theodore Ziolkowski, "An Ontology of Anxiety in the Dramas of Schiller, Goethe,

and Kleist," in *Lebendige Form. Festschrift für Heinrich E. K. Henel*, ed. Jeffrey L. Sammons and Ernst Schürer (Munich: Fink, 1970), 121–45.

64. Rudolf von Jhering, *Der Kampf um's Recht*, 13th ed. (Vienna, 1897), 64; Horst Sendler, *Michael Kohlhaas—gestern und heute*, Schriftenreihe der Juristischen Gesellschaft zu Berlin 92 (Berlin, 1985), 13–22.
65. Ziolkowski, *German Romanticism and Its Institutions*, 114–15.
66. In the draft of a letter of October 28–29, 1840 (probably never sent) to Balzac; Stendhal, *Correspondance*, vol. 3 (Paris: Pléiade, 1962–68), 401.
67. Richard Weisberg, "The Codification of Western Law and the Poethics of Disclosure," *Cardoza Studies in Law and Literature* 6 (1994): 157–70.
68. "Das öde Haus"; in E.T.A. Hoffmann, *Poetische Werke*, ed. Gerhard Seidel, vol. 2 (Berlin: Aufbau, 1958), 558.

Chapter Eleven
The Modern Crisis of Law

1. For an overview see Gustav Radbruch, *Grundzüge der Rechtsphilosophie* (Leipzig: Quelle und Meyer, 1914), 1–28.
2. Georg Jellinek, "Der Kampf des alten mit dem neuen Recht," in his *Ausgewählte Schriften und Reden* (Berlin: Häring, 1911), 2:392–427.
3. Dennis Lloyd, *The Idea of Law* (Baltimore: Penguin, 1964), 95–115; *Begriff und Wesen des Rechts*, ed. Werner Maihofer (Darmstadt: Wissenschaftliche Buchgesellschaft, 1973), 85–163.
4. Kelsen's *Reine Rechtslehre*, which gave the theory its title, was not published until 1934; but as he affirms in the preface to the first edition (reprinted in 2d ed. [Vienna: Franz Deuticke, 1960], III–VI), the main principles are clearly evident already in 1911 in his influential *Hauptprobleme der Staatsrechtslehre entwickelt aus der Lehre vom Rechtssatze*, 2d ed. (Tübingen: Wohr, 1923). See J. Walter Jones, *Historical Introduction to the Theory of Law* (Oxford: Clarendon, 1940), 222–34; and Kelsen's essays collected under the title *What Is Justice: Justice, Law, and Politics in the Mirror of Science* (Berkeley and Los Angeles: University of California Press, 1952), 266–302.
5. Lloyd, *The Idea of Law*, 199–225; *Begriff und Wesen des Rechts*, 164–308; and Niklas Luhmann, *Rechtssoziologie*, 3d ed. (Opladen: Westdeutscher Verlag, 1987).
6. Rudolf von Jhering, *Der Geist des römischen Rechts auf den verschiedenen Stufen seiner Entwicklung*, 8th ed., vol. 3 (Basel: Benno Schwabe, 1954), 321 (= bk. 2, sec. 2, para. 59).
7. Dietmar Moench, *Die methodologischen Bestrebungen der Freirechtsbewegung auf dem Wege zur Methodenlehre der Gegenwart* (Frankfurt am Main: Athenäum, 1971), 86–126. Kantorowicz published his fundamental position statement, *Der Kampf um die Rechtswissenschaft* (Heidelberg, 1906), whose title of course echoes Jhering's famous *Der Kampf um's Recht*, under the pseudonym Gnaeus Flavius; Ehrlich's *Grundlegung der Soziologie des Rechts* (Munich and Leipzig, 1913) was based on articles that he had been publishing since 1888.
8. In 1911, for instance, the leading legal journal featured a panel in which prominent figures—e.g., the philosopher Ernst Haeckel, the legal scholar Karl Binding, the classicist Ulrich von Wilamowitz-Moellendorff—expressed their opinions on the death penalty. See *Deutsche Juristen-Zeitung* 16 (1911), cols. 14–17.

9. See Walter Müller-Seidel, *Die Deportation des Menschen. Kafkas Erzählung "In der Strafkolonie" im europäischen Kontext* (Stuttgart: Metzler, 1986), 26–87.

10. O. W. Holmes, "The Path of the Law," in his *Collected Legal Papers* (New York: Harcourt, Brace, 1920), 167–202; here 179; the following citations from 170, 171–72, and 176.

11. Kelsen, *Hauptprobleme der Staatsrechtslehre*, 56.

12. Ferdinand Tönnies, *Gemeinschaft und Gesellschaft. Grundbegriffe der reinen Soziologie* (1887; 8th ed. Leipzig: Hans Buske, 1935), 241.

13. "Preusse und Österreicher. Ein Schema," in Hofmannsthal's *Prosa III* (Frankfurt am Main: S. Fischer, 1952), 407–9.

14. *Strafgesetzbuch für Österreich*, Regierungsvorlage aus der XXI Session 1912; 90 der Beilagen zu den stenographischen Protokollen des Herrenhauses, V; quoted in Claus Hebell, *Rechtstheoretische und geistesgeschichtliche Voraussetzungen für das Werk Franz Kafkas analysiert an seinem Roman "Der Prozess"* (Frankfurt am Main: Peter Lang, 1993), 31.

15. Robert Musil, *Der Mann ohne Eigenschaften*, in *Gesammelte Werke in neun Bänden*, ed. Adolf Frisé (Reinbek bei Hamburg: Rowohlt, 1978), 2:534–39; here 537. On Musil and law, see Heinz Müller-Dietz, *Grenzüberschreitungen. Beiträge zur Beziehung zwischen Literatur und Recht* (Baden-Baden: Nomos, 1990), 430–72.

16. Bleuler discussed the case extensively in his classic study, *Dementia Praecox, or the Group of Schizophrenia* (written 1908; published 1911). Freud wrote his "Psychoanalytic Notes on an Autobiographical Account of a Case of Paranoia (Dementia Paranoides)" in 1910 and read a postscript to the paper at the 1911 Congress of the International Psycho-Analytical Association in Weimar. See Freud, "Psychoanalytische Bemerkungen über einen autobiographisch beschriebenen Fall von Paranoia (Dementia paranoides)," in the *Studienausgabe* of his works, ed. Alexander Mitscherlich et al. (Frankfurt am Main: S. Fischer, 1973), 7:133–203.

17. Uwe Wesel, *Juristische Weltkunde: Eine Einführung in das Recht*, 5th ed. (Frankfurt am Main: Suhrkamp, 1990), 129–31.

18. Immanuel Kant, *Werke in zehn Bänden*, ed. Wilhelm Weischedel (Wiesbaden: Insel, 1956), 7:455 (= *Rechtslehre*, II. Teil, 1.E.).

19. On Gross, see the biographical sketch in *Neue Deutsche Biographie*, 7:139–41.

20. Müller-Dietz, *Grenzuberschreitungen*, 460–61.

21. Roland Graßberger, "Hundert Jahre reformierter Strafprozeß und die Entwicklung der Kriminologie in Österreich," in *Hundert Jahre österreichische Strafprozeßordnung 1873–1973*, ed. Viktor Liebscher and Otto F. Müller (Vienna: Springer, 1973), 17–28; here 18–21. This close relationship can actually be traced back to Rudolf von Jhering and the dramatic affirmation of legal practice represented by his *Der Kampf um's Recht*, which was originally delivered in 1872 as a talk before the Viennese Juristic Society and which made him "the hero of an entire generation of Austrian legal practitioners." See Herbert Hofmeister, "Jhering in Wien," in *Rudolf von Jhering: Beiträge und Zeugnisse*, ed. Okko Behrends, 2d ed. (Göttingen: Wallstein, 1993), 38–48; here 43.

22. It is no accident that this classic depiction occurs in a novel; the theater lends itself well to the procedures of the courtroom, but not to the quiet and less dramatic work of the examining magistrate. See in this connection Max Neuda, *Das Gerichtsverfahren im modernen Drama* (Vienna and Leipzig: Breitenstein, 1892). Neuda, an Aus-

trian lawyer, singles out as one of the major shortcomings of modern legal drama the neglect of "die geheimen Fäden der unsichtbaren Rechtsfindung im stillen Zimmer des Untersuchungsrichters" (12) and its preference for the bright light of the public trial.

23. Karl Kraus, *Sittlichkeit und Kriminalität*, ed. Heinrich Fischer (Munich and Vienna: Langen Müller, 1963), 18; the following quotations from 27 and 19. For Kraus's views on law see Harry Zohn, *Karl Kraus* (New York: Twayne, 1971), 42–47; and Müller-Dietz, *Grenzüberschreitungen*, 341–411.
24. *Sittlichkeit und Kriminalität*, 154.
25. I write these pages in the winter of 1994–95 during the frenzy of publicity surrounding the celebrity trial of star athlete O. J. Simpson for the murder of his wife. But similar examples are easily found: e.g., the controversy following the so-called Wolfenden Report on Homosexual Offences and Prostitution in England. For an account of the debate, see Basil Mitchell, *Law, Morality, and Religion in a Secular Society* (London: Oxford University Press, 1967).
26. *Sittlichkeit und Kriminalität*, 188.
27. Ibid., 285.
28. Ibid., 192.
29. Ibid., 164.
30. Ibid., 292.
31. Ibid., 256.
32. "Ist es eine Komödie? Ist es eine Tragödie?" in Thomas Bernhard, *Die Erzählungen* (Frankfurt am Main: Suhrkamp, 1979), 154–62; here 162: "Die ganze Welt ist eine Jurisprudenz."
33. Franz Kafka, *Der Prozeß* (New York: Schocken, 1935), 181. I quote from this edition in my own translation because the published English versions are not precise or consistent in their rendition of legal terminology.
34. Hildegard Emmel, *Das Gericht in der deutschen Literatur des 20. Jahrhunderts* (Bern and Munich: Francke, 1963), 12–15.
35. Peter U. Beicken, *Franz Kafka. Eine kritische Einführung in die Forschung* (Frankfurt am Main: Athenäum Fischer, 1974), esp. 175–225; Beicken's more recent account in *Kafka-Handbuch*, ed. Hartmut Binder (Stuttgart: Kröner, 1979), 2:798–810; and Theo Elm's chapter on *Der Prozeß* in *Kafka-Handbuch*, 2:420–441.
36. "Note from the Editors," *Yale Journal of Law and the Humanities* 1 (1988): v.
37. Since 1985, at least six books on the general subject of Kafka and law have appeared; but since they are almost wholly unaware of one another, there is a great deal of overlap and little consistent development of the topic: Ulf Abraham, *Der verhörte Held. Verhöre, Urteile und die Rede von Recht und Schuld im Werk Franz Kafkas* (Munich: Fink, 1985); Walter Müller-Seidel, *Die Deportation des Menschen. Kafkas Erzählung "In der Strafkolonie" im europäischen Kontext* (Stuttgart: Metzler, 1986); Lida Kirchberger, *Franz Kafka's Use of Law in Fiction: A New Interpretation of "In der Strafkolonie," "Der Prozess," and "Das Schloss"* (New York: Peter Lang, 1986); Piero Pajardi, *"Il Processo" di Kafka rivissuto da un giudice* (Rome: Editalia, 1992); Claus Hebell, *Rechtstheoretische und geistesgeschichtliche Voraussetzungen für das Werk Franz Kafkas* (Frankfurt am Main: Peter Lang, 1993); and Arnold Heidsieck, *The Intellectual Contexts of Kafka's Fiction: Philosophy, Law, Religion* (Columbia, SC: Camden House, 1994). Pajardi's book consists of ruminations on *The Trial* by a practicing judge; but

it makes no effort to analyze the legal aspects in any technical way or to locate the work in its proper (that is, fin-de-siècle Austrian) context.

Unfortunately, much of the speculation on Kafka and law produced by the Law-and-Literature movement in North American has been carried out in ignorance of the rich secondary literature, Kafka's own legal experience, and even the German text of his works: e.g., Robin West, "Authority, Autonomy, and Choice: The Role of Consent in the Moral and Political Visions of Franz Kafka and Richard Posner," *Harvard Law Review* 99 (1985): 384–428; and Frederick C. DeCoste, "Kafka, Legal Theorizing and Redemption," *Mosaic* 27 (1994): 161–78.

38. Klaus Wagenbach, *Franz Kafka. Eine Biographie seiner Jugend, 1883–1912* (Bern: Francke, 1958), 243–45; and Binder, *Kafka-Handbuch* 1:259–332.

39. On Kafka's teachers, see Binder, *Kafka-Handbuch*, 1:290–92; and Heidsieck, *Intellectual Contexts*, 105–14. On Gross in particular, see Müller-Seidel, *Die Deportation des Menschen*, 50–71; and Mark M. Anderson, *Kafka's Clothes: Ornament and Aesthetics in the Habsburg Fin de Siècle* (Oxford: Clarendon, 1992), 145–55. Both Müller-Seidel and Anderson stress the negative aspects of Gross's teaching: e.g., his prosecutorial view of the *Untersuchungsrichter* and his espousal of deportation as a suitable criminal punishment.

40. Binder, *Kafka-Handbuch*, 1:286–89; and Heidsieck, *Intellectual Contexts*, 107–9.

41. Hartmut Binder, *Kafka-Kommentar zu den Romanen, Rezensionen, Aphorismen und zum Brief an den Vater* (Munich: Winckler, 1976), 188.

42. Binder, *Kafka-Handbuch*, 1:380. We do not know whether or not Kafka attended Kraus's earlier reading in December 1910, at which he read among other things a piece on law and morality entitled "Das Ehrenkreuz" (cf. Heidsieck, *Intellectual Contexts*, 151 n. 31).

43. Binder, *Kafka-Kommentar*, 233.

44. Franz Kafka, *Amtliche Schriften*, ed. Klaus Hermsdorf (Berlin: Akademie-Verlag, 1984), 29. Kafka's brief is reprinted on 95–120.

45. Abraham, *Der verhörte Held*, chaps. 1 and 2.

46. Martha S. Robinson, "The Law of the State in Kafka's *The Trial*," *ALSA Forum* 6 (1982): 127–47; Hebell, *Rechtstheoretische Voraussetzungen*, 17–41; and Heidsieck, *Intellectual Contexts*, 114–19.

47. See the pseudonymous Czech author "Josef K." (= Josef Kroutvor), who reads *The Trial* as a representation of the shift from "the era of the state officials" to "the era of the functionaries"; cited by J. P. Stern, *The Heart of Europe: Essays on Literature and Ideology* (Oxford: Blackwell, 1992), 4–5.

48. For a summary of interpretations see Beicken's *Kritische Einführung in die Forschung*, 273–86. Hebell, *Rechtstheoretische Voraussetzungen*, 5–17, analyzes Kafka's general distrust of Habsburg institutions.

49. Max Brod, *Franz Kafka*, trans. G. Humphrey Robert and Richard Winston, 2d ed. (New York: Schocken, 1960), 178.

50. See Richard Weisberg, "Comparative Law in Comparative Literature: The Figure of the 'Examining Magistrate' in Dostoevski and Camus," *Rutgers Law Review* 29 (1976): 237–58. The process in Russia and France as described by Weisberg is close to that in Austria and Germany. But in Austria, thanks in no small measure to Hans Gross, the *Untersuchungsrichter* enjoyed a special prominence.

51. Hans-Heinrich Jescheck, "Neue Entwicklungstendenzen des deutschen Strafver-

fahrensrechts im Vergleich mit dem österreichischen Recht," in *Hundert Jahre österreichische Strafprozeßordnung 1873–1973*, 39–58; here 47.

52. Graßberger, "Hundert Jahre reformierter Strafprozeß," 26.

53. Franz Kafka, "Fürsprecher," in *Sämtliche Erzählungen*, ed. Paul Raabe (Frankfurt am Main: Fischer Taschenbuch, 1971), 322.

54. See Theodore Ziolkowski, "The Novel of the Thirty-Year-Old," in *Dimensions of the Modern Novel: German Texts and European Contexts* (Princeton, NJ: Princeton University Press, 1969), 258–88. Elsbeth Schmidhäuser, "Die Verhaftung des Josef K. Zum Verständnis von Kafkas Roman 'Der Prozeß,'" *Neue Juristische Wochenschrift* 23 (1991): 1455–60, reads the novel in a Freudian sense as a birthday prank played on K. by his friend, state's attorney Hasterer.

55. Binder, *Kafka-Kommentar*, 160–94, offers the most complete, albeit still conjectural, presentation of the order of composition and intended arrangement. See also Malcolm Pasley, "Kafka's *Der Process*: What the Manuscripts Can Tell Us," *Oxford German Studies* 18–19 (1989–90): 109–18. For the purposes of the present analysis I use the traditional order of chapters but refer to information contained in the uncompleted chapters as well as the excised passages.

56. Hebell, *Rechtstheoretische Voraussetzungen*, 21.

57. Heidsieck, *Intellectual Contexts*, 116–18.

58. Robinson, "The Law of the State," 131.

59. See the consternation of the Austrian lawyer Max Neuda, *Das Gerichtsverfahren im modernen Drama* (Vienna and Leipzig, 1892), 18. Pointing out a technical mistake in a contemporary legal drama, he stresses the fact that the state prosecutor has no place in the preliminary investigation. "Not only would his absence be no dereliction of his duty, but his presence would be an encroachment [*Übergriff*]; for the examining magistrate is not supposed to be influenced in his investigation by either party, the prosecution or the defense."

60. Robinson, "The Law of the State," 135–36. See also Heidsieck, *Intellectual Contexts*, 111–15.

61. Hans Gross, *Criminal Psychology: A Manual for Judges, Practitioners, and Students*, trans. from the 4th German ed. by Horace M. Kallen (Boston: Little, Brown, 1911), 106.

62. Robinson, "The Law of the State," 137.

63. Ibid., 127.

64. Heidsieck, *Intellectual Contexts*, 115.

65. The relevant passages are conveniently assembled in *Franz Kafka*, ed. Erich Heller and Joachim Beug, Dichter über ihre Dichtungen (Munich: Heimeran, 1969), 76–81.

66. There has been astonishingly little effort in Kafka scholarship to interpret this startling image. Kirchberger, *Kafka's Use of Law*, 85, mentions the representation of the image of Justitia on the frontispiece of Jhering's famous *Der Kampf um's Recht*, which Kafka no doubt knew, and the explanation of the figure's attributes on the first page, where Jhering mentions the sword and scales but does not cite the blindfold. But the image was so common, and the interpretation of the attributes so standard since the early seventeenth century, that the reference is not very helpful.

67. The text is reproduced in Otto Rudolf Kissel, *Die Justitia. Reflexionen uber ein Symbol und seine Darstellung in der bildenden Kunst* (Munich: Beck, 1984), 92.

68. Abraham, *Der verhörte Held*, 111–15; and Kirchberger, *Kafka's Use of Law*, 43–52. See also Eberhard Schmidhäuser, "Das 'Gesetz' in Franz Kafkas Roman *Der Prozeß*," in *Strafgerechtigkeit. Festschrift für Arthur Kaufmann*, ed. Fritjof Haft et al. (Heidelberg: C. F. Müller Juristischer Verlag, 1993), 803–17.
69. The expression "traduced" in the standard English translation by Edwin and Willa Muir does not capture the legal implications of the German word *verleumdet* ("slandered").
70. Graßberger, "Hundert Jahre reformierter Strafprozeß," 23.
71. *Strafgesetzbuch für das Deutsche Reich in der vom 1. Januar 1900 ab geltenden Fassung. Textausgabe von Paul Herold* (Halle: Otto Hendel, n.d.). See also *The German Penal Code of 1871*, trans. Gerhard O. W. Mueller and Thomas Buergenthal (South Hackensack, NJ: Fred B. Rothman, 1961).
72. On German law see, in contrast, Robert von Hippel, *Lehrbuch des Strafrechts* (Berlin: Julius Springer, 1932), 131 n. 2: "Im Gesetz selbst fehlt leider [. . .] eine Begriffsbestimmung des Vorsatzes."
73. *Das Strafgesetz vom 27. Mai 1852*, ed. Hans Hoyer, 2d ed. (Vienna: Manz, 1944). This edition includes various provisions added following the German annexation of Austria, including the notorious Nuremberg racial laws; but the language of the original code is clearly indicated.
74. Wesel, *Juristische Weltkunde*, 127–44; here 132–34.
75. For an overview see Reinhard Moos, *Der Verbrechensbegriff in Österreich im 18. und 19. Jahrhundert* (Bonn: Ludwig Röhrscheid, 1968); and Hans-Heinrich Jescheck, "Die Entwicklung des Verbrechensbegriffs in Deutschland seit Beling im Vergleich mit der österreichischen Lehre," *Zeitschrift für die gesamte Strafrechtwissenschaft* 73 (1961): 179–209.
76. See von Hippel, *Lehrbuch des Strafrechts*, 127: "Schuld ist ungenügende Berücksichtigung (Nichtachtung oder Nichtbeachtung) der Anforderungen des Rechts. . . ."
77. Döblin, *Die beiden Freundinnen und ihr Giftmord* (Reinbek bei Hamburg: Rowohlt, 1978), 79: "Eine leichte flimmernde Erinnerung an die Skala der Vorgänge durften die Geschworenen anklingen lassen: nach dem Tatbestand wurden sie gefragt, und dann: liegen mildernde Umstände vor?" In his epilogue (90–91) Döblin makes it clear that he wrote his account mainly in order to explore the very questions of motivation that played no role in the German criminal justice system.
78. Moos, *Der Verbrechensbegriff*, 49–53 and 504; Jeschek, "Die Entwicklung des Verbrechensbegriff," 198–203.
79. E. Kaufmann, "Strafe, Strafrecht," in *Handwörterbuch zur deutschen Rechtsgeschichte*, 32. Lieferung (Berlin: Erich Schmidt, 1990), 2025–28.
80. Moos, *Der Verbrechensbegriff*, 520–21.
81. Thomas Anz, "Jemand mußte Otto G. verleumdet haben . . . Kafka, Werfel, Otto Groß und eine psychologische Geschichte," *Akzente* 31 (1984): 184–91; Müller-Seidel, *Die Deportation des Menschen*, 65–70; and Anderson, *Kafka's Clothes*, 152.
82. See Theodore Ziolkowski, "Franz Kafka: *The Trial*," in *Dimensions of the Modern Novels: German Texts and European Contexts* (Princeton, NJ: Princeton University Press, 1969), 37–67.
83. Müller-Seidel, *Die Deportation des Menschen*.
84. See Müller-Seidel's brilliant interpretation of this story in ibid.; here 139–41.

Chapter Twelve
Twentieth-Century Legal Evolutions

1. Brook Thomas, *Cross-Examinations of Law and Literature: Cooper, Hawthorne, Stowe, and Melville* (Cambridge: Cambridge University Press, 1987), 254.
2. See also Hildegard Emmel, *Das Gericht in der deutschen Literatur des 20. Jahrhunderts* (Bern and Munich: Francke, 1963), 22–35.
3. The published text—Ferdinand Bruckner (pseud. of Theodor Tagger), *Die Verbrecher. Schauspiel in drei Akten* (Berlin: S. Fischer, 1929)—contains diagrams at the beginning of acts 1 and 2 indicating how the set is divided into three levels, each with various sections, to accommodate the seven simultaneous plot lines in the tenement house and in the court building.
4. See Hannah Arendt, *The Origins of Totalitarianism* (1951; 2d enl. ed. New York: Meridian, 1958), who attributes its rise to such factors as anti-Semitism, imperialism, and the emergence of previously nonpoliticized masses.
5. Herbert J. Spiro, "Totalitarianism," in *International Encyclopedia of the Social Sciences*, ed. David L. Sills, vol. 16 (New York: Macmillan, 1968), 106–13.
6. Hans Hattenhauer, *Europäische Rechtsgeschichte* (Heidelberg: C. F. Müller Juristischer Verlag, 1992), 705–11; here 707.
7. A speech at the German-Austrian meeting of National Socialists in Salzburg on August 7, 1920; in Hitler's *Sämtliche Aufzeichnungen 1905–1924*, ed. Eberhard Jäckel and Axel Kuhn (Stuttgart: Deutsche Verlags-Anstalt, 1980), 177.
8. Paper published for the General Members Assembly and Party Meeting of the National Socialist Party, Munich, January 23, 1922; in *Sämtliche Aufzeichnungen*, 551. On Hitler's attitudes toward the law, see J. P. Stern, *Hitler: The Führer and the People* (Glasgow: Collins, 1975), 116–29.
9. Rainer Zitelmann, *Hitler. Selbstverständnis eines Revolutionärs* (Hamburg: Berg, 1987), 173–94.
10. Cited by Hinrich Rüping, "Zur Praxis der Strafjustiz im 'Dritten Reich,'" in *Recht und Justiz im "Dritten Reich,"* ed. Ralf Dreier und Wolfgang Sellert (Frankfurt am Main: Suhrkamp, 1989), 181.
11. Quoted by Roland Freisler, *Nationalsozialistisches Recht und Rechtsdenken* (Berlin: Industrieverlag Spaeth & Linde, 1943), 67.
12. Ibid., 69.
13. "oder die nach dem Grundgedanken eines Strafgesetzes und nach gesundem Volksempfinden Bestrafung verdient"; cited from the Austrian penal code (*Strafgesetz*) as revised and edited by Hans Hoyer (Vienna: Manz, 1944) to accommodate the Nazi penal code.
14. Freisler, *Nationalsozialistisches Recht und Rechtsdenken*, 18–19.
15. Ibid., 54.
16. Ibid., 57: *"Es gibt keine andere letzte Quelle des Rechtes als das Gewissen des Volkes selbst."*
17. Ibid., 58: "Recht ist, was dem deutschen Volke frommt, Unrecht, was ihm schadet."
18. Ibid., 71.
19. Ibid., 98 and 106.
20. See Hattenhauer, *Europäische Rechtsgeschichte*, 676–83; and Hubert Rottleuthner,

"Rechtsphilosophie und Rechtssoziologie im Nationalsozialismus," in *Recht und Justiz im "Dritten Reich,"* 295–322; here 299–300.

21. Ingo Müller, *Hitler's Justice: The Courts of the Third Reich*, trans. Deborah Lucas Schneider (Cambridge: Harvard University Press, 1991), 68–81.
22. Joseph W. Bendersky, *Carl Schmitt: Theorist for the Reich* (Princeton, NJ: Princeton University Press, 1983).
23. "Der Führer schützt das Recht," *Deutsche Juristen-Zeitung* 39 (August 1, 1934): 945–50.
24. Freisler, *Nationalsozialistisches Recht und Rechtsdenken*, 94.
25. Bergengruen's novel appeared in English after the war under the title *A Matter of Conscience*, trans. Norman Cameron (London: Thames & Hudson, 1952).
26. Bergengruen has written about the composition of this novel in his memoirs, *Schreibtischerinnerungen* (Zurich: Arche, 1961), 160–78.
27. Ibid., 174–75.
28. *Der Großtyrann und das Gericht* (Zurich: Arche, 1949), 285; subsequent passages translated from this edition.
29. *Schreibtischerinnerungen*, 162.
30. See Hans-Jürgen Wipfelder, *Die Rechts- und Staatsauffassung im Werke Werner Bergengruens* (Bonn: Bouvier, 1969).
31. Published in English as *The Private Life of the Master Race*, trans. Eric Bentley (New York: New Directions, 1944).
32. Bertolt Brecht, *Gesammelte Werke in 20 Bänden* (Frankfurt am Main: Suhrkamp, 1967), 3:1103–1120. Emmel, *Das Gericht*, mentions this work only in passing (34) in her chapter on Brecht (36–55).
33. Cited here and elsewhere from the English translation by Anatol Murad: *Six of Them* (New York: Macmillan, 1945).
34. Published in the collection *Servitude et grandeur des Français: Scènes des années terribles* (Buenos Aires: Viau-Fougere, 1946), 195–262.
35. "The Fundamental Tasks of the Science of Soviet Socialist Law" (1938), in *Soviet Legal Philosophy*, trans. Hugh W. Babb (Cambridge: Harvard University Press, 1951), 303–41; here 329 and 317.
36. Berman, "Socialist Legal Systems—Soviet Law," in *International Encyclopedia of the Social Sciences*, 9:219.
37. Koestler's original German text of the novel was lost; the English translation by Daphne Hardy, published in England in 1940, is therefore the original edition. It is cited here according to the Modern Library edition (New York, n.d.). The quotation is found in Koestler's preliminary note.
38. In Koestler's contribution to *The God That Failed*, ed. Richard Crossman (1950; reprint, New York: Bantam, 1965), 11–66; here 61–62.
39. See my interpretation of Koestler's novel in *Fictional Transfigurations of Jesus* (Princeton, NJ: Princeton University Press, 1972), 207–14.
40. *The First Circle*, trans. Thomas P. Whitney (New York: Bantam, 1969), 348–49.
41. *The Trial Begins*, trans. Max Hayward (New York: Pantheon, 1960), 56.
42. Milan Kundera, *Testaments Betrayed*, trans. Linda Asher (New York: HarperCollins, 1995), 231. Kundera lists dozens of European intellectuals persecuted after the war for alleged pro-Nazi sympathies.
43. See *Recht und Justiz im "Dritten Reich,"* esp. 34–79 (Okko Behrends, "Von der

Freirechtsbewegung zum kontreten Ordnungs- und Gestaltungsdenken") and 323–54 (Manfred Walther, "Hat der juristische Positivismus die deutschen Juristen im 'Dritten Reich' wehrlos gemacht?").

44. Gustav Radbruch, *Rechtsphilosophie*, 4th ed. (Stuttgart: Koehler, 1950); and Helmut Coing, *Grundzüge der Rechtsphilosophie* (1950), 3d ed. (Berlin: De Gruyter, 1976). See also the essays in *Naturrecht oder Rechtspositivismus*, ed. Werner Maihofer, 3d ed. (Darmstadt: Wissenschaftliche Buchgesellschaft, 1981).

45. Otfried Höffe, *Politische Gerechtigkeit. Grundlegung einer kritischen Philosophie von Recht und Staat* (Frankfurt am Main: Suhrkamp, 1987), 125.

46. Quoted in Konrad Zweigert's preface to the 10th edition of Radbruch's *Einführung in die Rechtswissenschaft* (1929; Stuttgart: Koehler, 1961), 6. Radbruch died in 1949, but his reputation as the leading German philosopher of law continued to grow posthumously in Europe and the United States.

47. See in this connection the chapter "Der totale Ideologieverdacht" (300–320) of the monograph-length section "Deutsche Literatur seit Thomas Mann" (259–362) in Hans Mayer, *Zur deutschen Literatur der Zeit. Zusammenhänge, Schriftsteller, Bücher* (Reinbek: Rowohlt, 1967).

48. See the discussion and bibliography in Richard Weisberg, *Poethics and Other Strategies of Law and Literature* (New York: Columbia University Press, 1992), 127–87.

49. On May 23, 1995, the Bundesverfassungsgericht came to precisely the opposite conclusion when it determined that spies operating for the former German Democratic Republic could not be found guilty of crimes against the German Federal Republic since they were operating at the time under the laws of a legally constituted state.

50. Dennis Lloyd, *The Idea of Law* (Baltimore: Penguin, 1964), 103–5.

51. Hattenhauer, *Europäische Rechtsgeschichte*, 749–55; here 749.

52. Albert Camus, *The Rebel: An Essay on Man in Revolt*, trans. Anthony Bower (New York: Vintage, 1959), 240 and 243.

53. Jesse Levitt, "Justice in Two Novels: *The Stranger* and *The Plague* by Camus," in *Justice: Interdisciplinary and Global Perspectives*, ed. T. M. Thomas and Jesse Levitt (Lanham, MD: University Press of America, 1988), 103–32, includes a good survey of writings on Camus's concern with issues of justice. See also Martina Yadel, *La Chute von Albert Camus—Ansätze zu einer Interpretation* (Bonn: Bouvier, 1984), 17–21.

54. René Girard, "Camus's Stranger Retried," *PMLA* 79 (1964): 519–33, takes an unusually skeptical view of Meursault's "innocence."

55. Albert Camus, *The Fall*, trans. Justin O'Brien (New York: Knopf, 1957), 11. I cite the French text according to *La Chute* (Paris: Gallimard, 1956).

56. Richard H. Weisberg, *The Failure of the Word: The Protagonist as Lawyer in Modern Fiction* (New Haven: Yale University Press, 1984), 128, recognizes that "Clamence's 'fall' is that of a full generation of Europeans."

57. Carl A. Viggiani, "Camus and the Fall from Innocence," *Yale French Studies* 25 (1960): 65–71.

58. Herbert R. Lottman, *Albert Camus*, trans. Marianne Véron (Paris: Seuil, 1978), 572.

59. Philip Thody, *Albert Camus: A Study of His Work* (New York: Grove, 1957), 76–79, makes a compelling case for the ironic ambivalence of the novel.

60. I cite *Die Panne* in my own translation from Friedrich Dürrenmatt, *Werkausgabe in dreißig Bänden* (Zurich: Diogenes, 1985), 20:35–98.

61. W. Wolfgang Holdheim, *Der Justizirrtum als literarische Problematik: Vergleichende Analysen eines erzählerischen Themas* (Berlin: DeGruyter, 1969), 99–202, discusses "the ambivalence of modern guilt" in the light of Dürrenmatt's story. Eberhard Schmidhäuser, *Verbrechen und Strafe* (Munich: Beck, 1995), 209–30, is concerned more with Dürrenmatt's parody of justice.

62. *Die Panne. Eine Komödie*, in Friedrich Dürrenmatt, *Die Panne. Ein Hörspiel und eine Komödie* (Zurich: Verlag der Arche, 1980), 57–173.

63. Höffe, *Politische Gerechtigkeit*, 203–5. See also Noam Chomsky's introduction to Daniel Guérin, *Anarchism*, trans. Mary Klopper (New York: Monthly Review, 1970), vii–xx.

64. For the following paragraphs see Thomas Parker and Douglas Nelson, *Day by Day: The Sixties*, 2 vols. (New York: Facts on File Publication, 1983).

65. See Jason Epstein, *The Great Conspiracy Trial: An Essay on Law, Liberty and the Constitution* (New York: Random House, 1970). Until Black Panther Bobby Seale's case was severed because of his contempt of court and obstruction of justice, there were originally eight defendants.

66. David Lewis Stein, *Living the Revolution: The Yippies in Chicago* (Indianapolis and New York: Bobbs-Merrill, 1969), 18.

67. Ibid.

68. Ibid., 35–36.

69. Epstein, *The Great Conspiracy Trial*, 116.

70. Ibid., 306.

71. Heinrich Böll, "Einführung in 'Dienstfahrt' " (1967), in *Heinrich Böll Werke: Essayistische Schriften und Reden II*, ed. Bernd Balzer (Cologne: Kiepenheuer & Witsch, [1978]), 253–54.

72. I cite the text in my own translation from Heinrich Böll, *Ende einer Dienstfahrt* (Cologne: Kiepenheuer & Witsch, 1966); here 213.

73. See Böll's article on the value-added tax in *Die Zeit*, November 29, 1963; "Vom Mehrwert bearbeiteten Papiers," in his *Essayistische Schriften und Reden I*, 557–60.

74. See Robert C. Conard, *Heinrich Böll* (Boston: Twayne, 1981), 155–63; J. H. Reid, *Heinrich Böll: A German for His Time* (Oxford: Berg, 1988), 150–56; William J. Dodd, "Aufforderung zur Aktion," in *The Narrative Fiction of Heinrich Böll: Social Conscience and Literary Achievement*, ed. Michael Butler (Cambridge: Cambridge University Press, 1994), 153–75, esp. 162–75.

75. Heinrich Böll, *Frankfurter Vorlesungen* (Cologne: Kiepenheuer & Witsch, 1966).

76. Böll's letter requesting information was displayed in the exhibit mounted for the 1992 Cologne Symposium on Böll.

77. Böll commented on this in his 1971 interview with Heinz Ludwig Arnold, in *Interviews I*, ed. Bernd Balzer (Cologne: Kiepenheuer & Witsch, [1978]), 135–76; here 155–56.

78. Ronald L. Cohen, introduction to *Justice: Views from the Social Sciences*, ed. Ronald L. Cohen (New York: Plenum, 1986), 2.

79. Höffe, *Politische Gerechtigkeit*, 12–13.

80. On Rawls's central influence in the United States as well as Europe see Cohen,

Justice: Views from the Social Sciences, 3 and passim; Höffe, *Politische Gerechtigkeit*, 14–14, 46–49, 322–28, 451–53; and *What Is Justice? Classic and Contemporary Readings*, ed. Robert C. Solomon and Mark C. Murphy (New York: Oxford University Press, 1990), 6–7, 303–56.

81. David Miller, *Social Justice* (Oxford: Clarendon, 1976), 22–23.

82. On "legal moralism" see H.L.A. Hart, *Law, Liberty and Morality* (Stanford, CA: Stanford University Press, 1963), 6.

83. Reproduced in *Berndt Pfeifer. Holzschnitte 1980–1994*, the catalog for the exhibition at the Naturkundemuseum in Freiberg (Saxony) in October 1994 sponsored by the Kulturamt of the city of Cologne and the city of Freiberg.

INDEX